Practically Speaking

J. Dan Rothwell

CABRILLO COLLEGE, CALIFORNIA

New York   Oxford

OXFORD UNIVERSITY PRESS

Oxford University Press is a department of the University of Oxford.
It furthers the University's objective of excellence in research,
scholarship, and education by publishing worldwide.

Oxford   New York
Auckland   Cape Town   Dar es Salaam   Hong Kong   Karachi
Kuala   Lumpur   Madrid   Melbourne   Mexico City   Nairobi
New Delhi   Shanghai   Taipei   Toronto

With offices in
Argentina   Austria   Brazil   Chile   Czech Republic   France   Greece
Guatemala   Hungary   Italy   Japan   Poland   Portugal   Singapore
South Korea   Switzerland   Thailand   Turkey   Ukraine   Vietnam

Copyright © 2014 by Oxford University Press

Published by Oxford University Press
198 Madison Avenue, New York, New York 10016
http://www.oup.com

Oxford is a registered trademark of Oxford University Press

Library of Congress Cataloging-in-Publication Data
Rothwell, J. Dan.
    Practically speaking / J. Dan Rothwell, Cabrillo College, California.
        pages cm
    Includes bibliographical references and index.
        ISBN 978-0-19-533766-2 (main text : alk. paper)—ISBN 978-0-19-533767-9
(instructor's manual / test bank : alk. paper)—ISBN (invalid) 978-0-19-533768-6
(instructor's resource cd) 1. Public speaking. I. Title.
        PN4129.15.R68   2013
        808.5'1—dc23
                                                                2013014677
9 8 7 6

Printed in the United States of America
on acid-free paper

To my lovely wife, Marcy.
No better partner in life could be imagined!

BRIEF CONTENTS

CONTENTS

vii

CHAPTER 5 Attention: Getting People to Listen 68

CHAPTER 6 Introductions and Conclusions 84

CHAPTER 7 Outlining and Organizing Speeches 99

CHAPTER 8 Gathering Material 120

CHAPTER 9 Skepticism: Becoming Critical Thinking
Speakers and Listeners 134

CHAPTER 12 **Speaking Style 182**

CHAPTER 13 **Visual Aids 195**

CHAPTER 14 **Informative Speaking 216**

CHAPTER 15 Foundations of Persuasive Speaking 230

CHAPTER 16 Persuasive Speaking Strategies 245

CHAPTER 17 Speeches for Special Occasions 262

PREFACE

Lately, public speaking texts have taken two main approaches. One could be called the all-you-can-eat buffet approach. These works are resplendent with almost every conceivable tasty feature that only the most dedicated and motivated students will ever sample. They can be wonderful books as a kind of "everything you ever wanted to know about public speaking, and then some" reference work, but public speaking novices may see them as excessive. A second is the cookbook approach. These works offer little beyond a list of recipe steps for constructing and presenting a speech. Striving to cover "only the basics," they achieve this purpose, but few are likely to find the recipe approach interesting reading.

Each approach has its merits and supporters. *Practically Speaking*, however, offers a third approach for consideration. *Practically Speaking* is a relatively short text that is loaded with practical advice. It covers the essentials without sacrificing reader interest or scholarship. Understanding this third approach can be ascertained by addressing key objectives for both students and teachers.

OBJECTIVES FOR STUDENTS

Practically Speaking aims to address four key objectives for students: (1) readability, (2) clarity, (3) applicability, and (4) affordability. Regarding the first objective—readability—the wisdom of Samuel Johnson seems apt: "What is written without effort is in general read without pleasure." Maximum effort has been devoted to writing a textbook that might ignite the interest of student readers, not induce a coma. Textbooks are not meant to read like spy or mystery novels, but they need not read like an instruction manual for setting up your new flat-screen TV. Therefore, I attempted to practice what I teach about gaining and maintaining attention by using the attention-getting strategies discussed in Chapter 5. The text includes novel and humorous examples, stories, quotations, photos, and cartoons; intense, dramatic, and poignant illustrations; colorful and vivid language and metaphors; startling statistics and historical facts sprinkled throughout every chapter. The writing style is conversational, and the perpendicular pronoun "I" is used when relating personal narratives. First-person singular is more engaging than impersonal references such as "this author experienced" or "a student in the author's class." In addition, second-person pronoun references to "you" are employed frequently to address readers directly.

A second objective—**clarity**—is addressed in a variety of ways. The organization of each chapter follows the rules of good organizational logic presented in Chapter 7. Such logic can be examined by perusing the Table of Contents. In addition, headings and subheadings were carefully chosen and worded to produce maximum clarity as well as originality. Finally, copious illustrations and explanations are provided to clarify all important public speaking concepts and processes.

A third objective—**applicability**—requires concerted effort to demonstrate the practical utility for students of becoming competent public speakers. The first chapter addresses in detail such applicability. The remaining chapters elaborate on this important objective. Numerous pop-culture references and newsworthy events are used as illustrations, further revealing the applicability of competent public speaking for students.

A fourth objective—**affordability**—has become a national issue shared by students and faculty alike. A 2012 Oxford University Press national survey of 327 professors who teach public speaking at U.S. universities and community colleges revealed that almost 75% of respondents viewed price as an "extremely or very important" feature of a public speaking text. I am a longtime member of the bookstore/textbook committee on my campus that strives to find ways to make textbooks more affordable for students. Every effort has been exerted to make *Practically Speaking* an attractive but affordable alternative to other much more expensive choices. Oxford University Press is a non-profit publishing company, so this alone provides considerable price advantage for students surviving on tight budgets. The lean size of *Practically Speaking* also helps reduce the price.

OBJECTIVES FOR TEACHERS

Practically Speaking aims to address six different objectives for teachers of public speaking: (1) sound scholarship, (2) standard yet innovative coverage, (3) brevity, (4) recency, (5) logical organization, and (6) useful ancillaries. The first objective, **sound scholarship**, is critically important. Providing substantial theory and research to bolster the advice offered to novice student speakers counters the oft-heard, naive claim that public speaking is just "common sense." Without such theory and research, advice provided will appear as little more than the personal opinion of the author, easily trivialized or ignored and often at odds with the opinions of others. It is bound to strike the more alert student readers that authors who insist on inclusion of research and evidence for student speeches but include little research and evidence to support their advice offered in a textbook seem contradictory. We never want students to equate relatively short texts such as *Practically Speaking* with being "lightweight" or insubstantial. The careful scholarship in *Practically Speaking* is evident in every chapter. More than **500 references** are cited, and the communication competence model, carefully developed in Chapter 1, serves as the theoretical basis for all advice offered. In addition, Chapter 9 on skepticism is the only chapter of its kind in public speaking texts that so thoroughly explains the theoretical underpinnings of critical thinking for public speakers.

A second objective for public speaking teachers—**standard yet innovative coverage**—is addressed in several ways. All standard topics found in any reputable public speaking text and identified in the Oxford survey previously referenced are thoroughly developed in *Practically Speaking*. Innovative coverage includes the opening chapter on communication competence. There is a separate chapter on speech anxiety, offered in only a few public speaking texts. A full chapter on gaining and maintaining attention, not typically found in other public speaking texts, emphasizes that speakers must do far more than merely gain immediate attention of their audiences. The much greater challenge is to keep that attention throughout a lengthy speech. A full chapter on skepticism, already mentioned, is yet another innovation of *Practically Speaking*. Finally, two full chapters on persuasive speaking provide both a theoretical explanation for how persuasion works generally and specific strategies for persuading public speaking audiences. Results from the Oxford survey showed that three-quarters of respondents believed that a chapter on foundations of persuasion is "extremely or very important." A chapter on persuasive speaking strategies was similarly embraced by 85% of respondents.

A third objective—**brevity**—was identified by 72% of respondents to the Oxford survey as variously "important" to "extremely important." A significant 85% of respondents in the same survey also noted that "preparing students to start speaking right away" is important. In standard, lengthy texts, students have to read hundreds of pages before they learn the basics for a simple first or second speech. Standard texts typically do not cover introductions and conclusions, for example, until almost 200 pages of text have been read. Students will have read the bulk of *Practically Speaking* when they reach 200 pages. *Practically Speaking* gets students "up and running" quickly. Another related concern in the Oxford survey identified by almost half the respondents was that students do not read the text. Reading a textbook of 500 pages or more can be daunting. *Practically Speaking* is about half the size of most standard-sized public speaking texts. Its brevity is far less intimidating and more likely to be read.

A fourth objective—**recency**—is always a challenge because of the lag period between finishing a manuscript and completing the textbook production process that typically takes months. As someone with a Bachelors degree in American history, I value the use of historical examples for illustrations. I also see the applicability of recent events to clarify concepts and processes in public speaking. I have included both, some examples as recent as 2013 and others centuries old. Great speakers and powerfully illustrative events do not occur in only one brief time period. We can learn from both the old and the new. This is true for references as well. About half of the more than 500 references are between 2008 and 2013, while many of the rest are more "classic" citations.

A fifth objective—**logical organization**—produced some juggling of chapters. There is no perfect organization for any public speaking text. *Practically Speaking* is organized similar to most such texts. Several reviewers of *Practically Speaking*, however, suggested moving the chapter on delivery forward in the text. Their advice and rationale seemed cogent. Delivery is an immediate concern of students when they give their first speech. Addressing this concern early seems warranted. Consequently, the delivery chapter was moved from Chapter 13 to Chapter 3. Likewise, speech anxiety is addressed very early in Chapter 2 because it is an immediate and significant student concern. With the exception of Chapter 1 on communication competence, all chapters can be moved to a different order if so desired.

A final objective—**useful ancillaries**—is addressed in several ways. An instructors' manual, available online or as hard copy, accompanies *Practically Speaking*. Dozens of unique activities and exercises are provided to supplement what most teachers already use. More than a hundred website links to a wide variety of speeches and video resources are included for easy in-class access. A test bank, carefully prepared PowerPoint slides, a glossary of key terms, and online student resources are also included as ancillaries.

ACKNOWLEDGMENTS

My sincere thanks are extended to reviewers of this text. They include:
Jill Alcorn, Green River Community College
Marie Arcidiacono, California State University, East Bay
Diane Auten, Allan Hancock College
Jessica Barkl, Walla Walla Community College
Ray Bell, Calhoun Community College
Kathy Berggren, Cornell University
Marilyn Brimo, Mt. Hood Community College
Bryan Brown, Missouri State University
Megan Burnett, Alice Lloyd College
Dana Burnside, Lehigh Carbon Community College
Rebecca Carlton, Indiana University Southeast

Janet Colvin, Utah Valley University
David Mario Curio, St. John's University
Lisa Darnell, University of North Alabama
Quinton Dale Davis, University of Texas at San Antonio
Staci Dinerstein, Ramapo College
Ann Duncan, McLennan Community College
Danielle Endres, University of Utah
Charles Falcon, San Antonio College
Maxim Fetissenko, Northeastern University
Valerie Manno Giroux, University of Miami
Adam Gutschmidt, Wright State University
Michael J. Havice, Marquette University
Andrew Herrmann, University of Missouri
Carol S. Hopson, Southeastern Louisiana University
Pamm Killeen, University of Nebraska at Omaha
Theodore Matula, University of San Francisco
Tina Leisner McDermott, Antelope Valley College
Scott McLean, Arizona Western College/Northern Arizona University - Yuma
Richard A. Mercadante, Jr., St. Petersburg College
Laurie D. Metcalf, Blinn College
Donata Nelson, Rockingham Community College
Gyromas Westley Newman, University of Mobile
Karen Osgood, Santa Barbara City College
Tracey Elizabeth Powers, Central Arizona College
Marlene M. Preston, Virginia Tech
Brandi Queensberry, Virginia Tech
Dan C. Rogers, Cedar Valley College
Rita Rosenthal, Boston College
Tedro R. Rouse, South Carolina State University
Roy Schwartzman, University of North Carolina at Greensboro
Matthew Sciarrino, Jr, St. John's University
Alisa Shubb, American River College & University of California, Davis
Suzanne M. Uhl, Mt. San Jacinto College
Nadene N. Vevea, North Dakota State University
Catherine K. Wright, George Mason University
Jason Zenor, State University of New York at Oswego

I also want to thank the many professionals at Oxford University Press who worked to bring *Practically Speaking* to the marketplace. They include Mark Haynes and Peter Labella, Editors; Thom Holmes, Development Manager; Danielle Christensen, Development Editor; Theresa Stockton, Senior Production

Editor; Michele Laseau, Art Director; Caitlin Kaufman, Associate Editor; Grace Ross, Editorial Assistant; Kate McClaskey, Editorial Assistant; Courtney Roy, Editorial Assistant.

I want to make a final, special thanks to my wife, Marcy, for the wonderful custom cartoons. I gave her ideas and she produced beautiful, animated renderings. Artist, singer, writer, computer program analyst—her talents seem boundless.

ABOUT THE AUTHOR

J. Dan Rothwell is chair of the Communication Studies Department at Cabrillo College. He has a BA in American history from the University of Portland (Oregon), an MA in rhetoric and public address, and a PhD in communication theory and social influence, both from the University of Oregon. He has authored four other books in addition to *Practically Speaking*. They are *In Mixed Company: Communicating in Small Groups and Teams* (Cengage), *In the Company of Others: An Introduction to Communication* (Oxford University Press), *Telling It Like It Isn't: Language Misuse and Malpractice* (Prentice-Hall), and *Interpersonal Communication: Influences and Alternatives* (with James Costigan and published by Charles-Merrill).

Dr. Rothwell has received numerous teaching awards, including, among others, the 2010 "Ernest L. Boyer International Award for Excellence in Teaching, Learning, and Technology"; the 2010 Cabrillo College "Innovative Teacher of the Year"; the 2011 National Communication Association "Community College Educator of the Year" award; and a 2012 official resolution by the California State Senate acknowledging Dr. Rothwell's excellence in teaching. In 2012, the Western States Communication Association awarded the Cabrillo College Communication Studies department, under the leadership of Dr. Rothwell, the "Model Communication Program" award. The immensely talented faculty in the Communication Studies department at Cabrillo College, however, deserve most of the credit for this last award.

1

Communication Competence and Public Speaking

Freedom of speech is the bedrock of a democratic society. There is an inherent recognition in the First Amendment to the U.S. Constitution that articulate speech can give voice to the voiceless and power to the powerless. Eloquence has influenced the course of our history. The oratory of Martin Luther King and the eloquence of others were powerful instruments of the civil rights movement. The Tea Party that emerged in 2009 and the Occupy Wall Street protests that became the Occupy movement by 2012 both relied heavily on public speeches to marshal support. The entire history of student protest in this country exhibits the centrality of public speaking to evoke change. Even a single student gifted in public speaking can produce important change. For example, a student in my public speaking class gave a terrific persuasive speech that argued for a more restrictive campus smoking policy. I encouraged her to present her speech to various decision-making bodies, which she did. Her speech provoked a campus-wide debate and produced her desired result.

There are many other important reasons to become a competent public speaker. College courses in diverse disciplines increasingly assign oral presentations. One massive survey revealed that 90% of first-year college students and 95% of seniors gave formal class presentations. Among first-year students, more than two-fifths gave oral class presentations "often" or "very often" and two-thirds of seniors did likewise ("National Survey," 2012). Relatively few students, however, see themselves as proficient public speakers (Pryor et al., 2012). Whether viewing oral presentations with reluctance or relish, you will undoubtedly be required to give them in your classes, so, practically speaking, why not learn to do them well?

Teaching, law, religion, politics, public relations, and marketing also require substantial public speaking knowledge and skill. A survey of employers in a wide variety of occupations and professions shows that competent public speaking is highly desirable ("Top Skills," 2011). Employers, however, do not believe most job applicants possess such knowledge and skill (Driscoll, 2011; "Job Outlook," 2009).

Competent public speaking is useful in other circumstances as well. Average citizens are frequently called upon to give speeches of support or dissent at public meetings on utility rate increases, school board issues, and city or county disputes. Toasts at weddings or banquets, tributes at awards ceremonies, eulogies at funerals for loved ones, and presentations at business meetings are additional common public speaking situations.

Imagine if this critical right in a free society to speak your mind in public were taken from you? In earlier times, women did not have to imagine it; they had to fight for the right. In 17th-century colonial America, a woman who spoke publicly could be dunked in any available body of water. When raised, sputtering and breathless, she was given two choices—agree to curb her offending tongue or suffer further dunkings. In Boston during the same century, women who gave speeches or spoke in religious or political meetings could be gagged (Jamieson, 1988). The mere presentation of a speech by a female in public was considered "unwomanly" and invited scorn, ridicule, and humiliation. So intent were men on silencing women that in the 18th and 19th centuries a ridiculous fiction was propagated that women who insisted on giving public speeches would become infertile (Levander, 1998). Even as recently as the early 1970s, Congresswoman Patricia Schroeder felt it necessary to tell a hostile constituent during her speech, "Yes, I have a uterus and a brain, and they both work" (cited in Tolchin & Tolchin, 1973, p. 87).

Learning to be a competent public speaker is important for both women and men. Such speakers possess an impressive array of knowledge and skills. They know how to present complex ideas clearly and fluently, keep an audience's attention, analyze important issues, conduct research, make reasonable arguments, and support claims with valid proof. They entertain and also move people to listen, to contemplate, and to change their minds.

Given these bountiful benefits of effective public speaking, *the purpose of this chapter is to begin exploring public speaking from a communication competence perspective.* This chapter defines both communication and communication competence in the context of public speaking, and it provides general ways to achieve public speaking competence as a basis for more specific exploration in remaining chapters.

DEFINING COMMUNICATION

Communication is a transactional process of sharing meaning with others. **Public speaking** is fundamentally an act of communication in which a clearly identified speaker presents a message in a more formal manner than mere conversation to an audience of multiple listeners on an occasion to achieve a specific purpose. Explaining how public speaking functions as a transactional process begins our journey.

Communication as Transactional: Working with an Audience

Human communication is transactional. To understand the ways in which public speaking as a communication act is transactional, some basic elements need brief explanation. When you give a speech in class you are the *sender* who *encodes* your ideas by organizing and expressing them in a spoken language. The *message* is composed of the ideas you wish to express, such as what your college should do about rising tuition and fees. The *channel* is the medium used to share a message with receivers; they include oral (speaking), aural (listening), and visual (seeing) channels. The *receivers* are your classmates who *decode* your message by interpreting your spoken ideas. *Noise* is any interference with effective transmission and reception of your message. This might be a loud cell-phone conversation just outside the classroom, tardy students arriving in the middle of your speech, or the unfortunate periodic reappearance of corduroy pants and paisley blouses that all divert attention from the message transmitted.

Defining communication, and public speaking, as **transactional** means that the speaker is both a sender and a receiver simultaneously, not merely a sender or a receiver. (Listeners are likewise sender-receivers). As you give a speech, you receive *feedback* or responses, mostly nonverbal, from listeners. This feedback *influences* you while you are speaking. When Julian Castro, mayor of San Antonio, Texas, was delivering the keynote address at the 2012 Democratic National Convention, he delivered this line halfway through his speech: "*Que Dios te bendiga*—May God bless you." At that very moment, Castro's three-year-old daughter, sitting in the gallery with her mother, was shown on the giant television monitor behind Castro repeatedly flipping her hair. The crowd began to laugh at this adorable child's antic. Castro was clearly perplexed by this unexpected interruption, and he stopped for a moment. Afterwards, Castro said that he was startled and thought, "What? You are not supposed to laugh at this part" (quoted in "Julian Castro's Daughter," 2012). He thought he was receiving feedback from his audience about the speech he was presenting, and it affected him.

PHOTO 1.1 & 1.2 Julian Castro's daughter provides an adorable distraction (noise) during his 2012 keynote address at the Democratic National Convention.

The unexpected audience laughter acted as noise because it distracted Castro and momentarily disrupted the smooth rhythm of his speech.

The influence of audience feedback can also be seen when you give a speech in class. Imagine the difference between being enthusiastically applauded and angrily booed by your classmates. Being applauded is encouraging and may enhance the effective transmission and reception of your message, but being loudly booed is discouraging and likely acts as noise that diminishes your effectiveness.

Transactional communication also means that there is more to a speech than the *content* (information) of your message. You develop a *relationship*, an association, with audience members as you present your speech. If they like you, they may listen to you; if they dislike you, they may not. For example, I had a Vietnamese student in one of my public speaking classes whose English was difficult to understand. He was genuinely enthusiastic when giving his speeches, however, and he was universally well liked by the class. So, whenever he gave a presentation, classmates would strain to discern what he was saying, and they always gave him a rousing ovation after each speech, even though I am certain only the gist of his message, at best, was comprehended.

Effective public speaking blends excellent content with a strong audience connection. Neither one by itself is sufficient. An excellently constructed speech may fail if either you or your message does not resonate with listeners. Conversely, a strong connection with your audience may not compensate adequately for a poorly constructed, rambling, or indecipherable speech.

Communication as Process: The Continuous Flow

Viewing public speaking as a transactional *process* recognizes that nothing stands still, or as the bumper sticker proclaims, "Change is inevitable—except from a vending machine." You cannot understand the ocean by isolating a single wave in a photograph. The ocean is understood only as a dynamic event—its tides, currents, waves, plant and animal life interacting symbiotically. Similarly, public speaking as a communication event makes sense, not by isolating a word, sentence, gesture, facial expression, or body movement made while speaking, but by examining currents of thought and feelings expressed verbally and nonverbally as a total speech.

Because a speech is a process, speakers must learn to adapt to inevitable and persistent change. Your audience members may be bored one minute and attentive the next depending on the flow of your speech. They may agree one minute and, in a flash, disagree the next minute. Strong preparation and effective audience analysis can minimize the need for adaptive changes because you have properly prepared for what is likely to occur during your speech.

Communication as Sharing Meaning: Making Sense

Public speaking as a communication act requires more than the mere transmission of a message from a speaker to receivers. The speaker hopes to share meaning with his or her listeners. **Shared meaning** occurs when both the speaker and receivers have mutual understanding of a message (Anderson & Ross, 1994). Something is viewed as "meaningless" when it makes no sense. For example, consider the story of a Catholic nun teaching religion to her third-graders and conducting standard catechism drills. She repeatedly asked her students, "Who is God?" Her students were to respond in unison, "God is a supreme being." Finally, she decided to test the fruits of her patient labor and called on one of the boys in the class. When asked, "Who is God?" he promptly and proudly replied, "God is a string bean." Words were transmitted, but meaning was not shared. *Supreme being* to a third-grader is difficult to grasp as an abstract concept, but a *string bean* is a concrete understandable object, even if applying it to the divinity is a tad mysterious. Sharing meaning requires that you tailor your speech to your audience's ability to understand your intended message.Technical terminology or highly abstract presentations well beyond the knowlege and background of your listeners may merely confuse them making your speech fairly pointless.

Sharing meaning between cultures poses its own unique problems. Accurate translations between languages are notoriously difficult. Electrolux, a Scandinavian manufacturer, discovered this when it tried to sell its vacuum cleaners in the

United States with the slogan, "Nothing sucks like an Electrolux." Soon after the 9/11 terrorist attacks on the United States, George W. Bush observed during a press conference that "this crusade, this war on terrorism, is going to take awhile." Bush used "crusade" to mean a vigorous action, but crusade is an explosively offensive word in the Muslim world, conjuring images of the historic clashes between Christians and Muslims. There was a huge outcry around the world from those who feared a renewed "clash of civilizations" provoked by the thought of a new crusade (Ford, 2001). Recognizing his verbal gaffe, Bush immediately dropped the term in future speeches and press conferences.

Sharing meaning nonverbally between cultures can be equally problematic (Axtell, 1998, 2007; Mancini, 2003). World leaders, diplomats, and members of the business community have to be conscious of potentially embarrassing gestural misunderstandings when giving speeches. Bill Clinton has often flashed the thumbs-up gesture during and after speeches, but it means "up yours" in several cultures (Axtell, 1998).

In review, communication is a transactional process of sharing meaning with others. Public speaking as a communicative act is transactional because as a

PHOTO 1.3 Common hand gestures can be offensive in many cultures. The "hook-em horns" gesture displayed by George W. Bush, a reference to the University of Texas Longhorns, is a salute to Satan in Norway. In Italy, it is an accusation of adultery.

speaker you both send messages to listeners and receive messages (feedback) from your audience members simultaneously. You influence your listeners and they influence you as this constantly changing, dynamic process of sharing meaning unfolds.

Identifying and explaining public speaking as an act of communication, however, does not tell you how to become a competent public speaker. Many books, both academic and mass market, have been written that attempt to do just that. What they often have in common is extensive recipes for improving your public speaking, but they are devoid of a strong theoretical model for such proffered advice. This makes the advice seem more personal opinion and individual taste than sound practice based on research.

In contrast, the communication competence model is a well-conceived theoretical model grounded in solid reasoning and research. It should serve as your over-arching guide to public speaking excellence. Defining what it is and how to achieve it generally are the next two points of focus.

DEFINING COMMUNICATION COMPETENCE IN PUBLIC SPEAKING

Communication competence *is engaging in communication with others that is perceived to be both effective and appropriate in a given context* (Spitzberg, 2000). The previous section already defined communication. This section defines what it means to be both effective and appropriate when giving a public speech.

Effectiveness. Achieving Goals

Effectiveness is the degree to which speakers have progressed toward the achievement of their goals. In public speaking, you have general goals or purposes that you hope to achieve well, such as to inform, persuade, celebrate, entertain, inspire, or give tribute. Achieving your public speaking goals is a challenging process.

Degrees of Effectiveness: From Deficiency to Proficiency   Some of you would rather be dipped in molasses and strapped to an anthill than to give a public speech in front of your peers. Yet, giving a speech to an audience of strangers may invite no more than mild concern for success. Competence varies by degrees from highly proficient to severely deficient depending on the current set of circumstances. Thus, you may see yourself as moderately skillful giving a well-prepared informative speech but woefully deficient giving an inspirational speech. We are more to less competent, not either competent or incompetent. Labeling someone a "competent speaker" makes a judgment of that individual's degree of proficiency *in a particular speaking context*, but it does not identify an immutable characteristic of that person. Even the best public speakers occasionally fail in some situations.

Audience Orientation: You Are Not Talking to Yourself   To be effective, the key focus of any speech has to be on your audience. Topics that interest you may narcotize your audience. A speaking style that is florid with colorful language and weighted with complicated sentence structure and sophisticated vocabulary may confuse and frustrate listeners whose native language is not English.

Audience orientation can be complicated by today's ready access to information through multiple forms of media transmission. You may be speaking to an immediate audience present in front of you, but your speech may be transmitted to additional remote audiences, especially if it is posted on YouTube. For example, University of Iowa college student Zach Wahls gave a powerful 3-minute speech in 2011 to the Iowa State Legislature that was subsequently posted on YouTube and viewed more than 17 million times (*see* http://www.youtube.com/watch?v=FSQQK2Vuf9Q). His seemingly local speech went viral on the Internet, and Wahls' speech became one of the most talked about speeches by a college student ever presented.

National figures must also recognize that in this age of sophisticated information technology, remote audiences must be considered. Vice President Joe Biden, on August 14, 2012, triggered a controversy when speaking to a largely African American audience in Virginia. Biden asserted that Mitt Romney would "unchain" the big banks by deregulating them. Then departing from his prepared text, always a thrill ride of uncertainty, he claimed, "They're going to put y'all back in chains." His immediate audience roared approval, but most of the news media covering the speech and in the Twitterverse saw this as a gaffe that implied Romney favored slavery. Biden backtracked quickly to "clarify" his point and dampen outrage from many quarters beyond his immediate audience (Amira, 2012).

Being audience oriented does not mean that you must hide your true viewpoints and pander to the whims of your audience. There are times when challenging the views of your listeners is essential, especially when most of them believe what is patently false. Nevertheless, your topic choice, purpose in speaking, organizational structure and development of your speech, your style and delivery, and your use of supporting materials all must keep a focus on your audience's needs, views, and expectations. For example, *your first class speech* might be to introduce yourself. Your student audience is unlikely to find a long, rambling speech interesting. Provide relevant, interesting information about yourself. Basic background, such as your age, place of birth, length of time in your present location, places you have visited, reasons why you are in college, educational major, what you consider to be fun, what makes you laugh, and what you plan for a career are just some possible disclosures you might share with your audience. You want to be brief, conversational in style and delivery, interesting, and organized, because that is what your audience likely expects.

Appropriateness: Speaking by the Rules

Appropriateness is behavior that is perceived to be legitimate and fits the speaking context (Spitzberg, 2000). **Context** is the environment in which communication occurs: *who* (sender-receiver) communicates *what* (message) to *whom* (receiver-sender), *why* a message is presented (purpose), *where* (setting) it is presented, and *when* (timing) and *how* (channel) it is transmitted. We determine the appropriateness of our communication by analyzing all of these elements.

Every communication context is guided by rules. A **rule** "is a followable prescription that indicates what behavior is obligated, preferred, or prohibited in certain contexts" (Shimanoff, 1980, p. 57). College instructors take for granted that students will not interrupt the flow of a lecture by talking inappropriately with fellow students. This is an implicit rule, meaning one that is assumed but not stated directly. Occasionally, however, this implicit rule has to be made explicit, identified directly, to students whose enthusiasm for casual conversation outweighs their ardor for the classroom task of listening to the professor's lecture.

The relationship between speaking context and rules can be illustrated by an incident that produced a national controversy. During Barack Obama's speech to a joint session of the U.S. Congress on September 9, 2009, Congressman Joe Wilson shouted "You lie" when the president claimed that healthcare reform proposals did not permit health insurance coverage for illegal immigrants. Speaker of the House Nancy Pelosi shot a death stare at Wilson. Later she remarked, "There was a violation of the rules of the House. It needs to be resolved by an apology or a resolution" (quoted by Soraghan, 2009). A *USA Today*/Gallup poll showed that 68% of those who listened to the president's speech disapproved of Wilson's heckling, and a quarter were "outraged." Only 20% approved of the heckling (quoted in Murphy, 2009).

It was the president of the country (*who* was the target) being insulted (*what* was the message) by a member of Congress (*who* perpetrated the act) at a joint session of Congress (*where* it occurred) during the president's formal address (*when* it occurred), and the message was shouted (*how* it was communicated) to make a controversial point (*why* Wilson did it). All of these contextual elements dictate appropriateness or rules that apply. In addition, the Committee on Rules for Republicans instructs incoming party members of Congress that "it is not permissible to use language that is personally offensive to the President, such as referring to him as a 'hypocrite' or a 'liar'" ("Basic Training," 2009). Wilson, a Republican from South Carolina, was ordered by his party's leadership to apologize to the president, which he did.

In different cultures, the communication rules of civility and decorum can be strikingly different. Opposition members of the British Parliament regularly heckle the prime minister of Great Britain during parliamentary "debates," which often seem like verbal food fights. Comedian Robin Williams once likened the British Parliament to "Congress with a two drink minimum." Despite the raucous heckling often exhibited, even the British Parliament has an explicit rule against calling a prime minister a liar (Robinson, 2009).

There are no sacred, universal rules applicable to every speech situation, so such rules are matters of common agreement. You must know the operative rules, however, in any context. These contextual rules help you realize what to expect from your audience and what they expect from you. If you violate the rules of the speaking context, there will be consequences.

Rules, of course, can be changed if they do not achieve a common purpose. If Congress decides that its rules of decorum are too restrictive and stodgy, the rules can be loosened. Congress could operate more like the British Parliament. Even the rule that forbids members of Congress calling the president of the United States a liar could be eliminated. Whatever the prevailing rules, *communication becomes inappropriate if it violates rules when such violations could be averted without sacrificing a goal by choosing alternative communication behaviors* (Getter & Nowinski, 1981). Joe Wilson could have changed *what* he said by using more temperate language, such as "The president is dead wrong." He could have changed *where* and *when* he challenged the president by making a statement at a press conference after Obama's address. The issue then would have been who is right about the president's assertion on health care and immigration, which was Wilson's presumed goal, not whether it is appropriate to call the president a liar during a speech before Congress that is being televised to the nation.

ACHIEVING COMPETENT PUBLIC SPEAKING

Competent public speaking requires you to be both appropriate and effective when communicating your message to an audience. The appropriateness and effectiveness of your public speaking can be improved in five general ways. You can build *knowledge* about what works and what does not in any public speaking context, you can develop your public speaking *skills*, increase your *sensitivity* relevant to audiences, enhance your *commitment* to speak effectively, and you can apply *ethics* to your public speaking performances (see Figure 1.1). Consider each of these more specifically.

FIGURE 1.1 Communication Competence Model

Knowledge: Learning the Rules

Achieving communication competence begins with knowledge of the rules that create behavioral expectations and by knowing what is likely to work effectively given the rules of the situation. Communication can be *inappropriate and ineffective* and thus deficient in every respect. When Taylor Swift won the Best Female Video award at the 2009 MTV Video Music Awards, Kanye West interrupted her acceptance speech. He grabbed her microphone and proclaimed Beyoncé Knowles' video "one of the best of all time." West's communication was both inappropriate and ineffective. He seemed either clueless or unconcerned about basic rules of decorum at such an event. He hijacked 19-year-old Swift's moment in the spotlight. His boorish stunt went over like the pungent odor of effluent spewing from an overflowing sewer. He brought almost universal derision upon himself from the music and pop culture worlds (Martens, 2009).

Communication can also be *appropriate but ineffective*, such as when uncontrollable circumstances prevent achieving a goal despite following the rules. Parents and interested parties regularly appear at school board meetings across the nation in recessionary times to discuss and debate budget cutbacks. Even when participants give polite, well-reasoned, impassioned speeches beseeching board members to vote against budget cuts, school boards often see no other option because there simply is not enough money available.

Communication can also be *inappropriate but effective*. Lying, cheating, intimidating, or coercing others is inappropriate because it violates ethical rules, but it can be effective in achieving self-centered goals. Negative political advertising and speeches that lie about an opponent's record, character, and proposals often work to get candidates elected despite violating commonly accepted rules of ethical behavior (Westen, 2007).

Finally, communication can be *appropriate and effective* when goals are achieved while following the rules relevant to a context. When Beyonce won the 2009 MTV award for Video of the Year, she invited Taylor Swift back on stage and

PHOTO 1.4 In a stunningly inappropriate act, Kanye West seized the microphone from Taylor Swift, denying her the opportunity to give her acceptance speech at the MTV Music Awards. What implicit rules were violated by West? In 2013, Swift tweeted about her 2 VMA nominations, remarking that if she won, "I promise to keep a firmer grip on the mic this time."

she gave this short speech: "Thank you. I remember being 17-years-old, up for my first MTV Award with Destiny's Child, and it was one of the most exciting moments in my life. So I'd like Taylor [Swift] to come out and have her moment" ("Kanye West Acts Like a Jerk at VMAs," 2009). Beyonce received widespread acclaim for her generous gesture, and Taylor Swift got an opportunity to thank her fans.

Which of these four possibilities is most likely to occur largely depends on your knowledge of the rules and the communication strategies that work in a public speaking situation. This text aims to provide that necessary knowledge.

Skills: Showing Not Just Knowing

A **communication skill** is "the successful performance of a communication behavior . . . [and] the ability to repeat such a behavior" (Spitzberg & Hecht, 1984, p. 577). Clearly, fluently, concisely, eloquently, and confidently speaking to an audience are examples of such skill. Knowledge about public speaking without speaking skills will not produce competence. You can read this entire text and excel on every exam, but there is no substitute for skill gained by the practice and experience of speaking in front of an audience. Knowing that speaking with long pauses and vocal fillers such as *ums* and *uhs* is unskillful and ineffective does not automatically translate into an ability to speak fluently. You will continue *uming* and *uhing* unless you hone your speaking skills with practice.

Sensitivity: Developing Receptive Accuracy

Can you accurately perceive the difference between a look of disgust, anger, joy, agreement, frustration, or contempt from members of your audience? **Sensitivity** is *receptive accuracy* whereby you can detect, decode, and comprehend signals in your social environment (Bernieri, 2001). Sensitivity can help you adapt your messages to a particular audience in an appropriate and effective manner. Competent speakers develop sensitivity to the subtleties of communication transactions and respond to them. Failure to recognize and comprehend signals can severely diminish your effectiveness (Hall & Bernieri, 2001). Weddings all too often provide opportunities for members of the wedding party, relatives, or friends to offer cringe-worthy toasts to the bride and groom. Toasted on too much alcohol, they make sexually suggestive comments, use vulgar language, and generally give an R-rated speech to a G-rated audience which usually includes children. Despite obvious signals from offended listeners, the pickled presenters plod ever onward apparently unaware or unconcerned about their inappropriate behavior.

A major aspect of sensitivity is being mindful, not mindless, about your communication. You are **mindful** when you think about your communication and concentrate on changing what you do to become more effective (Griffin, 2012). You are **mindless** when you are not cognizant of your communication with others or simply do not care, so no improvement is likely. This text encourages mindfulness at every stage of speech preparation and presentation.

Commitment: Acquiring a Passion for Excellence

Commitment is a passion for excellence—that is, accepting nothing less than the best that you can be and dedicating yourself to achieving that excellence. To exhibit commitment, *attitude is as important as aptitude.* In sports, athletes develop a high level of skill when they commit themselves to hard work, study, and practice. Academic success also does not come from lackluster effort. You make it a priority in your life. The same holds true for competent public speaking. You have to want to improve, to change, and to grow more proficient, and you must be willing to put in the effort required to excel. You do not wait until the last minute to think about your speech, and you do not try to "wing it" with no preparation. "Winging it" just means flying blind with predictable results.

Ethics: Determining the Right and Wrong of Speaking

Humans ponder the moral implications of their behavior. It is one of the characteristics that separates humans from the beasts-as-feasts daily killing field that occurs on the African Serengeti. Consequently, you should consider whether your communication in the public speaking arena is ethically justifiable.

Ethics is a system for judging the moral correctness of human behavior by weighing that behavior against an agreed upon set of standards of right and wrong. The National Communication Association's "Credo for Ethical Communication" identifies five ethical standards (see also the Josephson Institute of Ethics publication, "Making Ethical Decisions," 2013):

1. **Respect.** Treating others as you would want to be treated is a central guiding ethical standard in "virtually all of the major religious and moral systems" (Jaksa & Pritchard, 1994, p. 101). Consequently, you should be respectful when others are speaking. Resist the temptation to text, tweet, or trifle with your Facebook page when other students are giving speeches.

2. **Honesty.** All ethical systems condemn lying and dishonesty (Jaksa & Pritchard, 1994). Plagiarism—stealing someone else's words and ideas and

attributing them to oneself—is clearly dishonest and is discussed later in the text. One study of intercollegiate informative speaking contests discovered that among the six student finalists, there were 18 instances of fabricated evidence and 10 instances of distorted evidence (Cronn-Mills & Schnoor, 2003). This is clearly dishonest.

3. **Fairness.** A debate in which one side was allowed to speak for 15 minutes but the opposing side was permitted only 5 minutes would be labeled as unfair. Fairness requires equal treatment and opportunity. "Playing by the rules" means avoiding favoritism. Whatever the rules, they should be applied without prejudice.

4. **Choice.** Our communication should strive to allow people to make their own choices, free of coercion (Cheney et al., 2011; Jaksa & Pritchard, 1994). Persuasion allows free choice among available options. Coercion forces decisions without permitting individuals to think or act for themselves. Shouting down speakers so they cannot give their speech is a bullying tactic that denies choice.

When is heckling ethical or unethical?

⑤ Responsibility. You have an obligation to consider the consequences of your speeches on others (Jensen, 1997). Competent speakers must concern themselves with more than merely what works. For example, provoking listeners to engage in unlawful violence is irresponsible.

In the abstract, these standards may seem straightforward and noncontroversial, but any list of standards for judging the ethics of public speaking, applied without exceptions, is bound to run into difficulty. For example, what if being honest shows disrespect and lack of concern for the feelings of others ("Yes, most members of this audience are fat and unattractive")? Heckling a speaker is disrespectful, but are there never occasions when heckling is the only means of communicating disagreement with a speaker? The Occupy movement's tactic dubbed "the human microphone," in which an individual rises in an audience during a speaker's presentation and calls out "mic check" and others do likewise has created quite a stir on many college campuses where it is most popular. As the original heckler barks out a sentence in protest to the main featured speaker, fellow Occupy protesters repeat each sentence to amplify their message. "The primary purpose of Occupy's use of the human microphone at public speaking events is not to disrupt, but to be heard. It is not an assault on free speech but a tactic for obtaining it" (Rey, 2012). Occupiers argue that the powerful easily gain access to the speaker's podium to express their ideas (they have a choice), while the less powerful must fight for the right to be heard (fairness) (Reguillo, 2013).

Others strongly disagree with the human microphone tactic. Andrew Bernstein, a visiting professor of philosophy at Marist College who gave a lecture disrupted by the human microphone strategy at University of Massachusetts Amherst claimed, "That behavior is simply uncivilized, and should not be tolerated by anybody on any campus, certainly not on a college campus where freedom of intellectual expression should be sacred" (quoted in Grasgreen, 2011).

Applying ethical standards is not always clear-cut and obvious. Despite these difficulties, however, all five ethical standards—respect, honesty, fairness, choice, and responsibility—are strong values in our culture, and they serve as important guidelines for ethical public speaking.

SUMMARY

Competent public speaking is an essential element of any democratic society. It also provides many practical benefits. The communication competence model serves as a theoretical guide throughout this discussion of practical public speaking. Public speakers must make choices regarding the appropriateness and likely effectiveness of topics, attention strategies, style and delivery, evidence, and persuasive strategies. When you are giving a speech, you must be sensitive to the signals sent from an audience that indicate lack of interest, disagreement, confusion, enjoyment, support, and a host of additional reactions. This allows you to make adjustments during the speech, if necessary. Finally, the effectiveness of a speech must be tempered by ethical concerns. What works may not always be honest, respectful, responsible, non-coercive, or fair.

2

Speech Anxiety

Ricky Henderson, longtime baseball star for the Oakland Athletics, fretted before giving a speech at the ceremony inducting him into baseball's Hall of Fame at Cooperstown on July 26, 2009. As he described it, giving a speech, especially of this magnitude, is like "putting a tie too tight around your neck . . . I've sweated to death about it and then wondered why" (quoted in Steward, 2009a, pp. C1, C5). Henderson wisely sought help from speech instructor Earl Robinson at Laney College. He also received critiques from Robinson's students, who were taking a summer public speaking class and heard Henderson's speech. He practiced his speech for 2 weeks. One journalist, who listened to Henderson's 14-minute presentation at the Hall of Fame ceremony, offered this assessment: "He seized the stage in Cooperstown, N.Y., and commanded it as he did as a player. . . . He wasn't perfect, but he was pretty close. Moreover, he was gracious, highly effective, and suitably entertaining" (Poole, 2009, pp. 1A; 6A).

The purpose of this chapter is to discuss speech anxiety as a potential problem that you can address effectively. Toward that end, this chapter discusses the magnitude of the challenge of speech anxiety, its symptoms, causes, and potential solutions.

SPEECH ANXIETY AS A CHALLENGE

Speech anxiety is fear of public speaking and the nervousness that accompanies that fear. Why address speech anxiety so early in this text and devote a chapter to it? There are two reasons. First, when a speech assignment is given, the immediate concern you may have is fear of speaking in front of an audience, especially to a gathering of your peers. In fact, the instant a speech assignment is announced, many students manifest high levels of anxiety (Behnke & Sawyer, 1999a). This anxiety can preoccupy your thoughts and adversely affect your ability to prepare your speech. Postponing a thorough discussion of speech anxiety would only increase the common response to such anxiety—avoidance (Richmond & McCroskey, 1995). Some students may drop a public speaking course early in the term if speech anxiety is not addressed promptly. Second, managing speech anxiety effectively requires specific preparation. If you wait until you actually give your speech before considering what steps need to be taken to manage your anxiety, it is usually too late. Simply put, you need a clear plan for managing your speech anxiety, one that is developed very early in the public speaking process.

Pervasiveness of Speech Anxiety: The General Population

Mark Twain once remarked, "There are two types of speakers: those who are nervous and those who are liars." Overstated perhaps, but about 85% of the population fears public speaking (Motley, 1995), and of these, almost three-quarters experience moderately high to very high speech anxiety (Richmond & McCroskey, 1995). This holds true for both face-to-face and web-based "online" speeches given to remote audiences (Campbell & Larson, 2012). Some surveys show that many people fear public speaking more than they fear death (Bruskin & Goldring, 1993; Thomson, 2008), prompting Jerry Seinfeld to quip that if you attend a funeral you would prefer being in the casket to delivering the eulogy. These "death before public speaking" survey findings are dubious at best (Davies, 2011). Can you imagine anyone choosing the firing squad to the firing line in front of an audience if provided this forced choice? Surely you would want to "say a few last words" (give a speech) to stall the firing squad? These death-preference survey results, however, are a reflection of some individuals' intense speech anxiety. Public speaking is a challenge, but not a fate worse than death, and it should not be avoided at all costs.

Anxiety and Professionals: Not Just the Novices

Speech anxiety is not a challenge only novice speakers must address. A substantial majority of experienced speakers also have anxiety before presentations (Hahner et al., 1997). Even college instructors must manage it (Gardner & Leak, 1994).

The "death before public speaking" poll results undoubtedly are more figurative than literal. Who would actually choose death? Nevertheless, irrational fear of public speaking can make it seem like a fate worse than death. This makes it an issue worth addressing right away.

Famous speakers throughout history such as Cicero, Daniel Webster, Abraham Lincoln, Eleanor Roosevelt, Winston Churchill, and Gloria Steinem overcame their fear of public speaking by taking every opportunity to mount the speaker's platform. Actor Harrison Ford feared public speaking his entire career. Even when the character he was playing in a movie was required to make a speech as part of the script (e.g., *Air Force One*), he admitted to feeling speech anxiety (Bailey, 2008). Jennifer Aniston, Cheryl Cole, Courtney Cox, Matt Damon, Ellen DeGeneres, Reese Witherspoon, Leonardo DiCaprio, Beyonce Knowles, Natalie Portman, Julia Roberts, Adam Sandler, and Charlize Theron are just a few of the celebrities who have confessed to fear of public speaking. NFL wide receiver, Marvin Harrison, a future Hall-of-Famer, made this surprising revelation: "When people talk about the Hall of Fame, the first thing I say is, "Do I have to give a speech?' If I'm not inducted, that will be fine with me because that means I'm not going to give a speech" (quoted in Demasio, 2007, p. 43). Harrison could profit from Rickey Henderson's example by seeking help from a speech instructor before giving his Hall of Fame presentation.

SYMPTOMS: FIGHT-OR-FLIGHT RESPONSE

Howard Goshorn observed, "The human brain is a wonderful thing. It operates from the moment you are born until you stand up to make a speech." "Going blank" is one of the most common concerns of novice speakers. Why does the human brain seem to stop working when giving a speech? Learning to manage your speech anxiety begins with identifying its common symptoms and explaining why these symptoms occur.

Basic Symptoms: Your Body's Response to Threat

The physiological defense-alarm process triggered by stress is called the **fight-or-flight response** (Cannon, 1932). The myriad physiological changes that are activated by a perceived threat prepare both animals and humans either to fight the foe or flee the fear-inducing threat.

The fight-or-flight response produces a complex constellation of physiological symptoms. Some of the more pronounced symptoms are accelerated heart beat and increased blood pressure that increase oxygen supply; blood vessel constriction in skin, skeletal muscles, brain, and viscera that cuts off blood supply to less necessary functions; increased perspiration that enhances cooling; increased respiration that supplies oxygen; inhibited digestion that stalls unnecessary energy drain; stimulated glucose release from the liver that increases energy supply; increased blood flow away from extremities and to large muscles that supplies oxygen and glucose to major muscles used to fight; stimulated adrenal gland activity that improves alertness, motion, and strength; spleen release of red blood corpuscles that aids in clotting a wound; and bone marrow stimulation to produce white corpuscles that fights possible infection (Passer & Smith, 2011).

Some of the more prominent corresponding verbal and nonverbal symptoms are quivering, tense voice and weak projection from constricted throat muscles; frequent dysfluencies such as "ums" and "uhs" and, of course, going blank from restricted blood flow to the brain causing confusion of thought; rigid, motionless posture from constricted muscles of legs and torso; dry mouth from digestive system shutdown that makes speaking difficult, even long pauses and silence from being scared speechless (Lewin et al.,1996).

Appropriateness of Symptoms: Relevance to Public Speaking

The physiological symptoms of the fight-or-flight response make sense if you are about to grapple with a crazed grizzly or run with the bulls at Pamplona.

Increased perspiration (cooling), respiration (oxygen), glucose (energy), and blood flow to major muscles (strength) would certainly help with the grappling and running. There are few times, however, in which fighting or fleeing would be an appropriate response to speech anxiety. There is little likelihood that you will be grappling with anyone during your speech, and it is doubtful that you would sprint from the classroom when called to begin a speech. Granted, if the speech is lengthy, the room hot and stuffy, and the occasion momentous, increased glucose, respiration, perspiration, and adrenaline will help sustain you throughout your presentation. Adrenaline can also assist you in performing at a peak level, very similar to athletes "psyching up" for an important contest. Clothes saturated with perspiration, increased red and white corpuscles, nausea, a pounding heart, a quivering voice, dry mouth, and rigid posture, however, are unnecessary and often distracting when making a speech—unless your life is in jeopardy, an unlikely classroom occurrence. Nevertheless, your sympathetic nervous system, which controls the fight-or-flight response, does not pick and choose relevant symptoms (Wilson, 2003). When the response is triggered, you get the whole package. Thus, *the useful approach to speech anxiety is to moderate the fight-or-flight response, not hope to activate only selective symptoms.*

PHOTO 2.1 The fight-or-flight response is quite useful if you are running from the bulls at Pamplona, Spain. It is not so helpful when giving a speech. Fighting or fleeing would be a strange response to giving a speech in class.

CAUSES OF DYSFUNCTIONAL ANXIETY

Dysfunctional speech anxiety occurs when the intensity of the fight-or-flight response prevents an individual from giving a speech effectively. **Functional speech anxiety** occurs when the fight-or-flight response is managed and stimulates an optimum presentation. *The degree of anxiety and your ability to manage it, not anxiety itself, determines the difference.* Individuals who experience low to moderate anxiety that is under control typically give better speeches than individuals who experience little or no anxiety (Motley, 1995). As much as you may think eliminating your speech anxiety would be terrific, *do not make zero anxiety your goal.* Low to moderate anxiety means you care about the quality of the speech. Anxiety can energize you and enhance your presentation. You present a more dynamic, exciting presentation when energized than when you feel so comfortable that you create an impression of almost sleepwalking through your speech.

The first step in learning to maintain your anxiety at a functional level is to understand the causes of dysfunctional anxiety. Causes of dysfunctional speech anxiety fall primarily into two categories: self-defeating thoughts and situational factors.

Self-Defeating Thoughts: Sabotaging Your Speech

Some individuals see giving a speech as a challenging and exciting opportunity, whereas other individuals see it as an experience equivalent to being swallowed by a python. How you think about speaking to an audience will largely determine your level of speech anxiety (Cho et al., 2004). Self-defeating thoughts that can sabotage your speech are grounded in the excessive concern that your audience will judge and reject you (Cunningham et al., 2006).

Catastrophic Thinking: Fear of Failure   Wildly exaggerating the magnitude of potential failure is a common source of stress and anxiety (Ellis, 1995; 1996). Those with irrational fears predict not just momentary memory lapses of no real consequence but a complete mental meltdown. They fear that audiences will laugh and hoot them off the stage and view them as irredeemable fools. Minor problems of organization during a speech are magnified in the speaker's mind into graphic episodes of total incoherence and nonstop babbling.

Predictions of public speaking catastrophes are unrealistic because they are highly unlikely to occur (Seligman, 1991; Peterson, 2000). I personally have listened to more than 20,000 student speeches. I have witnessed some unimpressive

Catastrophic thinking increases speech anxiety and magnifies minor mistakes into major mental meltdowns.

presentations, but not more than a handful of these qualified as outright unforgettable disasters, and the obvious cause of the disaster in each case was a complete lack of preparation.

Catastrophic thinking sees only failure, not an opportunity for exhilarating success produced by embracing challenges. Thomas Edison made more than 2000 attempts to invent the electric light bulb. When asked how it felt to fail so many times, Edison responded, "I never failed. It just happened to be a 2000 step process." Do not paralyze yourself with catastrophic, unrealistic thinking.

Perfectionist Thinking: No Mistakes Permitted   Perfectionists anguish over every perceived flaw, and they over-generalize the significance of even minor defects. For example:

> "I tanked—I forgot to preview my main points."
> "I feel so stupid. I kept mispronouncing the name of one of the experts I quoted."

Flawless public speaking is an unreasonable goal. Even the most talented and experienced public speakers make occasional errors in otherwise riveting and eloquent speeches. Martin Luther King Jr. stumbled twice during his famous "I Have a Dream" speech. These were only fleeting blips in an otherwise smoothly delivered masterpiece. Ironically, the imperfections so glaring to perfectionists usually go unnoticed by their audiences.

Desire for Complete Approval: Trying Not To Offend   It is highly unlikely that you will please everyone who listens to your speech, particularly if you take a stand on a controversial issue. Making complete approval from your audience a vital concern sets a standard for success at unreachable heights. Few speeches are universally praised. Lincoln's Gettysburg Address, for example, was effusively praised by the *Springfield Republican* newspaper as "a perfect gem" that was "deep in feeling, compact in thought and expression, and tasteful and elegant in every word and comma" (quoted in Prochow, 1944, p. 17). The *Chicago Times*, however, editorialized: "The cheek of every American must tingle with shame as he reads the silly, flat and dishwatery utterances of the man who has to be pointed out to intelligent foreigners as the President of the United States" (quoted in Sandburg, 2002, p. 445).

The Illusion of Transparency: Being Nervous about Looking Nervous   Substantial research shows that individuals often are overly worried about appearing nervous in front of an audience: "My knees were shaking. The audience must have thought I contracted rabies." Speakers who experience high levels of anxiety often fall victim to the *illusion of transparency*—the overestimation of the extent to which audience members detect a speaker's nervousness. As difficult as it may be for you to believe, your anxiety is not as obvious as you may think it is (MacInnis et al., 2010) . The speech by Zach Wahls referred to in the previous chapter is such a case. Wahls confessed on the Ellen DeGeneres Show that he was so nervous that he was shaking while presenting his "Two Mothers" speech to the Iowa state legislature. You simply cannot tell this from looking at his speech on YouTube. He appears very composed and confident.

Nevertheless, this illusion of transparency greatly increases a speaker's anxiety. You become "nervous about looking nervous" (Savitsky & Gilovich, 2003, p. 619). Unlike telling a person not to be nervous about giving a speech, which is unhelpful advice, informing a speaker about the illusion of transparency can free individuals from the cycle of anxiety and help them present better speeches because they worry less about appearing nervous (Savitsky & Gilovich, 2003).

Anxiety-Provoking Situations: Considering Context

Several anxiety-provoking situations are relevant to public speaking. There are three principal ones: novelty, conspicuousness, and types of speeches.

Novelty of the Speaking Situation: Uncertainty   We often fear what is unpredictable or unfamiliar (Witt & Behnke, 2006). For inexperienced speakers, the mere novelty of the speaking situation may trigger speech anxiety (Kelly & Keaten, 2000). What if your listeners seem bored? Is your speech too long or too short? Is the audience likely to be supportive or hostile? What if someone heckles? Based on **uncertainty reduction theory**, as you gain experience speaking in front of groups, the novelty wears off, uncertainty is reduced, and anxiety consequently diminishes because you gain a reservoir of knowledge from giving speeches that helps you handle almost any situation that might occur (Roby, 2009).

Conspicuousness: In the Spotlight   When asked what causes their speech anxiety, most students identify being "on stage" or "in the spotlight." Being conspicuous, or the center of attention, can increase your anxiety. You feel as if you are under a microscope being meticulously examined. As the size of an audience grows, conspicuousness increases in most individuals' minds. Gaining confidence from experience speaking often to a variety of audiences large and small is a strong antidote for alleviating speech anxiety provoked by conspicuousness.

Types of Speeches: Varying Responses   Types of speeches combined with situational challenges affect whether you experience anxiety. Telling a story in front of a class of fellow students may give you no pause, but giving a lecture as a teaching demonstration while interviewing for an important job may be an anxiety-producing situation (Young et al., 2004). Suddenly being asked to "say a few words" with no warning typically stirs greater anxiety than giving a more prepared speech (Witt & Behnke, 2006). Giving a speech to an audience hostile to your expressed point of view may also engender high levels of anxiety (Pertaub et al., 2002).

All of these causes of speech anxiety, both self-defeating thoughts and anxiety-provoking situations, can produce a spiraling effect that feeds on itself. If you begin by viewing a speech as a performance, you have already created unrealistic expectations for yourself. This, in turn, stimulates a physiological fight-or-flight arousal. If you then interpret the physical symptoms as fear, this can trigger catastrophic thinking which stimulates more intense physical symptoms, greater fear, and so forth (Motley, 1995). *A key to managing your speech anxiety is to prevent the spiral of fear from ever occurring.*

STRATEGIES FOR MANAGING SPEECH ANXIETY

One surefire way to experience absolutely no anxiety prior to and during a speech is not to care about the quality of your speech. You will be very relaxed, but you will also give a poor speech. Many individuals, from famous actors to celebrities of various kinds, have suggested strategies for managing speech anxiety. These include swearing at your audience backstage, sticking a pin in your backside (pain as diversion), and imagining members of your audience naked or clothed only in their underwear or in diapers. Although dubious solutions, these suggestions may indeed work for you, but there is no good evidence that they have widespread application. If there were such evidence, speech instructors across the nation would be passing out pins to their anxious students for them to stick in their backsides before giving speeches. These suggestions are unquestionably limited at best because they are diversionary tactics rather than strategies that directly address the primary causes of speech anxiety. This section discusses several ways to manage your speech anxiety that are supported by research.

Prepare and Practice: Transforming Novelty into Familiarity

As in most social situations, whether making small talk with strangers at parties or playing a musical instrument in front of a crowd, you tend to be less anxious when you are confident of your skills. You fear making a fool of yourself when you do not know what you are doing. First and foremost, do not delay preparing and practicing your speech until the night before you give it. Procrastination increases anxiety (Behnke & Sawyer, 1999b).

When you are adequately prepared, you have removed most of the novelty and uncertainty from the speaking situation. This reduces your anxiety (Menzel & Carrell, 1994). So prepare your speech meticulously. Begin the necessary research well in advance, organize and outline your speech carefully, and practice your presentation. Practice your speech while taking a shower. Give it in your car on your way to class. Give it to your dog; they are eager listeners (cats not so much). *Practice, practice, practice!* When you have practiced your speech "enough," practice it again. Do a dress rehearsal for friends or family members, or video record your performance and play it back so you can study parts to improve (Svoboda, 2009).

Giving speeches to a variety of audiences will gradually build your confidence and reduce your anxiety (Finn et al., 2009). Speaking experience, of course, will not reduce anxiety if you stumble from one traumatic disaster to the next. If you make speech after speech, ill prepared and untrained, your dread of public speaking will likely become dysfunctional. "Practice makes perfect" if it is practice based on knowledge of effective public speaking for appropriate skill building. Without requisite knowledge, practice will make perfectly awful any speech that you give because you will be rehearsing incompetent public speaking.

Poor physiological preparation also will sabotage the most carefully prepared and practiced speech. You require appropriate nutrition to manage the stress of public speaking. Do not deliver a speech on an empty stomach. Complex carbo-hydrates such as whole grains, pastas, and legumes work well to stoke your energy, but eat lightly. You want blood traveling to your brain, not to your stomach. Avoid the empty-calorie foods such as doughnuts. High intake of caffeine, simple sugars, and nicotine can stoke the physiological symptoms of fight-or-flight (increased heart rate, sweating). I once had a student with significant speech anxiety who drank a 32-ounce "Big Gulp" cola and chain smoked before each speech. He was a wreck each time he presented his speech, as were those of us who had to endure his agitated, overwrought, staccato presentation. Despite my best efforts, he continued to ignore proper physiological preparation necessary for effective public speaking.

Alcohol and tranquilizers are also counterproductive solutions. Alcohol restricts oxygen to your brain and dulls mental acuity. Tranquilizers can send you on a valium vacation in which you feel pleasantly numb but mentally dumb. You never want to take even a mild amphetamine. Speed kills a speech. It will increase your heart rate beyond what anxiety already induces.

There is no substitute for preparation and practice. If you do both, most of your anxiety will melt away, and your confidence will soar (Ayres & Hopf, 1995). Read the chapters in this text. Listen to the advice of your instructor as you prepare and present speeches.

Gain Realistic Perspective: Rational Not Irrational Thinking

Understanding the progression of your speech anxiety can give you a realistic perspective on what is a reasonable amount to expect. It will improve naturally. There are four phases to speech anxiety symptoms (Witt et al., 2006). There is the *anticipation phase*, when your symptoms elevate just prior to giving your speech. The *confrontation phase* occurs when you face the audience and begin to speak. There is a tremendous surge of adrenalin, heart rate soars—sometimes to 180 beats per minute—perspiration and other symptoms increase. Next the *adaptation phase* kicks in, about 60 seconds into the speech. Adaptation takes place even more swiftly for low-anxiety speakers, usually 15 to 30 seconds into the speech. During this phase symptoms steadily diminish, reaching a more comfortable level within a couple of minutes. Finally, there is the *release stage*—the 60 seconds immediately following the finish of the speech.

Recognizing that your anxiety will diminish dramatically and quickly as you speak should provide some comfort. By learning to monitor your adaptation, you can accelerate the process. As you begin to notice your heart rate diminishing, say to yourself, "It's getting better already . . . and better . . . and better." *Anxiety*

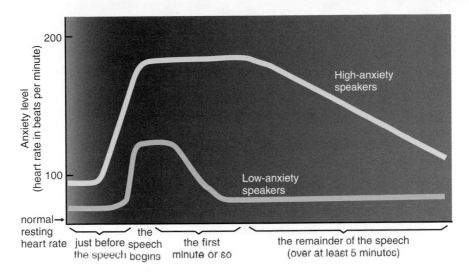

FIGURE 2.1 Heart-Rate Patterns of Typical High- and Low-Anxiety Speakers (Motley, 1995).

levels, even for the inexperienced, high-anxiety speaker, will diminish rapidly during the course of your speech.

Another aspect of gaining realistic perspective is learning to recognize the difference between rational and irrational speech anxiety. A colleague of mine, Darrell Beck, concocted a simple formula for determining the difference: *the **severity** of the feared occurrence times the **probability** of the feared occurrence.* This formula gives a rough approximation of how much anxiety is rational and when you have stepped over the line into irrational territory. Severity is approximated by imagining what would happen if catastrophic failure did occur. Peggy Noonan (1998), speechwriter for Ronald Reagan and political pundit on numerous television news shows, puts possible failure into perspective this way: "If I fail utterly, if I faint, babble or spew, if people walk out flinging the heavy linen napkins onto the big round tables in disgust . . . my life continues as good as it was. Better. Because fewer people will ask me to speak. So flopping would be good for me. The minute I remember this I don't flop" (p. 191).

Typically, when I ask my students for their worst imagined case of speech anxiety they offer examples such as stuttering, flop sweating, knees and hands shaking violently, forgetting everything, even fainting or vomiting in front of the class. Imagine all of this occurring, not just one or two of these manifestations of catastrophic failure, but the entire mess. Would you renew your passport and make plans to leave the country? Would you hide from friends and family, afraid to show your face? Would you drop out of college? Would you join a monastery and take a vow of silence? None of these choices seems likely. You might drop the class, but even this choice is unlikely. Students are an understanding lot (this is not high school), and you will have other opportunities in class to redeem yourself. Even a disastrous speech does not warrant significant life changes. A few moments of disappointment, mild embarrassment, or discouragement because of a mediocre grade is about as severe as the consequences get.

Then consider the probability of this nightmare scenario happening. It is highly improbable that all of these feared occurrences would transpire. No one has ever fainted or vomited in my classes despite the thousands of speeches I have witnessed. If you stutter and it is not an actual speech pathology, you can gain control by deliberately slowing your rate of speech and carefully enunciating your words. Other occurrences are mitigated with conscientious preparation and practice. When you consider the probability of the "worst-case scenario," you should realize that there is not much to concern you. *Concentrate on the probable (low-severity occurrences), not the improbable (high-severity occurrences).*

Even individuals for whom English is a second language will benefit from gaining a realistic perspective on their speech anxiety. Giving a speech in a second language can increase anxiety (McCroskey et al., 1985; Tan Chin Keok, 2010). There is an unrealistic expectation that English should be spoken perfectly. I have witnessed hundreds of speeches by non-native speakers of English. Never once has an audience of college students been rude to that speaker because his or her English was not perfect. Normally, students admire a speaker who tries hard to give a good speech in a relatively unfamiliar language. They usually listen more intently as well. Working yourself into a lather over an impending speech simply lacks a realistic perspective.

Adopt A Noncompetitive Communication Orientation: Reframing

Desiring complete approval, engaging in perfectionist thinking, and fretting over your conspicuousness onstage all occur when you view public speaking as a **performance**—an attempt to satisfy an audience of critics whose members are focused on evaluating your presentation (Motley, 1997). Giving a speech is not an Olympic event; you are usually not competing to score more points than someone else or to earn a gold medal and get your face on a cereal box. Your audience will not hold up cards indicating your score immediately after you sit down. Granted, your speech instructor will likely give you a grade on your speech, but even here the performance orientation is counterproductive. No speech instructor expects silver-tongued oratory from novice speakers. You are expected to make mistakes, especially during your first few speeches. Speech classes are learning laboratories, not speech tournaments.

Giving a speech is not an Olympic event. The communication orientation concentrates on clarity of your message to address speech anxiety not a performance orientation.

Reframe the performance orientation with a communication orientation. The **communication orientation** focuses on making your message clear and interesting to your listeners. Motley (1995) makes the case for reframing to the communication orientation: "I have never encountered an anxious speaker who did not have a performance orientation, or one whose anxiety was not substantially reduced when the communication orientation replaced it" (p. 49).

The irony is that you will perform more effectively as a speaker if you move away from the competitive performance orientation (Motley, 1995, 2011). Your speaking style and delivery will seem more natural, less forced and stiff. When conversing with a friend or stranger, you rarely notice your delivery, gestures, and posture. You are intent on being clear and interesting, even having some fun. Approach your speech in a similar way. Choking under pressure occurs most often when you overthink your performance while it is occurring (e.g., "vary your voice," "use gestures," "don't pace," "look at your audience," etc.). Scrutinizing your performance while speaking is counterproductive (Svoboda, 2009). Research on *attentional control* shows that high-anxiety public speakers concentrate on the threat associated with performance failure. Low-anxiety public speakers concentrate on that which does not heighten anxiety (Jones at al., 2012). Simply concentrate on communicating your message clearly to your audience and the rest will follow if you have prepared and practiced. Peggy Noonan (1998) reveals that one bad experience speaking in front of her peers in seventh grade caused her to lose her voice and induced panic. She had a performance orientation. She did not give another public speech until she was 40 years old. She became an accomplished speaker by focusing less on herself and more on communicating clearly the content of her speech.

One way to develop the communication orientation is to practice your speech conversationally. Choose a friend or loved one with whom you feel comfortable. Find a private location and sit in chairs or on a couch. Using a conversational style, just begin describing the speech that you have prepared. Do not actually give the speech. Merely talk about the speech—what the speech covers and how you plan to develop it. Use notes if you need to, but refer to them infrequently. In subsequent practice sessions with your listener, gradually begin to introduce elements of the actual speech, such as an introduction. Eventually, deliver the entire speech while sitting down. Finally, present the entire speech standing, using only an outline of the speech for reference.

Does the communication orientation work? *When compared to other methods of anxiety reduction and control, the communication orientation is the most successful* (Motley, 1995, 2011). Simply concentrating on communicating with an audience, not impressing them, reduced anxiety levels of speakers from high to moderately low.

These methods for reducing and controlling your speech anxiety work so well that little else needs to be said. Nevertheless, here are some remaining methods you can use because they are your insurance policy.

Use Coping Statements: Rational Reappraisal

Negative self-talk leads to catastrophic thinking. If you stumble at the outset of your speech and say to yourself, "I knew I couldn't do this well" or "I've already ruined the introduction," you are immediately scrutinizing your performance. Negative, catastrophic thinking triggers high anxiety. A rational reappraisal can help you cope effectively with your anxiety (Ellis, 1995; 1996). Try making coping statements when problems arise. "I'm past the tough part," "I'll do better once I get rolling," and "The best part is still ahead" are examples of positive coping statements. Coping statements shift the thought process from negative to positive self-talk. Make self-talk constructive, not destructive.

Use Positive Imaging: Visualizing Success

Mental images can influence your anxiety either positively or negatively (Holmes & Mathews, 2005). Prepare for a speech presentation by countering negative thoughts of catastrophe with positive images of success, sometimes called **visualization**. This can be a very effective strategy for addressing your speech anxiety (Ayres et al., 2001; Ayres, 2005; Martin et al., 1999). Novice speakers typically imagine what will go wrong during a speech. To avoid this pitfall, create images in your head that picture you giving a fluent, clear, and interesting speech. Picture your audience responding in positive ways as you give your speech. Exercise mental discipline and refuse to allow negative, disaster thoughts to creep into your consciousness. Keep imagining speaking success, not failure.

Use Relaxation Techniques: Reducing Fight-or-Flight Response

A number of simple relaxation techniques can reduce physiological symptoms of the fight-or-flight response (O'Donohue & Fisher, 2008). First, deep, slow, controlled breathing is very helpful. Five to seven such breaths per minute are optimum (Horowitz, 2002). Do not allow yourself to breath in rapid, shallow bursts. This will likely increase your anxiety.

Relaxing your muscles through a series of tense-and-relax exercises also can be beneficial, especially right before giving a speech if you can be unobtrusive about it—perhaps backstage or outside. Lifting your shoulders slowly up and down, then rotating them slowly is relaxing. Wiggling your facial muscles by moving your cheeks, jaw, mouth, nose, and eyebrows, and by smiling broadly may seem silly, but it loosens tight muscles. Even big, exaggerated yawns can help. Tensing then relaxing sets of muscles in your diaphragm, stomach, legs, and arms is another muscle relaxation exercise.

Finally, sitting in a hot bath can be very soothing and infinitely relaxing. This, of course, is a rather impractical technique right before giving a speech. You will not launch into your speech immediately after exiting the bathtub, but the relaxing effects can last for an hour or two, so you might be able to squeeze it in just before class. If not, a restful night's sleep induced by a hot bath will keep you mentally alert before giving your speech the next day.

Try Systematic Desensitization: Incremental Relaxation

Systematic desensitization is a technique used to control anxiety, even phobias, triggered by a wide variety of stimuli (O'Donohue & Fisher, 2008). The technique operates on the principle that relaxation and anxiety are incompatible and do not occur simultaneously (Wolpe, 1990). Systematic desensitization involves incremental exposure to increasingly threatening stimuli coupled with relaxation techniques. This method of managing anxiety is very effective (Spiegler & Guevremont, 1998). It is time-consuming, however, so you must be committed to this technique of anxiety reduction.

Applied to giving speeches, systematic desensitization involves making a list of perhaps 10 progressive steps in the speaking process, each likely to arouse increased anxiety. Find yourself a comfortable, quiet place to sit. Read the first item on your list (e.g., your speech topic). When you experience anxiety, put the list aside and begin a relaxation exercise. Tense your muscles in your face and neck. Hold the tensed position for 10 seconds, then release. Now do the same with your hands, and so on until you have tensed and relaxed all the muscle groups in your body. Now breathe slowly and deeply as you say the word "relax" to yourself. Repeat this for 1 minute. Pick up the list and read the first item. If your anxiety remains pronounced, repeat the process. If your anxiety is minimal, move on to the second item (e.g., gathering your speech material) and repeat the tense-and-relax procedure. Work through your entire list of 10 items, stopping when you are able to read the final item (e.g., beginning the introduction of your speech) without appreciable anxiety. Use systematic desensitization several days in a row before your actual speech presentation. Your anxiety level should fall to lower levels. The final step is exposure to the actual anxiety-provoking stimulus—giving the speech.

SUMMARY

Most people experience some speech anxiety. A key to managing your anxiety begins with understanding the fight-or-flight response to perceived threat and moderating the physiological symptoms through a variety of techniques and approaches. Self-defeating thoughts and anxiety-provoking situations are primary causes of dysfunctional speech anxiety which can trigger intense fight-or-flight responses. Preparation, practice, and perspective are some important approaches to managing speech anxiety. In addition, you can try the communication orientation, coping statements, visualization, relaxation techniques, and systematic desensitization to fortify your management of speech anxiety.

3

Delivering Your Speech

Cornell University psychology professor Stephen Ceci had been receiving average student evaluations of his teaching. He decided to change his delivery of class lectures. He spoke more loudly than usual, varied the pitch of his voice more dramatically, and gestured more emphatically than normal. Simply put, he exhibited a more animated delivery. The student ratings for his class and his instruction went up noticeably, from an average of between 2 and 3 on a 5-point scale to a 4-plus (Murray, 1997). Ceci was perceived by students to be more effective, knowledgeable, and organized because of the change in delivery. Students also believed they had learned more material even though their test scores were identical to those of previous classes where his delivery was commonplace. Does delivery make a difference? Unquestionably it does.

The moment that you are assigned your first class speech, competent delivery becomes an immediate concern. Waiting to discuss delivery until much later in this text seems rather tardy. Whether your very first class speech is to introduce yourself or a fellow classmate, to identify a person you admire, to present a "how to" speech, or simply to tell a brief story, competent delivery is a key element. At its most basic, a competent delivery seems natural, is intelligible, establishes connection with an audience, is lively, and avoids distractions. These and many other features of competent delivery are explored in this chapter. Thus, *the purpose of this chapter is to explain how you can develop a competent speech delivery.* Methods of delivery and overcoming delivery challenges with effective strategies are discussed.

METHODS OF COMPETENT DELIVERY

There are several methods of delivery, each with its own pros and cons, depending on the purpose of your speech and the difficulty of each method. The four methods discussed here are manuscript, memorized, impromptu, and extemporaneous speaking.

Manuscript Speaking: Looking for Precision

Speakers often refer to "writing their speeches." It is very difficult to write a speech for oral presentation that would not sound like an essay read to an audience. A read manuscript has a distinct sound and rhythm, and it can sound stilted and overly formal (more on this in the style chapter). If the use of a manuscript becomes obvious, it can be a distraction, even in a fairly strong speech. Jane Lynch, actress and star in the television series *Glee*, gave the 2012 commencement address at Smith College. The speech was humorous and at times provocative. Unfortunately, despite the generally positive response she received from her audience, the constant waving of her typed manuscript, obtrusively held in her right hand while she read from it, was distracting. She stumbled over words repeatedly while delivering her speech. (Access her speech at: http://www.youtube.com/watch?v=RwuNfHSOxZI /).

A manuscript speech may be an appropriate method of delivery in certain situations. If you must be scrupulously precise in your phrasing for fear of being legally encumbered or causing offense, then a manuscript with all your precise thoughts in black and white may be necessary. Political candidates spend millions of dollars for television and radio ads. They cannot tolerate mistakes in phrasing or wordy speeches. Their speeches are precisely written and often delivered from a teleprompter. The teleprompter is an electronic device that scrolls a manuscript speech, line by line, for the speaker to read while looking right at the audience or the television camera. A television audience does not see the manuscript scrolling in front of the speaker.

Actor and director Clint Eastwood demonstrated the risk of speaking without a manuscript or even notes when he gave a rambling, disjointed speech to an empty chair at the 2012 Republican National Convention. Conservative host Joe Scarborough of "Morning Joe" said "a great night for Mitt Romney just got sidetracked by Clint Eastwood. Wow. That was bad" (quoted in Cassata, 2012). The Twitterverse went into hyperdrive mocking Eastwood's meandering, halting, improvisational speech, and numerous spoofs went viral on YouTube. Political pundits and media sources were so focused on commenting about Eastwood's awkward, empty-chair speech that they largely ignored Marco Rubio's nominating speech that followed.

A manuscript can be useful, but it takes extensive practice to present a manuscript speech in such a way that an audience is not aware that the speaker is reading, even if a teleprompter is available. A chief drawback of manuscript speaking is that the speaker will appear too scripted, and ownership of his or her ideas becomes suspect. On February 19, 2010, Tiger Woods read a carefully scripted apology to his fans, colleagues, sponsors, employees, and family members for cheating on his wife with multiple sexual partners. One columnist called it "an infomercial" and a "weirdly scripted and strangely robotic appearance" that "had all the soul of one of his prepared releases" and "looked like a bad Saturday Night Live skit" (Dahlberg, 2010, p. C3). Another said that Woods "stayed too on script" and that "it was as awkward to watch as it must have been painfully uncomfortable for him to deliver" (Inman, 2010, p. 1D).

Another drawback is that digressions from the prepared manuscript are difficult to make smoothly, yet such changes may be critical if your audience does not respond well to a portion of the speech. I once witnessed a speaker at a union meeting get interrupted in mid-speech by a heckler who shouted, "Why should we trust anything you say? You're licking the boots of management." The speaker hesitated, then continued with her prepared speech that was wholly unresponsive to the heckler's allegation. The audience subsequently joined the heckler and began chanting "Sit Down!" The speaker became discombobulated and, finally, she sat down to the cheers of the audience. She failed to adapt to the unfolding circumstances because she was wedded to her script.

A final drawback of manuscript speaking is that the speaker easily gets buried in the manuscript and fails to establish eye contact with an audience. Reading to your audience can disconnect you from your listeners. Generally, manuscript speaking can be effective with plenty of practice, but it is best suited to professional speakers who have substantial experience using this difficult delivery method.

Memorized Speaking: Memory Do Not Fail Me Now

Some speakers attempt to memorize their speeches. A short toast at a wedding, a brief acceptance speech at an awards ceremony, or a few key lines in a lengthy speech may benefit from memorization, especially if what you memorize is emotionally touching or humorous (no one wants the punch line of a joke to be read). Memorizing a speech of 5 minutes or more, however, is a bit like stapling oatmeal to a ceiling—it takes lots of energy, it is usually pointless, and it probably would not stick anyway. It is too likely that you will forget portions of your speech; your script will not stick in your mind. Have you ever grown frustrated or felt uncomfortable when someone tries to remember a joke or funny story and keeps forgetting important details, then, following an agonizing oral search for the correct version ("Oh wait, that's not the way it goes."), he or she finally flubs the punch line? Forgetting can be painful for listeners and speaker alike. Awkward silences while you desperately attempt to remember the next sentence in your speech can be embarrassing. Also, making a memorized speech sound natural not artificial and robotic requires considerable experience. Those who have acted on stage know this well. Generally, do not memorize your speech.

Impromptu Speaking: Off-the-Cuff Presentations

An **impromptu speech** is a speech delivered without preparation, or so it seems. You are asked to respond to a previous speaker without warning, or to say a few words on a subject without advance notice. One advantage of impromptu speeches is that audience expectations are likely to be lower than for speakers given adequate time to prepare. If you give a strong impromptu speech, audiences will be impressed. Although impromptu speeches can be challenging, a few simple guidelines can help.

First, *anticipate impromptu speaking.* If you have any inkling that you might be called on to give a short speech, begin preparing your remarks. Do not wait until you are put on the spot. You will deliver it off-the-cuff without notes, but your main points are at the ready.

Second, *draw on your life experience and knowledge for the substance of your remarks.* F. E. Smith once observed that "Winston Churchill has devoted the best years of his life to preparing his impromptu speeches." Churchill had clarified his ideas and points of view in his mind. When called on to speak in an impromptu fashion, he was already prepared. Life experience is preparation for impromptu speaking. Draw from that experience.

Third, *formulate a simple outline for an impromptu speech.* Begin with a short opening attention strategy—a relevant story, a humorous quip you have used successfully on other occasions, or a clever quotation you have memorized. State your point of view or the theme for your remarks. Then quickly identify two or three short points that you will address. Finally, summarize briefly what you said. You are not expected to provide substantial supporting material for your points during an impromptu speech, but if you have some facts and figures memorized, you will impress your audience with your ready knowledge. Impromptu speaking is usually more informal than a standard speech, so be conversational in tone and presentation.

Extemporaneous Speaking: The Virtues of an Outline

Most public speaking classes stress extemporaneous speaking, often called "extemp" speaking for short. An **extemporaneous speech** is delivered from a prepared outline or notes. There are several advantages to this method of delivering a speech. First, even though fully prepared in advance, *an extemporaneous speech sounds spontaneous* because you do not read from a manuscript but instead you glance at an outline or notes, then you put your thoughts into words on the spot. In this sense, extemporaneous speaking falls between impromptu and manuscript speaking. It sounds impromptu and has the detail and substance of a manuscript speech without being either.

Second, *extemporaneous speaking permits greater eye contact with the audience.* You are not buried in a manuscript with your head down. Of course, an outline can take on the form of a manuscript if it is too detailed. It is possible to write an entire speech, word for word, on a 3 × 5 index card. In such cases, the manuscript is merely tiny, and not very useful.

Eye contact is easy when speaking from brief notes or a brief outline. Typically, you prepare an extemporaneous speech by constructing an outline composed of full sentences (see Chapter 7 on outlining). You deliver the speech, however, from an *abbreviated version* of the full sentence outline. This *presentation outline* is composed of simple words or phrases that trigger complete thoughts and ideas. Keep your presentation outline as brief as possible, highlighting key words and phrases. Use full sentences only for exact wording of main points or if you are quoting someone verbatim. Statistics and their sources, especially if there are a substantial number, may be included as well.

Here is a brief sample comparing preparation and presentation outlines:

PREPARATION OUTLINE	PRESENTATION OUTLINE

I. Texting while driving is extremely dangerous.
  A. Texting while driving is distracting
  B. Severe accidents, injuries, even deaths result from texting while driving.
	I. Texting dangerous
	  A. Distracting
	  B. Accidents, injuries, deaths

Third, *extemporaneous speaking allows the speaker to respond to audience feedback as it occurs.* You can adjust to the moment-by-moment changes in audience reactions much more so than with manuscript or memorized speeches.

The chief drawback to this method of delivering a speech is that learning to speak from notes or an outline takes practice. Inexperienced speakers tend to worry that they will forget important elements of their speech if every word is not written down. Keep your outline concise. There is no substitute for practicing extemporaneous speaking.

DEVELOPING COMPETENT DELIVERY

The method of delivery does not resolve many of the delivery challenges you face when presenting a speech and specific ways to address these challenges. This section discusses these challenges with copious tips on how to improve your delivery.

Eye Contact: Connecting with Your Audience

Eye contact is an important element of a speaker's credibility (Neal & Brodsky, 2008). Even across cultures a fair amount of eye contact during speaking is important to enhance credibility and to connect with listeners (Johnson & Miller, 2002). Direct, penetrating eye contact can be quite intense. If you doubt this, try staring at someone for a prolonged period of time. Good luck with that. When you zero in on listeners, it is difficult for them to ignore you, sometimes to the point of annoyance if prolonged. When you do not look directly at your audience, listeners' minds can easily wander. This is often the case when speakers make

PHOTO 3.1 Direct eye contact is a critical part of effective delivery. You cannot connect well with an audience if you are buried in a manuscript, always looking down. Here North Carolina state senator Don Davis exhibits direct eye contact and is not chained to a manuscript, which permits animated facial expressions.

PowerPoint presentations. They look at the slides, not the audience. Inexperienced speakers have a tendency to look at the ground, above the heads of their listeners, at one side of their audience or the other but not both, or they bury their head in a manuscript. When you rarely look at your audience, you allow your listeners' attention to drift. You lose connection with your listeners.

There are simple ways to improve your eye contact when delivering a speech. First, be very familiar with your speech so you avoid getting pinned to your notes or manuscript. Second, practice looking at your entire audience, beginning with the middle of your audience, then looking left, then right, and then to the middle again. Do not ignore a section of your audience by looking only left or right. Also, do not focus on a single listener (e.g., instructor grading your speech). Gradually sweep across your audience as you speak. With practice, even with an imaginary audience, your eye contact will become automatic.

Voice: Developing Vocal Variety

Using your voice effectively is an important aspect of speech delivery (Mayer, 2003). Strive for vocal variety called **inflection**. Raise and lower the pitch of your voice. **Pitch** is the range of your voice from high to low sounds. The singing voice has a range of pitch from soprano to bass. Similarly, you can vary your speaking voice by moving up and down the vocal range from high sounds to lower sounds and back. Of course, you are not trying to hit the extreme highs and lows. Guys do not want to switch into a falsetto or sound like a 3-year old on helium, and women do not want to sound like they are digging for the deep bass sound. Just vary your voice enough to avoid a monotonous sameness to your pitch.

Monotony can also be avoided by varying the **volume** of your voice from loud to soft. A loud voice signals intense, passionate feelings. It will punctuate portions of your presentation much as an exclamation point punctuates a written sentence. Do not be excessive, however. As Mark Twain noted, "Noise proves nothing. Often a hen who has merely laid an egg cackles as if she laid an asteroid." Incessant, unrelenting, bombastic delivery of a message can irritate and alienate your audience. Speak loudly only when you have an especially important point to make. All points in your speech do not deserve equal attention.

Speaking softly can also induce interest. When you lower the pitch and loudness of your voice, the audience must strain to hear. This can be a nice dramatic twist to use in a speech, if used infrequently. Michelle Obama, when delivering her 2012 speech to the Democratic National Convention, occasionally used just such a technique. As Media critic Howard Kurtz (2012) observed, "Michelle Obama took the tack of lowering her voice, perhaps prompting people to listen more intently."

Vocal variety signals shifts in mood and does not permit an audience to drift into the hypnotic, trance-like state produced by the white noise of the monotone voice. Practice vocal variety on your friends during casual conversations. Experiment with different voice inflections and volume.

Fluency: Avoiding Excessive Vocal Fillers

A common delivery challenge is to exclude **vocal fillers**—the insertion of *um, uh, like, you know, know what I mean, whatever,* and other variants that substitute for pauses and often draw attention to themselves. Such dysfluencies are common in normal conversations, comprising on average about 6% of speech (Bortfeld et al., 2001). Vocal fillers are also common during college class lectures (Fox Tree, 1995).

Despite how common they are, vocal fillers when giving a speech are not always problematic (Arnold et al., 2003; Collard et al., 2008). They often go unnoticed by listeners (Christenfeld, 1995). Actually, error-free speaking may strike some audiences as too slick and insincere (Erard, 2008).

Practice reducing dysfluencies in your everyday conversation and they will diminish when giving a speech.

Nevertheless, when your audience begins to notice these "vocal hiccups," it can divert attention and reduce your credibility (Croucher, 2004). A Geneva, Nebraska High School senior, Jessica Reinsch, won a $1000 prize in the Nebraskaland Foundation's "you know" contest for recording a 15-minute radio interview during which that phrase was used unintentionally 61 times ("Best English Lesson," 1999). A website called InterviewStream.com produced a top-ten list of "all-star" vocal-filler users among celebrities, politicians, and athletes. Britney Spears made the list for uttering 73 "likes" and "ya knows" in a 5-minute interview shown on YouTube. A companion website, UmmLike.com, included Eminem, who also like, you know, likes to use "like" and "ya know." (Kitchen, 2007). If you slip into a habit of using vocal fillers frequently in your conversations, you will very likely suffer the same problem when giving a speech. It can be a tough habit to break.

The fluency of your delivery suffers mightily when vocal fillers are used more than occasionally. Almost all speakers use vocal fillers once in a while. When they become frequent, however, it may be the only part of your speech that is memorable. Practice not using vocal fillers during casual conversation with friends and family. Rid yourself of the habit. Focus on noticing how often other people use vocal fillers. Practice your speech in front of a friend, or video record it. Have your friend tap a pencil on a table every time you use a vocal filler during your speech. When you review the video recorded practice speech, count the number of vocal fillers. With time, you will eliminate the habit.

Speaking Rate: Finding the Right Pace

Sean Shannon, a Canadian residing in Oxford, England, recited the famous soliloquy "To be or not to be . . ." from Shakespeare's Hamlet at 650 words per minute (wpm). Talking at 650 wpm is clearly possible, but how fast should you speak to an audience? Moderately fast and fast speaking rate (180–210 wpm) increases the audience's perception of you as intelligent, confident, and effective compared to slower-paced speakers (Smith & Shaffer, 1995). Speaking rapidly shows that you are quick on your feet and can handle ideas swiftly. Conversely, linguist Deborah Tannen (2003) notes that a very slow speaking rate (less than 100 wpm) is stereotyped as slow-witted and unintelligent in every culture studied.

Some listeners, however, may not be able to keep pace with you if you are attempting to speak at the pace of someone who has downed three hyper-caffeinated energy drinks. Listeners' comprehension of speech declines rapidly once the speaking rate exceeds 250 wpm (Foulke, 2006). Normal conversational speaking pace ranges between 140 and 180 wpm (McCoy et al., 2005). Because people generally are accustomed to a fairly standard conversational pace, speaking at a rate between 140 and 180 wpm is appropriate for most speaking situations. Audience members will find such a pace comfortable, easy to comprehend, and they will be unlikely to notice your pace, which avoids distraction. Without actually measuring your speaking pace, *you can get a rough idea by enunciating your words carefully and pausing to take breaths without gasping for air.* Proceed as you would in normal conversation. You can actually determine your rate by speaking into a recorder for exactly 1 minute, then counting the words.

Articulation and Pronunciation: Striving for Clarity of Speech

Sloppy speech patterns can make comprehending what you are saying tough for listeners (Mayer, 2003). When you mumble your words, who can tell what you said? Mispronouncing words and poor articulation are also common issues for speakers. Barack Obama regularly says "gonna" instead of "going to" and "ta" instead of "to." George W. Bush mispronounces "nuclear" (new-klee-er) as "new-cue-ler." Proper **articulation**—speaking words clearly and distinctly—and **pronunciation**—saying words correctly as indicated in any dictionary based on Standard English rules—can become a credibility issue. Mispronunciations can make a speaker an object of ridicule. The YourDictionary website identifies the 100 most often mispronounced words and phrases in English, and many are comical. Imagine an audience's reaction if a speaker said "it's a doggy-dog world" instead of the correct "dog eat dog world." It is not the male "prostrate" gland; it is the "prostate" gland, although the gland can make you want to lie flat at times. You do not "take for granite" unless you are into geology, you "take for granted." Another common mispronunciation is "preven*t*ative" instead of "preventive." It is "card*sharp*" not "cardshark." It is not "revelant" but "relevant," it is not "orientate" but "orient," and it is not "mispro*noun*ciation" but "mispro*nun*ciation." If in doubt, practice your speech in front of several people who know proper pronunciation and can listen for precise articulation.

Body Movements: Finding the Right Balance

Standing rigidly before your audience or moving around wildly can be very distracting. A straight upright posture exudes confidence and enhances credibility, but you do not want to appear statue-like. You should move some or your physical form will meld into the scenery. Strive for a balance between excessive and insufficient body movement. The general guideline is "everything in moderation." An animated, lively delivery can excite an audience to pay attention, but you do not want to seem out of control. Posture should be erect without looking like a soldier standing at attention. Slumping your shoulders, crossing and un-crossing your legs, and lurching to one side with one leg higher than the other call attention to awkward movements. Practice speaking in front of a mirror or record your practice speech to determine whether you have any of these awkward movements.

Regarding gesturing, *there is no need to plan gestures.* As Motley (1995) explains, gestures "are supposed to be non-conscious. That is to say, in natural conversation we use gestures every day without thinking about them. And when we do consciously think about gestures, they become uncomfortable and inhibited" (p. 99). Choreographing your gestures will make them appear awkward and artificial, thereby distracting audience attention. For example, consider Andrew Dlugan (2008), a self-described "award-winning speaker" and author of the "Six Minutes" website on "speaking and presentational skills." Delivering his "model" of how to choreograph gestures, there is an artificial and obviously staged quality to his gestures that is distracting. (Access this website at: *http://sixminutes. dlugan.com/speech-preparation-7-staging-gestures-vocal-variety/.*) Choreographing speech gestures is reminiscent of the old elocution movement of previous centuries that produced textbooks with graphics illustrating precisely coded poses and gestures for specific emotions. Elocution mostly disappeared because of its association with mere recitation of poems and readings and the mechanistic and unnatural appearance of bodily movements and gestures while speaking (Kirkpatrick, 2007).

Focus on your message and your audience, and the gestures will follow. When you are genuinely enthusiastic about your topic, for example, your gestures will naturally be enthusiastic. It is when you have to fake excitement that gestures become mismatched and look staged.

If, however, you realize that you have hyper-hands that wildly gesticulate when you experience anxiety, concentrate on relaxing (see Chapter 2). If this does not calm the hand and arm flailing, try purposely not gesturing at all when practicing your speech to calm the wandering appendages. This can train you for your actual speech.

Podium Usage: Avoiding the Lectern Lean

A lectern, or podium, is useful for placing your notes within easy view so you can avoid holding them for all to see. Rustling a stack of notes or sheets of paper distracts an audience. Teachers usually use a lectern for their lengthy lectures so their hands are free to write on the board, advance PowerPoint slides, access Internet sites, or present demonstrations to the class. The lectern, however, can easily become a crutch for inexperienced speakers, seeming to prop them up before they fall over. Student speakers often have to be advised not to lean on the

A lectern is not a crutch to lean on but a convenient place to set notes for your speech.

lectern. There is no need to embrace the lectern. It looks awkward. Just rest your notes on the podium, stand back slightly, and occasionally move beside it or toward your audience. Moving away from the podium entirely, perhaps occasionally glancing at notes to refresh your memory, has the distinct advantage of permitting a closer connection with your audience and seeming more conversational than stiffly formal.

Microphone Usage: Amplifying Your Delivery

Microphones amplify your voice and are essential if you are addressing a large audience in a big room, but that amplification can produce some tricky issues. A clip-on wireless microphone (called a lavaliere) must be placed just right on your clothing. If it is too close to your voice, it will be too loud for listeners, and if it is too far away, it will not amplify your voice sufficiently. You also have to be careful that your clothing does not rub against the microphone, creating a scraping sound. A stationary microphone, typically mounted on a stand or onto a podium, is also tricky to use. If you move away from the microphone, your voice fades, but if you speak too closely to it, you will blast your voice and distortion will occur. If you move towards and away from the microphone as you speak, your voice will fade in and out like a bad cell-phone connection, becoming quite annoying for your listeners. Audition with the microphone if possible. Work with the technician on producing a nice, even sound. Find the optimum distance from the microphone that produces the least distortion and the most natural sounding voice. Remember that microphones amplify all sounds, so shuffling papers, coughing, clearing your throat, and clicking a pen become more audible to listeners.

Distracting Behaviors: Avoiding Interference

This is a catchall category. There are numerous quirky behaviors that speakers can exhibit, often without realizing it (see "28 Distracting Mannerisms," 2011). Playing with your pen or pencil while speaking is one example. I once had a student who tapped a pencil loudly on the podium nonstop. For her sake and for the mental well-being of her audience, I had to stop her in mid-speech and tell her to put away the makeshift drumstick. Fiddling with change in your pocket, tapping

PHOTO 3.2 What delivery errors is this speaker committing?

fingers on the podium, and shifting your weight from right to left and back like a ship being tossed on the high seas are other distracters.

Distracting behaviors can easily be eliminated. If you do not hold a pen or pencil in your hand, you cannot click it, tap the podium with it, or wave it around while speaking. Take change out of your pocket before speaking if you have a tendency to jiggle coins when you put your hand in your pocket. Move away from the podium so you cannot tap your fingers. Practice standing erect, balanced on both feet, when rehearsing your speech, and you will eliminate the shifting weight problem. Distracting behaviors will not destroy a quality speech unless the behavior is beyond weird. Nevertheless, eliminating them makes your presentation more effective.

Audience-Centered Delivery: Matching the Context

Finally, *delivery should match the context for your speech*. Like every other aspect of public speaking, delivery is audience centered. The appropriateness of your delivery is dependent on certain expectations inherent to the occasion and purpose of your speech. A eulogy calls for a dignified, formal delivery. The speaker usually limits body movements and keeps his or her voice toned down as a sign of respect. A motivational speech, however, requires a lively, enthusiastic delivery, especially if you are speaking to a large audience. Your voice may be loud, pace fairly rapid, body movements dramatic, eye contact intense and direct, and facial movements expressive. During a motivational speech, the podium is usually moved aside or ignored and the speaker moves back and forth across a stage, sometimes even moving into the audience. An after-dinner speech or "roast" calls for a lively, comic delivery. Facial expressions consist mostly of smiles or gestures; they may be gross or exaggerated, and a speaker's voice may be loud, even abrasive, for effect. There is no one correct way to deliver a speech, but many effective ways. Match your delivery to the speech context and audience expectations.

SUMMARY

The general guidelines for effective delivery are these: use direct eye contact, vocal variety, few if any vocal fillers, moderate pace and body movement, and eliminate distracting mannerisms. Defer using manuscript and memorized speeches until you become an experienced public speaker. Extemporaneous speaking is the type of delivery to master for most occasions.

4

Audience Analysis

A competent speech is far more than good delivery. Your thoughts have to resonate with listeners. *Audience analysis and adaptation are at the core of any public speech.* A speech's effectiveness is determined from the standpoint of the audience. "I gave a great speech but the audience hated it" is uncomfortably close to "the surgery was a success but the patient died" analogy.

Almost 2,500 years ago, Aristotle wrote: "Of the three elements in speechmaking—speaker, subject, and person addressed—it is the last one, the hearer, that determines the speech's end and object" (quoted in Cooper, 1960, p. 136). Think of audience analysis as the process of discovering ways to build bridges between yourself and listeners, to identify with their needs, hopes, dreams, interests, and concerns and for listeners to identify with you. In general, you construct your speech with the audience always in mind. Thus, *the purpose of this chapter is to explore the essential role audience plays in constructing and presenting speeches.* Types of audiences, audience composition, audience adaptation, and topic choice are discussed.

TYPES OF AUDIENCES

Begin analyzing your audience by considering what type of audience will hear your speech. There are five general types of audiences: captive, committed, contrary, concerned, and casual. Each poses specific challenges for you the speaker.

Captive Audience: Disengaged Listener

A captive audience assembles to hear you speak because it is compelled to, not because listeners expect entertainment or intellectual stimulation. A required speech class is an example of a captive audience. Formal ceremonies, luncheon gatherings of clubs and organizations, and most meetings conducted in places of business are other examples. Listeners may attend a speech only because those with greater power (supervisors, teachers) insist.

Gaining and maintaining the interest of a captive audience is a primary consideration. Your sometimes ill-humored, captive listeners may prefer to be in the fiery furnace of Hades than listening to a speech. Snaring their attention and keeping them listening to you is no small accomplishment. (The next chapter discusses attention strategies necessary to meet this challenge.)

Committed Audience: Agreeable Listeners

A committed audience voluntarily assembles because they want to invest time and energy listening to and being inspired by a speaker. A committed audience usually agrees with your position already and is presumably interested since they voluntarily appeared to hear your speech. Listeners who gather for Sunday sermons, political rallies, and social protest demonstrations are all examples of committed audiences. Gaining and maintaining the interest and attention of a committed audience is not nearly as difficult as doing the same with a captive audience. Inspiring action, persuading, and empowering listeners to act decisively are primary challenges when speaking to a committed audience (subjects for later discussion).

Contrary Audience: Hostile Listeners

You do not usually get to choose your audience, so sometimes the audience that forms is initially hostile to your position on issues. School board meetings, public meetings of the county board of supervisors, meetings on public utility rates, and political gatherings often attract hostile listeners ready to do battle. Listeners of this sort are more likely to engage in **ambushing**—looking for weaknesses in your arguments and preparing to pounce on perceived mistakes in your facts. It is vitally important in such circumstances that you have researched your topic and are well prepared. Your demeanor when addressing a hostile audience must remain unconditionally constructive. Dealing with a hostile audience is adversarial. You want to defuse audience anger, not ignite it against you. Be prepared for personal attacks, but resist personal counter-attacks. Ask audience members who get rowdy to disagree without becoming disagreeable. (See discussion later in this chapter for more ways to address hostility.)

Concerned Audience: Eager Listeners

A concerned audience is one that gathers voluntarily to hear a speaker because listeners care about issues and ideas. A concerned audience is a motivated audience. Unlike a committed audience, however, listeners have not attended the speech to show commitment to a particular cause or idea. Concerned listeners want to gather information and learn. Listeners who gather for book and poetry readings or lecture series are examples of concerned audiences. Your main considerations are to present new ideas and new information in a stimulating and attention-getting fashion. Concerned listeners may eventually become committed listeners.

Casual Audience: Unexpected Listener

A casual audience is composed of individuals who become listeners because they hear a speaker, stop out of curiosity or casual interest, and remain until bored or sated. When I was in Bath, England, I happened upon a street performer, or busker as they are called in England. He gathered an audience mostly with clever banter, corny jokes, audience interaction, and whimsical tricks. Curious about the gathering crowd, I joined the audience. Within minutes I was picked out of the crowd to "assist" the busker in performing one of his "daring" tricks. My job was to tie the busker's hands tightly behind his back with a chain, put a bag over

PHOTO 4.1 This is an example of a casual audience. Audience members are free to leave at any moment, so keeping their attention is paramount.

his head, and count to 30 while the performer "escaped" from his confinement while on his knees with his head submerged in a two-gallon bucket of water. Not surprisingly, he performed this "underwater escape" successfully and garnered great laughter and applause from his casual audience.

Your primary consideration when addressing a casual audience is to connect with listeners immediately and create curiosity and interest. The busker did this well. Unlike a captive audience, members of a casual audience are free to leave at a moment's whim.

Each type of audience—captive, committed, contrary, concerned, or casual— presents its own challenges to a speaker. Each audience has its own expectations that a speaker must address both in preparing and presenting a speech to be successful.

AUDIENCE COMPOSITION

Your speech should be prepared with your audience always in mind, so knowing something about your audience is critical. An initial place to begin is by trying to ascertain the attitudes, beliefs, and values of your listeners. An **attitude** is "a learned predisposition to respond favorably or unfavorably toward some attitude object" (Gass & Seiter, 2011). An attitude is an evaluation, such as "Lawyers are dishonest" or "Cross country skiing is great if you live in a small country" (Steven Wright). A **belief** is what a person thinks is true or probable. "Women are more talkative than men" is a belief. This is an assertion of fact without evaluation. Objective evidence may contradict a belief. For example, women are not typically more talkative than men in mixed-sex groups (Crawford & Kaufman, 2006). Talkativeness depends on the situation. A **value** is the most deeply felt, generally shared view of what is deemed good, right, or worthwhile thinking or behavior. Values are general ideals that guide our lives. "Freedom" is a value that drives many competing attitudes on a wide range of topics, such as abortion, drug use, or health care.

You may have an opportunity to survey listeners and determine their basic values, beliefs, or attitudes. Often, however, you must make educated guesses about an audience based on **demographics**—characteristics of an audience such as age, gender, culture, ethnicity, and group affiliations. Even then audiences these days tend to be composed of diverse members, so often there are competing attitudes, beliefs, and values among listeners, making audience adaptation especially challenging. Recognize that few audiences are entirely of one mind.

Age: Possible Generation Gaps

The average age of an audience can provide valuable information for a speaker. College instructors, for instance, must speak to the experience of their students, and most of you were not even born before 1990. This means that most of you have no direct experience of the Vietnam War, Watergate, eight-track tapes, ditto machines, or manual typewriters. You have not experienced a time when space travel was not possible, color television was not available, ATMs were not readily accessible, computers would not fit on a desktop or in your hand, the Internet or cell phones and social networking sites were unavailable.

Generalizations based on generational differences should be embraced cautiously, but a study by the Pew Research Center (2009) reports the largest generation gap in the United States in 40 years. Individuals 65 years and older differ greatly from those 18 to 29 on issues such as religion, politics, marriage and social relationships, usage of technology, and many other topics (see also Leonhardt, 2012; "Same-Sex Marriage," 2013).

Generational differences do pose significant challenges for public speakers. An audience composed of a mixture of older members, teens and twenty somethings makes it difficult to interest everyone in your topic. References to mutual funds and retirement accounts do not speak directly to the experience of younger audience members as they do with older members. Conversely, do not assume older audience members are necessarily technologically proficient or view technology with the same attitude about its advantages and necessity as younger generations. Nevertheless, a topic on some aspect of technology, such as electric cars or solar energy, may bridge all generational groups. Stress management, immunity boosting steps to improve health, and unusual vacations for the entire family are other possible topics that span generational interests and may appeal to a diverse audience.

PHOTOS 4.2 & 4.3 There are generational differences reflected in these photos. A November 2011 Gallup poll found that Tea Party supporters are typically older and Occupy movement supporters are typically young (64% under the age of 35). Tea Party protesters blame big government for the nation's ills while Occupy protesters blame Wall Street and big business.

Gender: Go Beyond Simplistic Stereotypes

Gender differences in perception and behavior do exist (Dindia & Canary, 2006). Be careful, however, not to assume too much from these differences. For example, men generally find expressing feelings to be more difficult than passing kidney stones (Wong et al., 2006). However, men more easily express "negative emotions," such as anger or contempt, than "positive emotions," such as affection and joy. Women generally express emotions with greater ease, but they have more difficulty expressing negative than positive emotions (Simpson & Stroh, 2004).

Effective audience analysis means going beyond simplistic gender stereotypes ("Women express feelings; men don't"). Stereotypes are broad generalizations about a group, which in some instances may be more true than not (Lee et al., 1995), but they ignore individual differences of members within a group. Some men have little difficulty expressing the full range of human feelings and some women are emotionally restricted.

Although some gender differences exist, develop your speech to include all audience members. A speech on sexual harassment, for instance, could be linked to both men and women by discussing effects on victims who are typically women but increasingly men (Mattioli, 2010). The consequences to the victims of

Sexist language is inappropriate. According to the U.S. Census Bureau in 2013, 10% of registered nurses, almost 350,000 individuals, were male ("Male Nurses," 2013). Be inclusive not stereotypic.

sexual harassment should concern men and women alike. Consequences include psychological distress, depression, shame and embarrassment, and diminished job performance (Jorgenson & Wahl, 2000; Kelly, 2005). Why would anyone wish to ignore harassment of his or her partner, friend, or family member given such consequences?

In addition, sensitivity to an audience may require judicious attention to language when framing issues. Consistently referring to leaders as "he," "him," or "his," as in "A leader must inspire, and he must motivate his followers," excludes women. Similarly, referring to elementary school teachers as "she" or "her," as in "A third grade teacher works hard and she spends long hours with her students" excludes men. Try to speak in more inclusive, non-stereotypic terms, using "him or her" or plural forms such as "doctors . . . they."

Ethnicity and Culture: Sensitivity to Diversity

According to the U. S. Census, a third of the population of the United States is non-White. By 2042, minorities composed largely of Latinos and Mexican Americans, African Americans, and Asian Americans will constitute the majority of the population (Morello & Mellnik, 2012). Students who fail to analyze the multicultural makeup of college audiences can create embarrassing speaking situations. Despite my efforts to encourage sensitivity to individuals from diverse cultures, I have witnessed several student speeches that ignited awkward, even hostile, moments in class. One Jewish student referred to Palestinians as "terrorists and war mongers." This did not sit well with several Arab students in the class. Policies and issues can be questioned and debated without resorting to insults and sweeping generalizations that offend audience members.

One important hazard to avoid is **ethnocentrism**—the belief that customs, practices, and behaviors of your own culture are superior to any other culture. Ethnocentrism appears to be stronger among older adults than younger ones, according to a Pew Research Center (2004) study of 66,000 respondents in 49 countries. Avoid disparaging the customs, practices, and behaviors of cultures different from your own. Difference does not equal deficiency unless basic human rights are jeopardized.

Group Affiliations: A Window into Listeners' Views

The groups we belong to tell others a great deal about our values, beliefs, and attitudes. Membership in Save Our Shores indicates a strong belief in protecting our ocean environment. Working with Habitat for Humanity indicates an interest in charitable work and a concern for poor people with inadequate housing. Membership in clubs, sororities, fraternities, national honorary societies, or educational groups provides information about your listeners that can be helpful in shaping your speeches.

Be cautious, however, not to assume too much. Group affiliations suggest possible aspects to consider about your audience, but religious affiliations, for example, can be tricky. A huge majority of Catholics consistently disagree with the Vatican ban on contraception (Newport, 2012). A CBS/New York Times poll found that 62% percent of American Catholics believe same-sex marriage should be legal and 74% believe abortion should be available in some instances (Peoples, 2013). A quarter of white evangelicals, traditionally conservative and Republican, voted for Barack Obama in the 2008 election (Goodstein, 2008).

There are additional audience composition factors that can affect your audience analysis, such as sexual orientation, income, and education level. With some exceptions, however, these may not be so apparent. Some people purposely hide their sexual orientation or consider it nobody else's business, and others consider it rude to ask or discuss income level. Nevertheless, be sensitive to these elements of audience composition.

ADAPTING TO DIVERSE AUDIENCES

Analyzing your audience and breaking it into its constituent parts is only half the battle. The other half is taking this analysis and adapting effectively to audiences with diverse membership.

Establish Identification: Connecting with Your Audience

Identification is the affiliation and connection between speaker and audience. As discussed in the opening chapter, transactional communication means that as a speaker you establish a relationship with your audience. You want this relationship to be a positive one.

Likeability: I Can Relate to You   A key element of identification is the likeability of the speaker. Even when your audience is composed of highly diverse members, if your listeners grow to like you they are more inclined to listen. Compliance and assent on controversial positions are more probable if you are liked than if you are not liked (Perloff, 2013).

How do you enhance likeability? Praising and complimenting your audience ("This class did better on the exam than any previous class"), saying you like your audience ("What a great group"), and expressing genuine concern and showing empathy for problems and pain faced by audience members are just some quick ways (Cialdini, 1993). Telling stories well is also a very effective means of creating likeability, especially personal stories that resonate with audiences, such as tragedies faced and self-deprecating stories about funny mistakes made to seem more human. Substantial research shows that storytelling promotes **social cohesion**—it binds us together in mutual liking (Hogan, 2003). Our brains even seem to be wired to relish good stories. "Storytelling is one of the few human traits that are truly universal across culture and through all of known history" (Hsu, 2008, p. 46). An audience can be highly diverse, but who does not love a great story and like the person who tells it well. Both Ann Romney and Michelle Obama used a storytelling or narrative style when delivering their speeches to the Republican and Democratic conventions, respectively, in 2012. Both were highly personal narratives about their husbands. Both speeches were generally regarded, especially by less partisan commentators, as effective and well-received presentations.

Stylistic Similarity: Looking and Acting the Part   We tend to identify more closely with those individuals who appear to be similar to us. One way to appear similar is to look and act the part. This is called **stylistic similarity**. For example, when you go for a job interview, you should dress, look, and speak as an interviewer would expect from someone worthy of the job. Showing up in baggy pants and a T-shirt emblazoned with an imprint of your favorite local rock band when applying for a teaching job is unlikely to work in your favor. Using verbal obscenity during a teaching demonstration also is unlikely to charm an interview panel.

When the situation is formal, such as a valedictory speech at a graduation ceremony, dress and speak formally. Slang and offensive language should be avoided. When the situation is less formal, such as some classroom speeches, county fair presentations, many protest marches and public gatherings, however, you need to shift styles and speak, dress, and act more casually so your audience can relate to you.

Finding the appropriate level of formality can be tricky when the situation does not call for a clear-cut choice. For example, as a student, how do you respond to your instructor dressing formally, insisting you address him or her as "Professor" or "Doctor So-and-so," and being required to always raise your hand to be recognized before speaking? Would you relate better if your instructor were more casual, or do you appreciate the formality? A formal style communicates the seriousness of your intent and the significance of the event. An informal style communicates less seriousness, perhaps even playfulness, and sets a more casual atmosphere that encourages student participation. Your style needs to match your expectations and goals. Teachers make choices about formality or informality based on their goals for the class.

In June 2009, comedian Stephen Colbert exhibited the power of stylistic similarity in producing identification with an audience when he took his *Colbert*

PHOTO 4.4 Stephen Colbert's head shaving and camouflage suit created a strong identification with his audience of American soldiers in Iraq.

Report to Iraq and performed four shows for the troops. He dubbed the series of shows *Operation Iraqi Stephen: Going Commando*. To great applause and laughter from the assembled troops, Colbert marched on stage dressed in a camouflage business suit and tie. Later he had his head shaved by Gen. Ray Odierno to exhibit solidarity with the soldiers. The crowd roared its approval. One soldier, Ryan McLeod, remarked afterward, "Definitely the highlight was seeing him sacrifice his hair." Later Colbert declared, "By the power vested in me by basic cable, I officially declare we have won the Iraq war" (quoted in Baram, 2009).

Substantive Similarity: Establishing Common Ground   Highlighting similarities in positions, values, and attitudes also encourages identification. This **substantive similarity** creates identification by *establishing common ground* between speaker and audience. If listeners can say, "I like what I'm hearing," they can identify with the speaker. If you are speaking to a contrary audience, it is helpful to build bridges by pointing out common experiences, perceptions, values, and attitudes before launching into more delicate areas of disagreement. Listeners will be more inclined to consider your more controversial viewpoints if they initially identify with you.

Appealing to broadly accepted rights and values also works well to create identification. The United Nations Universal Declaration of Human Rights, originally adopted on a 48 to 0 vote with 8 nations abstaining, claims that every human being has the right to life, liberty, security, freedom of speech and belief, equal protection under the law, participation in the political process, a decent standard of living, necessary social services, and education (Harrison, 2000). Although not entirely without controversy, these values bind most nations and cultures. As Harrison (2000) notes, "The vast majority of the planet's people would agree with the following assertions: life is better than death, health is better than sickness, liberty is better than slavery, prosperity is better than poverty, education is better than ignorance, and justice is better than injustice (p. xxvi)." Here is your common ground. As Secretary of State, Hillary Clinton made such appeals in a December 6, 2011, speech in Geneva, Switzerland, to celebrate International Human Rights Day: "It is a violation of human rights when people are beaten or killed because of their sexual orientation." She continued, "Violence toward women isn't cultural; it's criminal. Likewise with slavery, what was once justified as sanctioned by God is now properly reviled as an unconscionable violation of human rights." She also noted, "Combating Islamaphobia or anti-Semitism is a task for people of all faiths" (Clinton, 2011).

Build Credibility: Establishing Believability

O'Keefe (1990) defines **credibility** as "judgments made by a perceiver (e.g., a message recipient) concerning the believability of a communicator" (pp. 130–131). In *The Rhetoric*, Aristotle identified the ingredients of credibility, or **ethos** in his terminology, as "good sense, good moral character, and good will." Recent research affirms Aristotle's observation and expands the list of dimensions somewhat. The primary dimensions of credibility are competence, trustworthiness, dynamism, and composure (Gass & Seiter, 2011; Pornpitakpan, 2004). All four are developed throughout a speech.

Competence refers to the audience's perception of the speaker's knowledge and experience on a topic. Competence addresses the question, "Does this speaker know what he or she is talking about?" You can enhance your credibility when you identify your background, experience, and training relevant to a subject. Citing sources of evidence, speaking fluently, and avoiding vocal fillers such as "uhm" and "you know" also enhance credibility (O'Keefe, 1990).

Trustworthiness refers to how truthful or honest we perceive the speaker to be. Trustworthiness addresses the question "Can I believe what the speaker says?" We hesitate to buy anything from a salesperson we perceive to be dishonest. One way to increase your trustworthiness is to argue against your self-interest (Pratkanis & Aronson, 2001). If you take a position on an issue that will cost you money, a job, a promotion, or some reward or benefit, most listeners will see you as presenting an honest opinion. In 2012, Billionaire Warren Buffett advocated higher taxes for the wealthy. He received accolades when he noted that his tax rate was lower than his secretary's and argued that this was wrong (Ody, 2012). Barack Obama, trying to capitalize on Buffett's credibility in his 2012 State of the Union speech, referred to his proposal to correct this claimed inequity in the tax code the "Buffett Rule."

Dynamism is a third dimension of credibility. It refers to the enthusiasm, energy, and forcefulness exhibited by a speaker. Sleepy, lackluster presentations lower your credibility. Over-the-top enthusiasm, however, can be equally problematic. Those who pitch products on infomercials are invariably enthusiastic, sometimes bordering on frenzied. Howard Dean killed his presidential campaign in 2004 when, after a disappointing showing in the Iowa caucuses, he gave what political pundits labeled his "I Have a Scream" speech when trying to whip up enthusiasm from his disappointed supporters. As his vocal volume escalated, he seemed almost maniacal. Former Michigan governor Jennifer Granholm's 2012 speech before the Democratic National Convention reminded some of Dean's speech. Although the speech whipped the partisan crowd into a frenzy, many critics on both sides of the partisan aisle mostly agreed that she was a tad "out of control," and that her delivery was too manic. She rocked her immediate audience, but the remote television audience was likely split on the effectiveness of her

PHOTO 4.5 Jennifer Granholm, an accomplished public speaker, nevertheless, by her own admission probably was overly animated in her delivery when speaking at the Democratic National Convention in 2012.

speech. Granholm admitted afterward that "I probably shouldn't have gotten so worked up" (quoted in Eggert, 2012). Too little dynamism can diminish your speech, but too much can backfire.

A final dimension of speaker credibility is **composure**. Audiences tend to be influenced by speakers who are emotionally stable and appear confident and in control of themselves. Cable news shows are notorious for shouting matches between political adversaries. To some, these episodes are entertaining, but it is doubtful that any listeners are impressed by witnessing two verbal combatants savage each other with cross-talk to the point where unleashing fire hoses on them to dampen their tempers seems almost appropriate. Displaying emotion overtly, however, does not always destroy a speaker's credibility. Too much composure may be perceived as hard-heartedness or insensitivity. Shedding tears while delivering a eulogy at a funeral or expressing outrage at an atrocity may enhance your credibility. *The appropriateness of displaying composure depends on the context.*

Adapt While Speaking: Exhibit Sensitivity

In Chapter One, sensitivity was identified as a key element of how to become a competent public speaker. Sensitivity means receptive accuracy, picking up the signals being sent by your audience. Although audience adaptation is largely an issue of preparation, it also needs to occur while you are presenting your speech. Inexperienced public speakers find this challenging. It is difficult to alter your speech on the fly when you have little experience doing so. Nevertheless, as you become more experienced, adapting to your audience while speaking becomes easier.

Public speaking is a transactional process, so your listeners are providing feedback indicating how your speech is being received. When your listeners seem to be losing interest, crank up your delivery by showing greater enthusiasm and animation. You may want to tell an interesting or humorous story, planned for later in the speech, much sooner. Some details may need to be dropped if you are running short on time. You do not want to increase the pace of your delivery to race through prepared material. When listeners appear confused, offer an additional example for clarification or explain your point in different, simpler terms. Adapting while presenting your speech is discussed in subsequent chapters, but for now, realize that with experience you can learn to respond to the unique circumstances every speech situation offers.

TOPIC CHOICE AND AUDIENCE ADAPTATION

If you become an expert on some subject, you may be asked to speak on that topic. Here the speech topic is chosen for you. In a speech class, however, the choice, within broad limits, will likely be up to you. In this section, how to choose a topic that is adapted well for you, your audience, and the occasion are discussed.

Exploring Potential Topics: Important Choice

Choosing bad topics produces bad speeches; choosing great topics is the first step toward producing great speeches. There are three primary ways to explore potential speech topics systematically.

Do a Personal Inventory: You as Topic Source   Begin your exploration of appropriate topics by looking at your own personal experiences and interests. Make a list. Do you have hobbies, such as woodworking, scrapbooking, or stamp collecting? What sports do you play? List any unusual events that have occurred in your life, such as getting caught in a tornado or witnessing a bank robbery. Have you done any volunteer work for charitable organizations? What form of entertainment interests you—romantic movies, rap music, dancing, rodeo, or car shows? Do you have any special skills, such as surfing, cooking, carpentry, or sewing? Have you traveled to any interesting places, such as Ayers Rock or Machu Picchu? Have you met any exciting people, such as a rock star, professional athlete, or famous actor? What is the worst thing that has happened to you? What is the best? This list contains many possible choices for a speech topic.

Brainstorm: New Possibilities   You may need to brainstorm additional topic possibilities beyond your personal inventory. Take your personal list, examine it, and then choose five topics that seem most promising. Write down each topic on a separate list, and brainstorm new possibilities for each topic. For example, brainstorm "trip to London" by letting your mind search for related topics, such as double-decker buses, driving on the left side of the road, the British accent, Parliament, royalty, Hyde Park, British money, and British rock groups. Now consider each one of these and try to brainstorm a more specific topic. British money, for example, might lead to a comparison of British and American currency. Driving on the left could lead to why the British drive on the left but we drive on the right. Parliament could trigger a comparison between the U.S. Congress and the British Parliament.

Scanning for Topics: Quick Ideas   Scanning books can help generate additional ideas for speech topics. This process can produce some real surprises. Consider, for instance, *The Hypochondriac's Pocket Guide to Horrible Diseases You Probably Already Have* by Dennis Diclaudio (2006). In it, the author identifies 45 terrible diseases—among them, alien-hand syndrome "in which your own hand may attempt to choke you to death" and cornu cutaneum "in which you grow a horn like a rhinoceros." This book, and others like it, could prove to be a useful resource for developing an interesting informative speech on hypochondria, or on serious diseases and prevention, or on a history of human disease epidemics.

Scan magazines, such as *Time, Consumer Reports, Ebony, Sports Illustrated, People, Psychology Today, O Magazine, Ms, Men's Health*, or *Scientific American Mind*. Look at the table of contents, and leaf through the articles. Do not spend time reading them. If you see a promising topic, write it down and note the magazine, the article, and the date. Do the same with newspapers. Scanning my local newspaper, I stumbled upon an Associated Press article with the headline, "Ecologists Alarmed by Rise in Bat Deaths" (Hill, 2009). Intrigued that anyone would be concerned about dying bats, especially given an unhappy experience I once had with a bat in my bedroom in the middle of the night, I discovered that white-nose syndrome, caused by a fungus, is killing whole caves full of bats in northeastern states. Bats can consume 1,000 disease-carrying mosquitoes in an hour, far more than any bug-zapper (Rogers, 2007). Exploring the alarming demise of bats could make an interesting speech.

Finally, scan blogging sites such as *Huffington Post*, which has a potpourri of articles and opinion columns on politics, sports, news items, gossip, comedy, business, entertainment, and fashion. If you cannot find a topic of appropriate interest after scanning this site, you are not looking hard enough.

Appropriateness of Topic: Blending Topic and Audience

Choosing a topic that is inappropriate for a particular audience virtually guarantees that your speech will be ineffective. Appropriateness is contextual. A speech topic that works in one instance may be an abysmal failure in another. There are three central elements to consider when analyzing the appropriateness of your topic choice: speaker, audience, and occasion.

Speaker Appropriateness: Suitability for You   If you find a topic uninteresting, then it is not appropriate for you, the speaker. It is a rare individual who can take a topic that he or she finds dull and successfully fake interest to an audience. If you think the subject is dull, what must your audience think? Choose a topic that interests or excites you.

Avoid choosing a topic that is a poor fit for you. A white person speaking about the "Black experience in America" is a poor fit. Similarly, young people talking about "what it's like being old" sounds goofy. Men speaking about female menopause or women discussing the care and feeding of the male prostate is awkward.

Describing what it is to be a Muslim in America when you have never been one lacks credibility. No matter how gifted you are as a speaker, some topics will sink your chances of presenting an effective speech.

Audience Appropriateness: Suitability for Your Listeners   Over the years, my colleagues have shared many horror stories about student speeches on topics that were startlingly inappropriate, such as "how to assassinate someone you hate," "spitting for distance," "harassing the homeless," "proper methods of inducing vomiting after a big meal" (with demonstration), "opening a beer bottle with your teeth," "constructing a bong," and "shoplifting techniques that work." These topics are inappropriate because they are offensive, trivial, demeaning, or they encourage illegal, unethical behavior. Most are pointless, adolescent silliness.

There are other reasons why a topic might be inappropriate. An audience may find a topic choice difficult to relate to or appreciate. Giving a speech on how to surf to an audience living in Kansas is a bit weird. A topic can also be too technical or complex. I once had a student try to explain string theory, a developing branch of theoretical physics, in a 5-minute speech. Not surprisingly, the speech was more confusing than clarifying for her audience unschooled in such things. A topic may also be overused. I have heard many reasons to legalize marijuana in

Some topics are inappropriate because they are trivial and offensive.

several hundred student speeches over many years. Although I am ambivalent on the topic, for me the strongest reason to legalize marijuana is to put an end to all speeches on the subject. Be wary of shopworn topics that might bore your instructor and your classmates.

Occasion Appropriateness: Suitability for the Event   The occasion usually defines the general purpose of your speech, so topic choice should be suited to that general purpose. A **general purpose** identifies the overall goal of your speech—to inform, describe, explain, demonstrate, persuade, celebrate, memorialize, entertain, or eulogize.

If you are asked to give a persuasive speech in class, merely explaining how to be successful when taking an online class, for example, is not appropriate. You have to promote a controversial position, such as arguing that online classes are inferior to traditional classes. A graduation ceremony invites topics such as "employment possibilities for the future," "skills for success," and "thinking in the future tense," not an unrelated series of jokes meant to entertain but not provide insight or inspiration for graduates. A sermon at a religious service warrants a topic related to moral behavior, not a political speech advocating for one political party or another. The occasion and its general purpose dictate the appropriateness of a topic choice.

Eleven days before the 2002 national election, Paul Wellstone, Democratic U.S. senator from Minnesota, died in a plane crash. With the expectation that former U.S. Senator Walter Mondale would replace Wellstone on the ballot, the memorial service for Wellstone, attended by 20,000 people, became a pep rally for the Mondale campaign. In a "eulogy" for Wellstone, Rick Kahn made this plea, "Can you not hear your friend calling you, one last time, one step forward on his behalf, to keep his legacy alive and help us win this election for Paul Wellstone" (Wilgoren, 2002). Most members of the crowd sprang to their feet and began chanting "Mondale! Mondale!" With many Republicans and independents in attendance, this burst of partisanship ignited a fierce controversy. Independent Party governor of Minnesota Jesse Ventura left in a huff, remarking that he found the transformation of a solemn memorial service into a political pep rally "disturbing." For days afterward, Republicans bitterly complained that the Democrats exploited a tragedy for political purposes. Jeff Blodgett, Wellstone's campaign manager, publicly apologized.

Narrowing the Topic: Making Subjects Manageable

Sometimes you are given a very broad topic on which to speak. Other times you find an interesting topic, but it is too broad and general for the time available. Narrowing your topic to fit the audience and the occasion is a significant task for the competent speaker.

Time constraints dictate to what extent a topic must be narrowed. President Woodrow Wilson took his public speaking very seriously. A reporter interviewed him once regarding his speech preparation. "How long do you spend preparing a 10-minute speech?" Wilson was asked. He replied, "About 2 weeks." "How long do you spend preparing an hour-long speech?" the reporter queried. "About a week," answered Wilson. Surprised, the reporter then asked Wilson how long he prepared for a 2-hour speech. He replied, "I could do that now." Giving a long-winded speech takes less effort than narrowing the speech to fit into a shorter time allotment.

Once you have settled on a general topic that is appropriate for you the speaker, your audience, and the occasion, begin narrowing the topic to fit your time limit. A 5-minute speech obviously requires much more narrowing than a 15-minute speech. Take the general topic and brainstorm more specific subtopics. For example, a broad topic such as "the cost of a college education," could be broken into these more specific subtopics: problems with financial aid, how to get a scholarship, part-time student employment, the high cost of textbooks, room and board fees for campus living, college tuition, and college fees. Each of these subtopics could be developed into an effective 5-minute presentation.

Staying within your time limit is critical. If you are asked to give a 15-minute address at a luncheon meeting of a civic organization, you will be addressing a roomful of empty chairs if you go much beyond the time limit. People attending luncheon meetings often have only an hour, of which your speech is but a small part.

Keeping within time limits was never Bill Clinton's strength. Clinton gave the nominating speech for presidential candidate Michael Dukakis at the 1988 Democratic National Convention. His speech lasted more than twice as long as scheduled. Television networks switched from showing the speech to shots of delegates drawing their forefingers across their throats in a "cut" signal. Clinton received an enthusiastic cheer when he said, "In closing . . ." Massachusetts delegate William Bulger joked, "When this started I was a young man." A network executive taped a sign onto the front of an Atlanta phone book that read: "Transcript of Gov. Clinton's Speech." As president, Clinton never seemed to learn from his disastrous 1988 speech. His 2000 State of the Union speech took 1 hour and 29 minutes—proving that he did not heed the observation of an anonymous wit: "The brain can absorb only what the seat can endure." Even his nominating speech at the 2012 Democratic National Convention went twice as long as scheduled, bleeding into the mainstream television networks prime-time schedule, although as a former president the immediate audience's reception was the opposite of his 1988 debacle.

Abraham Lincoln's Gettysburg Address, considered one of the great American speeches, lasted a little more than *two minutes*. Famed orator Edward Everett, who preceded Lincoln, gave a 2-hour-plus speech. He later wrote Lincoln: "I shall be glad if I could flatter myself that I came as near to the central idea of the occasion in two hours as you did in two minutes" (quoted in Noonan, 1998, p. 65). Although Barack Obama's State of the Union speeches have been nearly Clintonesque in length, he wisely patterned his January 20, 2009 inaugural address along the lines of Lincoln. His first speech as president, delivered outdoors to a massive crowd whose members endured frigid weather, lasted a mere 18 minutes. His second inaugural address delivered on January 21, 2013, was equally brief. On these occasions, Obama heeded the advice of another president, Franklin Roosevelt, who once said, "Be sincere; be brief; be seated."

SUMMARY

Audience analysis is the core of public speaking. Analyzing your audience begins with knowing the five types of audiences, discerning the composition of your audience, and then adapting your topic choice and development to meet the expectations and needs of your audience. You want to establish your likeability, credibility, and identification with your audience. Your topic choice should be appropriate for you as speaker, for your audience, and for the occasion. Narrowing your topic to fit the time limit of your speech is also important.

5

Attention: Getting People to Listen

The administration at my college campus hired a consultant to address safety in the workplace. The speaker opened with a personal story that illustrated the effects of traumatic experience on our ability to be safe. When driving from the cemetery after visiting the grave of her 5-year-old son, through tears from unimaginable sadness, she inadvertently ran a stop sign, pulling in front of another driver who had to brake hard to avoid a collision. The driver who screeched to a halt was a highway patrolman. The grieving mother pulled over to the curb. The officer got out of his patrol car and walked up to the passenger side of her vehicle. He tapped, indicating for her to roll down her window. He leaned over and asked, "May I get in?" She nodded her head, continuing to sob. The officer sat in the passenger seat for a few moments without saying a word, then he asked, pointing to the cemetery, "Do you have someone in there?" Her eyes welled with tears, but she found comfort in telling him about her little boy. When she finished, the officer asked her how far away she lived and then offered to follow her home to be sure she got there safely. He never mentioned the traffic violation.

The speaker drew numerous points from this simple narrative, but the overriding effect was to grab her listeners' attention immediately with lingering effect. Almost everyone who listened to the personal account of the grieving mother and the kindly highway patrolman subsequently admitted being profoundly moved. Throughout her hour-long presentation, with both poignant and humorous stories and examples, the consultant effortlessly and expertly kept her listeners' attention.

How important is gaining and maintaining the attention of your audience? One national survey of individuals from a wide variety of professions revealed that the top-ranked skill for preparing and delivering a speech was keeping an audience's attention (Engleberg, 2002). Corporate media consultant Steve Crescenzo (2005) observes, "In today's short-attention-span, sound-byte society, the one thing people cannot afford to be is boring" (p. 12). If your audience is not attentive, then you are talking to yourself. Why prepare and present a speech that induces a nap? You want your listeners excited, engaged, touched, and anxious to hear what comes next. You do not want them yearning for those signal words "In conclusion." It is a lesson every teacher learns when lecturing to students for an entire class period and every religious leader comprehends when delivering a sermon or homily to a congregation. Most speeches are not meant to be purely entertainment, but if listeners are bored when you speak to them about significant issues then your substantial ideas will not rouse lethargic listeners from slumber.

The next chapter addresses very specific ways to gain attention during the introduction to your speech that extend from this chapter's discussion. It is important to note here, however, that *grabbing your listeners' attention initially is far easier than maintaining attention for an entire speech.* Whether for 5 minutes or 55, keeping your listeners' rapt attention is a supremely difficult task, making it a topic worthy of considerable discussion and illustration. The rewards of presenting a truly galvanizing speech are considerable.

PHOTO 5.1 Gaining audience attention is a good start, but maintaining that attention of listeners throughout your speech is a huge challenge.

Capturing and holding the attention of your audience has to be an integral part of your speech development. Thus, *the purpose of this chapter is to explain ways to gain and maintain the attention of your listeners while presenting your speech.* This chapter discusses the nature of attention and rhetorical strategies that can ignite audience attention from the beginning of your speech to its conclusion.

NATURE OF ATTENTION

An enormously popular British ad that featured a sexy model acting seductively as she climbed inside a sleek automobile drew attention to the wrong stimulus. A study of this ad showed that the attractive model commanded attention while the automobile being advertised was virtually invisible to almost everyone watching (Clay, 2002). As a speaker, being seen in our kaleidoscopic world of images and heard above the clamoring din is your great task because you cannot afford to be boring. Understanding the nature of attention and how it works can be of great assistance in this endeavor.

Selective Attention of Listeners: Filtering Stimuli

Attention is unavoidably selective. **Attention** is the act of focusing on a specific stimulus to the exclusion of competing stimuli. By one calculation, your five basic senses are bombarded with 11 million bits of information *each second*, but at best you attend to only about 40 bits (Wilson, 2002). Gaining and maintaining attention is a process of directing listeners' awareness toward your message while steering them away from distractions. Herein lies your challenge. Minds easily wander, every chance they get (Kane et al., 2007; McVay & Kane, 2009). Professor Paul Cameron confirmed this in a study of students listening to a professor's lecture (cited in Adler & Proctor, 2007). Only 20% were mildly attentive to the lecture, and a mere 12% were actively listening. Others were pursuing erotic thoughts (20%), while the rest were reminiscing, worrying, daydreaming, or thinking about lunch or religion. A more recent study of 269 college students showed that 91% admitted to text messaging during class lectures. It is now the number one classroom distraction. Cell phones ringing was a close second (Mayk, 2010). Distractions from text messaging and cell-phone ringing significantly reduce students' classroom performance (Ellis et al., 2010; End et al., 2010). If listeners are staring out a window, doing a face plant onto the desktop, talking to the person next to them, doodling, texting on their cell phone, or accessing their social networking page when a speaker is talking, they send the message, "I'm not interested."

PHOTO 5.2 Multitasking diminishes your effectiveness on both tasks, in this case texting and driving. Texting while someone is speaking means you are only half-listening.

The challenge of attracting attention to your message and avoiding distractions is complicated by the fact that *listeners cannot attend to two competing stimuli simultaneously* (Dux et al., 2006). Someone engaged in an audible cell-phone conversation while you are trying to prepare your speech is incredibly distracting (Galvan et al., 2013). "Whatever has your attention pretty much has your undivided attention" (Myers, 2004, p. 232). A person can shift rapidly (in microseconds) back and forth between two competing stimuli (texting on a cell phone and driving), but this can result in performing both tasks more poorly than if only a single task received focus. For example, texting while driving is six times more dangerous than driving while under the influence of alcohol (Wilms, 2012). A driver is 23 times more likely to get into a crash while texting than drivers who do not ("Distracted Drivers," 2012). When audience members are texting while hearing a speech, their minds are weaving back and forth between two incompatible tasks. *Ironically, frequent multitaskers believe they are good at balancing two tasks at once, but research shows the opposite* ("Distracted Drivers," 2012). As Stanford psychologist Clifford Nass notes, "It turns out multitaskers are terrible at every aspect of multitasking. They're terrible at ignoring irrelevant information; they're terrible at keeping information in their head nicely and neatly organized; and they're terrible at switching from one task to another" ("Interview: Clifford Nass," 2010). Selectivity of listeners' attention highlights the magnitude of the challenge you face gaining and maintaining your audience's attention.

Mindful Listening: Focused Attention

Retention of information is an integral part of the listening process. If you remember little from a speaker's presentation, then of what value was it? If your goal is landing a high-paying job but you are daydreaming your way through school, you better get used to saying, "Do you want to super-size that drink?"

Retention is diminished when listening is *mindless*—little effort is made to attend to a speaker's message. Retention is enhanced when listening is *mindful*—careful attention is given to a speaker's message. *Mindful listening is active listening*; you are engaged in the communication transaction with others. You are not merely a passive observer.

Mindful listening requires focused attention. We do not remember what has not received our focused attention. The airline industry recognizes this. In an effort to get passengers to listen carefully to safety instructions at the beginning of flights (critical information if an emergency were to occur), flight attendants have tried singing the safety message accompanied by a ukulele, impersonating famous people while reciting the instructions, even performing a rap version of the safety message. Flight attendants have also added a little humor to their standard safety instructions, such as: "In the event of a sudden loss of cabin pressure, oxygen masks will descend from the ceiling. Stop screaming, grab the mask, and pull it over your face" and "Your seat cushions can be used for flotation, and in the event of an emergency water landing, please take them with our compliments" and "This is a non-smoking flight. If you wish to smoke in flight, please step outside of the aircraft" ("Airline Safety," 2010; Lim, 2012).

Do not expect listeners to be ideally prepared to focus on you and your message. "Just try harder" to pay attention is empty advice unless you provide compelling motivation for audience members to listen (Sanders, 1983; Pashler, 1998). If your listeners must force themselves to keep their eyelids from slamming shut, then you have failed as a public speaker. Avoid making listening tantamount to wisdom tooth extraction; make it a pleasurable experience. This requires a fairly sophisticated understanding of key stimulus triggers that can ignite listeners' attention involuntarily.

ATTENTION STRATEGIES: TRIGGERING LISTENING

Attention is both a voluntary and an involuntary activity. A sudden shrill scream will command your instant attention. That is involuntary. It is unexpected and unavoidable. Choosing to pay attention to a speaker whose topic may not interest you initially is voluntary. Key stimulus triggers that can ignite attention involuntarily include appeals to that which is novel, startling, vital, humorous, changeable, or intense (Passer & Smith, 2011). When direct effort is made by you to exploit such triggers, they become attention strategies.

Novelty: The Allure of the New

Novelty attracts attention (Escera et al., 1998; Poldrack, 2010). Audience members are naturally drawn to the new and different. They cannot help themselves. Conversely, the commonplace can produce a coma-like stupor. Recognizing this means never beginning your speech with a snoozer, such as "My topic is. . ." or "Today I'd like to talk to you about. . . ." Stimulate interest in your subject. There are several ways to make novel appeals to stimulate attention.

Unusual Topics: Choosing Outside the Box   In this age of high-tech weapons systems and sophisticated counter-terrorism tactics, sometimes it is the low-tech solutions that save lives. American troops in the Iraq War were constantly faced with potential booby-trapped dwellings. A solution? Shoot Silly String across a room before entering to locate possible tripwires attached to bombs. This is an unusual topic for a great speech: low-tech creative solutions to significant problems. For instructors who may have heard a gazillion speeches on the abortion controversy, unusual topics presented by students can be a refreshing experience. It is much easier to attend to unusual topics on substantial issues.

Unusual Examples: The Anti-Sedative   Sprinkle your speech with unusual examples that illustrate important points. For instance, consider using real examples such as these pulled from a newspaper story:

> "The check is in the mail" used to be the standard ploy to ward off bill collectors. Not so anymore. Delinquent customers have adopted more original stalling tactics. One woman claimed that she had run over her husband with a car, breaking both of his arms thereby making it impossible for him to write checks or pay by computer. A flower-shop owner insisted that she could not pay her bills until someone died and had a funeral. "Business should pick up soon," she said hopefully. These are silly excuses for failing to pay one's bills, but mounting personal debt is no laughing matter.

Compare this opening to the more commonplace "I want to talk to you about how to handle personal debt." The more novel opening with unusual examples invites attention. The commonplace opener does not.

Unusual Stories: Nothing Like a Good Tale   Everyone loves a good story, especially one they have not heard (Hsu, 2008). Storytelling can jazz up a potentially tedious speech. Corporations recognize the value of storytelling "as a way of enlivening speeches, sales pitches, training sessions, and other presentations on otherwise dry or technical topics" (Quinones, 1999, p. 4). Newspapers are filled with novel stories that can be used to snare listeners' attention. For example:

> Doctors who examined Hall of Fame Pittsburg Steelers' center Mike Webster estimated that he suffered the equivalent of 25,000 car crashes without a seatbelt in the 25 years he played football from high school through the NFL. After retiring, he experienced amnesia, dementia, and depression from his football-induced head trauma. Webster's experiences reflect a serious problem that until recently has received relatively little attention. Football at all levels, from high school to the NFL, is hazardous to your brain. Stronger regulation of football injuries must be implemented.

Stories such as these invite attention because they are not trivial, commonplace episodes we have heard many times. They make us sit up and take notice.

Unusual Phrasing: It Is in the Wording   Colorful phrasing or unusual wording can transform an ordinary statement into a novel, memorable one (Childers & Houston, 1984). For example:

> **Ordinary:** Most books are carried less than 60 days by bookstores unless they become bestsellers
> **Novel:** The shelf life of the average book is somewhere between milk and yogurt. (Calvin Trillon)
> **Ordinary:** Our office was way too small
> **Novel:** He and I had an office so tiny that an inch smaller and it would have been adultery. (Dorothy Parker)
> **Ordinary**: Sometimes you're the villain; sometimes you're the victim.
> **Novel:** Sometimes you're the windshield; sometimes you're the bug. (Mark Knopfler)

Startling Appeal: Shake up Your Listeners

The startling appeal is meant to stun your audience out of its complacency and motivate listening. There are several ways to startle your audience to enhance attention to your message.

Startling Statements, Facts, or Statistics: The "Oh WOW" Effect   A startling statement, fact, or statistic can rouse audience attention. Student Kathy Levine (2001) offers this startling revelation in her speech on dental hygiene:

As the previously cited *20/20* investigation uncovered, the water used in approximately 90% of dental offices is dirtier than the water found in public toilets. This means 9 out of 10 dental offices are using dirty water on their patients. Moreover, the independent research of Dr. George Merijohn, a periodontist who specialized in dental waterlines, found that out of 60 randomly selected offices from around the nation, two-thirds of all samples taken contained oral bacteria from the saliva of previous patients. *(p. 77)*

Startling statements, facts, and statistics can be unsettling. They are meant to alarm, shock, and astonish an audience into listening intently to what you have to say. Researchers David Brenner and Eric Hall of Columbia University attempted to raise an alarm about excessive use of diagnostic CT scans. They noted in a study reported in the *New England Journal of Medicine* that the radiation levels patients receive during each scan varies between 1,000 and 10,000 millirems. The average radiation dose for Japanese survivors of Hiroshima and Nagasaki who

You can be novel and startling, but make sure your strategy is appropriate for your speech purpose. Might this handstand ever be appropriate?

were a mile or two from the ground zero blast of atomic bombs during World War II was 3,000 millirems (see Sternberg, 2007). These are startling facts and statistics likely to cause real concern, especially since detection of minuscule radiation levels in the United States from the 2011 Japanese nuclear catastrophe following a tsunami sparked near panic in America. There was a run on potassium iodide pills to counteract the effects of radiation, even though such pills are not a cure-all for radiation poisoning (Goldwert, 2011).

Inappropriate Use: Beware Bizarre Behavior   Startling an audience should enhance your speech and your personal credibility with the audience, not detract and distract from these goals. Inappropriate use of the startling appeal can backfire. Every speech teacher remembers notable examples of student miscalculations when using a startling appeal. For instance, one student punched himself so hard in the face that he momentarily staggered himself and produced a large bruise under his eye (the speech was on violence in America). Another student shrieked obscenities to her stunned audience (the topic was the First Amendment).

The competent public speaker exercises solid judgment when choosing to startle his or her listeners. Your goal should not be to gain attention by being

PHOTO 5.3 You can bring an audience to its feet with a stunt such as giving a speech naked, but is this ever appropriate for a public speech? Explain.

outrageous, irresponsible, or by exercising poor judgment. Do not emulate the "American Idol" tryouts in which contestants appear intent on acting strange, even creepy just to get attention. You should consider the implied or stated rules of a speech context when choosing attention strategies. An audience can turn on you when angered or offended. Startle an audience, but be appropriate.

The Vital Appeal: Meaningfulness

You attend to stimuli that are meaningful to you, and you ignore stimuli that are relatively meaningless (Ruiter et al., 2006). Problems and issues that vitally affect your lives are meaningful. In this sense, audiences tend to be Me-oriented. Listeners heed warnings when a societal problem affects them personally. The AIDS epidemic was slow to seize the attention of the average American when it was erroneously thought to be a "gay disease." When the disease became rampant in the general population of heterosexual males and females, however, more people started to pay attention.

Student Nicolle Carpenter (2004) shows how to make your message vital and thus meaningful to your audience. After a brief opening story about a man named Jack Spratt who died of a food-borne illness caused by eating contaminated green onions at a restaurant, she proceeded with this effective vital appeal:

> What happened to Spratt and some 175,000 other people who are hospitalized each year due to contaminated produce is frightening; even more disturbing is the fact that it could happen to anyone.... In a November 23, 2003 *Seattle Times* news article Dr. Glen Morris, chairman of the department of epidemiology and preventive medicine at the University Of Maryland said, "Produce is emerging as an important cause of food-borne illness in this country, and we must understand how real the risk is". *(p. 5)*

Nicolle includes her entire audience as potential victims of food poisoning.

Instead of making a general appeal to the vital, citing the seriousness of the problem for nameless, faceless citizens, personalize the appeal to all of your listeners. Student Jake Gruber (2001) did exactly this when he stated in his speech on heart disease in women:

> "Whereas one in 28 women will die of breast cancer, one in five will die of heart disease. And guys, before you take the next nine minutes to decide what you'll eat for lunch, ask yourself one question: what would my life be like if the women who make it meaningful are not there? Clearly, this is an issue that concerns us all". *(p. 16)*

Humorous Appeal: Keep Listeners Laughing

"We've childproofed our house, but they keep finding a way in." This ironic, anonymous quip has been circulating on the Internet for years. Its humor gives it staying power. Humor is a superior attention strategy if used adroitly, probably the very best antidote to boredom (Banas et al., 2011). Using humor effectively, however, can be very dicey. It requires far more than chirpy advice such as "be funny." Complex issues of appropriateness and effectiveness are always present because "almost all forms of humor involve ridicule of something—a person, behavior, belief, group, or possession—at some level" (Greengross & Miller, 2008, p. 394). For example, Frieda Norris remarks: "Before you criticize someone, you should walk a mile in their shoes. That way, when you criticize them, you are a mile away from them, and you have their shoes." Norris is mildly ridiculing a standard aphorism about being empathic. Some will find this amusing; others may view this as trivializing an important communication concept. There are several guidelines for using humor competently as an attention strategy.

Do Not Force Humor: Not Everyone Is Funny   If you have never told a joke without flubbing the punch line, avoid humiliating yourself. Listening to a speaker stubbornly try to be funny without success can be an excruciatingly uncomfortable experience for all involved. Nevertheless, you can still use humor. *Use humorous quotations, tell funny stories or amusing occurrences* to amplify or clarify points. *Do not telegraph stories as intentionally humorous*, however, by using a risky lead-in, such as "Let me tell you a really funny story." Such a lead-in invites embarrassment if your listeners do not laugh. *Simply tell the story and let audience members laugh if they are so inclined.*

Use Only Relevant Humor: Stay Focused   Humor should amuse listeners while making a relevant point. It should not be an opportunity to insert an irrelevant political aside or merely to "loosen up" your audience with laughter. *Tie the humor directly to a main point or principal theme.* For example: "Someone once said, 'I want to die peacefully in my sleep like my grandfather, not screaming in terror like his passengers.' You've all experienced it—the nerve-wracking anxiety every time you see an elderly person driving a car. I want to convince you that greater restrictions on elderly drivers should be instituted." The humor is simple and it leads directly to the purpose of the speech.

Be Sensitive to Audience and Occasion: Humor Can Backfire   Don West, defense attorney for George Zimmerman in the Trayvon Martin murder case in 2013, began his opening statement to the jury with a knock-knock joke.

Legendary lawyer Alan Dershowitz commented afterward, "This is a murder case. The victim's family is sitting in the courtroom with tears in their eyes and he's telling a knock-knock joke? I just don't get it" ("Dershowitz," 2013). West later apologized to the jury for the inappropriate joke.

Humor can backfire. Sexist, racist, and homophobic "jokes" exhibit poor taste and lack of ethics. Coarse vulgarities, obscenities, and sick jokes are not everyone's idea of amusement. Humor that ridicules and demeans groups or individuals, such as when teachers put down students in class, usually backfires (Frymier et al., 2008). Humor that is negative or hostile may alienate vast sections of an audience, unless it is an official "roast" (Banas, 2011). A speaker I heard recently cracked this tired "joke" to his mixed-sex audience: "What's the difference between a terrorist and a woman with PMS? You can negotiate with the terrorist." Watching the audience's reaction was instructive. Some laughed. Some started to laugh, then thought better of it. Others not only did not laugh, they booed the speaker. The speaker seemed surprised by the mixed response and searched for a graceful recovery. He never found one.

Consider what amuses individuals in different cultures, and what might offend them. An Internet study called Laughlab attracted tens of thousands of respondents from 70 cultures that produced two million ratings of jokes to determine the world's funniest one (Wiseman, 2007). A favorite among American respondents, especially men, was this joke:

> **Texan:** Where are you from?
> **Harvard graduate:** I come from a place where we do not end our sentences with prepositions.
> **Texan:** Okay, where are you from, jackass?

The British liked: "A woman gets on a bus with her baby. The bus driver says: 'That's the ugliest baby I've ever seen.' The woman sits down fuming. She says to a man next to her: 'The driver just insulted me!' The man says: 'You go right up there and tell him off; I'll hold your monkey.'" The French liked: "You're a high-priced lawyer. If I give you $500, will you answer two questions for me? The lawyer responds, 'Absolutely! What is the second question?'"

Humor is subjective, and you may find these jokes less than thigh-slappingly funny, or harsh and not the best jokes you have heard, but Laughlab does not have to be representative of everyone's taste. It highlights that there are cultural differences, so be careful (Zhang, 2005). Generally speaking, sick jokes or dark humor do not travel well from culture to culture or even person to person (Lewis, 1996). Sarcasm, exaggeration, satire, and parody of others are usually unappreciated by Asians who value politeness and harmony. Jokes about religion, sex, and the underprivileged can also cause deep offense (Lewis, 1996). *Humor that is gentle or self-deprecating usually travels best.*

Consider Using Self-Deprecating Humor: "I'm Not Worthy"   Humor that makes gentle fun of your own failings and limitations, called **self-deprecation**, can be quite appealing because it communicates that you do not take yourself too seriously. You have enough confidence to recognize and note your flaws. Abraham Lincoln was a master of self-deprecation. During the famous Lincoln–Douglas debates, U.S. Senator Stephen Douglas called Lincoln "two-faced," whereupon Lincoln calmly replied, "I leave it to my audience. If I had another face, do you think I would wear this one?" Comedian Wendy Liebman on the David Letterman Show fired off a series of brief self-deprecating lines: "I've been getting back to nature . . . well I was evicted . . . from my parent's house . . . but we're still very close . . . genetically . . . I'm engaged now . . . it was so romantic . . . he turned off the TV . . . well he muted it . . . during the commercials." Liebman is both self-deprecating and other-deprecating, poking fun at herself and her boyfriend, as does Rita Rudner with this line: "My boyfriend and I broke up. He wanted to get married . . . and I didn't want him to."

Self-deprecating humor can disarm a hostile audience. On May 21, 2001, George W. Bush was the commencement speaker at the Yale University graduation. Bush faced his most hostile audience. More than 170 faculty members boycotted the graduation ceremony and scores of graduates greeted Bush with protest signs. Many thought he had "stolen" the election from Gore. Not known for his great oratorical abilities, Bush exceeded expectations using self-deprecating humor successfully. For example, referring to his party animal reputation while at Yale, Bush remarked, "If you're like me, you won't remember everything you did here. That can be a good thing." Making fun of his penchant for using tortured syntax and inventing words, Bush said, "As I recall, one of my academic advisers . . . said I should focus on English. I still hear that quite often" (quoted in "President George W. Bush," 2001). Bush likely did not change many people's minds, but he defused the overt hostility, and his audience listened to his speech because it is tough to be angry when the person you dislike is making you laugh.

Making fun of yourself instead of other people can work well with an audience, but, again, the advice is more complicated than simply "be self-deprecating" (Baxter, 2012). High-status individuals may benefit more from self-deprecation than lower-status individuals because self-deprecation exhibits lack of arrogance and ego without jeopardizing credibility and esteem (Greengross & Miller, 2008). George Bush as president of the United States could make fun of himself without jeopardizing his role as the most powerful leader in the world, but if you are self-deprecating during a job interview and teaching demonstration, you may handicap yourself compared to other job applicants who present a more capable image. Nevertheless, gentle self-deprecation can be attractive if not overdone.

Movement and Change: Our Evolutionary Protection

Attention to change is built into our brains. You do not pay attention to that which is static. "Is the carpet still the same? Is the paint on the walls unchanged? "Has the TV been moved?" These are not the questions we ask each day unless change occurs (the TV is gone). Why? Because change carries new information. Fast change especially provides important information. It warrants greater attention because it may indicate a potential threat to our well-being. Predatory animals move very slowly or remain still for long periods of time while stalking prey. If they move too fast before they are close enough to pounce, the prey notices and bolts.

Movement that represents change is noticeable and you attend to it (von Muhlenen et al., 2005). Too little movement when speaking can anesthetize an audience. A speaker stands before an audience, grabs the podium in a vise-like grip (white knuckles clearly visible to everyone), assumes an expressionless face reminiscent of a marble statue in a museum, and appears to have feet welded to the floor. This is an example of too little body movement and change. Aimlessly pacing like a caged panther, wildly gesticulating with arms flailing in all directions, or awkwardly wrapping legs and arms around the podium are examples of excessive body movement. Note the advice in Chapter 3 for achieving a balanced delivery with movement.

Intensity: Extreme Degree of a Stimulus

You attend to the intense (Pashler, 1998). **Intensity** is concentrated stimuli. It is an extreme degree of emotion, thought, or activity. Relating a tragic event, a moving human-interest story, or a specific instance of courage and determination plays on the intense feelings of your audience. The opening to this chapter references a consultant addressing the issue of safety in the workplace. What was left out was the context for this presentation. An instructor on my campus, a good friend of mine, was seriously injured when attacked with an ax handle by a mentally ill student of his. This was an intense, traumatic event for the campus community. Understandably, it riveted everyone's attention and became the subject of much discussion and debate. Consider another example:

A youth minister, Melvin Nurse, at the Livingway Christian Fellowship Church International in Jacksonville, Florida, during a sermon wanted to make his point emphatically that sin is like Russian roulette. His congregation of 250 parents and youngsters saw him place a .357-caliber pistol to his temple and pull the trigger. Nurse apparently expected that the blank cartridge in the pistol's chamber would cause him no harm. Unfortunately, in front of his wife and four daughters, the blank cartridge flew apart on impact and shattered Nurse's skull. He died instantly. His attempt to capture attention was successful, but with a horrifying result. *("Minister," 1998)*

These are two intense examples. Who could be callous or indifferent to such painful human drama? The examples, however, are also unpleasant, even disturbing, and this raises an important issue: *should speakers use unpleasant examples to capture attention?* Might your listeners be repelled by such stark, negative examples? There is often a potential risk when you employ intensity as an attention strategy. Any time deep human emotion is aroused, your listeners may respond in a variety of ways, both positive and negative. Nevertheless, research shows that highly unpleasant stimuli can be highly interesting and attention grabbing, while highly pleasant stimuli can be so uninteresting that attention is easily diverted (Turner & Silvia, 2006). Whether to use an unpleasant yet intense example is a judgment. Unpleasant examples are likely to work most effectively when they are used occasionally. A steady diet of unpleasantness can be mind numbing and counterproductive. Nevertheless, the extremely difficult challenge you face as a speaker to gain and maintain the attention of your audience may require moving beyond just happy stories and uplifting examples, as pleasant and comforting as these can be. Human interest runs the gamut from pleasant to unpleasant, so do not restrict yourself just to one or the other.

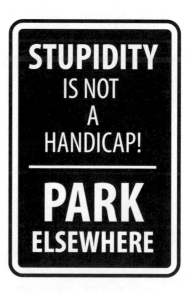

PHOTO 5.4 Which attention strategies are illustrated by this sign?

Sometimes the two, pleasant and unpleasant, seem to blend. Consider this example:

 What is love? There's romantic love with passion ignited. There's the love of a friend or companion. Then there's the simple, childlike love seen in the story of a four-year-old boy whose next-door neighbor had recently lost his wife. The man was crying in his backyard. The little boy came over, sat on the grieving man's lap. Asked later by his mother what he'd said to the man, the little boy replied, "Nothing, I just helped him cry."

The story of the grieving neighbor is unpleasant, but the little boy's act of love is pleasantly poignant.

SUMMARY

Gaining and maintaining the attention of your audience is a critical challenge for any speaker. Attention does not just happen; you have to plan it carefully. Although voluntarily making an effort as a listener to attend to a speaker's message is important, responsibility for attention resides mostly with the speaker. Involuntary stimulus triggers, such as appealing to what is novel, startling, vital, humorous, changeable, and intense, can provoke audience interest and keep listeners paying attention to your speech.

6

Introductions and Conclusions

The beginning and ending can be as important as the body of your speech. Creating a favorable first impression alerts your audience to expect a quality presentation. Ending with a bang leaves a lasting impression on your listeners. Student Kerry Konda (2006), began a speech delivered at the Interstate Oratorical Association contest this way:

> On the roof of an old airport hanger outside of Fallujah, the Marine credo, "No One Left Behind" is spelled with crudely arranged sandbags. Inside this hangar was where Marine Sgt. Daniel Cotnoir, father of two, tried to put that credo into practice. His job on the mortuary unit was to crawl along, sifting through the blood-soaked debris of blast areas, finding pieces of his fallen comrades, and then, put them back together. For his outstanding service in Iraq, the Marine Corps Times honored him as "Marine of the Year." However, this glory quickly faded. According to the *Boston Herald* on August 15, 2005, Cotnoir pointed a 12-gauge shotgun out his second floor window and fired a single shot into a crowd of noisy revelers who were leaving a nightclub and nearby restaurant in retaliation for a bottle that was thrown through his window. After police arrived, Cotnoir broke down crying saying he had to protect his family. Cotnoir is just one of the many soldiers returning from Iraq, who in military terms, has "temporary adjustment disorder," but in reality is suffering from something far greater. That something is PTSD, posttraumatic stress disorder. *(p. 74)*

This is a very powerful beginning to a speech. The story is novel, startling, and intense. Kerry's conclusion, however, is equally impressive:

Claiming posttraumatic stress disorder is just a temporary adjustment soldiers must go through is unacceptable. Our soldiers, like Daniel Cotnoir . . . , made it through the hell that is war, but we cannot lose them to the battles that still rage in their minds. As Americans we cannot sit idly by and deny them the right to lead a normal life when they sacrificed so much. Instead, we must do what is humanly possible and answer the call in their time of need; we must follow the example of Sgt. Daniel Cotnoir and leave no one behind *(p. 76)*

Tying the introduction and conclusion together with the Marine slogan "Leave no one behind" neatly packages the speech. The speech ends as poignantly as it began.

Recognizing the powerful impact a well-constructed beginning and ending to your speech can have on your audience, *the purpose of this chapter is to explore ways to construct effective speech introductions and conclusions.* Specific objectives for each are discussed.

OBJECTIVES FOR COMPETENT INTRODUCTIONS

There are five principal objectives for a competent introduction to a speech: gain attention, make a clear purpose statement, establish the significance of your topic, establish your credibility on the subject, and preview your main points. Please note that *these objectives are not rigid rules that must be followed without variation.* A wedding toast, a eulogy, or a speech that introduces another speaker usually does not need to identify the significance of the occasion or even preview the main points. The speech may be too brief to make that necessary. Some occasions also make a direct reference to significance unnecessary because the audience has assembled in recognition of the importance of the topic. A graduation ceremony and a commemoration for the victims of the 9/11 terrorist attacks are examples. Nevertheless, these five objectives apply well to most speaking occasions, especially informative and persuasive speeches.

Gain Attention: Focusing Your Listeners

In the previous chapter, general attention strategies were discussed that should be incorporated throughout your entire speech. For the introduction to your speech, however, more specific suggestions should be helpful.

Begin with a Clever Quotation: Let Others Grab Attention   Opening with a clever quotation can capitalize on the wit and wisdom of others. For example:

> President John F. Kennedy, in a speech at a White House dinner honoring several Nobel Prize winners, said: "I think this is the most extraordinary collection of talent, of human knowledge, that has ever been gathered together at the White House with the possible exception of when Thomas Jefferson dined alone." President Kennedy deftly complimented his esteemed honorees without becoming effusive in his praise. Complimenting others is an important but often overlooked way to cement interpersonal relationships, build teamwork, and promote goodwill among coworkers and friends. Giving compliments unskillfully, however, can provoke embarrassment and awkwardness between people. Today I will explain how to give compliments effectively.

Note that the quotation not only grabs attention with ironic humor, but it relates specifically to the purpose statement.

Use Questions: Engage Your Listeners   Asking questions of your audience can be an effective technique for gaining listeners' attention immediately. A question asked by a speaker that the audience answers mentally, but not out loud, is called a **rhetorical question**. Consider this example:

> The Scottish dish called haggis is a mixture of sheep innards blended with chunks of sheep fat, seasonings, and oatmeal, all cooked in the animal's stomach. If a Scottish friend offered this to you for dinner, would you eat it or would you try to politely decline the dish? If you were visiting East Africa and a local tribesman offered you a tall drink of fresh cow's blood, would you accept or decline the offer? If you were a contestant on a reality TV show that required you to eat worms, beetles, or other creepy-crawly insects, would you oblige? Some cultures find insects tasty. Culture teaches us what is food and what is not. Let me explain why cultures vary dramatically in their food choices.

These rhetorical questions engage an audience by inviting listeners to imagine what they would do. Rhetorical questions can also be quite powerful triggers of thought and emotion. "Who will be last to die for a mistake?" is a biting rhetorical question that challenges the very purpose served by continuing a flawed war policy that sacrifices human lives.

Make sure, however, that rhetorical questions are meaningful, not merely a commonplace device to open a speech. "Have you ever wondered why our college doesn't have a chess team?" may produce a "not really" mental reaction from the audience with a corresponding headshake. The question does not spark interest if interest is already lacking.

You may want to ask **direct questions** that seek overt responses. "How many of you have attended a rock concert—raise your hands?" or "Let's see a quick show of hands—have you tried an exercise program in the last year?" are examples. Student Daniel Hinderliter (2012) opened his speech at the Interstate Oratorical Association contest with these direct questions:

> By a show of hands, how many of your families have a hammer at home? If you think your neighbors to your left have a hammer, keep your hand up. Keep your hand up if you think your neighbors on your right have one. How about your neighbors across the street? That's four hammers, none of which, I'd be willing to bet, get used on a daily basis; the purchased quantity far outstrips any actual need. This disparity between need and ownership is emblematic of hyper-consumerism. *(p. 140)*

Polling an audience can be engaging and even amusing. "How many in this audience have used a dangerous, illegal drug in the past 6 months? Whoa, some of you actually raised your hand; that's a first. You might want to check the Fifth Amendment protections against self-incrimination. Americans revere the Bill of Rights, but how many of you can even identify the first 10 amendments to the

Is this a rhetorical question or a direct question? Although questions can engage listeners, they also may invite smart-aleck listeners to make abusive remarks. If you are uncomfortable with unexpected responses from an audience, use a different attention strategy.

U.S. Constitution?" This example uses both direct and rhetorical questions to engage the audience.

Expecting listeners to respond overtly to a question can be risky business. Asking an audience to cop to illegal behavior is questionable in its own right, even if it offers an opportunity for humor and playfulness with the audience. It could also easily produce an awkward silence with no hands raised. Conversely, you may expect (and hope) no hands are raised. A student began her speech this way: "How many of you have ever sewn your own clothes?" Almost every student raised a hand. "Wow, I didn't expect that response," blurted the speaker. Speakers faced with unexpected answers to questions may sputter, even get annoyed with the audience. Some listeners may see your question as an opportunity to heckle or ridicule you. "How many of you have difficulty losing weight?" might trigger "Not as much trouble as you seem to have." Only certain audiences would likely be so boorish (high school comes to mind), but skip polling your audience unless you feel comfortable ad-libbing quick responses.

Begin with a Simple Visual Aid: Show and Tell   Student Lauren Holstein (2012) began her speech with a simple visual aid apparent from the following: "I know I'm taking a chance here offering tomatoes to an audience at the beginning of a speech. But the difference between these two is the difference between a fair market and slavery. As consumers and vocal advocates for social change, we must work to bring this practice of slavery in the sunshine state to an end" (p. 34). Another example might be holding a smartphone for your audience to see, then noting:

> This tiny device has more computing power than the super computers of only 40 years ago that filled a large portion of a room. So why hasn't there been an equivalent downsizing of solar cells and enhancement of solar power in the same time period? Shouldn't we be able to replace huge, bulky solar panels with smartphone-size solar cells with the capacity to power an entire house? I'm going to explain why this hasn't occurred and what can be done to make greater progress.

Beginning with a simple visual aid can draw in your audience and also make a point.

Tell a Relevant Story: Use Narrative Power   Juan Roberto Melendez-Colon languished on Florida's death row for "17 years, 8 months, and 1 day." He became the 99th death-row inmate in the United States to be exonerated and freed since 1973. He told his story at the Los Angeles Religious Education Congress. The room was packed and transfixed to hear his tragic story of dehumanization, of wrongful imprisonment that nearly led him to commit suicide. As noted previously, story-telling can captivate the attention of audiences of all ages (Hsu, 2008).

A short, entertaining, real-life story is usually called an **anecdote**. Research shows that introductions that begin with an anecdote motivate your audience to listen and promote understanding and retention of your message (Andeweg & de Jong, 1998). Anecdotes that have a personal relevance can be particularly captivating. Student Buey Ruet (2006) gave this introduction that is not only novel but also intense:

> On October 15, 1994, a woman by the name of Workinsh Admasu opened a letter, which required her eight and 13-year-old boys to immediately report to military training camp. Three weeks after basic training, the boys along with another 300,000 eight to fourteen year olds, strapped on AK-47s that were half their body weight and headed off to fight in Sudan's civil war. . . . If you are wondering why I care about this topic so much, that eight-year-old boy was me. My 13-year-old brother and I were forced to experience things that no other child should ever have to experience. *(p. 49)*

The Sudan War can seem extremely remote for most Americans until a victim is standing in front of you telling his personal story of tragedy and outrage.

Refer to Remarks of Introduction: Acknowledging Praise   If you are introduced to an audience, you may need to respond briefly before launching into your prepared speech. A simple, clean reference to those remarks is sufficient. Walter Mondale, former U.S. senator from Minnesota, had a standard response when he was extravagantly introduced to an audience: "I don't deserve those kind words. But then I have arthritis and I don't deserve that either." Former President Lyndon Johnson also had a standard line prepared if the introduction of him to an audience was effusive in its praise: "That was the kind of very generous introduction that my father would have appreciated, and my mother would have believed." Following an underwhelming, bland introduction of him to his audience, Mondale would begin: "Of all the introductions I've received, that was the most recent" (quoted in Noonan, 1998, p. 148).

Make A Clear Purpose Statement: Providing Intent

As explained in Chapter 4, a **general purpose** identifies the overall goal of your speech. It tells the audience that you plan to inform, describe, explain, demonstrate, persuade, celebrate, memorialize, entertain, or eulogize someone or something. The general purpose will be given to you if your speech is a classroom assignment (e.g., give a demonstration speech). If given no direction from others, decide what general purpose is appropriate for the audience and occasion.

Once you have determined the general purpose, formulate your specific purpose. A **specific purpose statement** is a concise, precise infinitive phrase composed of simple, clear language that encompasses both the general purpose and indicates what the speaker hopes to accomplish with the speech. For example:

TOPIC: Cost of a college education
NARROWED TOPIC: The high cost of textbooks
GENERAL PURPOSE: To inform
SPECIFIC PURPOSE STATEMENT: To explain why textbooks are so expensive.

Once you have constructed your specific purpose statement, test its appropriateness and likely effectiveness. Ask the following questions:

(1) **Is your purpose statement concise and precise?** A long, wordy statement will confuse listeners. You should be able to phrase an effective purpose statement in about 15 words or fewer. If your purpose statement is much beyond 15 words, rephrase it until it is more concise.

(2) **Is your purpose statement phrased as a declarative statement?** Phrasing a purpose statement as a question, such as "Why are textbooks so expensive?" asks your listeners to provide the answers. Typically, although not always, you begin with an infinitive phrase, such as to explain, to inform, to persuade, to celebrate, to teach, to demonstrate, to eulogize. Then declare the direction of your speech. For example: "to explain why textbooks are so expensive" is a declarative, specific purpose statement.

(3) **Is your purpose statement free of colorful language?** Keep your purpose statement plain and direct. Colorful language is fine for the body of your speech, but it can be confusing in a purpose statement. For example, "To tell you why textbooks are the golden fleece of education" will likely leave some of your listeners scratching their heads and thinking "huh?"

(4) **Is your purpose statement more than simply a topic?** "To inform my audience about the cost of textbooks" is a topic statement not a specific purpose statement. Listeners are provided with no direction. Tell them specifically what you seek to accomplish. "To discuss the feasibility of a textbook rental program on campus" is a purpose statement with a direction.

(5) **Is your purpose statement practical?** Can your listeners accomplish what you ask them to do? "I want to teach you to be a top-notch computer programmer" will not happen in a single speech, even a lengthy one. It is too technical and complex, especially if audience members are mostly uninformed on the topic. Make your specific purpose statement practical: "I want to convince you that taking a computer programming course is worthwhile."

The specific purpose statement provides clear direction for your entire speech, guiding the audience members as they listen to the points you make. Imagine a classmate giving this introduction, and notice the blending of the opening attention strategy and the purpose statement:

> Matthew Shepard, a gay 21-year-old University of Wyoming student, was lured away from a bar in October 1998 by two young males pretending to be gay. Shepard was then robbed, beaten senseless, and tied to a fence outside of Laramie, Wyoming, and left for dead. He was found in a coma and he died 5 days later. This tragic instance of gay bashing aroused the entire nation. At his funeral, more than a thousand mourners paid their respects to "this gentle soul" as he was described by those who knew him. During the funeral, however, a dozen protesters stood across the street from the church holding signs that read, "No Tears for Queers" and "Get Back in Your Closet." It was a callously inappropriate protest. Soon after his death, a prominent conservative Christian church created a Web photo of Matthew Shepard burning, with a link allowing visitors to hear him "scream in hell."
>
> More than a decade after Matthew Shepard's tragic murder, hate speech continues unabated. The vileness of hate speech may incline us to support laws that ban it. However, I hope to convince you that outlawing hate speech, no matter how venomous, produces significant disadvantages.

The opening example invites attention because it is novel and intense, and it leads directly to a clear purpose statement.

The **central idea**, sometimes referred to as your *theme*, identifies the main concept, point, issue, or conclusion that you want the audience to understand, believe, feel, or do. The central idea becomes the one concise thought, separate from all the details provided in the speech, that audience members hopefully remember. A central idea is typically determined once you have investigated your specific purpose statement sufficiently to provide details. The Matthew Shepard introduction example never gets to the central idea, which is identifying the particular disadvantages of banning hate speech, such as that it drives hate speech underground, stifles freedom of speech, and so forth. The central idea for the purpose statement "to explain why textbooks are so expensive" would be: "Textbooks are expensive for three primary reasons: used books, ancillaries, and costly graphics." You want to keep your central idea uppermost in your mind as you prepare your speech. The central idea guides speech development.

Establish Topic Significance: Making Your Listeners Care

Establish the basis for why listeners should care about the problem, information, or demonstration central to your purpose. Listeners typically want to know "How does this affect me?" If you are an avid card player, quilter, or woodworker, your audience will see your enthusiasm for your topic. Why should the audience be enthusiastic, though, if they have never tried such activities or if they proved to be embarrassingly inept when they did try? Consider this example that ties the purpose statement to an audience's need to know its importance:

> Mark Twain once said that golf is a good walk spoiled. I beg to differ. Golf is a good walk, but it is only spoiled if you lack knowledge of the strategy behind the game and your skill level is embarrassingly bad. Understanding the strategy and learning to play golf well can make for an extremely enjoyable few hours of recreation in the bright sun and fresh air. Millions of dollars worth of business are negotiated on the golf links every day. Even old political rivalries can be resolved on the golf links. Barack Obama and Bill Clinton, two passable golfers, seemed to end their strained relationship left over from the 2008 primary battle between Hillary Clinton and Obama by playing a round of golf. The result was a rousing speech Bill Clinton agreed to deliver at the 2012 Democratic National Convention defending Obama's first-term record as president. To put it succinctly, golf can be entertaining and it can enhance your life physically, psychologically, economically, occupationally, and politically.
>
> I can't teach you to play golf well in a 5-minute speech. You'll want to find a qualified golf instructor to help you do that. I can, however, briefly explain important qualities to consider when choosing a golf instructor.

Some topics are more challenging to make relevant to an audience's interests than others. Nevertheless, without relevance listeners will quickly tune out and let their minds wander freely.

Establish Your Credibility: Why Listeners Should Believe You

Establishing your credibility is a process that develops over the course of an entire speech. Nevertheless, it is an important requirement of effective introductions for most speeches (eulogies, "roasts" and some other special occasions speeches may be exceptions). When you have real expertise on a subject, do not hide that fact.

In Chapter 4, elements of credibility—competence, trustworthiness, dynamism, and composure—were explored in detail. There are many ways to capitalize on these elements. Mentioning to your audience that you have surfed for 10 years, worked as an auto mechanic for 3 years, or have a degree in nursing, for example, would likely induce your listeners to grant you credibility on those subjects (competence). Presenting a commanding presence by exhibiting a confident, fluent, energetic delivery (competence and dynamism), sharing personal experiences that offer insight on a problem from an insider's viewpoint (competence and trustworthiness), or citing authoritative sources of initial information all can build credibility.

Consider, for example, how Ricardo, a former long-time gang member, establishes his credibility:

> I got my first tattoo when I was 11 years old—a skull. At 14, I had a Chinese character tattooed on my right forearm. It meant "trust no one." A dozen or more tattoos were added until, at 18, an ornate cross and rosary that memorialized my dead older brother killed in a rival gang hit was added to my left hand. Most of these tattoos symbolized transitional points into gang life. When my brother died, I vowed to leave gang life and find a productive path. When I searched for a job, however, my gang tattoos made employers wary of me. They would never come right out and say so; instead they would say, "Sorry, we don't have any openings," even though I knew they did. A Harris poll last month showed that 17% of tattoo wearers regret getting them. I speak from experience—be very cautious before getting any tattoo.

Ricardo establishes his credibility by identifying his personal experience with tattoos and by citing a reputable study. His audience listened intently to what he had to say in the rest of his speech.

Credibility can also be established even if you have no particular expertise or relevant experience on a subject. Here is an example:

> I've always been in favor of alternative sources of energy—biofuels, hybrid cars, wind power, solar energy and the like. "Going green" just sounds so Earth friendly and responsible. I even have a bumper sticker on my car that reads: "I'm a tree hugging dirt worshipper." Until I thoroughly researched this topic for my speech, however, I never much considered the downside to alternative energy sources. I know arguing against alternative energy sources currently being developed is not a popular idea today, but I hope sharing with you what I have learned from reputable scientific research might change your mind a bit on this subject.

Here, credibility is established by trustworthiness—arguing against a previously held position that reveals no bias, just a careful weighing of the relevant evidence. Reference to substantial, credible research also suggests competence on the subject. The research, of course, has to be truly credible and persuasive once presented or credibility will quickly swirl down the toilet.

Preview The Main Points: The Coming Attractions

A **preview** presents the coming attractions of your speech. A speech will normally have two to four main points that flow directly from the purpose statement. For example: "I want to explain how you can save money when purchasing a new car. There are three ways: First, you can save money by comparison shopping, second by lowering your interest payments, and third, by purchasing at the end of the year."

Although the purpose statement, explaining significance, and establishing credibility can be reversed, attention is always the first objective and the preview is typically last. Consider this *illustration of all five requirements*:

[**ATTENTION**] Orville Delong, a 57-year-old Canadian maintenance worker, was playing golf on July 12, 1998, when a meteorite the size of a baseball whizzed by his ear at an estimated speed of 124 miles per hour. "At first we thought somebody was shooting at us," commented Delong. On March 26, 2003, Colby Navarro was using his computer when without warning a meteorite 4 inches in diameter crashed through the roof of his home, struck the printer, bounced off a wall, and landed near a filing cabinet. It left a foot-wide hole in the ceiling. On January 2, 2007, Srinivasan Nageswaran walked into his bathroom and noticed a hole in the ceiling and debris on the floor. A small meteorite had crashed through the roof of his New Jersey home. Are these close calls merely freak events or do we all have something to fear from rocks falling out of the sky? [**PURPOSE STATEMENT**] I want to convince you that a space-based shield from meteorites is critical to our human survival.

[**CREDIBILITY**] I've researched this topic extensively and I completed an astronomy class last term, so let me share some insights I learned about the peril of meteorites and the necessity of this proposed space-based shield. Meteorites are fragments of meteoroids that reach earth before burning up in the Earth's atmosphere. Meteoroids streaking through the Earth's atmosphere are commonly referred to as shooting stars. [**SIGNIFICANCE**] Earth has already had many significant direct encounters with meteorites. In 1908 the famous Tunguska meteorite scorched a 20-mile area of Siberian forest and flattened trees. In 1947, a meteorite exploded into fragments in eastern Siberia, leaving more than 200 craters. In 1992, a 27-pound meteorite crumpled the back end of a Chevrolet in Peekskill, New York. Even more recently, on February 15, 2013, a meteorite the size of a bus, and estimated by NASA to be traveling at 40,000 miles per hour, exploded in Russia's Ural Mountains close to the city of Chelyabinsk with the force of an atomic bomb. More than a thousand people were injured by the blast. Fortunately, there was no direct impact on a populated area. The need to create a shield against meteorites is real and urgent.

[**PREVIEW**] I will explore three points to convince you that this is true. First, the probability of Earth experiencing a catastrophic collision with a meteoroid is very high. Second, current efforts to address this problem are woefully inadequate. Third, a space-based shield is the only sensible alternative.

This introduction provides the five elements of an effective introduction. It presents a novel attention strategy, the purpose statement is clear and concise, credibility is briefly addressed, significance is clearly developed by making the entire audience feel imperiled, and the preview is direct and concise and sets up the body of the speech. These are the makings of an effective introduction, but competent conclusions to your speech have their own requirements.

OBJECTIVES FOR COMPETENT CONCLUSIONS

You want your introduction to begin strongly, and you want your conclusion to end strongly. Your conclusion should create a sense of unity, like completing a circle. Be as organized about your conclusion as you are with your introduction. Consider three ways to finish your speech effectively.

Summarize The Main Points: Connecting The Dots

In your introduction you preview your main points as a final step. In your conclusion you summarize those main points, usually as a first step. For example, "In brief review, we learned a little history of the martial arts, I explained how to choose a qualified martial arts school, and I demonstrated some common martial arts defense techniques." Summarizing your main points during your conclusion reminds the audience of the most important points in your speech.

Refer to the Introduction: Bookending Your Speech

If you used a dramatic story or example to begin your speech, referring to that story or example in your conclusion provides closure. This is how student Amanda Brossart (2009) concluded:

 Justin Pearson was 24, close to the average age of many of us in this room. He was from Saint Cloud, Minnesota, less than 200 miles away from my hometown. Today, we looked at the dangers of counterfeit medications within the online pharmacy network, why they are used, and embraced solutions that can help stop the use of dangerous online pharmacies. Whitney Pearson, Justin's 18-year-old sister, says the life-threatening consequence of an online pharmacy is "just a click away." It is imperative that we tell others about the dangers of online pharmacies. *(p. 63)*

She finishes by making reference to her tragic opening example that she used to grab the attention of her audience. Bookending your speech by referring to an opening story or dramatic example is not always a requirement of an effective conclusion, especially if you did not use either in your introduction. If you have the opportunity to bookend, however, it can prove to be a very strong finish to your speech.

Make a Memorable Finish: Sizzle Do Not Fizzle

Surely one of the most powerful speech conclusions came in Martin Luther King's "I Have a Dream" speech in 1963. He concluded:

 When we allow freedom to ring, when we let it ring from every village and every hamlet, from every state and every city, we will be able to speed up that day when all of God's children, black men and white men, Jews and Gentiles, Protestants and Catholics, will be able to join hands and sing in the words of that old Negro spiritual, 'Free at last! Free at last! Thank God Almighty, we are free at last!

PHOTO 6.1 Martin Luther King's "I Have a Dream" speech had a powerful finish.

You begin your speech with an attention strategy, and you should end your speech in similar fashion. A strong quotation, a poignant rhetorical question, an intense statement, a moving example or story, or a humorous statement makes effective attention grabbers for introductions. They serve the same purpose for effective conclusions. Student Jenna Surprenant (2012) finished her speech on the dangers of the lobbying group called American Legislative Exchange Council with an expert reference and a quotation:

 Supreme Court Justice Louis Brandeis referred to states as the laboratories of democracy, speaking to the notion that every state is different and should have different approaches. As *The Nation* reports on July 12, 2011, we "rely on our elected representatives' efforts to restore what's left of the American Dream. But through ALEC, billionaire industrialists are purchasing a version that seems like a real nightmare for most Americans". *(p. 55)*

Student Shirae Christie (2011) uses a quotation and reference to her opening story to conclude her speech:

Plato asked the question in *The Republic*, and Alan Moore repeated it in his comic book: "Who watches the watchmen?" For Tasha Ford, a mom who wanted simply to protect her son, arrest and detainment were unexpected consequences. As Americans, we should not have to fear repercussions for keeping our eyes open to the things that happen around us and we most certainly should not have to fear those who are supposed to protect us. *(p. 20)*

One final note about conclusions: *do not end abruptly, or apologize for running short on time, or ramble until you fizzle like a balloon deflating.* Be concise and to the point when finishing your speech. Your conclusion should be no more than about 5% to 10% of your total speech. Do not diminish the effect of a great speech with a bloated, aimless conclusion. Student Tunette Powell (2012), winner of the 2012 Interstate Oratorical Association contest, effectively concluded her oration this way:

Now is the time to separate the war on drugs from the war on addiction. Today you've heard the problems, impacts, and solutions of criminalizing addictions. Bruce Callis is 50 years old now. And he is still struggling with his addiction. While you all are sitting out there listening to this, I'm living it. Bruce Callis is my father and for my entire life, I have watched our misguided system destroy him. The irony here is that we live in a society where we are told to recycle. We recycle paper, aluminum, and old electronics. But why don't we ever consider recycling the most precious thing on Earth—the human life?

She summarizes her main points, makes reference to her opening anecdote about Bruce Callis, and closes with a memorable revelation and poignant rhetorical question. Her conclusion was a forceful finish, not a fizzle.

SUMMARY

There are five objectives of a competent speech introduction: gain attention, provide a clear purpose statement, make the topic and purpose relevant to your audience, establish your credibility, and preview the main points of your speech. A competent conclusion should summarize your main point, make reference to your introduction if possible, and finish memorably. No matter how well you have prepared the body of your presentation, giving little preparation to your introduction and conclusion can significantly diminish the impact and effectiveness of your speech.

7

Outlining and Organizing Speeches

A colleague of mine, whose office was a perpetual disaster and a fire hazard because he would burn candles among mountainous stacks of papers, would justify his disorganization with the quip, "Being organized is the sign of a sick mind." If true, that would make him the most mentally healthy person on the planet. Although a disorganized, even chaotic office might be just quirky and innocuous, except for the fire hazard, a disorganized speech is not so forgivable. The quality of speech organization directly influences how well your listeners understand your key points (Thompson, 1960; Titsworth, 2004).

Speakers who are well organized impress listeners as more credible than speakers who are disorganized. A speaker who does not seem able to connect two thoughts together and continually circles before finally landing on a point does not inspire confidence (Chesebro, 2003). Recall how frustrating it is to listen to a disorganized instructor present a rambling lecture. Note taking becomes chaotic. Learning is impaired. Impressive research on a topic is mostly wasted effort if the speech is an incomprehensible verbal stew.

A disorganized speech creates confusion and misunderstanding. Actress Jodie Foster gave a rambling speech at the 2012 Golden Globes awards ceremony. Eric Sasson of the *Wall Street Journal* made this assessment: "Watching the show at a friend's apartment, many of us, some gay, some straight, had a strikingly similar reaction: the speech confused us. It disappointed us. It felt confrontational, defensive, disjointed" (quoted in Miller, 2013). Christy Lemure of the Associated Press gave this assessment: "Jodie Foster came out without really

PHOTO 7.1 A disorganized speech can be as confusing and pointless as this mess of road signs. Strive for clarity.

coming out, and suggested she was retiring from acting without exactly saying so, in a long, breathless and rambling speech" (quoted in Miller, 2013). Moments after her speech, Foster's *Wikipedia page* was "updated" to announce her retirement. The *L.A. Times* reporter Amy Kaufman, however, asked Foster whether she had in fact announced her retirement as an actress in her speech. Foster replied, "Oh, no, I could never stop acting. You'd have to drag me behind a team of horses" (quoted in "Jodie Foster Speech," 2013). Parts of her speech were impressive, but the organization was not one of them.

Mastering effective outlining methods and organizational formats is a significant skill for the competent public speaker. *The purpose of this chapter is to explain effective ways to outline and organize your speeches*. I discuss criteria for effective outlining and effective patterns of organization.

EFFECTIVE OUTLINING

The organizational process begins with an understanding of how to outline your thoughts and the underlying logic that guides outlining. The rudiments of effective outlining involve standard formatting, division, coherence, completeness, and balance.

Standard Formatting: Using Correct Symbols

Microsoft Word offers many outlining formats. The bulleted format is one of the most popular, especially for PowerPoint slides. The bulleted format, however, can easily become PowerPoint*less* when every point has a bullet in front of it (Mitchell, 2009). Thus, the standard outlining form is required in most speech classes because it is clear, precise, and logical, and it uses a specific set of symbols that more obviously demarcate main points from subpoints. Briefly, these symbols are the following:

I. *Roman numerals for main points*
   A. *Capital letters for primary subpoints*
   B. Another primary subpoint
      1. *Standard numbers for secondary subpoints*
      2. Another secondary subpoint
         a. *Lowercase letters for tertiary subpoints*
         b. Another tertiary subpoint
II. Second main point, and so forth

Each successive set of subpoints is indented to separate the main points visually from the primary, secondary, and tertiary subpoints. Thus, you would not format an outline as follows:

I. Main point
A. Primary subpoint
B. Primary subpoint
1. Secondary subpoint
2. Secondary subpoint
a. Tertiary subpoint
b. Tertiary subpoint
II. Main point

You can see that lack of indentation merges all of your points and can easily lead to confusion.

Division: Dividing the Pie

A purpose statement divides into a *minimum of two* main points, and main points divide into at least two subpoints. Logically, you do not divide something into just one. For example, "dividing" a pie into one means someone gets the whole pie and you get squat.

INCORRECT VERSION	CORRECT VERSION
I. Main point	I. Main point
A. Primary subpoint	A. Primary subpoint
II. Main point	B. Primary subpoint
A. Primary subpoint	II. Main point
1. Secondary subpoint	A. Primary subpoint
B. Primary subpoint	B. Primary subpoint
1. Secondary subpoint	1. Secondary subpoint
	2. Secondary subpoint

If you cannot divide a point into at least two subpoints, your point probably does not need division or the point is not substantial enough. It is time to rethink the development of your speech (see Box 8.1). *The following example shows proper division*:

PURPOSE STATEMENT: To inform you that obesity has become both a global and a national problem.

I. A huge proportion of the world's population is obese.
  A. An estimated 400 million adults are obese worldwide.
  B. An estimated 155 million children are also obese.
II. The countries with the highest obesity rates are in the Western Pacific.
  A. Nauru has an obesity rate of 80% for its men and 78% for its women.
  B. Tonga shows a 47% obesity rate for its men and 70% for its women.
  C. Samoa is also high at 33% for its men and 63% for its women.
III. In the Americas, the United States has the most severe obesity problem.
  A. Obesity rates are 31% for adult males and 33% for women, highest in the Americas.
  B. Being overweight portends an increasing obesity problem in the United States.
    1. The rate of being overweight in the United States is about equal to the rate of obesity.
    2. Being overweight often is a precursor to obesity.
    3. Being overweight is nearly as dangerous as being obese.

Even when you have only a single example to illustrate a point, the principle of division still applies, as illustrated in this example:

I. Professional baseball players' salaries are astronomical.
  A. Average player salaries are slightly more than $3 million per year.
  B. Example: Alex Rodriguez makes $25 million per year.

You cannot generalize from a single example so do not let it dangle as a subpoint all its own.

Coherence: Logical Consistency and Clarity

Logical consistency and clarity are qualities of an effective outline. Your outline should flow from your purpose statement. When developing your outline, think of your speech as an inverted pyramid with the base on top and the apex on the bottom (see Figure 7.1).

Begin with your topic, narrow the topic to your specific purpose statement, and develop main points from that purpose statement, which break down further into subpoints. Work from the most general to the most specific. For example:

[TOPIC] The aging U.S. population
[PURPOSE STATEMENT] To explain ways longer lifespans pose new challenges
   for America.
I. [MAIN POINT] Americans are living longer than ever before.
II. [MAIN POINT] Longer lifespans stress fragile support systems for the elderly
   in three significant ways.

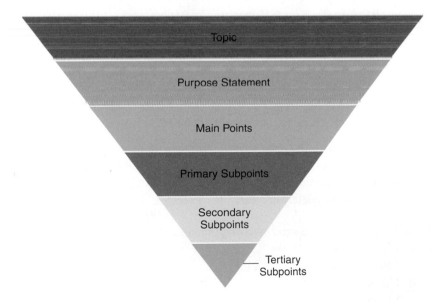

FIGURE 7.1 The Organizational Logic for Developing an Outline

Coherence requires that main points flow directly from the purpose statement. Subpoints, however, should also flow from main points. For example, look at the development of Main Point I:

I. [MAIN POINT] Americans are living longer than ever before.
   A. [PRIMARY SUBPOINT] Average lifespan of an American is at its highest level in history.
   B. [PRIMARY SUBPOINT] Americans are living increasingly to 100 years old and beyond.

Each primary subpoint flows from the main point on "living longer."

Each primary subpoint can be further divided into secondary subpoints that flow from primary subpoints. Note the following example:

A. [PRIMARY SUBPOINT] The average lifespan of an American is at its highest level in history.
   1. [SECONDARY SUBPOINT] Average lifespan of an American is a record 78 years old.
   2. [SECONDARY SUBPOINT] Average lifespan of an American has increased from 69 years old just two decades ago.
B. [PRIMARY SUBPOINT] Americans are living increasingly to 100 years old and beyond.
   1. [SECONDARY SUBPOINT] A record 100,000 Americans are 100 years old or older.
   2. [SECONDARY SUBPOINT] The U.S. Census Bureau projects that more than 800,000 Americans will be 100 years old in the year 2050.

Working from the most general to the increasingly specific will assure coherence.

Completeness: Using Full Sentences

Your first attempt to outline your speech will prove to be more successful if you use complete sentences (see p. 39, preparation outline). Complete sentences communicate complete thoughts. A word or phrase may suggest a thought without communicating it completely or clearly. For example:

PURPOSE STATEMENT: To explain hazing (initiation rituals).
I. Hazing
   A. Campus hazing
   B. Military hazing
   C. Corporate hazing
II. Solutions
   A. Laws

B. Policies
C. Penalties
D. Education

This word and phrase outline creates informational gaps and questions that cannot be answered by merely referring to the outline. The purpose statement provides no direction. What will be explained? Will you explain what hazing is? Why it is a problem? How it can be controlled?

The main points and subpoints are no clearer. Main point I is about hazing, and subpoints indicate three types: campus, military, and corporate. Still, no direction or complete thought is communicated. Are these three types of hazing serious problems? Should they be prevented? Should we find them amusing? Should we encourage hazing on campus, in the military, and in the corporate world? Main point II suffers from the same problem. Solutions are suggested, but solutions imply a problem has been described when no problem is indicated in the previous main point or in the purpose statement. If a problem exists, what type of legal, policy, and educational solutions are offered? The point of the speech remains unclear.

Consider how much more complete a full sentence outline is when compared to the incomplete and confusing word and phrase outline:

PURPOSE STATEMENT: To explain specific ways to prevent the significant problem of hazing.
I. Hazing is a growing problem in the United States.
   A. More than 50 deaths and numerous injuries have occurred from hazing in just the last decade.
   B. The number of hazing incidents requiring intervention by authorities has doubled in the last decade.
II. There are several ways to prevent hazing.
   A. Hazing could be outlawed in all states.
   B. College, corporate, and military policies could specifically ban hazing rituals.
   C. Penalties for violations of laws and policies could be increased.
   D. Students, employees, and soldiers could receive instruction on the dangers of hazing and the consequences of violating laws and policies banning the practice.

Balance: No Lopsided Time Allotment

Each main point deserves substantial development. This does not mean that you have to allot an equal amount of time during your speech to each main point. Nevertheless, you want a relatively balanced presentation. If you have three main points in the body of your speech, do not devote 4 minutes to the first main point and only a minute or less to your two remaining main points. Such a lopsided time allotment means either that your second and third main points are not really main points at

BOX 7.1 A Student Outline: Rough Draft and Revision

Constructing a competent outline can be a struggle, especially if appropriate outlining form and criteria are not well understood. Initial attempts to outline a speech may prove difficult, and your first attempts may produce seriously flawed results. Do not despair. Outlining is a process that trains your mind to think in an orderly fashion. It takes time to learn such a sophisticated skill.

Compare this rough draft of a student outline to the revised outline constructed by the same student (my comments appear in *italics*):

Rough Draft Outline

PURPOSE STATEMENT: To eliminate the drug problem by making drug testing mandatory. (*Where is your attention getter? Where is your central idea? You overstate the potential outcomes of mandatory drug testing. Try significantly reducing drug use, not "eliminating the drug problem." General purpose is only implied—will you try to convince us? Also, you are missing significance, credibility, and preview of main points.*)

I. The drugs among society. (*No clear direction is provided. What do you want to say about "the drugs among society?" This is also not a complete sentence.*)
   A. The effects of drugs. (*Are you concerned with only negative effects? Unclear! This is not a complete sentence.*)
      1. The immediate effects of drugs.
      2. The permanent effects of drugs. (*1 and 2 are not complete sentences.*)
   B. The effects of using drugs. (*This seems to repeat A above. Do you have a different idea in mind? Unclear! This is not a complete sentence.*)
      1. Memory loss.
      2. Addicted babies
      3. Brain damage.
      4. Physical harm. (*1–4 are not complete sentences.*)
II. Ways to solve drug abuse. (*Your purpose statement indicates only one solution: mandatory drug testing. Stay focused on your purpose statement. Also, not a complete sentence.*)
   A. The first step is to be aware of the problem. (*"Awareness" does not seem related to mandatory drug testing. Let your purpose statement guide your entire outline.*)
      1. Establish drug testing in all companies.
      2. Establish stricter laws against drug users.
      3. Start more drug clinics. (*Good use of complete sentences. Subpoints 1–3 do not relate directly to "A"—they are not kinds of awareness. Subpoints 2 and 3 also seem unrelated to mandatory drug testing. These are coherence problems.*)

(You have an A point without a B point—problem of division. Also, main point II is less developed than main point I—problem of balance. Where is your conclusion? One final note: You have not included your bibliography of credible sources.)

Revised Version
INTRODUCTION

ATTENTION STRATEGY: I tell my personal story of battling drug abuse. *(Without the actual personal story written here, it is difficult to judge its effectiveness. Potentially powerful; are you comfortable with such a revelation?)*

CENTRAL IDEA: Drug use in the workplace is a serious problem requiring a new approach to solving this problem. *(Is mandatory drug testing really a "new approach?")*

PURPOSE STATEMENT: To convince my audience that every place of employment should start a mandatory drug testing program. *(This is a much improved purpose statement. "Every place of employment," however, seems a bit drastic. Are there a lot of drugged out teachers? Try narrowing the application of your proposal to workers who might jeopardize the health and safety of others if drugs were used—airline pilots, bus drivers.)*

SIGNIFICANCE: Drug use in the workplace potentially affects all workers. *(Vague)*

CREDIBILITY: My experience using drugs in the workplace gives me a special perspective.

PREVIEW: I offer two main points:

I. Drug use in the workplace is a serious problem.

II. Mandatory drug testing in the workplace will reduce drug abuse. *(Good, concise preview)*

BODY

TRANSITIONAL STATEMENT: Let me begin with my first main point:

I. Drug use in the workplace is a serious problem. *(Good clear main point.)*

    A. Drug use in the workplace is widespread.

        1. Many employees in large companies use drugs.

        2. Many employees in factories use drugs.

    B. Drug use in the workplace is dangerous.

        1. Workers injure even kill themselves.

        2. Customers have been injured and killed. *(Does not the risk go far beyond customers? If a plane crashes on a neighborhood because the pilot was loaded on drugs, dead and injured include far more than customers.)*

(This entire main point with its subpoints is much improved?)

TRANSITIONAL STATEMENT: Clearly, drug use in the workplace is a serious problem. This brings me to my second main point: *(Nice transition)*

continued

BOX 7.1   Continued

II. Mandatory drug testing in the workplace will reduce drug abuse.
(*This is a solid second main point that flows nicely from your purpose statement.*)
  A. Drug testing will catch drug users.
    1. Testing is very accurate.
    2. Drug testing will provide absolute proof of drug use by workers.
       (*"Absolute proof" seems overstated. Try "solid proof."*)
  B. Drug testing will prevent drug use in the workplace.
    1. Workers will worry about getting caught using drugs.
    2. Drug testing can prevent drug users from being hired.
(*The second main point is coherent, balanced, divided appropriately, and complete sentences were used throughout. One final question: What do you propose should happen to employees who use drugs? Rehabilitation? Immediate job termination?*)

CONCLUSION

I. In summary, drug use in the workplace is a serious problem, and mandatory drug testing in the workplace will significantly reduce this problem. (*Good, concise summary*)

II. I opened with a personal story of my own battle with drug abuse and what it did to my ability to remain gainfully employed. (*Good reference to opening attention strategy*)

III. I am proud to say that I have won my personal war with drugs; I have a great job with lots of responsibility; my future looks bright; and as a nation, we must forcefully addressed this scourge of drug abuse in the workplace. (*Pretty good, memorable finish*)

BIBLIOGRAPHY

U.S. Department of Transportation, Office of Drug and Alcohol Policy and Compliance. (2009). Best practices for DOT random drug and alcohol testing. [Online]. Available at: Http://www.gov/ost/dapc/testingpubs/final_random_brochure.pdf

National Conference of State Legislatures. (2009). Statutes on drug testing in the workplace. [Online]. Available at: http://www.ncsl.org/default.aspx?tabid=13395

U.S. Department of Health and Human Services, Office of Applied Studies. (June 16, 2008). An analysis of worker drug use and workplace policies and programs. [Online]. Available at: Http://www.oas.samhsa.gov/wkplace/toc.htm

Reisner, R. (2008, September 16). Issue: Drug abuse in the workplace. *Business Week*. [Online]. Available at: http://www.businessweek.com/managing/content/sep2008/ca20080916_40029

U.S. Department of Labor, Occupational Safety & Health Administration. (2009, May 26). Workplace substance abuse. [Online]. Available at: http://www.osha .gov/SLTC/substanceabuse/index.html
(*Solid bibliography; credible and recent sources; APA style used correctly—good.*)
NOTE: The APA style for source citation in outline bibliographies is one of the popular choices. There are others, such as the MLA style. Your instructor will direct you regarding which style to use with your outline.

PHOTO 7.2 Effective organization provides clear direction for your speech. Disorganization leads you into the darkness of confusion.

all or that you have not developed your last two main points sufficiently. Increase the development of main points given insufficient treatment, combine points insufficiently developed into a single point, and give the point some beef or drop the two under-developed points and replace them with more substantial points.

Competent outlining requires proper use of symbols, appropriate division of points, coherence, completeness, and balance. An outline maps the flow of a speaker's ideas.

EFFECTIVE ORGANIZATION: CREATING PATTERNS

There are several patterns for organizing the body of your speech into an outline. The most common ones used in U.S. culture are topical, chronological, spatial, causal, problem-solution, problem-cause-solution, comparative advantages, the motivated sequence, and the narrative pattern.

Topical Pattern: By the Subjects

A topical pattern is appropriate when your information falls nicely into types, classifications, or parts of a whole. Your main topic divides easily into significant subtopics. You are not exploring a problem or looking for a solution. You are not explaining a step-by-step process or a spatial relationship. For example:

PURPOSE STATEMENT: To provide a basic explanation of the Islamic religion
I.   There are several basic Islamic beliefs
II. The Quran is the primary source of every Muslim's faith and practice.
III. There are five pillars of Islam.

A topical pattern does not necessarily suggest a particular order of presentation for each main point, as does a chronological pattern. You could begin with the Quran, then discuss the five pillars, and end with additional basic beliefs.

Chronological Pattern: According to Time

Some speeches follow a time pattern. A chronological pattern suggests a specific sequence of events. When speeches provide a biographical sketch of an individual, explain a step-by-step process, or recount a historical event, chronological order is an appropriate pattern of organization. For example:

PURPOSE STATEMENT: To explain the renovation plan for our local downtown city center.
I.   The old Cooper House and Del Rio Theatre will be demolished.

II. Main Street will be widened.

III. A Cinemax theatre complex will replace the Del Rio Theatre.

IV. A new, twice-as-large Cooper House will replace the old Cooper House.

Each main point follows a logical sequence. You do not replace buildings on the same sites until the old buildings are demolished. There is a temporal sequence that must be followed.

Spatial Pattern: Visualization

Some speeches provide information based on a spatial pattern. This spatial pattern may be front to back, left to right, north to south, top to bottom, bottom to top, and so forth. Explaining directions to a particular place requires a spatial order, a visualization of where things are spatially. Directions from your college campus to the local mall, for example, would begin from campus and move spatially ever closer until your destination is reached. You would not begin at the mall and work backward, because that would be difficult to visualize clearly and logically. Consider this example:

PURPOSE STATEMENT: To explain space allocation in the new communication building.

I. There are four main, average-size classrooms on the ground floor.

II. There are two large lecture halls on the second floor.

III. Faculty offices are mostly adjacent to the large lecture halls.

IV. A student study and meeting facility is also located on the second floor at the north end.

The outline helps listeners visualize specific locations spatially in relation to each other. A visual aid showing a diagram of the floor plan of the entire building as you explain each section of the building would be especially useful.

Causal Pattern: Who or What Is Responsible

Humans look for causes of events. A standard organizational pattern is causes-effects or effects-causes. The causes-effects pattern is most appropriate when you are discussing why things happen and their consequences. The following is an example:

PURPOSE STATEMENT: To explain the causes and effects of high national unemployment.

I. There are several causes of high national unemployment.

II. High national unemployment has serious consequences for our country.

Your speech can also begin with the effects of an event and then move to what caused the event. For example:

> PURPOSE STATEMENT: To show that poverty is a devastating global problem.
> I. The effects of global poverty are widespread, many, and severe.
> II. The causes of global poverty are complex.

Problem–Solution Pattern: Meeting Needs

The problem-solution organizational pattern is most appropriate when you explore the nature of a problem and propose a solution or possible solutions for the problem. Consider this example:

> PURPOSE STATEMENT: To argue for stricter regulation of the food supply in the United States.
> I. The food supply in the United States is too often contaminated.
> II. More stringent FDA regulation of the U.S. food supply would significantly reduce the problem.

Problem–Cause–Solution Pattern: Knowing Why and How

The problem-cause-solution organizational pattern expands on the problem-solution pattern and the causal pattern by exploring causes of the problem and addressing these causes in the solution. This is especially appropriate when the problems are complex and the causes are not immediately obvious to an audience.

> PURPOSE STATEMENT: To argue for a government-sponsored program to prevent hearing loss among teens and young adults.
> I. Teenagers and young adults are suffering serious hearing loss.
> II. There are several causes of this hearing loss.
> III. A government-sponsored program to prevent hearing loss is critical.

Comparative Advantages Pattern: Who or What Is Better

Sometimes the best organizational pattern is to compare two things and argue that one is significantly better than the other for specific reasons (resulting in advantages). It is not that some policy, program, person, or practice is terrible or

It makes sense to be logically organized. As you would not put your shoes on before your socks, so also you would not propose a solution before identifying a problem. That is why the organizational pattern is called "problem–solution" not "solution–problem."

completely non-functional. It may be, however, that significant advantages can be achieved, so why not make the better choice? The following example illustrates the comparative advantages:

> PURPOSE STATEMENT: To explain why women often make better leaders than men in the service industry.
> I.   Women typically exhibit greater team leadership skills.
> II. Women offer more social support and are better at it.
> III. Women are better suited to the team-oriented business climate in the service industry.

It is not that men are completely terrible team leaders. Many may be very good. You are simply arguing that women may be better suited to the task in the service industry than most men. That is a comparative advantages approach.

Monroe's Motivated Sequence: Five-Step Pattern

Monroe's motivated sequence, not surprisingly, was formulated by a speech professor named Alan Monroe, who synthesized sales techniques and basic principles from motivational psychology into five basic steps (McKerrow et al., 2007):

I. *Attention*: Create interest; use attention strategies (see Chapter 5).
II. *Need*: Present a problem to be solved, and relate it to your audience.
III. *Satisfaction*: Provide a solution to the problem that will satisfy your audience.
IV. *Visualization:* Provide an image for your audience of what the world will look like if your solution is implemented.
V. *Action:* Make a call to action; get your audience involved and committed.

The motivated sequence is essentially a problem-solution organizational pattern with the added step of helping your audience visualize the benefits of your solution, such as: "Increasing the number of student representatives on the College Board will provide a stronger voice for students on this campus. We will have greater influence on decision making that affects all of us as students." The final step is a call to action on your proposed solution, such as: "Sign this petition to be presented to the Board that seeks additional student representation on the College Board." An extensive, more complex example of this organizational pattern is presented in **Appendix B**.

Narrative Pattern: Telling a Story

Speeches are sometimes arranged as a narrative. The speech consists of a story that has a plot, characters, settings, and a theme. Your story, however, may incorporate other organizational patterns as well. You may tell the story chronologically or you may tell it in an effect-cause pattern (telling first the effect of a crime committed then telling the cause by digging into the background and experiences of the perpetrator of the crime). The focus is on telling a story to make a point. For example,

PURPOSE STATEMENT: To explain how the early life of Mohatma Ghandi transformed him into the world's foremost advocate of nonviolent protest.
I. Ghandi's childhood in India was one of poverty and deprivation.
II. Ghandi's education raised important questions for him.
III. Ghandi's experiences with the British in India had a significant impact on his thinking.

CONNECTING THE DOTS: ADDITIONAL ORGANIZATIONAL TIPS

When giving a speech, you have to connect your ideas and create a flow so your listeners can comprehend and remember your message. Here are a few ways to accomplish these goals.

Provide Definitions

Key terms, especially unfamiliar or technical ones, should be defined clearly and precisely. For example, student Adam Childers (1997) defines *endocrine disruptors* as "human-made chemicals that have an uncanny ability to mimic some of the human body's most powerful hormones" (p. 103). Even though most people have a passing familiarity with the term hormone, many may have a difficult time giving a precise definition. Childers anticipates this and defines hormones as "little more than messengers of the endocrine system. They are released by the pituitary gland, and then they circulate throughout the body, telling different cells what

PHOTO 7.3 Ill-defined messages lack clarity and precision.

to do. For example, the hormone adrenaline tells our heart when to beat faster" (p. 104). This is a nice definition and explanation of hormones. You can picture what hormones do.

Use Signposts

A **signpost** is an organizational marker that indicates the structure of a speech and notifies listeners that a particular point is about to be addressed. Often signposts are numerical markers. Student Joseph Jones (2011) provides an example: "*The first cause* is that for-profit universities are willing to mislead students to persuade them to enroll" and "*A second cause* for the launch of this new wave of secondary education is that innocent people are intrigued by false advertising" (p. 74). Student Sneha Polisetti (2012) provides these three slightly different signposts: "*First,* in order to prevent mistakenly removing children from families, foster care systems need to start placing an emphasis on keeping families together," then "*Next,* in order to ensure that Native American children are placed with Native American foster parents, the ICWA must be reformed," and "*Finally,* in instances where a child cannot be kept with the family or placed with a Native American family, a third-party service should be offered" (p. 165).

Make Transitions

A **transition** uses words or phrases to connect what was said with what will be said. It is a bridge between points. Student Andrew Eilola (2012) provides this transition: "*Now that we've delved* into the problems of veteran homelessness, *let's examine* the causes that enable them to remain in existence today" (p. 81). Student Joy Minchin (2012) offers this transition: "*Having examined* the problem and diagnosed the causes, *let's now turn* to prescribing solutions" (p. 29). Student Michael Kelley (2012) provides this slightly different transition: "*So if* jobless discrimination creates so much damage, *the reasonable question is* why do employers pursue this policy?" (p. 57). Each of these examples uses transitional words and phrases that provide transitional statements between ideas. These transitions state the point you are leaving and the point you are about to explore. Box 7-2 offers examples of typical signposts and transitional words and phrases that are part of complete signposts and transitional statements.

Use Internal Previews

An **internal preview** is just like a preview in your introduction, except it appears in the body of your speech. Student Stephanie Stovall (2012) provides this transition

BOX 7.2   Developing Communication Competence

Signposts and Transitional Words and Phrases

SIGNPOSTS

My first point is

My second point is

Next

There are three points to explore

The key points are

There are two ways to view this

Finally

My final point is

TRANSITIONS

So what does this mean?

For example

Nevertheless

In summary

Consequently

Conversely

However

Why should we care?

Along the same lines

Therefore

Granted

But

(italicized) and internal preview (underlined): "*Now that we have explored* the extent of the problem with juvenile crime, *we can discuss* <u>two of its primary causes: a lack of understanding about juvenile brain development and inadequate</u> responses to juvenile crime" (p. 137). She connects her previous point with her next point. Student Angela Wnek (2012) similarly provides a transitional statement and an internal preview on "honey laundering": "*Why isn't* our government doing more to stop honey laundering? <u>Two forces are driving the laundering: first, money, and second, the FDA's lax policies</u>" (p. 144).

Give Internal Summaries

When you say "summary," most people think of a final wrap-up to a speech or essay. There is another type, however, called an internal summary, which is useful for especially informative and persuasive speeches. An **internal summary** is the reverse of an internal preview. Instead of indicating what is about to be addressed, an internal summary reminds listeners of the points already made. It occurs in the body of the speech, not in the conclusion. Internal summaries help listeners follow the sequence of ideas, connecting the dots so the picture drawn by the speaker comes into focus. "To review, wildfires cause serious damage to homes, they result in deaths and injuries, and they require huge resources to combat. So let me offer some ways to protect homes from wildfires" is an internal summary followed by a transitional statement. Here, main points already discussed are summarized as a preparation for proposed solutions that follow.

CULTURAL CHALLENGES

All of the organizational patterns discussed here are commonly used in the predominant U.S. culture. Other cultures, however, may use additional patterns (Jaffe, 1998). Space does not permit an explanation of these less standard, though valid, forms of speech organization. Additionally, it would be a rare opportunity for you to use any of these non-standard organizational patterns, so learning the standard forms of organizing is an excellent beginning for you as a novice public speaker. Nevertheless, it is useful for speakers and listeners to understand some basic differences among cultures regarding organizational patterns.

The basic structure of most speeches, but especially informative ones, divides the speech into an *introduction, body,* and *conclusion.* The introduction grabs attention, explains the significance of the topic to the audience, provides a clear purpose statement, develops your credibility, and previews the main points of the speech. The body of the speech, which takes the most time to present, develops the main points previewed in the introduction. The conclusion provides a quick summary of the main points, often makes a reference to the introduction, and offers a memorable finish. This basic structure may seem unusual to individuals from cultures accustomed to high-context communication patterns, such as those living in Asian countries. In *high-context cultures* characterized by a preference for indirect verbal expression, speakers typically do not provide such explicit organization when communicating messages to audiences (Hall, 1981; Hofstede & Hofstede, 2005). A purpose statement and main points will not normally be precisely stated. Listeners are expected to understand the principal message of a speech from the cultural context. Previous knowledge about the speaker and the message help listeners interpret meaning.

The United States, however, is a *low-context culture* characterized by a preference for precise, direct, and explicit verbal expression (Hall, 1981; Hofstede & Hofstede, 2005). There is a general expectation that messages will be communicated explicitly and that ambiguity will be kept to a minimum. Because of this prevailing expectation, individuals from high-context cultures will be more effective public speakers in the United States if they organize their speeches explicitly, fulfilling standard requirements for a competent introduction, body, and conclusion. Explicit organization by a speaker can also help listeners from cultures whose native language is not English to understand the speaker's message.

SUMMARY

Effective and appropriate outlining and organization are important elements of successful public speaking. The criteria for effective outlining include proper use of a standard symbol system, coherence, completeness, balance, and division. The primary organizational patterns include topical, chronological, spatial, causal, problem-solution, problem-cause-solution, comparative advantages, motivated sequence, and narrative. Satisfy the criteria for effective outlining and choose the appropriate organizational pattern and you will be on the road toward a successful public speech.

8

Gathering Material

The advent of electronic technologies has ushered in the Information Age. You have greater access to information than at any time in human history. This makes gathering credible material for your speech especially challenging. The research firm IDC (International Data Corporation) calculated that the total global digital data available in 2010 was 1.2 million petabytes, an increase of 62% from 2009 (Gantz & Reinsel, 2010). A petabyte is a million gigabytes. So, 1.2 million petabytes is roughly equivalent to "the digital output from a century's worth of constant tweeting by all of Earth's inhabitants" (Wray, 2010), a scary thought indeed! The amount of information available digitally by 2020, however, is estimated to be *50 times greater* than that available in 2010 (Gantz & Reinsel, 2012). The word *staggering* does not seem sufficient to capture the size of the challenge we face in coming years with information overload. As Nate Silver (2012) notes, most of this abundance of information is useless noise. Your challenge is to mine the nuggets of credible information that are buried in the cavernous refuse of misinformation and trivialities.

Gathering useful information for your speech takes effort and know-how. Consequently, *the purpose of this chapter is to provide advice and insight on how to research speech topics effectively.* This chapter discusses using the Internet and the library, conducting interviews to generate your own relevant information, and avoiding plagiarism, which is an unethical shortcut that avoids labor-intensive research.

PHOTO 8.1 The Library of Congress is the world's largest library, housing more than 155 million items in 470 languages. About 11,000 items are added to the collection each day. Conveniently, many of the Library's resources (and these facts) are available online at www.loc .gov. "I couldn't find anything on my speech topic" is hardly a plausible excuse these days.

THE INTERNET: ONLINE RESEARCH

The Internet has quickly become a primary source for research by college students. A UCLA survey of almost 200,000 first-year college students at 270 four-year colleges revealed that 81% frequently used the Internet for research (Pryor et al., 2012).

Search Engines

A **search engine** is an Internet tool that computer generates indexes of Web pages that match, or link with, key words typed in a search window. There are far too many search engines to provide an exhaustive list here. A comprehensive list of search engines can be found at the Library of Congress website (http://www.lcweb .loc.gov/global/search.html). These are some of the more popular search engines:

> Google (http://www.google.com)
> Lycos (http://www.lycos.cs.cmu.edu)
> Bing (www.bing.com)

If one engine fails to provide what you are looking for, try another one.

Two search engines focus on scholarly articles and academic and scientific information:

> Google Scholar (http://scholar.google.com)
> Scirus (http://www.scirus.com/)

Directories

A **directory** is an Internet tool in which humans edit indexes of Web pages that match, or link with, key words typed in a search window. The important difference between a search engine and a directory is that a directory has a person trained in library or information sciences choosing prospective sites based on the quality of the site. *Search engines are more likely than directories to provide overly broad, often irrelevant sites.* These are three popular directories:

> TradeWaveGalaxy (www.einet.net)
> Yahoo (http://www.yahoo.com)
> About (www.about.com)

Metasearch Engines

A **metasearch engine** sends your key word request to several search engines at once. *They work best when your request is a relatively obscure one*, not a general interest topic. When you want to narrow your search to about a dozen sites, try using a metasearch engine. Here are some popular metasearch engines:

> Dogpile (http://www.dogpile.com)
> Ask Jeeves (www.ask.com)
> MetaCrawler (www.metacrawler.com)
> Excite (www.excite.com)

Virtual Libraries

Because much on the Internet is irrelevant, misinformed, or plain nutty, virtual libraries have been created to provide more selective, higher-quality information. A **virtual library** is a search tool that combines Internet technology and standard library techniques for cataloguing and appraising information. Virtual libraries are usually associated with colleges, universities, or organizations with strong reputations in information dissemination. Unlike other search tools, virtual libraries provide fewer websites and a more narrow focus, but the information has been carefully screened so it is more credible. These are some of the more popular virtual libraries:

Internet Public Library (http://www.ipl.org)
Social Science Information Gateway (http://www.sosig.ac.uk)
WWW Virtual Library (http://vlib.org)

Internet Search Tips

Researching your topic on the Internet should be a focused undertaking to avoid information overload. Broad topic searches will not prove helpful. For example, typing *smoking* into the Google search window produced 491 million hits when I last checked.

Several tips will aid you in narrowing your search. First, narrow your topic. Instead of *smoking*, narrow to perhaps *smoking cigarettes*. That produced 36 million hits when last checked. This is still far too many hits, although the first sites that appear may prove useful. Narrow the topic further to perhaps *smoking cigarettes on college campuses*. That produced 1.5 million hits. Using quotation marks further refines your search. By putting "smoking cigarettes on college campuses" in quotation marks, seven hits appeared. Finally, look at the source of the site. Governmental sites are more likely to provide useful and accurate information than blogging sites.

Wikipedia: Credible Scholarship or Mob Rule?

Wikipedia is sometimes cited as a credible reference. This online collaborative encyclopedia is the most widely used general reference source on the Internet. By June 2013, *Wikipedia* had accumulated 27 million articles in 286 languages. The English *Wikipedia* reached 4.3 million articles ("*Wikipedia* Statistics," 2013). This is more than 50 times the size of the next largest English-language encyclopedia, *Encyclopedia Britannica* (see http://en.wikipedia.org/wiki/Wikipedia:Size_comparisons). As Association for Psychological Science President Mahzarin Banaji (2011) notes, "It is the largest collaboratively produced knowledge repository that has ever existed."

One serious problem with *Wikipedia* is that it takes contributions from almost anyone willing to make entries. Information can be unreliable, even wrong. An assessment in 2011 by the Project on Psychology of 935 articles on *Wikipedia* found that only 2% were above "B level" in quality, and many were embarrassingly inadequate, even inaccurate (Banaji, 2011). Sources of articles contributed are often omitted. Even though *Wikipedia* articles often include links to valid and credible sources, and some articles are first-rate scholarly works, nevertheless you may be quoting merely an interested party with no expertise and a decidedly biased view. This "anyone can contribute and edit" approach runs the risk of providing misinformation (Banaji, 2011).

In late 2011, Wikimedia Foundation, the caretaker of *Wikipedia*, commissioned a study by Epic, a United Kingdom-based e-learning company, and Oxford University to determine the quality and accuracy of *Wikipedia* articles with an eye toward improvement (McNamara, 2011). Results of this study showed that *Wikipedia* did well on accuracy and citing references for factual claims (Taraborelli, 2012). Nevertheless, the sample of articles studied was very small (only 22), and the study was a pilot project of limited scope.

Despite genuine concerns about the accuracy of articles contributed to *Wikipedia* that still remain, Duke University interdisciplinary studies and English professor Cathy Davidson (2007) views *Wikipedia* as "the single most impressive collaborative intellectual tool produced at least since the *Oxford English Dictionary*" (p. B20). She further claims that criticisms are overblown. She notes that errors on *Wikipedia* can be corrected sometimes within hours of discovery. *Wikipedia* "is not just an encyclopedia. It is a knowledge community, uniting anonymous readers all over the world who edit and correct grammar, style, interpretations, and facts" (p. B20). As a starting point for research, *Wikipedia* can be "a quick and easy reference before heading into more scholarly depths" (p. B20). Davidson's points have merit. Nevertheless, be cautious using *Wikipedia*. It is probably best to use *Wikipedia* as Davidson suggests—as one possible starting point for your research, but not as a primary, reliable reference.

Blogging Sites: Be Very Choosy

Although of limited breadth, some blogging sites can be useful as sources of very recent political and world news stories and popular culture events and issues. Blogging sites provide news, commentary, and opinion. These sites are usually accessible from computers in your college library, even on your smartphones. The opinions offered by bloggers are sometimes interesting, even amusing, and often incendiary, but they are not credible sources of information. Many blogging sites, however, include detailed articles by reputable authors with frequent links to online newspapers and magazines. Potentially useful blogging sites include the following:

> CNN Politics (http://www.cnn.com/POLITICS)
> Huffington Post (www.huffingtonpost.com)
> Politico (www.politico.com)
> Real Clear Politics (http://realclearpolitics.com)
> Salon (http://www.salon.com)
> The Conservative Voice (http://www.theconservativevoice.com)

Be very careful using these blogging sites, however. To greater or lesser extent, they all have a certain political leaning. They are best for getting you started on recent political and social events, but they are not credible sources in and of themselves. You should not offer *Huffington Post*, for example, as your primary source. Look for credible sources that write articles included on the site (e.g., Paul Krugman, Nobel prize-winning economist).

Evaluating Internet Information: Basic Steps

Despite the prevalent use of the Internet by college students to conduct research, only 41% of these students evaluate the quality or reliability of the information garnered from the Internet (Pryor et al., 2012). The Internet can be a phenomenal resource for finding high-quality information, but there is also great potential for spreading misinformation. For example, I received from a friend the following attachment in an email:

 These are actual comments made on student's report cards by teachers in the New York City public school system.

1. Since my last report, your child has reached rock bottom and has started to dig.
2. I would not allow this student to breed.
3. Your child has delusions of adequacy.
4. Your son is depriving a village somewhere of an idiot.
5. Your son sets low personal standards and then consistently fails to achieve them.
6. The student has a "full six-pack" but lacks the plastic thing to hold it all together.
7. This child has been working with too much glue.
8. When your daughter's IQ reaches 50, she should sell.
9. The gates are down, the lights are flashing, but the train isn't coming.
10. If this student were any more stupid, he'd have to be watered twice a week.
11. It is impossible to believe that the sperm that created this child beat out 1,000,000 others.
12. The wheel is turning but the hamster is definitely dead.

Confident that public school teachers would not have written these "actual comments," especially on a report card, I used the Internet to check on the credibility of this report. I chose one of the comments, typed it verbatim in the Google search window, and located websites that printed the same list of comments but claimed that the list was garnered from British military officer fitness reports, employee performance evaluations, military performance appraisals, and appraisals of federal employees. There were 672 Google hits dating as far back as 1997 that printed this list of comments attributed to various sources. The list is almost certainly fabricated. How would anyone have gathered these comments?

As humorist Will Rogers reportedly said, what gets us into real trouble is "what we know that ain't so." Consult snopes.com to correct urban myths and misinformation such as the spiders and sex statistics that "ain't so."

Who has unfettered access to student report cards and would publicize such personal information at the risk of legal action?

Then there is the oft-repeated Internet hoax that Congress is considering passage of the "Americans with No Abilities Act." The act would defend millions of Americans who "lack any real skills or ambition." Originally a political satire published by *The Onion* in June 1998 that lampooned the Americans with Disabilities Act, the satirical piece has been circulating for more than a decade on the Internet as a serious news story constantly "updated." It is a joke!

The Internet is a rich source of rumor, gossip, and hoaxes, so you should exercise extreme caution when using it for serious, credible research. How do you separate the high-quality information on the Internet from the hokum? In general, follow four easy steps (see also "Evaluating Information Found on the Internet," 2012).

(**1**) *Consider the Source.* The specific source of the information is not always clear from accessing a website. Are you looking at medical information from the Mayo Clinic or from an anonymous source? If no source is evident other than the name of a website, be very suspicious. Even an author's name without accompanying credentials is dubious. You may be able to find the credentials of an author by consulting *Biography Index* or by logging on to Virtual Reference Desk (www.refdesk.com) or ProfNet's Expert Database (www.profnet.com). Check and see if sources are cited in the article, and make a quick check of some of them to see if they exist or are from credible sources.

② *Consider Source Bias.* No matter the source, if the website uses a hard sell to peddle products, therapies, or ideas, be wary. Look for sites that have no vested interest, no products to peddle, and no axe to grind. Look at the website address. If it ends in *gov* or *edu*, the website is sponsored and maintained by a governmental or educational institution with a reputation to protect. If the address ends in *com*, it is a commercial site with varying levels of credibility from strong to weak. If such sites are offering fact-checking information, then their credibility and profitability are dependent on accuracy. Website addresses ending in *org* are sponsored by organizations and also have varying credibility depending on the reputation of the organization.

③ *Determine Document Currency.* Not everything on the Internet is recent. Look for current information. Websites sometimes indicate when the site was last updated. Many documents indicate the date at the top or at the end of the document. You can also make a rough estimate of the currency of the document from the currency of the information contained in the article and from any sources cited in the article. If the source references are all outdated (at least 5 years old or older), you can deduce that this site has not been updated recently. We live in a fast-changing world. You will want to use the most recent information, not what may have been true at one time but may no longer be true now.

④ **Use Fact Checking Sites.** The validity of many claims can be checked for accuracy at a number of sites. Potential urban myths and hoaxes, such as "90% of people in the U.S. marry their high school sweethearts" and "Coca-Cola is an effective spermacide" can be checked at Snopes (*http://www .snopes.com*). Most political claims, especially when made in the heat of a political election, can be checked for accuracy at nonpartisan sites such as PolitiFact (www.politifact.com), FactCheck (www.factcheck.org), and The Fact Checker (www.washingtonpost.com/blogs/fact-checker). Medical claims can be checked for accuracy at such sites as Centers for Disease Control and Prevention (www.cdc.gov), Web MD (www.webmd.com), and Health Central (www.healthcentral.com). News events can be checked at reputable news agencies' sites such as the *New York Times* (www.nytimes .com) and CNN (www.cnn.com).

LIBRARIES: BRICKS-AND-MORTAR RESEARCH FACILITIES

The Internet is a wonderful virtual resource, but the bricks-and-mortar library buildings still house books, documents, and reference works that cannot be found on the Internet. College libraries also are computerized, and most allow students to access the Internet on library computers. Thus, college libraries provide "one-stop shopping" for information on speech topics.

Every college library offers one or more tours of its facility. Take the tour. Even if you are already knowledgeable about using a library, the tour will familiarize you with where materials are located in a specific library.

Librarian: Expert Navigator

Begin researching early. A frenzied attempt to research your speech topic in the library the night before your presentation will jump-start your anxiety and prove to be a less than satisfactory experience. If you do not know quite where to begin, ask the librarian; there is no better single source of information on researching a speech topic. I have consulted the reference librarians at my college on dozens

PHOTO 8.2 Although the Internet is a repository of vast and useful information, it can also be a vast wasteland of misinformation. Do not ignore traditional libraries in your search for high-quality information for your speeches.

of occasions while researching this textbook. They are the experts on information location. Use them. Do not expect the librarian to do your research for you, but he or she will guide you on your journey through the maze of information if you get stuck.

Library Catalogues: Computer Versions

For decades, the card catalogue was a standard starting point for most research. The card catalogue, listing all books contained in the library on 3 × 5 cards by author, title, or subject, has become antiquated. The old card catalogues have been computerized in almost all libraries in the United States.

The computer catalogue, like its predecessor, lists books according to author, title, and subject. An important distinguishing characteristic of the computer catalogue is that you can do a keyword search. Type in "mountain climbing," and a list of titles appears related to this subject. You can also keyword search by author names. Computer catalogues also indicate whether the book is available or checked out, saving you time.

Periodicals: Popular Information Sources

The Reader's Guide to Periodical Literature provides current listings for articles in hundreds of popular magazines in the United States. Articles are listed by both author and subject. There is also a computer version of *The Reader's Guide*. It is entitled *Reader's Guide Abstracts and Full Text*. This computer version is faster to use, and it includes a brief abstract, or summary, of the listed magazine articles and full-text articles from more than 100 periodicals. There are many other periodical indexes. Check with your librarian to discover which are available at your college library.

Newspapers: An Old Standby

Despite their recent economic struggles, newspapers are still one of the richest sources of information on current topics. Your college library will undoubtedly subscribe to the local newspaper. The *New York Times Index* is a valuable resource. Database indexes for newspapers include *Newsbank Index*, the *InfoTrac National Newspaper Index*, and *UMI's Newspaper Abstracts*. In addition, every major newspaper (e.g., *New York Times, L.A. Times, Boston Globe, Chicago Tribune, Wall Street Journal*) has its own website that includes major news stories online each day for up-to-the-minute information on breaking news and an archive of past articles on topics.

Reference Works: Beyond *Wikipedia*

Encyclopedias are standard references in libraries used for researching a wide variety of topics. Unlike *Wikipedia*, articles appearing in encyclopedias such as *Encyclopedia Britannica, Colliers's Encyclopedia, World Book Encyclopedia*, and *Encyclopedia Americana* are solicited from scholars in the appropriate fields, and their contributions are subject to peer review for accuracy. You can access many encyclopedias by computer.

Other useful general reference works available in most college libraries besides encyclopedias are *Statistical Abstracts of the United States, World Almanac, Monthly Labor Review, FBI Uniform Crime Report, Vital Statistics of the United States, Facts on File, The Guinness Book of World Records*, and *Who's Who in America*. References for government related information include *Monthly Catalogue of United States Government Publications, Congressional Quarterly Weekly Report, The Congressional Record, The Congressional Digest*, and *The Congressional Index*.

INTERVIEWING: QUESTIONING EXPERTS

Research interviews are sometimes a very productive resource for your speeches. Interviewing local artists about painting techniques or about standards for determining the difference in quality between a Picasso painting and a 3-year-old's crayon drawing could be quite useful. Interviewing an expert on hybrid car technology might be a great place to begin your research on this topic. Experts can often guide your search by telling you where to search and what to avoid.

Student speakers often assume that no expert would want to be interviewed by just a student. That is usually untrue, especially when you consider how many experts are college professors on your campus. If your topic is a campus issue, such as parking problems or theft of car stereos, an interview with the campus chief of security could provide valuable information.

Interview Plan: Be Prepared

No research interview should be conducted without a specific plan of action. Your plan should include what you hope to find, whom you will interview and why, a specific meeting time and place arranged with the interviewee, and prepared questions that will likely elicit helpful information. Avoid questions that ask the obvious or tell you what you already know. Avoid leading questions such as, "You couldn't possibly believe that this campus has no parking problem, could you?" Also avoid hostile or belligerent questions such as, "When you screwed up the arrest of that student accused of stealing car stereos on campus, did you make the arrest because you are biased against Middle Eastern people?" Ask difficult questions if you need to, but be respectful to the interviewee. Open-ended questions are usually a good way to begin a research interview. Consider a few examples:

> Do you believe we have a parking problem on campus?
> What actions have been taken to address the parking issues on campus?
> What more should be done about campus parking?

Interview Conduct: Act Appropriately

The manner in which you conduct yourself during the interview will usually determine whether the interview will be a success and provide useful information. Dress appropriately for the interview. Sloppy or bizarre dress will likely insult the interviewee. Always be on time for your meeting. If you are late, the interview may be cancelled. Never record your interview without the expressed permission of the interviewee. This is not ambush journalism or an undercover operation with hidden cameras trying to catch an interviewee telling a lie. Stay focused and avoid meandering into unfruitful side discussions. Take careful notes. Stay within the allotted time for the interview. Thank the interviewee for answering your questions. Review your notes after the interview, and write down any additional clarifying notations that will help you remember what transpired during the interview.

Interviewing by Email: Surprise Yourself

Not all interviews need to be in person. You might be surprised by how readily experts from around the world are happy to answer a few short questions posed to them by inquiring, eager students. Students from various places in the United States and even from distant countries have contacted me by email to ask a few pertinent questions regarding communication concepts and issues. I am always flattered to be contacted and willing to respond. Many experts have home pages with an email address. Make a short, initial inquiry about being interviewed. Lengthy emails may go unread. If the expert agrees to answer questions, be brief and concise. Ask only a few well-phrased, precise questions. Proofread every email for proper spelling and grammar. Fewer questions are more likely to get answers than a lengthy survey.

PLAGIARISM AND ETHICS: CUTTING CORNERS ON RESEARCH

In 1987 when Joe Biden was a U.S. senator from Delaware, he ran for president of the United States. Biden, a gifted orator, was given a decent chance of securing the Democratic nomination. His candidacy went into the dumpster, however, when news accounts revealed that Biden had plagiarized his conclusion to a speech he gave at the Iowa State Fair. He lifted his conclusion almost verbatim from a speech by British Labor Party leader Neil Kinnock. Biden had even cribbed Kinnock's personal history. For example, Kinnock asked rhetorically, "Why am I the first Kinnock in a thousand generations to be able to get to university? Why is Glenys [his wife] the first woman in her family in a thousand generations to be able to get to university?" (cited in Jamieson, 1988, p. 221). Biden's conclusion asked rhetorically, "Why is it that Joe Biden is the first in his family ever to go to a university? Why is it that my wife, who is sitting out there in the audience, is the first in her family to ever go to college?" (p. 222). Biden was not the first in his family to receive a college education (Jamieson, 1988).

Confronted with the charge of plagiarism, Biden claimed that the similarity between his speech and Kinnock's was merely coincidental. The news media, however, sensed a bigger story and discovered that Biden had also lifted passages from speeches by Hubert Humphrey and Robert Kennedy. Biden was further damaged by his admission that he had plagiarized when he was a law student at Syracuse University. Biden's presidential campaign came to a screeching halt, and he did not attempt another presidential bid until the 2008 campaign, ultimately winning the consolation prize—vice president.

Some might pass off Biden's plagiarism as a lot of huffing and puffing about very little. Plagiarism, however, is unethical behavior. Speaking someone else's words without giving attribution is dishonest and disrespectful and, therefore, incompetent communication (see Chapter 1 discussion). How do we know who the real Joe Biden is if he speaks the unattributed words of another and even assumes someone else's personal history to sound eloquent?

The issue of plagiarism emerged again in the political realm when journalist Geoffrey Dunn (2009) accused Sarah Palin of lifting whole passages of a November 1, 2005, article written by Newt Gingrich and Craig Shirley. In a speech she gave in June 2009 at the Alaska Center for the Performing Arts, Palin very closely paraphrased the article ten times, making this vague attempt to reference her paraphrases: "Recently, Newt Gingrich, he had written a good article about Reagan." She made one further oblique reference to the Gingrich article later in the speech. Is this plagiarism? Jonathon Bailey (2009), who founded the website Plagiarism Today, thinks not. Technically, he is correct. Palin would have been guilty of plagiarism if she had never attributed anything she said in her speech to Gingrich. Nevertheless, her attempt at attribution is extremely vague, and it makes it impossible for her audience to know which are her words and which specifically are those of Gingrich. She also never references the second author of the article, Craig Shirley. That is not acceptable. It is not strictly plagiarism, but it certainly is extremely sloppy and unprofessional. Merging your words and those of others without clearly identifying the difference is inappropriate.

With the explosive growth of the Internet and the easy availability of whole speeches by others, student plagiarism has become an increasing problem (Noguchi, 2008). Documented cases of students stealing lines, even entire passages, from the graduation speeches of other students for use in their own graduation speeches have produced lively debate on YouTube, a frequent resource used by students for such plagiarism.

These student speakers and Joe Biden were guilty of selective plagiarism, or stealing portions of someone else's speech or writings. That is bad enough, but plagiarism becomes even more serious when entire speeches are stolen and presented as one's own. Some students attempt such blatant theft of another's words usually because development of a speech has been left until there is too little time to conduct adequate research. Research early and remove any temptation to plagiarize. Stealing someone's words is pilfering a part of that person's identity. That is never an inconsequential act.

SUMMARY

Gathering relevant, credible material for your speech is not a casual event. You should begin early and have a focused plan of attack. Although the Internet is an amazing, plentiful source of information, it is also a source of abundant misinformation, hoaxes, gossip, and nutty opinions by all sorts of individuals, some identified and others anonymous. The library is still a major resource for speech research. Knowing how to use it efficiently and effectively can save you time and prove enormously productive. Finally, avoid plagiarism by eschewing the temptation usually triggered by procrastination followed by panic when little time is left to research effectively.

9

Skepticism: Becoming Critical Thinking Speakers and Listeners

All beliefs are not created equal. People used to think that the Earth was flat, that pus healed wounds, that ground-up mummies had curative powers, and that bloodletting cured diseases. In 1622, a German physician, Daniel Bockher, published a popular book entitled *Medicus Microcosmos*. In it, he touts the healing properties of urine, excrement, tapeworms, and earwax. A 1902 publication authored by a group of "the best physicians and surgeons of modern practice" entitled *The Cottage Physician* claimed that cataracts on the eye could be removed by generous doses of laxatives. These physicians claimed that problems urinating could be relieved by marshmallow enemas, and tetanus could be treated effectively by "pouring cold water on the head from a considerable height" (quoted in Weingarten, 1994, p. B7).

We hear a dizzying array of weird and wild claims every day that beg to be questioned. For example, 70% of people surveyed believe that most people use only 10% of their brains (Chabris & Simons, 2010). If you surgically removed the "inactive" 90% of your brain, what do you think might happen? "There is no reason to suspect evolution—or even an intelligent designer—would give us an organ that is 90 percent inefficient" (Chabris & Simons, 2010, p. 199). Then there are the claims of some anti-government fringe groups that the government has constructed a thousand concentration camps for its own citizens and that 30,000 guillotines have been stockpiled to execute anti-government critics (Thomma, 2009). Surely there is a simpler way to commit murder, and who has been constructing these big, clunky guillotines without being noticed? As speakers and listeners, you need to be capable of separating the prime rib from the baloney, fact from fiction. No speaker should feel comfortable presenting implausible claims to his or her audience, and no listener should feel comfortable accepting such claims.

Faced with staggering challenges both foreign and domestic, critical thinking from those who mount the public podium to offer wisdom and insight has never been more essential. Thus, *the primary purpose of this chapter is to explain and promote the process of skepticism.* Skepticism is distinguished from true belief, which is the opposite of critical thinking. *This chapter also serves as the justification for the next two chapters,* and it provides the fundamental basis for the practical public speaking advice offered in those chapters.

SKEPTICISM, TRUE BELIEF, AND CYNICISM

Skepticism is a *process of inquiry* whereby claims are evaluated by engaging in a rigorous examination of evidence and reasoning used to support those claims (Sagan, 1996; Shermer, 2013). The term skeptic is derived from the Greek *skeptikos* which means *thoughtful or inquiring, not doubtful and dismissive.* Skepticism is a process for acquiring beliefs and changing them when warranted. *Skeptics are not of one mind on controversial issues.* Skeptics can be politically liberal, moderate, or conservative. They can be devoutly religious or atheistic. (See Dowd, 2008, for an excellent discussion of the compatibility of religious faith and skepticism.)

Conversely, **true belief** is a willingness to accept claims without solid reasoning or valid evidence and to hold these beliefs tenaciously even if a mountain of contradictory evidence proves them wrong. As Winston Churchill commented, a true believer is "one who can't change his mind and won't change the subject." True belief is a closed-minded system of thought in which facts and truth are not desired goals. Columnist Leonard Pitts (2011) puts it aptly when he observes that the "new media" are overrun "by true believers for whom accuracy is subordinate to ideology and facts useful only to the degree they can be bent, shaped or outright disregarded in service to ideology." This true belief results in "an empty shouting match better suited to a fifth-grade schoolyard than to adults analyzing the great issues of the day" (p. A13).

Cynicism is nay-saying, fault-finding, and ridiculing. H. L. Mencken once described a cynic as someone who "smells flowers and looks around for a coffin." They are quick to mock human frailties and imperfections and to deride the beliefs of others. Cynics do not seek truth; they seek their next target. Skepticism, unfortunately, is often confused with cynicism. The two are significantly different. In some instances, skeptics have exhibited condescension and arrogance when commenting on questionable beliefs, acting more like cynics and justly deserving criticism. Gentle teasing and mild sarcasm have their place in public speaking, but vicious, personal attacks so often witnessed in political speeches are inappropriate. Skepticism requires humility because no one's ideas and beliefs are immune to challenge (Hare, 2009).

Finally, true belief does not simply mean "strong belief." Skepticism also does not mean "no belief" (Shermer, 2013). Advocates for truth and justice in all spheres of life are often passionate in their beliefs, and rightly so. This does not make them true believers. *The key distinction between a true believer and a skeptic is the process used to arrive at and maintain a belief.* "It is not the embracing of an idea that causes problems—it is the refusal to relax that embrace when good sense dictates doing so" (Ruggeiro, 1988). Skepticism is a profoundly positive intellectual journey that seeks knowledge and understanding while avoiding the dangers of true belief.

DANGERS OF TRUE BELIEF

The dangers of true belief are real and extensive (Lewandowsky et al., 2012). There are at least six serious harms: a decline in scientific literacy and critical thinking; an inability to make informed decisions; monetary losses by a substantial number of people; a diversion of society's resources that could be used to solve serious problems; the promotion of simplistic answers to complex problems that may result in needless deaths; and the creation of false hopes and unrealistic expectations (Beyerstein, 1998). Succinctly put, "People suffer" from true belief (Sherman, 2009, p. 35).

Consider just one example. Thousands of scientific studies support the link between HIV and AIDS. The Centers for Disease Control, the National Institutes of Health, the Pasteur Institute and others all conclude that this link is conclusive (see "The Evidence," 2010; Moore & Nattrass, 2006). Nevertheless, Christine Maggiore, with no scientific background or even a college degree, waged a vigorous campaign to discredit the HIV-AIDS link (France, 2000). Having tested positive for AIDS, she nevertheless often gave speeches and appeared at medical conventions on AIDS to protest. She garnered surprisingly widespread support for her views (France, 2000). She refused to take any antiviral drugs that could have prevented passing the AIDS virus during pregnancy to her two children, and she breastfed them, thereby increasing the odds of transmitting the virus. She adamantly maintained that a healthy lifestyle provides sufficient protection, and she discouraged use of condoms. Tragically, her 3-year-old daughter, Eliza Jane, died in 2005 from what the Los Angeles Coroner's report deemed pneumonia caused by AIDS. Dr. James Ribe, the senior deputy medical examiner called the autopsy report's conclusion "unequivocal" ("Did HIV-Positive Mom's Beliefs," 2005).

Maggiore disputed the findings and continued her campaign even after the death of her child (note the tenacity of true belief). Maggiore died in December 2008 from pneumonia. No autopsy was performed, but it seems likely that her pneumonia, like her daughter's, was AIDS related.

True belief may not always lead to harm. Reading your daily horoscope may simply be entertaining if you never act on it. Also, practitioners of true belief are not always hucksters looking to con a gullible public or fanatical speakers raving about conspiracies to audiences of rabid supporters. Many true believers are well-meaning, caring individuals who firmly believe they can help others, but good intentions and the strength and tenacity of one's beliefs do not negate the serious harm they can do. Christine Maggiore was probably well meaning, but she and others of like mind do damage nevertheless. True belief is a poor pattern of thinking when listening to a speaker, and it is a deeply flawed basis upon which to build a speech.

THE PROCESS OF TRUE BELIEVING

True beliefs vary widely. They can even be contradictory. Nevertheless, despite the differences in the details, true believers all operate in essentially the same way, as discussed in this section.

Confirmation Bias: Searching for Support

Confirmation bias is the tendency to seek information that supports one's beliefs, and to ignore information that contradicts those beliefs. One of the hallmarks of true belief is confirmation bias (Lilienfeld et al., 2009). *True believers are belief-driven, not evidence-driven.* Their beliefs are formed first, and then they look for confirming evidence. Studies show that confirmation bias is pervasive (Taber & Lodge, 2006; Nickerson, 1998). One such study took self-described "strong" Democrats and Republicans prior to the 2004 presidential election between George W. Bush and John Kerry and presented statements made in their public speeches and debates in which each candidate clearly contradicted himself. Democrats consistently ignored contradictions by Kerry and Republicans consistently did the same for Bush, but both partisan groups were keenly aware and strongly critical of the contradictions from the opposing candidate (Westen et al., 2006). Individuals generally do not give themselves a chance to spot faulty claims from speakers because they search for and listen to assertions and information that support their beliefs, and they ignore contrary information (Schittekatte & Van Hiel, 1996; Taber & Lodge, 2006).

When researching your speeches, you want to seek information reflecting various points of view, then weigh the evidence and decide which point of view makes the most sense. Defending the indefensible because of a biased search for confirming information is public speaking in service to true belief, not an admirable desire to search for what is true and accurate. Such a one-sided search also leaves you unprepared for counter-arguments and research that might be used against you in a debate or an exchange with audience members after your speech.

Rationalization of Disconfirmation: Clinging to Falsehoods

There is a story of a client with an odd problem who came to see a therapist. The client believed that he was dead. The therapist made several tries to convince the client that he was not dead. Nothing worked. Finally, the therapist asked her client, "Do dead men bleed?" The man said no. The therapist then took a pin out of the drawer in her desk, grabbed the man's hand, and stabbed it. Blood spurted. The man looked at his bleeding hand and responded, "Well, I'll be damned; dead men do bleed." The man could not be dissuaded from his belief that he was dead. Like the man who believed he was dead, even when true believers are confronted with strong, disconfirming evidence, they usually cling to their beliefs (Lewandowsky et al., 2012).

For example, Ronald Reagan famously asserted in a 1981 speech, "Trees cause more pollution than automobiles do." (This provoked an anonymous wit to hang a sign on a tree in California that said: "Chop me down before I kill again."). The claim is wildly false because trees consume carbon dioxide, they clean the air, but car exhaust expels pollution into the air. Reagan was advised of his mistake. Nevertheless, he repeated the false statement in two ensuing speeches. In this instance, he acted like a true believer.

True believers hold firmly to unwarranted beliefs by using **rationalization of disconfirmation**—inventing superficial, even glib, alternative explanations for contradictory evidence. For example, a preacher named Harold Camping adamantly predicted that the Rapture—Judgment Day—would occur on May 21, 2011. He posted 5,000 billboards around the country that cost more than $5 million to advertise his prediction and gave numerous speeches warning of the impending Rapture (Gafni, 2013). The popular media gave Camping's prediction wide coverage. As you know, his prediction did not come true. Did he admit his mistake and accept that his prediction was based on no credible evidence? He did not. Instead, he "revised" the date to October 21, 2011, claiming that May 21 was the "spiritual" Rapture and that October 21 would be the "physical" Rapture. Again, you know he was wrong. This time, however, Camping apologized to his followers for his mistake but said it was God's will, which is unprovable, that the predicted Rapture did not occur ("Harold Camping Apologizes," 2011). To his credit, however, Camping eventually acted less like a true believer than previously

PHOTO 9.1 Harold Camping predicted the end of the world and posted 5,000 billboards to announce it.

by admitting to his radio congregation in a March 2012 letter that he was wrong to predict the Rapture. He even claimed it was "sinful" for him to make such a prediction and that he would never do it again (Leclaire, 2012). It took him 20 years and three unmistakable disconfirmations of his predictions, however, to change his mind. In 1992, he predicted Judgment Day would occur on September 6, 1994 (Kaleem, 2011). The tenacity to true beliefs is noteworthy.

Shifting the Burden of Proof: Whose Obligation Is It?

As a speaker, whenever you make a claim to an audience, you assume the **burden of proof**, that is, your obligation to present compelling evidence and reasoning to support your claim (Freeley & Steinberg, 2013). You are not being reasonable if you challenge your audience to disprove your claims that you have not sufficiently defended with evidence and logic. This is **shifting the burden of proof**, inappropriately assuming the validity of a claim unless it is proven false by another person who never made the original claim (Verlinden, 2005). Shifting the burden of proof is common among true believers (e.g., "Prove I'm not a psychic"). This approach is inappropriate because skeptics would have to disprove all manner of absurd, unsupported claims. I once had a student who gave a speech in which he challenged his audience to disprove his claim that life is merely a dream and nothing is real. It was an amusing speech that consisted mostly of raising funny questions and speculating, but I had to remind him afterwards of that annoying burden of proof, which he clearly shifted inappropriately to his audience. *Those who make the claim have the burden to prove the claim.*

The burden of proof can be a tricky business to nail down. For example, Senate Majority Leader Harry Reid asserted in a speech on the U.S. Senate floor in July 2012 that Mitt Romney paid no federal taxes for 12 years ("Harry Reid," 2012). In interviews and press conferences he later asserted that Romney paid no taxes for 10 years prior to 2010, based on an anonymous "highly reliable" source. The Romney camp went ballistic and Romney correctly challenged Reid to "put up or shut up" about his supposed source for the allegation. At this point, the burden of proof was on Reid to reveal his source. He did not. Democrats, however, challenged Romney to disprove Reid's claim by releasing his tax returns in question. Although perhaps a cagey political strategy, this incorrectly shifts the burden of proof to Romney to disprove an assertion by Reid that was never supported with tangible evidence. To defend himself, Romney later claimed in a campaign speech that he had "never paid less than 13%" in the past 10 years ("Romney Says," 2012). Romney assumed the burden of proof to provide evidence (his tax returns) to support this new claim. He, like Reid, produced no such evidence.

In addition, *extraordinary claims require extraordinary proof* (Gracely, 2003; Shermer, 2013). Extraordinary claims increase a speaker's burden of proof. If your claim requires rewriting the laws of physics, for example, no ordinary evidence will do. Motivational speaker Tolly Burkan, founder of the Firewalking Institute for Research and Education, introduced firewalking in America. Participants walk barefoot across red-hot coals to convince themselves that any obstacle can be overcome with the proper mindset (Carroll, 2010; see also *firewalking.com*). Mega-inspirational speaker Tony Robbins, who built a financial empire on his super-charged motivational speeches and self-help advice, was introduced to firewalking by Burkan, and he regularly uses it in his huge workshops as a final "proof" that "People change their physiology by changing their beliefs" (quoted in Anderson, 2012). If participants can walk barefoot over burning coals without injury, so goes the argument, surely they can accomplish anything by willing it with their minds.

The mind-over-matter explanation is hard to swallow, however, because "the very idea that brain activity could alter the physical properties of burning carbon compounds or the reactivity of skin cells to extreme heat contradicts volumes of well-established scientific data" (McDonald, 1998, p. 46). As physicist David Willey explains, wood coals are poor thermal conductors, unlike metal rods (Noelle, 1999). If you decided to walk on hot metal rods, the moment your feet hit the metal you would hear the same sound a steak makes when it first hits the barbecue grill—SIZZLE. Note that firewalking is not called fire *standing*, but if

PHOTO 9.2 It is called firewalking, not firestanding, however, because simple physics makes it apparent that you will be horribly burned if you do not keep moving briskly across the hot coals. Extraordinary claims require extraordinary proof. Firewalking is not "mind over matter."

minds truly can control matter, why do participants have to move at all? In fact, 21 participants at Robbins motivational workshop in San Jose, California, in the summer of 2012, suffered burns to their feet when they apparently did not walk briskly enough over hot coals. One participant rationalized his burns by stating that he "didn't get into the right state of mind" (Anderson, 2012). A commonplace firewalk does not begin to prove the extraordinary mind-over-matter claim. Much more impressive, credible evidence is required to contradict what volumes of scientific evidence support.

THE PROCESS OF SKEPTICISM: INQUIRING MINDS WANT TO KNOW

There are essentially two general ways of knowing: intuition and skepticism (Alter et al., 2007; Myers, 2004a). You could base your claims primarily on *intuition*, that "immediate knowing without reasoned analysis," but substantial research shows that intuition is often inaccurate and unreliable (Myers, 2004a; see also Chabris & Simons, 2010). If you want to know whether using strong fear appeals in a speech are more persuasive than using weak fear appeals, your intuition is a poor substitute for scientific studies that yield an answer (see Chapter 16).

There is no need to invalidate intuition in all areas of your life. As Myers (2004a) explains, "Intuition works well in some realms, but it needs restraints and checks in others... it feeds our creativity, our love, and our spirituality" (pp. 247–248). Nevertheless, intuition should not substitute for careful reasoning and use of credible evidence to support claims in a speech. Additionally, *Practically Speaking* puts the emphasis on "practical" instruction in public speaking. Skepticism can be taught in public speaking courses, intuition not so much. Thus, this section discusses the skepticism process and encourages its practical speech application.

Probability Model: Likely but Not Certain

The process of skepticism begins with the probability model. Claims speakers assert can vary in degrees of likelihood from *possibility* to *plausibility*, to *probability* and all the way to *certainty* (Freeley & Steinberg, 2013). Any informative or persuasive speech you present requires your determination of how strong a claim, and what degree of likelihood, you want to defend. Remember: *The stronger the claim the greater is your burden of proof.*

Few things in this world are certain. Death and your dryer will eat your socks are two that come to mind, but these are rare exceptions. Decision making and problem solving are best based on probabilities (Silver, 2012). Skeptics do not claim certainty because skepticism is an open system of thought and inquiry. Skeptics seek the highest degree of probability attainable. Thus, skepticism is based on a probability not a certainty model.

Possibility: Could Happen, but Do Not Bet on It   That you could receive an "A" in a public speaking class despite flunking all your speeches, failing all your tests, and missing most class sessions is possible, but highly unlikely. There could be a clerical error by the instructor or a computer glitch. True belief often rests on the "anything is possible" rationale. This allows for no distinctions to be drawn between fact and fiction. Thus, claims based on possibility require no diligent research preparing a speech or use of compelling evidence during a speech.

Suppose, for example, a stranger offers you $1,000 to walk blindfolded across a busy highway. Would you do it? Hey, it is possible you could succeed! What if you saw someone else do it without getting hit by a car? Now would you do it? One successful crossing proves that it is possible to cross a busy highway blindfolded and not get catapulted into the next county by a speeding automobile. It is possible but not likely. "Anything is possible" is insufficient justification for gambling with your life or with your educational future. It is also a woefully inadequate basis for any speech you might present.

Basing your decisions on only a possibility is silly in the extreme. It makes the weakest "possible" argument for a speech.

Plausibility: Making a Logical Case   The next step up from possibility is plausibility. For a claim to be plausible, it must at least seem to be logical. When the cause of AIDS was first determined to be a virus, only the most plausible theories on how to attack it were likely to gain federal grants to conduct research. Implausible theories (drink lots of orange juice) provide no logical basis for distributing scarce resources for research.

Plausibility alone is a basis for inquiry when substantial evidence is lacking, but it is an insufficient basis for acceptance of a claim. In the wake of the horrendous, incomprehensible massacre of 20 young children and 6 adults at the Sandy Hook Elementary school in Newtown, Connecticut, in December 2012, the Executive Vice-President and chief spokesman for the National Rifle Association, Wayne LaPierre, gave a much anticipated, nationally televised speech. He asserted, "The only thing that stops a bad guy with a gun is a good guy with a gun" (quoted by Castillo, 2012). He called for an armed security guard in every school in America. LaPierre's proposal was predicated on plausibility. Do not "gun free school zones," as LaPierre asserted in his speech, simply announce to deranged individuals that "schools are their safest place to inflict maximum mayhem with minimum risk?" He continued his plausibility argument by noting, "We protect our banks with armed guards. American airports, office buildings, power plants, courthouses—even sports stadiums—are all protected by armed security" (quoted in "Full Text," 2013). Plausible arguments such as LaPierre's can be convincing. A Washington Post/ABC poll showed that 55% of those surveyed supported LaPierre's proposal ("Post-ABC Poll," 2013).

Claims that rest on plausibility alone, however, can seem logical and persuasive when left unquestioned. LaPierre's speech implied that armed guards reduce violence in banks, sporting events, and other venues and thus should reduce violence in schools, but he did not actually offer any supporting evidence that shows such reductions or that these venues are comparable to public schools. Consequently, many media sources and numerous legislators offered a plausible case of their own, countering LaPierre's speech. They noted that there were two armed police officers at Columbine High School when a massacre of 12 students and a teacher occurred in 1998. Virginia Tech University had its own police force on campus composed of more than four-dozen armed officers at the time of the 2007 massacre in which 32 lives were lost and 17 more were injured. With approximately 100,000 public schools in the United States, providing even a single armed guard for every school would cost billions of dollars annually. What would prevent the guard, armed only with a hand gun, from becoming the first target of a mass murderer armed with assault weapons intent on causing mayhem (Burke & Chapman, 2012)?

The point here is not to resolve who is right in this most contentious, complex debate based only on plausibility. In the absence of careful research and bountiful evidence beyond a few selective examples to support claims, *plausibility alone on this or any other controversial topic serves as an insufficient basis for drawing any useful conclusions.* Plausibility may rightly provoke a dialogue and debate on controversial issues, but plausibility should not end the dialogue and the search for truth.

Probability: What Are the Odds?   *Your strongest speech arguments are both plausible and highly probable.* This means offering claims that are both logical and supported with abundant, high-quality evidence. If your claim cannot even pass the plausibility test, if it is demonstrably implausible, further consideration and evidence gathering seem unwarranted. For example, one of the world's best known "alternative medicines" is homeopathy, which is based on the "law of infinitesimals." The more diluted the medications, so goes the reasoning, the more effective they are. "Homeopathic medications are often so literally watered-down that they don't contain a single molecule of the original medicine or substance"

(Radford, 2013, p. 33). In March 2012, the British Science and Technology Select Committee reported on an extensive analysis of homeopathy, declaring that "the existing scientific literature showed no good evidence of efficacy" and that homeopathy, the no-medicine medicine, is "scientifically implausible" (quoted in Radford, 2013; see also Ernst, 2012).

Assuming your argument passes the plausibility test, you then move to probability to make a strong argument. Probability is a concept not well understood by most people (Silver, 2012). There is high probability that unusual events will occur, but that is no reason to give them special significance. For example, Ethem Sahin was playing dominoes with his friends in a coffee house in Ankara, Turkey, when a cow fell on him breaking his leg and gashing his forehead. The coffee house was built on the side of a hill and the cow wandered onto the roof, which caved in from the cow's weight ("Falling Cow Injures Coffee House Customer," 2001). It is doubtful that you will agonize about suffering a similar incident in a coffee house, but it did happen. With more than 7 billion people in the world, weird things will occur to some of them, "sometime somewhere." This demonstrates the **Law of Truly Large Numbers** with large enough numbers almost anything is likely to happen to *somebody, somewhere, somehow, sometime* ("Law of Truly Large Numbers," 2012). On August 14, 1992, a small meteorite hit a boy in Uganda (Krieger, 1999). The odds of this specific little boy being hit by a meteorite are astronomical. The odds of someone at some time being struck by a meteorite are likely.

Recognizing the Law of Truly Large Numbers, you should avoid making a speech that rests primarily on a handful of vivid, extraordinary examples. Remember, the unusual is likely to happen to someone, but that is poor justification for generalizing to a much broader population from "news of the weird." It is weird because it is improbable but not impossible. *Base your speech claims, not on the improbable, but on the highest degree of probability attainable.* For example, polio vaccinations have a 99% probability of preventing the disease ("Vaccine Effectiveness," 2010). Thus, the effectiveness of a polio shot is both plausible, based on previous experience with vaccines used against diseases in general, and probable, based on extensive studies on polio vaccines in particular. Do careful research to discover strong evidence that bolsters the probability of your claims. Chapter 10 discusses in detail how to determine the strength of your evidence.

Certainty: Without Exception   Claims of true believers are frequently stated as absolute certainties. A true believer by definition exhibits no doubt. *Skeptics, however, can aspire to no stronger claim than very high probability.* As a speaker, you do not want to make a claim that is absolute, certain. Practically speaking, a claim asserting certainty requires only a single exception to disprove it. Why set such an argumentative trap for yourself? "Highly likely" avoids the trap of certainty because exceptions do not disprove strong probability.

Skepticism discourages claims that any phenomenon is "impossible," although some skeptics have intemperately done so. What first appears to be impossible may prove to be disastrously incorrect. For example, the Fukushima nuclear reactor was designed to withstand an earthquake up to 8.6 in magnitude, in part because some seismologists thought it impossible that any earthquake larger than this could occur at this location (Silver, 2012). In addition, the plant was built on the expectation that no tsunami wave from a major earthquake could rise higher than 5.7 meters. On March 11, 2011, Japan experienced the "impossible," suffering a 9.0 magnitude quake that resulted in a 15-meter-high tsunami wave that engulfed the reactor, producing a meltdown and a severe radiation leak that together claimed almost 20,000 lives (Aldhous, 2012).

Skepticism and Open-Mindedness: Inquiring Minds, Not Empty Minds

Although skeptics avoid claims of certainty, this does not open the door to the everything-is-possible "open-mindedness" justification for true belief (Petrovic, 2013). Years ago, I explored a variety of alternative medical treatments and New Age therapies partly from curiosity and partly from a need to help a sick friend. I investigated herbal remedies, homeopathy, psychic healing, polarity therapy, crystal healing, iridology, pyramid power, radiasthesia, dowsing, marathon fasts, megavitamin therapy, therapeutic touch, and faith healing. Whenever I expressed doubt concerning the validity of these alternative approaches to health and disease, I was denounced as "closed-minded." It seemed that open-mindedness was equated with never discounting any claim no matter how poorly supported or implausible.

Open-mindedness does not require us to entertain obviously false claims made by speakers or to give them a forum for expression (Hare, 2009; Shermer, 2013). Do you really want to listen to a speaker argue that the world is flat or that gravity does not exist? As the bumper sticker says: "Gravity: Not just a good idea; it's the law!" An open mind should not equate with an empty mind. *"What truly marks an open-minded person is the willingness to follow where evidence leads"* (Adler, 1998, p. 44).

We do not always follow where the evidence leads, however. A Zogby survey of 1,200 Americans in May 2001, reported on the NBC "Today" show, revealed that 7% of respondents did not believe that the Apollo astronauts ever landed and walked on the moon, and an additional 4% were not sure. Since there are about 240 million adult Americans ("Quick Facts," 2012), these results suggest that about 17 million adult Americans think the moon landing was a hoax, and an

PHOTO 9.3 Shirley Phelps-Roper, member of the controversial Westboro Baptist Church, loudly and visibly proclaims her beliefs. Open-mindedness, however, does not mean that you have to listen to hateful bigotry spouted, for example, at funerals for dead soldiers. This same group threatened to picket actor Cory Monteith's funeral in July 2013 and tweeted that Monteith's girlfriend and fellow *Glee* actor, Lea Michele, should "kill herself."

additional 10 million think it might have been faked. A more recent survey of British respondents found that a whopping 25% believed the moon landing was a hoax (Bizony, 2009). Eleven of the respondents who believed the moon landing did occur, however, thought Buzz Lightyear was the first to step onto the moon, apparently confusing Edwin "Buzz" Aldrin, the second astronaut to step onto the moon's surface, with the animated character in *Toy Story*.

Attempting to capitalize on this apparent confusion and doubt, the Fox TV network aired "Conspiracy Theory: Did We Land on the Moon?" Striving for the sensational and achieving the nonsensical, the program clearly intimated that the U.S. government faked the moon landing. The Internet is replete with sites alleging the moon landing was a hoax.

Here is how, in preparing a speech, you sort the nonsense from common sense on an issue such as the moon hoax claim. Scientists from around the world documented the moon landing. The whole world was watching. It was one of the most thoroughly documented events in human history, thus establishing extremely *high probability* of its occurrence. A moon hoax conspiracy is also *highly implausible* because it would have to involve thousands of NASA collaborators, none of whom has ever blown the whistle in more than four decades. If Soviet scientists who were monitoring the Apollo moon flights had discovered any credible evidence of fakery, they surely would have announced it to the world. The Soviet Union was our Cold War nemesis and was racing us to the moon. Thus, the moon hoax conspiracy does not even pass the plausibility test.

If you engage in a debate with those who deny the moon landings, or other equally discredited claims such as Holocaust denial, that is your choice, and you may just be exercising your intellectual muscles for fun. Remember, though, that all claims are not created equal, and being open-minded does not mean giving an equal hearing to speakers espousing false claims that have already been demolished by careful reasoning and abundant evidence. Be open-minded by following where the evidence leads you, both as a speaker and as a listener. This requires *self-correction of erroneous beliefs* (Hare, 2009; Shermer, 2013). Self-correction should be embraced, not resisted. Defending a belief you know to be untrue before an audience inclined to embrace the error raises an ethical red flag. It is pandering. Ethical public speaking requires honesty (see Chapter 1), and honesty demands self-correction of mistaken ideas. Skepticism mandates tough choices and the courage to correct error.

SUMMARY

Skepticism is a process of inquiry whereby claims are evaluated by engaging in a rigorous examination of the evidence and reasoning used to support those claims. Skeptics seek to present plausible arguments that are also highly probable based on substantial, high-quality evidence. They recognize that those making claims have the burden of proof. They must engage in self-correction when beliefs are contradicted by compelling logic and evidence. Possibility or surface plausibility, however, is sufficient for true believers to accept claims. True believers engage in confirmation bias, rationalization of disconfirmation, and shifting the burden of proof inappropriately to skeptics. As a practical public speaker, it is your responsibility to embrace skepticism in both the preparation and presentation of your speeches. The practical public speaker strives to do much more than simply speak fluently and present points with impact. You want to communicate substantial, well-supported ideas. Skepticism should guide your search and construction of these substantial ideas.

10

Argument, Reasoning, and Evidence

You live in a world of claims. Hyper-caffeinated pitchmeisters on infomercials proclaim the wonders of cordless vacuums with the sucking power of a tick. Products are advertised as medical breakthroughs, yet suspiciously, these break-throughs are announced on TV instead of in professional medical journals. Weight-loss diets and pills promising a thin body without effort emerge almost daily. Hard-to-believe, get-rich-quick real estate programs and business schemes are exuberantly promoted. You are asked to purchase the latest electronic marvel because it is faster, cheaper, or has more options. Competing political candidates slander each other with negative ads. What is a person to believe? That is where skepticism serves you well.

In the previous chapter, differences between true believers and skeptics were identified. The justification for carefully reasoned and well supported claims was carefully developed. This chapter expands on the practical ways you can implement skepticism as a public speaker or as someone listening to those who give speeches. This is skepticism in action. Thus, *the purpose of this chapter is to explain ways to distinguish degrees of strength or weakness in reasoning and evidence used to support claims.* This chapter discusses the structure of an argument and the criteria for determining fact from fallacy in reasoning and evidence.

AN ARGUMENT: STAKING YOUR CLAIM

Remember that skepticism is the process of inquiry that scrutinizes arguments based on reasoning and evidence. Aristotle used the term *logos* when referring to persuasive appeals that rest on reasoning and arguments. An **argument** "implicitly or explicitly presents a claim and provides support for that claim with reasoning and evidence" (Verlinden, 2005, p. 5). **Reasoning** is the thought process of drawing conclusions from evidence. **Evidence** consists of statistics, testimony of experts and credible sources, and verifiable facts. Developing a sound argument begins with understanding how reasoning and evidence mesh logically.

Syllogism: Formal Logic

In formal logic, the basic structure of an argument is called a **syllogism**. A syllogism contains three parts: a major premise, a minor premise, and a conclusion. A standard example of a categorical syllogism is

> Major premise: All humans are mortal.
> Minor premise: Bridgett is human.
> Conclusion: Bridgett is mortal.

Not all categorical syllogisms make sense. Consider this bumper sticker syllogism:

> Major premise: Nobody's perfect.
> Minor premise: I'm nobody.
> Conclusion: I'm perfect.

It almost seems logical. The meaning of terms used twice in a syllogism, however, must be identical. Here "nobody" in the major premise means "no one at all," but in the minor premise it means "a person of no consequence." The syllogism should actually be written this way to see its illogic clearly:

> Major premise: All people are imperfect.
> Minor premise: I'm a person of no consequence.
> Conclusion: I'm perfect.

In the formal logic of categorical syllogisms, you can reach certainty because premises are stated categorically, and conclusions logically follow from those absolutes. Consider this example:

> Major premise: All individuals who kill another human being deliberately and with malice aforethought are guilty of first-degree murder.

Minor premise: Tom Higgins killed Alfonso Carbonati deliberately and with malice aforethought.

Conclusion: Tom Higgins is guilty of first degree murder.

As discussed in the previous chapter, however, human decision making and problem solving navigate in a sea of varying uncertainty. High probability, not certainty, should be your goal. In the above example, a jury must determine that Tom Higgins is guilty of first degree murder "beyond a reasonable doubt" but not with certainty. Thus, informal logic described by British philosopher Stephen Toulmin more aptly depicts how people usually conduct argumentation and decision making based on probabilities (Freeley & Steinberg, 2013; Verlinden, 2005).

Toulmin Structure of Argument: Informal Logic

Toulmin's (1958) description of informal logic identifies and explains the six elements of an argument:

1. *Claim*—That which is asserted and requires support.
2. *Grounds* (Reasons/Evidence)—Reasons to accept a claim and the evidence used to support those reasons. Reasons justify the claim, and evidence provides firm ground for these reasons.
3. *Warrant*—The reasoning that links the grounds to the claim. It is usually implied, not stated explicitly.
4. *Backing*—The reasons and relevant evidence that support the warrant.
5. *Rebuttal*—Exceptions or refutation that diminish the force of the claim.
6. *Qualifier*—Degree of truth to the claim (possible, plausible, probable, highly probable).

Everyday reasoning follows this pattern known as the Toulmin structure of argument. For example, suppose you are a guy who wants to date a supermodel. Your train of reasoning might proceed as follows:

Claim: I can date supermodel Jasmine.

Grounds: I am a brainy, average looking, very nice, sensitive guy with an average income. (*At this point, the logical question that should pop into the mind of a skeptic is: "Why would someone so described have any chance of dating a supermodel?" Thus, your warrant must supply that logical connection.*)

Warrant: She dates brainy, average looking, very nice, sensitive guys with average incomes so she will date me. (*Next question worth asking is: "What evidence do you have that this stated warrant is true?"*)

Backing: The last three guys she dated were brainy. Two of them had college degrees, and one had a Ph.D. All three were average looking according to five girls I asked at random. All three had very average incomes and drove 3- or 4-year-old sedans. I read interviews with Jasmine in which she said that all of these guys were very nice, sensitive, caring human beings, and that was attractive to her.

Rebuttal: She is a supermodel who could date almost any guy she wanted. I am a stranger to her. I do not know anyone who is friends with her who could introduce me. She has a bodyguard who could rearrange my internal organs if I tried to approach her. I cannot just call her. She might think I am a stalker. (*Now you must weigh the pros* [*grounds, warrant, and backing*] *and cons* [*rebuttal*] *and judge the strength of the claim by providing a qualifier.*)

Qualifier: Jasmine would *possibly* accept a date—when pigs can fly and taxes are abolished.

From this example you can see how each element of the Toulmin model illustrates a train of reasoning relevant to an overall claim that is advocated by a speaker. (For an additional example of the Toulmin structure of an argument, see Figure 10.1.)

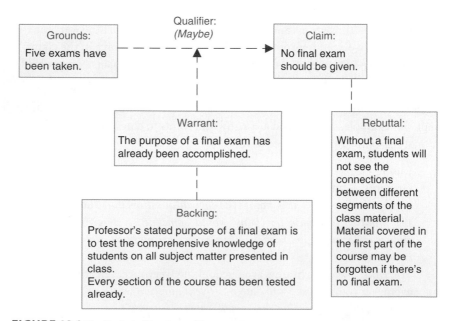

FIGURE 10.1 The Toulmin Structure of Argument

Notice that the connections between each element of an argument must make logical sense. Consider the following argument:

Claim: Bob should get a better grade than Scott.
Grounds: Bob studied harder than Scott.
Warrant: Students who study harder get better grades.

Note that using either of the last two statements as the claim is not reasonable. "Bob studied harder than Scott" is not supported by either of the other two statements. Where is the evidence of studying harder? Likewise, "Students who study harder get better grades" is also unsupported by either of the other two statements. "Bob studied harder than Scott" does not indicate that he actually got a better grade.

CRITERIA FOR REASONING AND EVIDENCE: IS IT FACT OR FALLACY?

The Toulmin structure of an argument blends well with the skepticism perspective. For a skeptic, the more probable the claim, the more valuable it is as a basis for decision making, provided that the speaker making the claim meets his or her burden of proof. You determine whether the burden of proof has been met by evaluating the reasoning (warrants) and the evidence (grounds; backing) supporting the claim. Then you assign a qualifier to the claim based on how well the burden of proof has been met. Any fallacies diminish the warrant for the claim.

The term fallacy is derived from the Latin *fallere* which means *to deceive*. A **fallacy** is any error in reasoning and evidence that may deceive your audience. This section explains the three principal criteria for evaluating evidence and reasoning: credibility, relevance, and sufficiency. Fallacies that commonly occur when these criteria are poorly met are discussed.

Credibility: Should We Believe You?

The **credibility** of evidence refers to its believability as determined by consistency and accuracy. *Consistency* means that what a source of information says and does are in agreement. A source of information should not be quoted as support for claims if that source says one thing but does another or has not been truthful in the past. *Accuracy* means that the evidence has no error; it is free of fallacies. If cited "facts" prove to be inaccurate, the credibility of the source of those inaccuracies should suffer. Quoting the Centers for Disease Control on the likelihood of a serious outbreak of the West Nile virus or the flu is credible because the CDC is both consistent and accurate. The CDC is consistently objective, relying on scientific studies to support claims about diseases. The CDC also provides highly accurate information. It is an internationally recognized authority often called upon to investigate outbreaks of diseases worldwide.

Evidence used to support claims is often not credible, however. Several fallacies discussed next significantly diminish the credibility of evidence presented and therefore do not warrant the claim based on the evidence. As a speaker, you want to build a speech with strong reasoning and evidence, not weaken it by using fallacious reasoning and evidence.

Questionable Statistic: Does It Make Sense? When giving a speech, you will likely include statistics while attempting to inform or persuade your audience. Be careful, however, that the statistics you use to support your claims make sense. Do not fall victim to confirmation bias by grabbing the first statistic that supports your claim without analyzing its credibility. Dr. Edgar Suter (1994), for example, who ironically was the chair of the Doctors for Integrity in Research and Public Policy, opposed gun control by claiming: "The overwhelming predominance of data we have examined shows that between 25 and 75 lives may be saved by a gun, for every life lost to a gun." This claim has been repeated by other sources (Elder, 2000; Faria, 2002) and appears recently on many pro-gun blogging sites. There have been more than *1 million gun deaths* in America in the 40 years prior to 2012 (Weir, 2012). If Suter's claim is correct, then as many as *75 million Americans* would have died in the same 40-year period if guns had not been available to Americans to protect themselves (1 million × 75). This is almost *60 times more deaths* than the total American lives lost in combat in *all the wars in U.S. history* ("Numbers of Americans Killed," 2011). One can only wonder why Great Britain, with its strong gun control, had only a few *thousand* homicides during the same 40-year period ("United Kingdom," 2013). The skeptic must ask, "Does this statistic of Suter's make sense?" A reasonable argument supported by credible evidence can be made for opposing gun control in a speech (see Kates et al., 1994; Kleck, 2005). Suter's statistics, however, are implausible.

Then there is the claim asserted every year by the Academy of Motion Picture Arts and Sciences, and repeated in opening remarks by the hosts, as Seth MacFarland did for the 2013 Oscars, that a billion people worldwide watch the Academy Awards. It is highly likely that this statistic is pure nonsense. Consider just a few facts: only 40.3 million Americans saw the Oscars presented in February 2013, according to a Nielsen ratings survey (Collins, 2013); the Academy Awards are probably of greater interest to Americans than to other countries because most movies nominated for Oscars are American; the program is aired in English, which is not the language of most other countries; it is broadcast in most other countries on satellite or cable feeds which have very few subscribers; and there are typically only about 7 million viewers of the Oscars tracked in China—which has one-sixth of the world's total population (Radosh, 2005). The one billion viewers claim is almost certainly a preposterously inflated statistic.

This is an implausible statistic. Check snopes.com for an explanation. Even usually credible newspapers have repeated this bogus statistic.

Finally, consider one additional example to emphasize how widespread is the problem of questionable statistics and how often they go unchallenged. The headline "Shocking numbers behind cell phone usage" appears on hundreds of websites (see especially Tennant, 2012). The most shocking number was that "*200 trillion text messages* are received in America *every single day.*" Simple arithmetic shows that for this to be true, every person (including infants) in the United States (315 million) would receive, on average, *634,920* text messages *each day* or more than *440* messages *each minute* of each day. The statistic is wildly implausible.

Biased Source: Grinding an Ax   Special interest groups or individuals who stand to gain money, prestige, power, or influence if they advocate a certain position on an issue are biased sources of information. Do not quote them in your speeches because they lack credibility (Reynolds & Reynolds, 2002). *Look for a source to bolster your claims that has no personal stake in the outcome, a source that seeks the truth, not personal glory or benefit.*

Websites are often biased. For example, any website providing nutritional information while pushing vitamins, minerals, and other "health" products is biased (e.g., GNC, Vitacost, Vitamin World, etc.). Although these sites may cite reputable sources for medical and health claims, they are unlikely to provide studies that debunk the value of certain supplements and products sold on the website. In contrast, WebMD, HealthCentral.com, and MayoClinic.com are three more neutral sites that do not push products, and they provide useful medical and health-related information.

In one of the more outlandish examples of a biased source, tobacco companies such as Philip Morris and R. J. Reynolds launched highly publicized *anti*-smoking campaigns that discouraged teenage smoking. As a skeptic, you have to wonder immediately why any tobacco companies would launch anti-smoking campaigns when they are in the business of selling cigarettes. The supposed anti-smoking campaigns proved to be little more than a public relations ploy to forestall restrictive anti-smoking legislation by seeming to be a responsible industry (Landman et al., 2002; Assunta & Chapman, 2004). The industry programs were not only found to be ineffective, but they also subtly encouraged smoking among teens by making it seem as though smoking is only for adults and therefore it marks a passage into adulthood (Landman et al., 2002; Wakefield et al., 2006).

Incomplete Source Citation: Something to Hide?   Every source used in your speech should be cited completely. "Studies show" or "research indicates" is woefully incomplete because you are not an expert interpreting the latest evidence in your area of expertise. Which studies and what specific research is being referenced? Student Anastasia Danilyuk (2011) made this mistake in an otherwise strong speech on "alternatives to imprisonment": "According to criminology, more than 70% of inmates return to prison" (p. 97). That is a critical statistic given only a very vague citation. A complete citation of the source of your information enhances your credibility and persuasiveness as a speaker if your source is qualified. *A complete citation includes, as a minimum*: (1) the name of the source, (2) the qualifications of the source if not obvious, (3) the specific publication or media citation where the evidence can be found, and (4) the relevant date of the publication.

Student Katie Donovan (2012) illustrates how to cite a source completely but concisely in her speech on supporting gay youth: "As Dan Savage, co-founder of the 'It Gets Better' campaign,' wrote in *The Stranger Magazine*, September 28th, 2011 . . ." The source is named, qualifications are provided, the place of publication is apparent, and the date is included. Note that merely citing "Dan Savage"

Vague references to "studies" and "research" are incomplete citations. What studies and whose research support the speakers' claims?

would be too vague a reference for listeners to discern the credibility of this source. (See Box 10.1 for additional examples of effective citation of various sources.)

Expert Quoted Out of Field: No Generic Experts Allowed   Quoting experts outside their field of expertise runs the substantial risk of promoting inaccurate claims supported by invalid and unreliable evidence. For example, Iben Browning, the chief scientist for Summa Medical Corporation, has a doctorate in physiology and a bachelor's degree in physics and math. He predicted a major earthquake for December 3 and 4, 1990, along the New Madrid Fault in the Midwest. Schools in several states dismissed students for these 2 days as a result of Browning's prediction. Browning had some scientific expertise, but not in the area of earthquake prediction. In fact, earthquake experts, with geotechnical engineering degrees and experience in seismology, denounced Browning's predictions because those who study earthquakes cannot accurately predict them (Roach, 2013). No earthquake, large or small, occurred on the dates Browning predicted, and no major earthquake on the New Madrid Fault has occurred in more than two decades since his prediction. The first sizable earthquake on the Madrid fault since Browning's prediction occurred on April 17, 2008, and it was considered "moderate" by quake experts, and caused little damage.

Consider a second example of citing a credible source outside of its field of expertise. Student Grant Anderson (2009), a finalist at the Interstate Oratorical Association national competition, cited the *Quarterly Journal of Speech* as his source for claiming "22,000 people donate blood every day" and that donors are

---

BOX 10.1 Oral Citation of Sources

Here are some examples from student speeches on how to cite a variety of sources concisely and effectively:

Website	"The Centers for Disease Control and Prevention website, last accessed April 4, 2012, reports ..."(Stephanie Stovall, 2012, p. 136).
Academic Journal	"[Law] Professor Robin Feldman explains in the *Stanford Technology Law Review* on January 23, 2012 that ..." (Katie Lese, 2012).
Television Program	"As CBS News detailed on January 9, 2010, the average person ..." (Jeremy Johnson, 2012, p. 174).
Magazine	"Before discussing solutions to what *Newsweek* of June 27, 2011 calls ..." (Holly Abers, 2012, p. 176).
Personal Interview	"As Roberta Sklar, the spokeswoman for the National Coalition for Anti-Violence programs states in a personal interview on February 16, 2011 ..." (David DePino, 2012, p. 45).
Newspaper	"*The New York Times* of July 26, 2011 explains ..." (Michael Kelley, 2012, p. 56).
Organization	"According to a 2011 Public Safety Performance Project conducted by the *Pew Research Center* ..." (Tunette Powell, 2012, p. 101).
Book	"As author John Nichols describes in his 2011 book *The Death and Life of American Journalism* ..." (Jenna Surprenant, 2012, p. 54).

---

asked potentially embarrassing questions (p. 32). *QJS* is a wonderful source for all sorts of things rhetorical, but it is not an authority on blood donation statistics and procedures. The American Red Cross would be a far better source on this topic. His citation is also incomplete because someone, not *QJS*, wrote the article that appeared in *QJS*.

Relevance: Does It Follow?

Evidence used to support claims must have relevance—it must relate directly to those claims, or the claims are unwarranted. A classic type of fallacy is called a **non sequitur**, which is Latin for "it does not follow." A conclusion that does not follow from its premises is a non sequitur fallacy. The non sequitur is a kind of general fallacy that encompasses many more specific fallacies in which claims do not follow (are unwarranted) from evidence and reasoning. Consider two common non sequiturs: ad hominem and ad populum fallacies.

Ad Hominem Fallacy: Diversionary Tactic   In December 2006, Rosie O'Donnell, apparently irked that business tycoon and beauty pageant sponsor Donald Trump allowed Miss USA Tara Conner to keep her beauty crown despite revelations of underage drinking and drug use, attacked Trump. She noted, "Left his first wife, had an affair, left the second wife, had an affair. Had kids both times, but he's the moral compass for 20-year-olds in America." Later she called Trump a "snake-oil salesman," "a hot bag of wind with bad hair," and a "pimp," and she made fun of his "comb-over" hairdo. Trump fired back by calling O'Donnell "a loser," "a degenerate," "a fat slob," "ugly," a "mental midget," and "a stumbling buffoon" ("Donald and Rosie," 2007; "Donald Trump Tells FNC," 2006; "Trump vs. Rosie," 2006). These are ad hominem (Latin meaning "to the person") attacks. They are personal assaults, but are they ad hominem fallacies?

The **ad hominem fallacy** is a personal attack on the messenger to avoid the message. It is a *diversionary tactic* that is irrelevant to the primary message. In the Rosie-versus-Donald kerfuffle, O'Donnell challenges Trump's "moral authority" to speak to young people about second chances. Trump's response is pure vitriol. He is using diversion, not a reasonable or relevant response to her initial claim. In effect, Trump is making the irrelevant argument, "Your allegation is weak because you're a fat, ugly slob." O'Donnell, on the other hand, diminished the validity of her main claim that Trump has no credibility as a "moral compass" by mixing in irrelevant personal attacks. Both parties, then, were guilty of the ad hominem fallacy.

Not all personal attacks are ad hominem fallacies. If a claim raises the issue of a person's credibility, character, or trustworthiness, the attack is not irrelevant to the claim being made. Criticisms that led to the impeachment and removal from office of Illinois governor Rod Blagojevich in 2009 for trying to "sell" to the highest bidder Barack Obama's vacant U.S. Senate seat when Obama became president involved legitimate questions about Blagojevich's character and credibility. The Illinois state senate apparently felt the charges were credible and relevant; it voted 59-0 to remove Blagojevich from office. On December 7, 2011, Blagojevich, following a high-profile trial, was sentenced to 14 years in prison for corruption.

Ad Populum Fallacy: Arguing from Public Opinion   A national survey conducted by a research team at UCLA found that 63% of almost 220,000 first-year college students agreed that "only volunteers should serve in the armed forces"

("This Year's Freshmen at Four-Year Colleges," 2010). Advocating that the U.S. army remain all volunteer because a majority of first-year college students felt this way is an example of the **ad populum fallacy**—basing a claim on popular opinion. Whether the military remains voluntary or becomes mandatory should not be decided just on the basis of popular opinion at some moment, even the opinion of the most affected group. Popular opinion, be it the majority or a vocal minority, can be fickle and unsound. Student Kate Ryland (2012) notes this very point in her speech on vaccine exemptions: "Twenty-one states now allow exemptions from school-required vaccinations due to 'philosophical reasons,' which just puts all of the children in danger" (p. 59).

Although popular opinion may reflect good policy and solid decision making, it can also ignore or be ignorant of the best reasoning and evidence. Majority opinion also can be shamefully wrong. At one time in our history, majorities favored slavery and segregation for African Americans in restaurants, schools, housing, and public transportation; they opposed voting rights for women and minorities as well as women serving on juries or owning property or receiving credit cards in their own names. Speech claims should be weighed on the basis of valid reasoning and substantial high-quality evidence, not merely on the whim of the majority or a vocal minority.

PHOTO 10.1 The ad populum fallacy occurs when a person argues from popular opinion not reasoning and evidence. Even an enormous crowd supporting a claim does not improve the credibility of the claim. Ever see a mob do something stupid?

Sufficiency: Got Enough?

As explained in Chapter 9, the person who makes a claim has the burden to prove that claim. This means that sufficient evidence and reasoning must be used to support a claim you make. Insufficient evidence in a court trial, for example, warrants a "not guilty" verdict for the defendant or dismissal of the charges. Sufficiency requires judgment. There is no precise formula for determining sufficiency. Generally, strong, plentiful evidence and solid reasoning meet the sufficiency criterion. Almost three decades ago 40,000 studies had already been conducted that showed cigarettes are a serious health hazard ("Advertising Is Hazardous," 1986). Thousands more have since been added to the list. Now that is sufficient proof. Several fallacies, however, clearly exhibit insufficiency.

Self-Selected Sample: Partisan Power   To achieve sufficiency, any poll or survey must use a random sample. A **random sample** is a portion of the target *population,* the entire set of individuals of interest, chosen in such a manner that every member of the entire population has an equal chance of being selected. Any poll or survey that depends on respondents selecting themselves to participate provides results that are insufficient to generalize beyond the sample. This **self-selected sample** attracts the most committed, aroused, or motivated individuals to fill out surveys on their own and answer polling questions. Printing a survey in a magazine and collecting those that have been returned is an example of a self-selected sample. Calling an 800-number to answer questions about politics or social issues is another example.

Results of surveys and polls conducted with a self-selected sample and a random sample can be vastly different. For example, on January 19, 2007, an MSNBC online poll that asked whether George W. Bush should be impeached as president showed startling results. Using a self-selected sample of 390,122 respondents, the poll showed: 87% for impeachment and the rest opposed it or were not sure ("Politics," 2007). Surveys conducted at about the same time using random samples showed a deeply divided country on the impeachment question, but most showed only a strong minority favored impeachment. The Daily Kos, a liberal blogging site, posted results of an online survey it conducted for the 2012 presidential election. Results showed that 4,268 respondents (94%) supported Barack Obama for president and a mere 99 respondents supported Mitt Romney (2%) ("Poll," 2012). Actual results of the election were far closer to say the least: Obama received 51% and Romney received 47% of the total vote (Wasserman, 2013).

Why the difference? Online political surveys attract partisan respondents. In fact, some political groups have purposely organized campaigns to rig the results by flooding online surveys with partisan voters. In 2004, the American Family

Association, a conservative organization that supports a constitutional amendment banning gay marriage, posted an online survey on gay marriage for its followers. The organization hoped to use anticipated strong opposition to gay marriage to bolster its case with Congress for a constitutional ban. Gay activist groups, however, encouraged their constituents to flood the online survey with a massive vote supporting gay marriage. The result was that 60% of more than half a million respondents favored "legalization of homosexual marriage" and another 8% favored civil unions for gays.

Surveys using self-selected samples are insufficient to support general claims, not because the sample size is inadequate, but because it represents only a narrow, biased population. Self-selected samples often involve huge numbers of respondents. Increasing the number of respondents does not improve the results, unless you survey everyone in the population, because the sample comes from the most motivated, committed individuals. The indifferent or non-partisan, which may be a majority, are less likely to participate in the survey or poll.

Inadequate Sample: Large Margin of Error   Almost every day you read in the newspaper or hear on radio or television about some new study that "proves" coffee is dangerous, certain pesticides sprayed on vegetables are harmful, power lines cause cancer, or massive doses of vitamin C prevent colds. A consistent problem in this regard is the propensity of the mass media to sensationalize each new study that gets published. *A single study, however, proves very little and is insufficient to draw any general conclusion.* In science, studies are replicated before results are given credence because mistakes can be made that may distort the results. The greater the number of carefully controlled studies that show similar or identical results, the more sufficient is the proof.

So what is an adequate sample size for a survey? In general, the **margin of error**—a measure of the degree of sampling error accounted for by imperfections in sample selection—goes up as the number of people surveyed goes down. Margin of error applies only to random samples, not self-selected samples that are inherently biased. An adequate sample size will have a margin of error no greater than plus or minus 3–4%. A poll of 1,000 people randomly selected typically has a margin of error of about plus or minus 3%. This means that if the poll says that 65% of respondents approve of the job the president is doing, the actual result, if every adult American were surveyed, would be between 62% and 68%. No poll is without some margin of error. It is usually impractically expensive and time consuming to survey every person in a population, but increasing the sample size improves the chances that the poll is accurate if the sample is random, not self-selected.

Hasty Generalization: Arguing from Example   Television producer Gary David Goldberg once sardonically observed, "Left to their own devices, the networks would televise live executions. Except Fox—they'd televise live naked executions" ("TV or not TV," 1993, p. 5E). The graphic, gruesome, and grand event can galvanize our attention. When an outrageous, shocking, controversial, and dramatic event distorts our perceptions of the facts, this is called the **vividness effect** (Glassner, 1999). The vividness effect can fallaciously distort your perception of events because the shocking example can negate a mountain of contradictory evidence (Sunstein & Zeckhauser, 2009). For example, a single airline disaster can provoke fear of boarding a jetliner and induce many people to choose driving their automobile instead. Yet the odds of perishing in a plane crash are 1 in 11 *million*, whereas the odds of dying in a car crash in the United States are 1 in 5 *thousand* (Ropeik, 2008).

When individuals jump to a conclusion based on a single or a handful of examples, especially vivid ones, they have made a **hasty generalization** (Govier, 2010). How many times have you avoided a class based solely on the claim of another student that the professor was "incredibly boring" or "sexist" or "terribly unfair"? Perhaps the student told a startling tale of poor behavior from the teacher. You might reply, "Wow! I hadn't heard that. Thanks. I'll make sure not to take his class." A sample of one is hardly conclusive evidence to warrant such choices, yet such choices are made. If you seek out other students' opinions of the same professor, many may actually have very positive things to say, completely countering the single student with the negative opinion. There are exceptions,

PHOTO 10.2 The vividness effect is illustrated by a dramatic event. The crash of Asiana Flight 214 at the San Francisco International Airport on July 6, 2013 is such an event.

however, in which you may need to take seriously a vivid tale, even if told by only one person. If you hear that someone is dangerous and potentially violent, even if it proves to be erroneous, it deserves to be considered seriously until proven wrong. In general, however, avoid hasty generalizations, especially those based on vivid examples.

Correlation Mistaken for Causation: X Does Not Necessarily Cause Y Humans are intensely interested in discovering causes of events that remain unexplained. For example, why do some people live to be a hundred years old, and others die at a much younger age? Scientists, journalists, and health seekers have visited Vilcabamba, Ecuador, for a half-century to discover the causes of their unusual longevity. Manuel Picoita, 102 years old, thinks getting along with his neighbors is the cause of his reaching centenarian status. "There is tranquility and solidarity among us" (Kraul, 2006, p. 16A). Josefa Ocampa, 104, believes the secret to her long life is that each morning she drinks a glass of goat's milk with a bit of her own urine added. Aurora Maza, a mere 96, attributes her longevity to working in the fields all her life. Legendary comedian George Burns was fond of arguing that he made it to 100 years old because he smoked a cigar and drank martinis every day. Henry Allingham, who died as the world's oldest man at 113 on July 18, 2009, attributed his long life to "cigarettes, whiskey, and wild, wild women" (quoted in Kirka, 2009, p. B8). Pinning down exact causes of phenomena can often be illusive.

Everyone is prone to draw causation (*x* causes *y*) from mere correlation (*x* occurs and *y* also occurs either sequentially or simultaneously). "The invalid assumption that correlation implies cause is probably among the two or three most serious and common errors of human reasoning" (Gould, 1981, p. 242). A **correlation** is a consistent relationship between two variables. A **variable** is anything that can change. Finding a strong correlation between two variables does not prove causation. A large research team explored variables that might determine causes of contraceptive use in Taiwan (Li, 1975). The team found that the number of electric appliances (ovens, irons, toasters) found in the home correlated most strongly with birth control use. As the number of appliances increased, use of contraceptives also increased. So, based on this study, do you think distributing free toasters would likely reduce teen pregnancies? Most likely, this correlation merely reflects socioeconomic status that is also strongly correlated with contraceptive use and is a better candidate for causation.

Correlations suggest *possible* causation, but correlations alone are insufficient reasons to claim *probable* causation (Sherman, 2009; Silver, 2012). "The vast majority of correlations in our world are, without doubt, noncausal" (Gould, 1981, p. 242). For example, kids with big feet are better readers than those with small feet. Why? Is it because big feet cause reading proficiency? Not likely.

Children with big feet are usually older, and older children have had more experience reading.

Even a perfect correlation does not mean there is causation. For instance, what if you surveyed 100 college students and found that none of the 55 who regularly eat breakfast dumped their girlfriend or boyfriend in the past 2 years, but all of the 45 students who regularly skip breakfast did? Here is a perfect correlation—no exceptions. Eat breakfast—keep your girlfriend/boyfriend; avoid breakfast—dump your girlfriend/ boyfriend. Would you assert in a speech that this perfect correlation was sufficient proof that skipping breakfast causes a person to dump his or her girlfriend or boyfriend? Only a cereal manufacturer might try this to boost sales.

False Analogy: Mixing Apples and Oranges   A claim based on an analogy alleges that two things closely resemble each other. Thus, both things should be viewed in similar ways. Historically, marriage recognized by the state exempted husbands from any criminal charge of rape against their wives, even if sex was obtained by force. These laws began to change in the United States in 1975, primarily based on analogical reasoning. Those who supported marital rape laws argued: Is there any essential difference between rape by a stranger and rape by a spouse? Both acts involve non-consensual sexual penetration achieved by force and violence. This should be viewed as rape in either instance. The analogy was a good one, and marital rape laws have been passed in all 50 states.

False analogies occur when a significant point or points of difference exist despite some superficial similarities between the two things being compared (Govier, 2010). Both George W. Bush and Barack Obama have been characterized by opponents in numerous fiery speeches as the new Hitler. Protesters have prominently displayed posters showing each with Hitlerian mustaches and swastikas. "If you hate Hitler, you should hate this guy because they are so similar" goes the strained analogy. Whether referring to measures taken to fight

PHOTOS 10.3 & 10.4 Comparing George W. Bush and Barack Obama to Hitler is a false analogy. Avoid making foolish and indefensible comparisons.

terrorism (Bush) or the health care legislation passed in 2009 (Obama), analogies to "Gestapo tactics" and "big government" enforced by the "jack-booted Nazis" are false analogies. The comparison in both cases boggles the mind of any reasonable person. Hitler was a mass murderer of unparalleled infamy. He systematically exterminated whole populations and instituted a worldwide reign of terror. In what universe of perverse thinking, regardless of political leanings, do either Bush or Obama compare to this madman? Disagree passionately with their policies, or the policies of any other person you dislike, even warn of potential dangers in their ideologies and practices when speaking to audiences, but do not accept or use the analogy to Hitler. Former *Newsweek* editor Jon Meacham (2009) said it well, "We are in danger of turning evil itself into a triviality when we draw on the images of Hitler's Germany to make political points in debates that are in no way comparable to the terrors of Nazism" (p. 9). The analogy to Hitler is grossly misapplied in speech after speech and is false because the dissimilarities are enormous.

This concludes the discussion of specific fallacies. Only the most common fallacies among the hundreds that could be identified have been examined. These examples should serve you well, however, in constructing speeches and discussing and debating controversial issues.

SUMMARY

The previous chapter laid out the fundamental justification for skepticism, for why you need to think critically as a public speaker and listener and how to do it generally. This chapter specifically illustrates skepticism in action. The formal logic of syllogisms is not as applicable to constructing speeches as Toulmin's structure of arguments model. The six elements of the model—claim, grounds, warrant, backing, rebuttal, and qualifier—can be applied to a single argument or to an entire debate on an issue. Understanding the connections between each element clarifies the importance of reasoning and evidence to the validity and probability of a claim. There are three main criteria for evaluating reasoning and evidence: credibility, relevance, and sufficiency. Fallacies, those errors in reasoning and evidence, suffer from lack of credibility, irrelevance, or insufficiency.

11

Presenting Supporting Materials

Faux conservative Stephen Colbert, a self-described "well-intentioned, poorly informed, high-class idiot," (quoted in Solomon, 2005) pretends to be contemptuous of facts while favoring "truthiness," that is, asserting what one wishes were true even though it is not. As Colbert amusingly noted on his Comedy Central show "The Colbert Report," "I'm not a fan of facts. You see, facts can change, but my opinion will never change, no matter what the facts are" (quoted by Peyser, 2006). Unlike satirist Colbert's fake character, one of your chief concerns should be the facts and the supporting materials that bolster your facts.

Without supporting materials, you would have the mere shell of a speech, empty and insubstantial. **Supporting materials** are the examples, statistics, and testimony used to bolster a speaker's viewpoint. Chapter 10 explained the fallacious use of examples, statistics, and testimony. Remember, *criteria for evaluating supporting materials are credibility, relevance, and sufficiency.* Avoiding fallacies, however, does not necessarily mean that you have used supporting materials effectively. You can provide a fallacy-free list of numerous statistics during a speech and still come off as a crashing bore. Recite a lengthy quotation from a government document and watch your classmates' heads snap backward as they slip into unconsciousness.

The purpose of this chapter is to explain ways to present supporting materials effectively. Types of supporting materials and their effective use are discussed. Using supporting materials is an audience-centered process. The three primary questions your listeners are likely to ask and you need to answer during your speech are: "What do you mean?" "How do you know?" and "Why should we care?" Thus, supporting materials accomplish four specific goals: to clarify points, to support claims, to gain interest, and to create impact.

USING EXAMPLES COMPETENTLY

Examples are specific instances of a general category of objects, ideas, people, places, actions, experiences, or phenomena. The principle purposes of examples are to improve understanding and to support points made in your speeches. This section discusses the types of examples used in speeches and how to use them appropriately and effectively.

Types of Examples: Specific Illustrations

The well-chosen example makes your speech memorable and it may have a great impact on listeners (Baesler & Burgoon, 1994). There are four main types of examples: hypothetical, real, brief, and extended.

Hypothetical Examples: It Could Happen   A **hypothetical example** describes an imaginary situation, one that is concocted to make a point, illustrate an idea, or identify a general principle. Hypothetical examples help listeners envision what a situation might be like. They tap into similar experiences listeners have had without having to cite actual occurrences or historical events that may not be readily available. *As long as the hypothetical example is consistent with known facts, it will be believable.* For example:

> Imagine that you are at work. Suddenly the air is filled with ammonia fumes, chemical acetate, hydrogen sulfide, methane gas, hydrogen cyanide, nitric oxide, formaldehyde, and dozens of other substances that are irritants, poisons, or carcinogens. Would you shrug your shoulders and endure these potentially lethal toxins produced by cigarette smoke? Would you support "smokers' rights" to pollute your air? Although laws have been passed across the United States banning smoking in the workplace, the one workplace where employees typically cannot escape the hazardous risks of second-hand smoke is the local pub. Congress must ban smoking in all bars and taverns.

Here the impact on listeners is persuasive. The hypothetical example seeks to change listeners' attitudes about smoking in bars and taverns. The example is based on known facts.

A hypothetical example can also help an audience visualize what might occur. Imagine what it would be like to experience a hurricane, tornado, or tsunami. In what ways would your life be changed if you suddenly lost your job, were laid up in a hospital for 3 months, or became permanently disabled? These hypothetical examples help listeners picture what might happen and motivate them to take action that might prevent such occurrences. When a real example is not available, a hypothetical one can be a useful substitute.

Real Examples: It Did Happen   Actual occurrences are **real examples**. A chief benefit of using a real example is that it cannot be easily discounted by listeners as simply "made up" or that it "won't occur." Unlike hypothetical examples, real examples can sometimes profoundly move an audience. For example, during the tumultuous protests in Iran following the disputed presidential election in June 2009, 26-year-old Neda Agha-Soltan stepped from her car to get fresh air while caught for an hour in traffic clogged by mass protests. Within seconds she was shot in the chest by a suspected government sniper ("Who Was Neda?" 2009). Caught on a video cell phone by a bystander, her agonizing death almost instantly became a rallying cry for the anti-government protesters in the streets. The video was posted on YouTube and was seen by millions around the world. Protesters brandished copies of a picture showing her last moment of life. Mehdi Karroubi, an opposition leader and presidential candidate, called Neda a martyr. "A young girl, who did not have a weapon in her soft hands, or a grenade in her pocket, became a victim of thugs who are supported by a horrifying intelligence apparatus," he wrote (quoted by Fathi, 2009). Neda Agha-Soltan became a symbol of the Iranian uprising.

PHOTO 11.1 Protests erupted around the world when Neda Agha-Soltan was shot and killed during the Iranian uprising in 2009. This one occurred in Tokyo. Real examples can be quite powerful.

Real examples have an immediacy and a genuineness that hypothetical examples typically lack. Just picture the different response you would have to "I could become an alcoholic and so could you" and a speaker saying, "I am an alcoholic, and if it happened to me it could happen to you." Real examples have more credibility than hypothetical examples.

Brief Examples: Short and to the Point   Sometimes you can make a point quickly with a **brief example** or two: "The best examples of suspension bridges in the United States are the Golden Gate Bridge and the Brooklyn Bridge." Brief examples can quickly combine comedy and a serious point. Consider this brief example of Chris Rock exhibiting this very point: "Gun control? We need bullet control! I think every bullet should cost $5,000 dollars. Because if a bullet cost $5,000, we wouldn't have any innocent bystanders." Ellen Degeneres likewise intersects comedy with a serious point in this brief example: "I ask people why they have deer heads on their walls. They always say because it's such a beautiful animal. There you go. I think my mother is attractive, but I have photographs of her." With short attention spans and information overload, brief examples work well to maintain your audience's interest.

Extended Examples: Telling a Story   Sometimes a story is so profound and so moving that only a detailed, **extended example**, can do it justice. Consider this extended, real example:

> Genie was 13 years old when she was discovered in a suburb of Los Angeles in 1970. From the time she was 20 months old, Genie had been imprisoned in a bare room with the curtains drawn. She was strapped naked to a potty chair and sometimes tied in a makeshift straitjacket by her abusive father. Genie had minimal human contact. If she made noise, her father did not speak to her but literally barked or growled, or beat her with a stick. Genie's mother, almost blind and fearing her husband's brutality, left Genie isolated and deprived.
>
> When Genie was discovered, she could not walk, talk, stand erect, chew solid food, or control her bodily functions. She was about four-and-a-half feet tall and weighed about 60 pounds. Despite years of intensive training, Genie never lost her unnatural voice quality, and she never learned to master language. Her very ability to communicate with other humans was forever impaired. *(See Rymer, 1993)*

A briefer version of this touching, tragic story could be told, but which details would you delete and with what effect? A story's length must fit the time constraints for your speech, but for full impact a story sometimes must have at least minimal elaboration.

HOW to Use Examples: Choose Carefully

Using examples effectively requires skill. The well-chosen example can make a speech come alive. Here are some basic tips.

Use Relevant Examples: Stay on Point　Examples must be relevant to the point you make. A young Abraham Lincoln, acting as a defense attorney in a courtroom trial, explained what "self-defense" meant by using a relevant story to clarify his point. He told the jury about a man who, while walking down a country road with pitchfork in hand, was attacked by a vicious dog. The man was forced to kill the dog with his pitchfork. A local farmer who owned the dog asked the man why he had to kill his dog. The man replied, "What made him try to bite me?" The farmer persisted, "But why didn't you go at him with the other end of the pitchfork?" The man responded, "Why didn't he come at me with the other end of the dog?" (cited in Larson, 2012). Lincoln made his point that the degree of allowable force is dependent on the degree of force used by the attacker.

Choose Vivid Examples: Create Images　Examples usually work best when they are vivid. A vivid example triggers feelings and provokes strong images (Pratkanis & Aronson, 2001). Student Kittie Grace (2000) uses a vivid example to evoke a strong image on her main theme that hotels in America are unsanitary:

> According to the August 8, 1999 *Hotel and Motel Management Journal* or
> *HMMJ*, in Atlantic City, New Jersey, two unsuspecting German tourists
> shared a motel room which had been cleaned that morning, but a foul smell
> permeated through the room. After the third complaint, housekeeping
> cleaned under the bed finding the body of a dead man decomposing, all
> because housekeeping failed to clean under the bed in the first place.
> *(Grace, 2000, p. 86)*

This example is so vivid that it quite likely will come to mind the next time you stay at a hotel.

Use Representative Examples: Reflect What Is Accurate　Examples should be representative. Was the example of the dead body under the hotel bed representative? Kittie Grace presented voluminous evidence that significant numbers of people are getting sick and dying from unsanitary conditions in hotels in the United States because of negligent housekeeping. The example of the dead body graphically represents just how negligent the housekeeping can be. She does not claim that dead bodies will be found under hotel beds on a regular basis, or even imply such. Nevertheless, its representativeness can be called into question. Most of us do not discover dead bodies under hotel beds in our entire lifetime. For this we can be thankful.

Vivid examples can influence an audience far beyond their legitimacy as proof (Glassner, 1999). In the previous chapter, this was termed the *vividness effect*. When vivid examples are unrepresentative, they have the power to distort the truth. Make sure that any vivid examples you use in your speeches are truly representative. Almost any example that related the desperate plight of victims in the hurricane Sandy disaster in 2012, for instance, was representative because the devastation was so widespread and caused an unprecedented upheaval along the eastern portion of the United States. It would be difficult to find someone in that part of the country who was not personally impacted by this major weather event.

Stack Examples: When One Is Not Enough Sometimes a single example does not suffice to make a point clear, memorable, interesting, or adequately supported. Note the value of using plentiful examples stacked one on top of another in the following:

> Words are human creations. You have the power to invent new words. For example, in the late 1800s, male residents of Boonville, California, created a lingo of their own called Boontling, mostly to talk around women without them understanding what was being said. The rules for Boontling with its more than 1300 words are those of English. Those individuals who *harp Boont* (speak Boontling) concocted some colorful words. Examples include: *grey-matter kimmie* (college professor), *tongue-cuppy* (vomiting), *scotty* (heavy eater), *wheeler* (lie), *shoveltooth* (medical doctor), and *high-split* (very tall, slender man). Knowing just these few Boont words gives you the ability to translate this sentence: "The high-split, grey-matter kimmie told a wheeler to the local shoveltooth about his supposed tongue-cuppy experience resulting from being a scotty." There are still a few speakers of Boontling, but most have *piked to the dusties* (died).

In this instance, using only one or two examples of Boontling would not adequately clarify the main point, create much impact, support the claims, or spark much interest.

Choosing apt examples and using them competently can mean the difference between a mediocre or memorable speech. Never underestimate the importance of picking your examples for maximum clarity, accuracy, and impact.

USING STATISTICS COMPETENTLY

Statistics are measures of what is true or factual expressed in numbers. For example, the total outstanding student loan debt for college students in the United States surpassed $1 trillion by 2013, according to the Consumer Financial Protection

Bureau. This is a record amount of student debt (Driscoll, 2013). A college student has accumulated, on average, more than $26,000 of debt upon graduation, and this amount is rising rapidly ("Education," 2013).

Proficient speakers use statistics as a primary supporting material for a variety of reasons. Statistics can provide magnitude, frequency, and allow comparisons. For example, the first Internet website was *info.cern.ch*, created by Tim Berners-Lee in December 1990 ("How We Got," 2008). The number of websites (not Web pages) worldwide jumped to 24 million by 2000, and by March 2010 it exploded to more than 200 million sites ("March 2010 Web Server Survey," 2010). The magnitude of the Internet today and its astronomical growth in just two decades (comparison) is exhibited by these statistics. A well-chosen statistic can support claims, show trends, correct false assumptions, validate hypotheses, and contradict myths, perhaps not as dramatically and memorably as a vivid example, but often more validly and effectively (Lindsey & Yun, 2003).

In this section, specific types of statistics—mean, median, and mode—that do more than just quantify the magnitude or frequency of something are discussed. Ways to use statistics competently beyond just avoiding statistical fallacies are also explored.

Measures of Central Tendency: Determining What Is Typical

Statistics can tell us what is typical about a group, phenomenon, event, or population. When you are attempting to determine a **measure of central tendency**—how scores cluster so you can get a sense of what is typically occurring—you can use three main statistics. They are mean, median, and mode.

Mean: Your Average Statistic   The **mean** is commonly referred to as the arithmetic average, determined by adding the values of all items and dividing the sum

PHOTO 11.2 & 11.3 The mean (average) price of these two homes would be grossly misleading if claimed to be the typical price of homes.

by the total number of items. For example, grades are typically averaged to determine your final course grade. If your scores for the term on all speeches and exams are 97, 78, 95, 88, 78, 96, and 98, the total is 630. Your mean is 90% (630 divided by 7). A mean score is typically used to figure term grades because it usually gives a fairly accurate indication of your overall achievement. This is not always true, however. Suppose your grades for the term are 92, 91, 89, 88, and 35 (sometimes life intrudes in negative ways). Your total is 395 and your mean is 79%. Your one bad grade, perhaps the result of an illness, accident, or emotional event in your life, takes you from a low "A" (90%) to a high "C" (79%) for the class. In this case, using the mean is not entirely reflective of your achievement and effort in the class. Instructors faced with a skewed score such as this might use a different measure of central tendency, such as the median, to reflect more accurately your work and achievement.

Median: An in-the-Center Statistic   The statistical median is like the median on a freeway—it is the center divide. It is in the middle. The **median** is the middle score. If your term grades were the scores just discussed—92, 91, 89, 88, and 35, then the median would be 89. There are two scores above and two scores below, so it is right in the middle. This is more reflective of your typical work in the class than the mean score of 79. The median does not typically work well as a measure of central tendency for term grades unless there is one grade that is markedly different from other scores. Also, *when the mean does not reflect reality, such as the average family has 2.2 children, the median is more representative.* Since real estate prices can range drastically from extremely high to very low, using the mean as a measure for typical real estate prices in a particular area of the country is not very useful. This is why most real estate values are measured in median prices. An $8 million house selling at the same time as a dozen houses selling for $250,000 each yields a mean value of $846,000. This mean value hardly reflects what most houses typically cost in the area. The median would be $250,000, and so would the mode in this case.

Mode: Most Frequent Statistic   The **mode** is the most frequent score in the distribution of all scores. If your term grades are 91, 93, 75, 93, 75, 93, 82, your mode is 93 because it appears three times, more than any other score. Undoubtedly, you would prefer using the mode in this case. Your term grade would be higher than your mean score (mean = 86%). Nevertheless, your scores are somewhat inconsistent, and there are no very high or very low scores to skew the result, so the mean, not the mode, is a better measure. *The mode might be a better measure if you had mostly consistent scores with only a single very high or very low score,* such as the real estate values in the previous section. Ultimately, you want to choose the measure of central tendency—mean, mode, or median—that best reflects what is occurring with the least distortion.

How to Use Statistics: Beyond Numbing Numbers

Statistics do not have to be dull and mind numbing. In fact, research shows that they can be very persuasive when used properly (Allen & Preiss, 1997; Kazoleas, 1993). Here are a number of tips for using statistics effectively in your speeches.

Use Accurate Statistics Accurately: No Distorting   A statistic itself should be accurate, but the speaker should also use an accurate statistic carefully to avoid misleading an audience. You may have heard the news media and even health care professionals claim that a woman's chance of developing breast cancer is 1 in 9. That, however, is the cumulative probability of getting breast cancer if a woman lives to an age of 85 years or older. The chances of developing breast cancer by age 50, however, are about 1 in 52, or less than 2% (Paulos, 1994). The risk gradually increases beyond the age of 50. Both probability statistics are accurate, but the latter provides a more accurate picture of what is true for young women, helping them make a more informed decision regarding whether they should get yearly mammograms.

Consider one more example. A major study found that the mean teacher salary for non-college instructors in 2007 was $51,009, a $16,005 improvement from the mean salary in 1993. When adjusted for inflation, however, the actual improvement in "real dollars" which allows for cost-of-living increases was $23 (DiCarlo et al., 2008). The report went on to note that, using data from the U.S. Bureau of Economic Analysis, teachers earned only 70% of the mean salaries of 23 professional occupations requiring an equivalent education. The $16,005 salary increase is an accurate statistic, but it would not be accurate to claim from this statistic that teacher salaries have improved dramatically in the decade-and-a-half period based only on raw salary increases, or that teacher salaries are competitive with other comparable professions.

Make Statistics Concrete: Meaningful Numbers   Large statistics do not always communicate meaning to listeners. For example, the difficulty in sending a spaceship to Alpha Centauri, the nearest star system to Earth, is its distance—4.4 light years from the Sun. That is equal to about 26 trillion miles (Angier, 2002). These statistics are so large that they have little meaning beyond "really big." Dr. Geoffrey Landis of the NASA John Glenn Research Center in Cleveland, however, provides a more concrete description. Referring to the Voyager interplanetary probes, the fastest objects humans have ever launched into space, he explains: "If a caveman had launched one of those during the last ice age, 11,000 years ago, it would now be only a fifth of the way toward the nearest star" (Angier, 2002). By providing this concrete description of a number beyond big, he helps make the numbers meaningful to the average person.

Make Statistical Comparisons: Gaining Perspective Making a meaningful statistical comparison can provide real perspective for your audience. Consider this example on federal mandatory minimum prison sentences used by student speaker Sarah Werner (2005). She noted that Weldon Angelos was convicted of selling marijuana, a first-time offense, and was sentenced to *63 years* in prison "despite the fact that a jury of his peers—the jury that convicted him—favored a sentence of 15–18 years." She further noted that "the federal maximum sentencing for hijacking an airplane is 24 1/2 years, for detonating a bomb in a public place, 19 1/2 years" (p. 60). The comparison greatly enhanced the impact of her central claim that mandatory minimum sentences are unjust.

Stack Statistics: Creating Impact A particularly effective strategy is to stack statistics, especially statistics that also show comparisons. For example:

> Women have made significant strides toward gender equality in the United States. According to a *Time* magazine special report, October 26, 2009, women for the very first time occupied more than 50% of the middle management positions in U.S. businesses and organizations. *Time* goes on to report that in 1972, 43% of college students were women. Now it is 57%. Women also now earn 58% of Bachelors degrees, 60% of Masters degrees, and half of all Doctoral degrees. In an information-based economy, possessing college degrees gains you access to higher-paying jobs. Gender inequality still remains an issue in the United States, but these statistical comparisons suggest a basis for optimism.

Stacking statistics, however, should be used sparingly and only to create an impact on the central points in a speech. An audience will quickly tune out if you stack a mountain of statistics repeatedly.

Use Credible Sources: Build Believability As explained in Chapter 10, biased sources diminish the quality and the credibility of a statistic. *Objectivity* and *accuracy* are essential for sources to be credible. Sources exhibit objectivity by having no stake in the outcome of their inquiries. They just want to report the facts accurately with no agenda to advance.

Speakers often cite credible sources for some, but not all, statistics used. Make it an automatic practice that *every time you use a statistic you cite a credible source for that statistic* unless the statistic is common knowledge, such as the United States has 50 states. Listeners should never be given the opportunity to wonder, "Where did the speaker get that statistic?"

Statistics can be enormously useful, even powerful as a supporting material for your speeches. Choosing the most apt statistic and using it competently, however, are key concerns.

USING TESTIMONY COMPETENTLY

Testimony, derived from the Latin word for *witness*, is a first-hand account of events or the conclusions offered publicly by experts on a topic. In this section, several kinds of testimony that you can use to support your points are discussed, and ways to use testimony competently are explored.

Types of Testimony: Relying on Others

There are three principal types of testimony you can use as a supporting material. Testimony of experts is probably the most commonly used, but testimonies of eye witnesses and testimony of non-experts are also effective.

Testimony of Experts: Relying on Those in the Know   Expert testimony was discussed in some detail in the last chapter. Recall that testimony from experts provides important supporting material and that such testimony can be persuasive (Petty & Wegener, 1998). Experts can help laypeople sort fact from fantasy. Should you worry about heart disease before you reach 30 years old? Listen to the experts at the American Heart Association.

The Internet is a rich source of expert testimony, but the Internet itself is not an authority. It is a medium of communication. "According to the Internet . . ." is like saying "According to my iPhone . . .". Be careful citing specific websites that are unfamiliar to you. They may be hugely biased, even inflammatory and bigoted in their presentation of information. Use credibility tests discussed in Chapter 10. Citing a specific NBC news program on TV, however, or a specific issue of a particular newspaper or magazine, is better. Quoting the actual experts on the program or in the articles is best.

Eyewitness Testimony: You Had To Be There   Using the testimony and accounts of those who have observed some event or activity is a staple of criminal and civil trials. Eyewitnesses support factual claims for both sides in the courtroom, and their testimony is often critical to the outcome of a case. Eyewitnesses can also be a source for news events. In the June 2009 disputed presidential election in Iran, hundreds of thousands of protesters hit the streets of Tehran in defiance of the ruling regime. In an attempt to control global perceptions of these exploding events, the Iranian government expelled foreign journalists. Major news networks and cable shows scrambled for any bits of news that they could garner. Twitter became an important source of eyewitness messages from protesters clashing with the police and the government (May, 2009). Twitter was scheduled to be shut down for maintenance, but the U.S. State Department made the highly unusual request that Twitter remain in service to keep the limited information from Iran flowing (Hannah, 2009). Protesters sent tweets continually as events were occurring to counter the spin coming from official news sources within the Iranian government.

Similarly, uprisings across the Middle East and North Africa arose starting in Tunisia in December 2010 and spread to Egypt, Yemen, Algeria, Morocco, Libya, and other countries. By 2012, Tunisian President Zine El Abidine Ben Ali fled his country, Egypt's President Hosni Mubarak resigned after 30 years in power and was arrested and put on trial, Libya's leader Muammar Gaddafi was overthrown and killed, and other leaders announced plans to step down from power. The Arab Spring protests were fanned by cell phone videos posted on YouTube and Facebook and by Twitter tweets sent to the outside world. A study at the University of Washington of these firsthand accounts from protesters concluded, "The Arab Spring had many causes. One of these sources was social media and its power to put a human face on political oppression" (Howard et al., 2011).

Testimony of Non-Experts: Ordinary Folks Adding Color to Events You do not have to be an expert or an eyewitness to world events to add compelling testimony to your speech. Follow the example of newspapers, television news media, and documentary films. They all use interviews with "common folks" to spice up a story and personalize coverage of events. When General Motors and Chrysler declared bankruptcy in 2009, tens of thousands of workers lost their jobs and thousands of dealerships were closed. Interviews with those directly affected by this momentous economic trauma was a powerful source of information to support a claim that the U.S. automobile industry was in serious trouble, and so was the country.

How to Use Testimony

When you cite testimony to support your speech, you have to decide whether to quote exactly or merely paraphrase. Typically, you use a direct quotation when the statement is short, well phrased, and communicates your point more eloquently or cleverly than you can. Paraphrasing is appropriate when a direct quotation is not worded in an interesting way, such as in most government documents, or when a quotation is very lengthy and needs to be shortened. Whether directly quoting or merely paraphrasing, there are a couple of ways to present testimony appropriately and effectively during your speech.

Quote or Paraphrase Accurately: Consider Context It is imperative that you not misquote or inaccurately paraphrase either an expert or an eyewitness supporting your claims or an opponent in a debate or discussion. When quoting someone's testimony, do not crop the quotation so it takes on a different meaning than communicated in context. Do not delete important qualifiers from any statement. During the 2012 Republican presidential campaign, Mitt Romney claimed in a speech a day before the New Hampshire primary, "I like being able to fire people who provide services to me." Despite the clumsiness of the statement, taken in context Romney clearly meant that he liked firing health insurance companies that provide bad service to consumers. Nevertheless, his Republican opponents jumped on the statement, clearly distorting it. John Huntsman retorted, "Governor Romney enjoys firing people; I enjoy creating jobs." Rick Perry offered his supporters a downloadable ring tone for their cell phones that repeatedly played Romney's edited comment as "I like to fire people" (Madison & Boxer, 2012).

During the same campaign, Romney distorted a speech made by Barack Obama. In one of his attack ads, he quoted Obama saying, "If we keep talking about the economy, we're going to lose." The quote, however, was taken from the 2008 presidential campaign but made to seem current and it omitted a key statement. The entire quote states: "*Senator McCain's campaign actually said, and I quote,* 'If we keep talking about the economy, we're going to lose'" (Huffington, 2011). Obama clearly wanted to talk about the economy in 2008 because it favored his election. Editing Obama's statement made Obama seem to be saying the exact opposite of what his claim actually was. Editing quotations to change the meaning of the speaker's intended message is unethical. It is dishonest, and as explained in Chapter 1, honesty is an essential criterion for ethical public speaking.

Use Qualified Sources: Credibility Matters   You should be skeptical of any expert testimony that does not include citation of the expert, his or her qualifications, and the publication source and date (see previous chapter). Testimony from non-experts and eyewitnesses can be doubly dubious. Abundant research shows the unreliability of eyewitness testimony (Wells et al., 1999; Wright et al., 2009). The Twitter tweets from Iranian "eyewitnesses" on the 2009 uprising could not be verified. News organizations often took these accounts as factual, yet some of these tweets could have been government plants trying to confuse the issue and create seeds of doubt for outsiders. Others may only be reporting gossip or hearsay, not direct observations of events. As Mark Glaser, host of PBS's online show "Media Shift," observed about the Twitter phenomenon in Iran, "I feel like I'm not getting what I get at the BBC's site with confirmed sources" (quoted in May, 2009).

GENERAL CONSIDERATIONS ACROSS TYPES

There are several basic tips for using supporting materials effectively that apply to all types. Use them to choose interesting supporting materials, abbreviate source citations, and combine types of supporting materials.

Choose Interesting Supporting Materials: Counteracting Boredom

Your first consideration when choosing supporting materials should be their credibility and strength. Nevertheless, strong, credible, but also interesting supporting material is the best of all choices. Do as student Ted Dacey (2008) does when speaking about bottled water:

> Rocky Anderson, mayor of Salt Lake City, Utah, detailed the true cost of bottled water to NPRs *Talk of the Nation* on July 23, 2007. He explained: "We're told we should drink eight glasses of water a day. If you filled that glass from a tap in any major city, it will cost you about 49 cents a year. To get that same amount of bottled water, it will run around $1400 every year". *(p. 54)*

That fact is startling, and it is an interesting comparison from a credible source. He follows this with another interesting comparison from a credible source: "According to *Business Week* of April 14, 2008, to produce a 1 year's supply of water bottles for the American market, it takes 17 billion barrels of oil each year, or enough to fuel 1 million cars for an entire year" (p. 55). He provides credible but also interesting supporting materials.

Abbreviate Source Citations: Brief Reference Reminders

The initial citation of a source should be complete, but subsequent references to the same source can be abbreviated to avoid tedious repetition, unless the abbreviation might cause confusion, such as two articles from the same magazine. Student Alisha Forbes (2012) abbreviates this way: "According to the previously mentioned *New York Times* article . . ." (p. 104). After qualifying her source earlier in her speech, student Angela Wnek (2012) makes this secondary reference: "According to Scheider's article . . ." (p. 143). Student Laura Streich (2012) makes this abbreviated reference: "During the previously cited interview with Leah Holmes, she stated . . ." (p. 147). Abbreviating secondary citations makes your speech flow more smoothly.

Combine Examples, Stats, and Quotes: The Power of Three

Sometimes you can combine examples, statistics, and quotations to provide real impact. For example, a case that texting among teens has become excessive could be made as follows:

> Reina Hardesty, a California teenager, accumulated a staggering 14,528 text messages in a single month. Her online statement from AT & T ran 440 pages,

according to a January 11, 2009 *New York Post* article. Reina "explained" her 484 text messages per day or 1 every 2 minutes of her waking hours with "It was winter break and I was bored." A 2010 survey by Nielsen Media Research found that most teenagers do not reach the heights of Reina, but they do average 3,339 text messages per month. Katie Keating, a representative of AT & T, responded to inquiries about Reina's prodigious texting with this observation cited in the January 7, 2009, *Orange County Register*: "Texting is becoming more and more popular, and growing at a spectacular rate. Text-messaging is now hard-wired into our culture."

In a short space, a specific and dramatic example was offered, specific statistics were offered, and two direct quotes were used from reputable sources. Combining three types of supporting materials makes a nice package.

SUMMARY

There are four primary reasons to use supporting materials generously in your speeches: to clarify points, support claims, gain interest, and create impact. There are three chief forms of supporting materials: examples, statistics, and testimony. Each has its strengths and weaknesses. Examples can be very vivid and powerful but limited in applicability. Statistics can establish the magnitude of a problem or event and provide perspective, but they can also seem dull and tedious. Testimony can personalize problems and issues, but it can also be inaccurate and unreliable. In each case, consider the many tips offered for using each supporting material effectively.

12

Speaking Style

She crawled on her hands and knees across the courtroom floor. She kicked the jury box, cried, flailed her arms, and screamed. One journalist said she "behaved like she needed a rabies shot during the trial" (Hutchinson, 2002, p. 9A). Her marathon two-and-a-half hour opening statement was verbose and rambling. Defense attorney Nedra Ruiz's style, exhibited before the jury in the emotion-charged trial of Marjorie Knoller and Robert Noel in the highly publicized 2002 dog-mauling murder case in Los Angeles, became a subject of considerable comment. Laurie Levenson, a law professor at Loyola University in Los Angeles remarked, "Most people I talk to just shook their heads. To put it mildly, her style is unusual. It's borderline bizarre" (quoted in Curtis, 2002, p. A4). As Levenson explained during the trial, "There's a pretty decent defense here, but it's getting lost in her (Ruiz) mannerisms and her theatrics. She's not smooth. She's not polished. She crosses the line from what I think is effective advocacy to cheap theatrics" (quoted in Curtis, 2002, p. A4). Ruiz lost the case.

This is an instance of style subverting substance. It illustrates the importance of a competent public speaking style. An inappropriate style can undermine your effectiveness. One of the jurors, Don Newton, remarked after the trial that Ruiz's flamboyant performance was "in some ways counterproductive. She was so scattered at times and it threw you off" (quoted in May, 2002, p. 8A).

British author Oscar Wilde once remarked, "One's style is one's signature always." Your speaking style reveals an identity and makes your speech memorable. It is achieved primarily by the way you use words to express your thoughts and bring them to life for an audience. A verbose style may tag you as boring or confused, a clear and detail-oriented style as knowledgeable and instructive, a vivid style as exciting, even inspiring, and a personal, conversational style as approachable

PHOTO 12.1 Lawyer Nedra Ruiz's style was vivid and memorable during her animated defense in a California dog mauling trial. Nevertheless, she was more distracting than effective.

and belonging to the group. Take your style seriously. It may leave a more lasting impression than any specific points made in your speech.

The purpose of this chapter is to explain the elements of a competent speech style. Distinctions between oral and written style, effective style in the electronic age, and standards of competent style are discussed.

ORAL VERSUS WRITTEN STYLE

There are distinct differences between oral and written style. First, *oral style usually uses simpler sentences than written style.* Simpler sentences allow an audience to catch your meaning immediately. In contrast, when you read, you can review a sentence several times if necessary to discern the correct meaning. You may even consult a dictionary if you do not know the meaning of unfamiliar words. This is not the case while listening to a speech. Audience members cannot rewind a speech as they listen unless they are watching it on YouTube. Very complex sentence structure can confuse your listeners.

Second, *oral style is highly interactive; written style is not.* When speaking, you can look directly into the faces of your listeners. If you sense that they do not understand your point, you can adjust by rephrasing your idea, adding an example, or even asking your listeners if they are confused. Feedback, especially nonverbal, is immediate from listeners, but feedback from readers is delayed and often nonexistent. (For example, I cannot know how you are responding to this chapter as you read it now, nor am I likely ever to hear from you.) The speaker and the audience influence each other directly. For example, if you crack a joke and no one laughs, you may decide to dump other such attempts at humor.

Third, *oral style is usually less formal than written style*. Effective writing style adheres to the appropriate use of grammar, includes well-constructed sentences and proper punctuation and spelling. Even highly educated individuals diminish their credibility when they send emails with obvious spelling and grammatical mistakes. Such errors may jump off the page and can be repeatedly reread. My auto insurance company sent me a letter with this sentence in the opening paragraph: "You may not know that the reputation of our Auto Insurance is equally outstanding." The obvious typographical error is ironic considering it appears in a sentence touting an "outstanding reputation." Oral style tends to be more conversational, including shorter sentences, even sentence fragments. Grammatical errors may be less noticeable and thus less damaging to a speaker's credibility.

Being generally less formal compared to written style, however, does not mean that oral style should never exhibit formality. Nedra Ruiz used a style stunningly inappropriate to the formal occasion of a serious courtroom trial. She could have been conversational and still have remained cognizant of the formalities and expectations inherent in a criminal trial. Some occasions are formal by nature (e.g., trials, some ceremonies) and require a more formal oral style than is typical of most speaking situations. Using slang, obscenities, and being too casual and familiar in addressing certain individuals (e.g. referring to a court judge during trial by his or her first name, as in "Hey Pat"), is inappropriate style. Match your style to the occasion.

STYLE IN THE ELECTRONIC AGE

With the rise of the electronic age characterized by the influence of television and more recently YouTube, social networking sites, and text messaging and Twitter tweets, the traditional model of eloquent speaking style clashes with newer expectations from audiences. The traditional model is "factual, analytic, organized, and impersonal." The newer model is more narrative, personal, self-disclosive, dramatic, and vivid (Jamieson, 1988; and Levander, 1998; Frobish, 2000). Electronic media, especially television and YouTube, thrive on vivid pictures, terse, compelling storytelling, and clever soundbytes (Cyphert, 2009). The adversarial, competitive, data-driven, impersonal, traditional speaking style can come across on visual media as abrasive, unfriendly, and sometimes bland (e.g., an uninteresting, detailed policy discussion). It can disconnect you from your audience unless audience members are looking for someone to express their anger forcefully. During the 2012 presidential debates among Republicans, Newt Gingrich resonated with many conservative voters because "his in-your-face style has excited GOP voters" who wanted "a scrappy fighter to take on President Barack Obama" (Fouhy, 2012). Gingrich's style provided many terse, vivid soundbytes well suited to the electronic media. His style was adversarial but not data-driven and impersonal. It ran the risk, however, of appearing unfriendly and divisive, so his appeal was ultimately limited.

Does this mean that your speaking style should pander to the requirements of visual media such as television and YouTube and bend to the necessarily abbreviated messages of our Twitter environment? Nedra Ruiz's melodramatic, personal, narrative style might make good television or YouTube viewing for those drawn to the bizarre, but her style was excessive, especially given the seriousness of the occasion. A woman was torn to shreds by vicious dogs and Ruiz was defending two people on trial for murdering this defenseless victim. Ruiz's flamboyant style seemed to make light of a horrible tragedy.

Ronald Reagan helped legitimize the personal, narrative, dramatic style (Jamiesen, 1988). Reagan was a great storyteller, and he loved to spin a yarn. He was criticized, however, for being overly narrative, sometimes telling tales that were contradicted by facts and evidence (Greider, 2004). You do not want to sacrifice accuracy just to tell a great story. Barack Obama has an essentially narrative speaking style. "Storytelling is at the core of Obama's public speaking" (Dorning, 2009, p. 2A). This narrative style works well for inspirational speeches, particularly to adoring crowds. It is more difficult to use effectively in most televised debate formats restricted by tight time constraints and formal rules of turn taking. Obama, by almost every account, did poorly in the first presidential debate with Mitt Romney on October 3, 2012. He seemed lethargic and detached, not dramatic and vivid. He opted mostly for an impersonal, professorial style, attempting to teach his audience instead of persuade his listeners and viewers. Issues and ideas became muddled. Romney, however, did far better on style because he came across to most listeners as energetic and more "factual, analytical, and organized" than Obama, but with a bit of passion mixed in occasionally. These widely held impressions of Romney's performance based on style, however, do not mean that Romney was factually accurate and that his analysis of issues was necessarily deep and correct. Style and substance do not always mesh. You can appear to be factual by asserting "facts" without being accurate. Fact-checking groups did not give Romney, or Obama either, particularly high marks for factual and analytical accuracy in the first debate ("Fact Checking," 2012).

The challenge for you as a speaker is to blend the traditional with the more contemporary styles, merging the best of both. Ultimately, blending the two styles, the factual/analytic and the narrative/dramatic, is best suited for most speaking situations that you will face in the electronic age (Jamieson, 1988, 1995). Advice offered throughout this text instructs you on how to blend these styles.

STANDARDS OF COMPETENT ORAL STYLE

Style is your signature, but learning how to make that signature is the subject of this section. Oral style is effective and appropriate when it fulfills certain criteria. In this section, criteria and some examples of competent oral style are discussed.

Clarity: Saying What You Mean

Oral style works most effectively when language is clear and understandable. *Clarity comes from a simple, concise style.* John F. Kennedy asked his speechwriter, Ted Sorensen, to discover the secret of Lincoln's Gettysburg Address. Sorensen noted this: "Lincoln never used a two- or three-syllable word where a one-syllable word would do, and never used two or three words where one word would do" (quoted in National Archives, 1987, p. 1). There are 701 words in Lincoln's Second Inaugural Address, of which 505 are one syllable and 122 are merely two syllables (Zinsser, 1985). Inexperienced speakers may think that big ideas require big words. When listeners start noticing the big words, however, the big ideas shrink into the dark shadows of obscurity. Do not try to impress your audience with a vocabulary that sounds as though you consulted a thesaurus repeatedly. Remember, oral style requires greater simplicity than written style.

A clear style is simple, but not simplistic. Lincoln's Second Inaugural Address included this memorable line: "With malice toward none, with charity for all, with firmness in the right as God gives us to see the right." The words are simple, yet the meaning is profound, even moving. Including an occasional complex sentence or more challenging vocabulary, however, can also work well. Although Lincoln used a simple, clear style, his sentence structure and phrasing were not always simple. In his Gettysburg Address, he included several lengthy, complex sentences. He also included this sentence: "We cannot dedicate, we cannot consecrate, we cannot hallow this ground." He could have said, "We cannot set aside for the special purpose of honoring, we cannot make holy this ground." Sometimes more challenging vocabulary provides an economical use of language. By occasionally using more sophisticated vocabulary, Lincoln spoke more concisely, clearly, and eloquently. If in doubt, however, default to simple sentence structure and vocabulary.

This often means avoiding **jargon**—the specialized language of a profession, trade, or group. Jargon is a kind of verbal shorthand. When lawyers use terms such as *prima facie case* and *habeus corpus,* they communicate appropriately to other attorneys and officers of the court very specific information without tedious, verbose explanation. "To the initiated, jargon is efficient, economical, and even crucial in that it can capture distinctions not made in the ordinary language" (Allan & Burridge, 1991, p. 201). Jargon used orally, however, can be inappropriate for those who do not understand the verbal shorthand. Jurors may not fully understand legal jargon when lawyers address them in opening and closing statements. Parents, for example, can be forgiven if they are confused by jargon used by educators to "explain" their child's strengths and shortcomings, such as *phonemic sequencing errors, phonological process delays, normed modality processing, morphosyntactic skills, word attack skills, psychometrics, deficit model,* and *additive model* (Helfand, 2001). To most parents, this bushel basket of buzzwords probably sounds closer to Klingon than any language they speak. Student Nick Phephan (2011) notes the problem of jargon in his speech on "hospital speak" that produces common patient overcharges. Jargon such as "fog reduction elimination device" which is a small "piece of gauze used to wipe condensation off of stethoscopes" creates its own foggy use of language no patient is likely to decipher. Use jargon only when necessary, and then explain terminology that is likely to be unfamiliar to your listeners. If you use the medical term "tinnitus," explain immediately to a lay audience that this means "ear ringing."

Euphemisms can also confuse listeners. A **euphemism** is an indirect or vague word or phrase used to numb us to or conceal unpleasant or offensive realities. Substituting a euphemism such as *passed away* for *dead* when giving a eulogy at a funeral may cushion an ugly reality for grieving relatives and friends. This is probably harmless, even compassionate. Nevertheless, euphemisms can create unnecessary, even purposeful, confusion. Members of Congress prefer to cumouflage a "tax increase" proposal by euphemizing it as a "revenue enhancement" or a "fee" when speaking to constituents. Repeatedly the mass media refer to "wardrobe malfunctions" when celebrities have difficulty keeping their clothes from falling off their bodies. The military has repeatedly euphemized civilian casualties in war as "collateral damage." Generally, avoid using euphemisms in your speeches.

Finally, use slang sparingly. **Slang**, the highly informal speech not in conventional usage, can be employed when you are confident that your listeners will comprehend and identify with such casual speech, the speech occasion is meant to be relatively informal, and using slang will not brand you as ridiculously out of touch. Slang typically works more effectively in oral than in written presentations because you are speaking directly to a specific audience whose members you already know may actually be familiar with the slang. In written communication, your slang may be understood by only a small fraction of your audience. If you are unfamiliar with your audience, stick to more standard colorful

Euphemisms blunt unpleasant realities but they can also confuse listeners. Would you ever guess that "preparation for success" refers to a failed test?

language use. Using terms, such as *eyeolating, web glow, ear worm, trash jenga, cobra yawn, carbo bloating, bodybooking,* and *familiated* when speaking to an unfamiliar audience may leave your listeners in a state of confusion (check www .urbandictionary.com for translations). Slang also can become dated quickly, making you sound hopelessly uncool. If in doubt, skip slang.

Precision: Picking the Apt Words

Baseball great Yogi Berra once observed this about the game that made him a household name: "Ninety percent of this game is half-mental." Yogi also said, "When you get to a fork in the road, take it," and "Our similarities are different."

Yogi was not renowned for his precise use of the English language (or his mastery of arithmetic). Deborah Koons Garcia, wife of the Grateful Dead's Jerry Garcia, was equally imprecise when she remarked, "Jerry died broke. We only have a few hundred thousand dollars in the bank" (quoted in White, 1998). Most people would probably love to be that broke.

Everyone occasionally misuses a word or gets tangled on syntax. Unfortunately for George W. Bush, his mangling of the English language became notorious. For example, he coughed up such linguistic hairballs as: "Republicans understand the importance of bondage between a mother and child" and "Families is where wings take dream" (quoted in Weisberg & Ivins, 2004). You should strive to be as precise in your use of language as possible. *Choose your words carefully and know their exact meaning.* Adlai Stevenson, twice a candidate for president of the United States, had just finished a speech before the United Nations when a woman approached him excitedly and said, "I really enjoyed your talk; it was without exception *superfluous!*" ("superlative" might have been the word she meant to use). Before Stevenson could respond to the woman's unintended characterization of his speech as *unnecessary,* she continued, "Will it be published?" "Yes," replied Stevenson. "Posthumously." "Good," said the woman. "The sooner

PHOTO 12.2 Use language precisely. This sign is ambiguous.

the better" (quoted in Rand, 1998, p. 282). Stevenson probably did not feel flattered by the woman's unintended encouragement that he die soon so his speech could be published after his demise. Using words imprecisely or inaccurately diminishes your credibility and can make you appear foolish.

Lack of precision is one strong reason sexist language should be avoided (see also Chapter 4 discussion). Aside from the bigotry, sexist language is imprecise and often inaccurate language usage. Terms such as businessman, policeman, fireman, and postman were mostly accurate depictions of a society with few female executives, police officers, firefighters, and letter carriers. This is no longer accurate, so such terms are sexist and imprecise. *Eliminate sexist language.*

Sometimes our attempt to be precise leads to redundant phrases such as "twelve noon," "true fact," "circle around," "close proximity," "end result," "revert back," and "the future to come." Also be careful when using acronyms that you do not add pointless words such as "ATM machine" (**A**utomatic **T**eller **M**achine machine), "HIV virus" (**H**uman **I**mmunodeficiency **V**irus virus), and "AIDS syndrome" (**A**cquired **I**mmune **D**eficiency **S**yndrome syndrome). *Eliminate redundant words and phrases.*

Vividness: Painting a Picture

Simple, concise, and precise use of language does not mean using words in a boring fashion. A vivid, visual style paints a picture in the minds of listeners and makes a speaker's ideas attention-getting and memorable (Childers & Houston, 1984). William Gibbs McAdoo, twice an unsuccessful candidate for the Democratic nomination for president, vividly described the speeches of President Warren G. Harding this way: "His speeches left the impression of an army of pompous phrases moving over the landscape in search of an idea." The words are simple and the point is clearly drawn. The style, however, is quite vivid. Oscar-winning actor George Clooney, speaking about his real passion for directing movies, once remarked, "Directing is the key to filmmaking. Everything else is just paint" ("As 'Sexiest Man Alive,'" 2006, p. 2A). Student Sarah Hoppes (2008) notes that a proposal to sell ad space on the Golden Gate Bridge to cover an $80 million deficit would turn a national landmark into "The Google Gate Bridge." Student Melody Carlisle (2011) uses vivid language in her speech on bed bugs when she remarks that "bed bugs might be the world's greatest hitchhikers" and sarcastically refers to these "creepy crawlies" as "enchanting houseguests" (p. 138). Each of these examples leaves a visual impression in the listener's mind, grabbing attention and remaining memorable.

There are many ways to make your speech style vivid. Here are a few suggestions for you to consider.

PHOTO 12.3 Clever wording shows style. This sign is a play on the oft-repeated "separation of church and state."

Metaphor and Simile: Figures of Speech

Two main figures of speech that can add vividness to your speeches are metaphors and similes. A **metaphor** is an implied comparison of two seemingly dissimilar things. In a speech delivered on January 6, 1941, Franklin Roosevelt said that selfish men "would clip the wings of the American eagle in order to feather their own nests" (quoted in Waldman & Stephanopoulos, 2003). Hillary Clinton, addressing the 2008 Democratic National Convention as the runner up candidate for president, used metaphor when she described the "Supreme Court in a right-wing headlock and our government in partisan gridlock" ("Transcript," 2009). Patrick Buchanan, in a speech at the Republican National Convention in 1992, characterized the Democratic National Convention held weeks before as a "giant masquerade ball [where] 20,000 radicals and liberals came dressed up as moderates and centrists in the greatest single exhibition of cross-dressing in American political history" (quoted in Meyer, 2004). Buchanan was a speechwriter turned presidential candidate who knew how to use words vividly.

Be careful not to mix your metaphors, otherwise your vivid imagery may sound laughable. A **mixed metaphor** is the use of two or more vastly different metaphors in a single expression. Famous movie producer Samuel Goldwyn once remarked, "That's the way with these directors. They're always biting the hand that lays the golden egg." Then there is the example of Alabama Senator Jeff Sessions who, in his opening statement at the Judiciary Committee confirmation hearings for Sonya Sotomayor as Supreme Court justice in July 2009, argued for a "blindfolded justice calling the balls and strikes fairly and objectively" (quoted in Goodman, 2009, p. A13). A blindfolded justice metaphorically symbolizes lack of bias, but a baseball umpire, making inherently subjective perceptual judgment calls, surely does not. Even more to the point, would you ever want an umpire of any sort to be blindfolded when they "call the balls and strikes?" Mixing metaphors can sound goofy.

A **simile** is an explicit comparison of two seemingly dissimilar things using the words *like* or *as*. Curt Simmons described what it was like pitching to Hank Aaron: "Trying to get a fastball past Hank Aaron is like trying to get the sun past a rooster." "She was as sharp as a box cutter and twice as deadly" and "Listening to him is like fingernails on a chalkboard" are also similes. Student Melody Carlisle (2011) uses a nice simile in her speech on bed bugs: "Sherri and her little girl were sick of being treated like human buffets" (p. 138).

Similes and metaphors can enhance a speech by being vivid and memorable, but not if they become clichés. A **cliché** is a once-vivid expression that has been overused to the point of seeming commonplace. "Naked as a jaybird," "dull as dishwater," "dumb as a post," and "smooth as a baby's butt" are a few similes that long ago became clichés. "It's not rocket science," "It's an emotional roller coaster," and "I'm between a rock and a hard place" are metaphors that have become shopworn from massive overuse. A survey of 5,000 individuals in 70 countries conducted by the British-based Plain English Campaign, showed that "at the end of the day" is the most annoying cliché in the English language across all cultures. Other clichés vying for most annoying are "thinking outside the box," "pushing the envelope," and "singing from the same hymn sheet" ("Cliches," 2009). Additional nominees for most annoying cliches include "doubling down," and "tipping point" (Corbett, 2013).

Create your own unique similes and metaphors, but do not create picturesque figures of speech that offend and insult listeners. Similes and metaphors can be offensive. Hitler once compared Jews to "maggots on rotting flesh." His point was disgusting and so was his figurative language. Play with language, but play with it carefully.

Alliteration: Several of the Same Sounds

The repetition of the same sound, usually a consonant sound, starting each word is called **alliteration**. It can create a very vivid and effective cadence. Classic examples of alliteration were spoken by the wizard in the movie "Wizard of Oz." He called the Tin Man a "clinking, clanking, clattering collection of caliginous junk." He referred to the Scarecrow as a "billowing bale of bovine fodder." Student Joy Minchin (2012) gave a speech on medical errors that she referred to as "death by doctor." Student Curt Casper (2011) uses simple alliteration in his speech on suicide when he says, "I realize this is a tough topic to talk about" and refers to "a simple solution" to "suicide survival" and he advocates "survivor support" (p. 87).

When Spiro Agnew was vice president of the United States during the Nixon presidency, he became famous for phrases such as "nattering nabobs of negativism" and "pusillanimous pussyfooters." The problem with Agnew's use of alliteration, however, was that most listeners could not decipher what he had said because he loved to use silver-dollar words when nickel and dime words would have been more effective.

Alliteration can create a captivating cadence, especially when delivered orally. Do not overuse alliteration, however. A little alliteration is appropriate. Frequent alliteration could become laughable.

Repetition: Rhythmic Cadence

Reiterating the same word, phrase, or sentence, usually with parallel structure, is called **repetition**. Barack Obama's "Yes We Can" theme repeated in almost every campaign speech he gave in 2008 was memorable. It provided a rhythmic cadence for his speeches, unified a series of ideas, and created a powerful, vivid, emotional effect with his audience. His listeners would often shout, without prompting, "Yes we can" during his speech. Such repetition in a written essay to be read would lose some of its rhythmic cadence, and no opportunity for an audience response is available.

Here are some other examples of effective oral repetition:

> Today, we have a vision of Texas where opportunity knows no race or color or gender. . . . Tomorrow, we must build that Texas.
> Today, we have a vision of a Texas with clean air and land and water. . . . Tomorrow, we must build that Texas.
> Today, we have a vision of a Texas where every child receives an education that allows them to claim the full promise of their lives. Tomorrow, we must build that Texas. *(Ann Richards, former Governor of Texas)*

> We shall fight on the beaches.
> We shall fight on the landing grounds.
> We shall fight in the fields and in the streets.
> We shall fight in the hills.
> We shall never surrender. *(Winston Churchill)*

> We will not waiver; we will not tire; we will not falter; and we will not fail. Peace and freedom will prevail. *(George W. Bush on the 9/11 terrorist attacks)*

As is true of any stylistic device, a little goes a long way. *Be careful not to overuse repetition and become boringly redundant.*

Antithesis: Using Opposites

Charles Dickens began his famous novel, *A Tale of Two Cities*, with one of the most memorable lines in literature: "It was the best of times; it was the worst of times." This is an example of the stylistic device called **antithesis**—a sentence composed of two parts with parallel structure but opposite meanings to create impact. Former First Lady Barbara Bush (1990) offered this example of antithesis in a commencement address at Wellesley College: "Your success as a family, our success as a society, depends not on what happens at the White House, but on what happens inside your house." Hillary Clinton, when running for president in 2008, used this example of antithesis: "In the end the true test is not the speeches a president delivers, it's whether the president delivers on the speeches" (quoted by Johnson, 2008). Perhaps the most famous example of antithesis in public speaking is from John F. Kennedy's inaugural address in 1961: "Ask not what your country can do for you, ask what you can do for your country." He also used this example of antithesis: "Let us never negotiate out of fear, but let us never fear to negotiate."

The effectiveness of antithesis is in the rhythmic phrasing. Four months before his inaugural address, Kennedy made this statement: "The new frontier is not what I promise I am going to do for you. The new frontier is what I ask you to do for your country." This also used antithesis, but it was not memorable. It seems more verbose and bland. Be concise when using antitheses.

SUMMARY

Style is the distinctive quality that makes your speech memorable. The principal standards of stylistic effectiveness are clarity, precision, and vividness. You can learn much about style by examining competent speakers who follow these standards. Ultimately, however, your style must be your own. Work on clarity, precision, and vividness by listening to successful speakers, but explore what fits you well. Metaphors and similes may come easily to you, but antithesis may seem artificial and awkward. Develop your own style by experimenting. Try including metaphors in your conversations with others. Play with language informally before incorporating stylistic devices in your formal speeches. Remember, style is your signature.

13

Visual Aids

I once had a student who realized 5 minutes before his speech that a visual aid was required for the speaking assignment. I actually saw him take his lunch bag, pour out the contents, take a black marker pen, and quickly sketch a drawing for his visual aid. When he gave his speech and showed his lunch bag drawing, audience members had to stifle their laughter. When discussing visual aids, it is important that you recognize both words in that term. The visual part is necessary, but so is the aid part. You do not choose just anything visual to show during your speech. You choose that which actually aids your presentation and does not invite ridicule or serve as a distraction.

There is little reason to use visual aids if the choice of aids serves no useful purpose. A speech on apple farming, for example, does not require a picture of an apple split in half unless the speaker plans to present information at a much deeper level than merely identifying readily apparent parts of this common fruit. Visual aids can be exceedingly helpful, however. *The purpose of this chapter is to explain how to use visual aids appropriately and effectively.* The benefits and types of visual aids available, presentational media, and the guidelines for competent use of visual aids are discussed.

BENEFITS OF VISUAL AIDS: REASONS TO USE THEM

Effective visual aids provide several benefits for a speaker. First, they *clarify difficult points* or descriptions of complex objects. Actually showing an object to an audience helps listeners understand. Try explaining a motherboard for a computer or the internal combustion engine without a visual aid. Second, effective visual aids *gain and maintain audience attention.* A dramatic photograph of an anorexic teenager can capture attention during the opening of a speech on eating disorders. Third, visual aids *enhance speaker credibility.* Presenting impressive statistics in a graph, chart, or table drives home an important point in your speech. You appear knowledgeable. Fourth, visual aids can *improve your delivery.* Novice speakers find it difficult to stray from notes or a manuscript. When you are showing a visual aid, however, you can move away from reading your speech, and you assume a more natural delivery when you explain your visual aid to your listeners. Finally, effective visual aids can be *memorable.* Demonstration speeches rely heavily on visual aids. You can remember a magic trick, a martial arts move, the proper way to arrange flowers, or how to decorate wedding cakes when you have actually seen them demonstrated.

TYPES OF VISUAL AIDS: MAKING APPROPRIATE CHOICES

There are several types of visual aids. Each must be considered for how it either contributes to or detracts from the purpose of your speech. This section discusses making appropriate visual aids choices, and identifies both strengths and limitations of each type.

Objects: Show and Tell

Sometimes there is no substitute for the actual object of your speech. For example, giving a speech on playing different types of recorders really requires demonstrating with the actual musical instruments. "Bass and tenor recorders have very different sounds" just does not work if you merely show a photograph of the instruments. You must actually play the recorders. An awards ceremony requires presenting the physical trophy, plaque, certificate, or check to the recipient. A handshake and a promise do not work as well.

There are limitations, however, to the use of objects as visual aids. Some objects are too large to haul into a classroom. One student in my class wanted to show how the size of surfboards has changed over the years, so he brought in four different-sized boards. His immediate problem was that his long board hit the ceiling when it was placed on its end, punching a hole in the ceiling tiles. Some objects are also impractical to bring to most speaking venues. A speech on building a bullet train in the United States may benefit from a visual aid, but you surely cannot drive a real train into a classroom or auditorium.

Some objects are illegal, dangerous, or potentially objectionable to at least some audience members. One of my students brought in a live marijuana plant he had been cultivating as a "show-and-tell" object. The speech had to be halted

PHOTO 13.1 Showing an oversized object can be a very effective visual aid. Here U. S. surfer Carissa Moore holds an oversized check over her head while on the winner's podium.

because the object was illegal. Firearms, poisons, or combustible liquids are dangerous. Simply *exercise responsible judgment.* Check for rules or laws that could invite trouble before using any visual aid that seems questionable.

Inanimate objects are usually preferable to living, squirming objects. Puppies are unfailingly cute and great attention grabbers, but they are also very difficult to control. A student of mine brought a puppy to class for her speech. The puppy whined, barked, and howled throughout her presentation. At first it was cute. After 5 minutes the audience was thoroughly annoyed. My student ended her speech as the puppy urinated on the classroom carpet.

Some living objects can frighten audience members. A live snake, especially one not in a cage, will make some audience members extremely uneasy, even agitated. One student brought a live tarantula to class for her speech. She let the spider walk across a table as she presented her informative speech. Audience members were transfixed—not by what she was saying but by the hairy creature moving slowly in front of them.

Models: Practical Representations

When objects relevant to your speech are too large, too small, expensive, fragile, rare, or unavailable, models often act as effective substitutes. A speech on dental hygiene requires a larger-than-normal plastic model of a human mouth full of teeth. You want to avoid asking for a volunteer from the audience to open wide so the speaker can show the volunteer's teeth. The teeth will be too small to see well, and such a demonstration will also be extremely awkward. The speaker may have to point out tooth decay, gum disease, and fillings in the volunteer's mouth—not something most people want others to notice, much less have spotlighted.

Demonstration speeches on cardiopulmonary resuscitation (CPR) require a model of a person. You cannot ask for an audience member to serve as a victim for the demonstration. Pushing forcefully on a person's chest could be dangerous and potentially embarrassing.

Graphs: Making Statistics Clear and Interesting

When your speech includes several statistics, merely listing those statistics can be tedious and confusing for your audience. A graph can clarify and enliven statistics. A **graph** is a visual representation of statistics in an easily understood format. There are several kinds. Figure 13.1 is a *bar graph,* which compares and contrasts two or more items or shows variation over a period of time. Bar graphs can make a dramatic visual impact. Figures 13.2 and 13.3 are line graphs. A *line graph* is useful for showing a trend or change over a period of time. A *pie graph,* as shown in Figure 13.4, depicts a proportion or percentage for each part of a whole. A pie graph should depict from two to six "pie pieces." Much more than this will make the pie graph difficult for your audience to decipher.

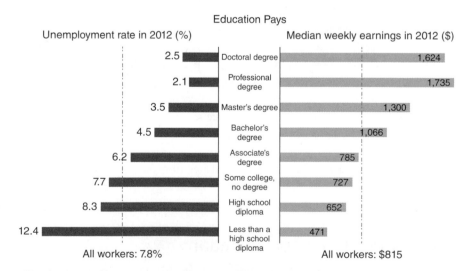

FIGURE 13.1 A bar graph illustrating the monetary advantage of education. Trends (unemployment rates and median weekly earnings) are visually apparent. (Source: Bureau of Labor Statistics, 2013).

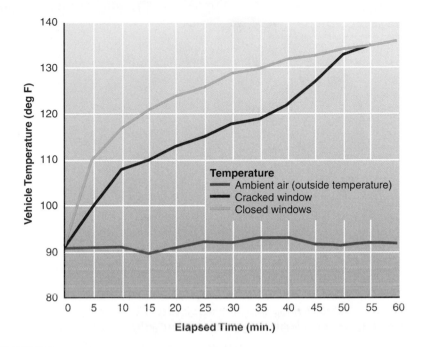

FIGURE 13.2 A line graph comparing interior temperature over time in cars with closed or "cracked" windows. (Source: McLaren et al., 2005).

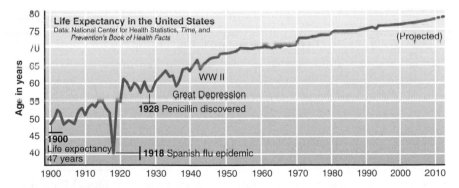

FIGURE 13.3 A line graph illustrating life expectancy in the United States. (Sources: San Jose Mercury News and CDC, "National Vital Statistics," 2012).

Graphs are effective if they are uncluttered. Too much information in a graph makes it difficult for an audience to understand. More detailed graphs published in print media can be effective because readers can examine the graphs carefully. During a speech, however, this is neither possible, nor desirable.

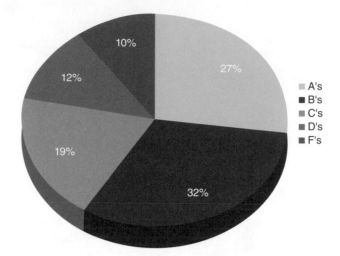

FIGURE 13.4 This is a pie graph depicting breakdown of grades in a public speaking class.

Maps: Making a Point Geographically

When geography is central to your speech or a key point, there is no good substitute for a map. Imagine teaching a geography class without showing maps. "Picture the Arabian Peninsula" does not work for a geography-challenged audience. Commercial maps are often too detailed to be useful as a visual aid. The most effective maps are large, clear, and directly relevant to the speaker's purpose. Some speakers attempt to draw their own maps, but the proportions and scale of continents, countries, or bodies of water are often badly represented. A map should be exact to be effective. You do not want the United States to look three times bigger than Asia.

Tables: Factual and Statistical Comparisons

Tables are effective for depicting blocks of information. A **table** is an orderly depiction of statistics, words, or symbols in columns or rows. Tables 13.1 and 13.2 are examples. A table can provide easy-to-understand comparisons of facts and statistics. Tables, however, are not as visually interesting as graphics, and they can become easily cluttered with too much information.

Tables will be a visual distraction if the headings are too small to read, the columns or rows are crooked, and the overall impression is that the table was hastily drawn. With readily available computer technology, there is little excuse for amateurish looking tables.

TABLE 13.1

Average Annual Major League Baseball Salaries 2002–2012

YEAR	AVERAGE ANNUAL SALARY
2002	2.38 million
2003	2.58 million
2004	2.49 million
2005	2.63 million
2006	2.83 million
2007	2.92 million
2008	3.15 million
2009	3.26 million
2010	3.27 million
2011	3.32 million
2012	3.43 million

SOURCE: *USA TODAY* (2013)

TABLE 13.2

World's Deadliest Earthquakes in the Last 100 Years

	LOCATION	MAGNITUDE	DEATHS
1.	Haiti Region (2010)	7.0	316,000
2.	Tangshan, China (1976)	7.5	243,000
3.	Sumatra, Indonesia (2004)	9.1	228,000
4.	Haiyuan, China (1920)	7.8	200,000
5.	Kanto, Japan (1923)	7.9	143,000
6.	Turkmenistan (1948)	7.3	110,000
7.	Eastern Sichuan, China (2008)	7.9	88,000
8.	Northern Pakistan (2005)	7.6	86,000
9.	Chimbote, Peru (1970)	7.9	70,000
10.	Western Iran (1990)	7.4	50,000

SOURCE: U. S. Geological Survey (2013). Note: Statistics are rounded off for easier reading.

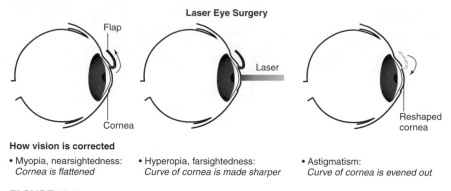

FIGURE 13.5 Drawing illustrates Laser eye surgery. (Source: Eye Surgery Education Council)

Photographs: Very Visual Aids

The many photographs included in this textbook underline the effectiveness of this visual aid to make a point, clarify a concept, and draw attention. When objects are too big, fragile, unwieldy, or unavailable to use as visual aids, photographs may serve as effective substitutes. Instead of bringing the wiggling, fussing, barking, urinating puppy to class, try showing several photographs of the cute pet. Instead of displaying a marijuana plant, show a photograph of it.

Photographs have some drawbacks. They may need to be enlarged for all to see. Technological advances with digital photography and Photoshop have made enlarging relatively easy if you have access to the technology and know how to use it. Postage-stamp-size photographs are worthless as visual aids. When a speaker says, "As you can see in this photograph," and no one can, the photo becomes not an aid but a cause for snickering.

Drawings: Photo Substitutes

When photographs are unavailable, a careful drawing might be an effective substitute (see Figure 13.5). Drawings of figures performing ballet moves or an athlete pole vaulting could be instructive for an audience. If the drawings are sloppy, distorted, small, or appear to have been drawn by a 5-year-old with no artistic talent, find a different visual aid.

VISUAL AIDS MEDIA: SIMPLE TO TECHNOLOGICALLY ADVANCED

There are many media, or means of communicating, with visual aids. Tables or graphs, for example, can appear on chalkboards, posters, PowerPoint slides, or other media. Choosing the appropriate visual medium should take into consideration what you are comfortable using, whether your speech really requires a visual aid, and what best suits your audience. A multimedia presentation may be too complicated for you to master in time for your speech, or the proper equipment may not be available. Showing very simple visual aids to an audience of experts may be viewed as condescending. Ask yourself, "Do I need a visual aid and, if so, which medium works best to accomplish my purpose?"

Chalkboard and Whiteboard: All Dinosaurs Are Not Extinct

Every student is familiar with the chalkboard or whiteboard. Despite its "dinosaur" reputation of late, chalkboards and whiteboards are appropriate when time and resources do not permit the use of more sophisticated media. Chalkboards and whiteboards are widely available and allow great flexibility. Tables, drawings, and graphs all can be drawn on them. Lecture material can be outlined. Mistakes can be immediately, and easily, erased. The evolving flow of an idea or process can be drawn in an as-you-go technique. This can allow for nice interaction with your audience. If you have real artistic ability, this art-in-progress can be quite impressive.

Words written on either a chalkboard or whiteboard should be printed if your cursive handwriting is difficult to decipher. Always write or draw images large enough for audience members sitting in the back rows to see easily. It is usually best to use proper outlining form (see Chapter 7) when listing main ideas and their subpoints. You do not want topics and ideas to appear unconnected.

Chalkboards and whiteboards do have several serious drawbacks. The quality of the table, drawing, or graph is usually inferior. Students sometimes draw on a chalkboard or whiteboard during their speech, consuming huge portions of their allotted speaking time. If a student uses the chalkboard or whiteboard prior to his or her speech, the class waits impatiently while the speaker creates the visual aid. It is too time-consuming. Turning to write or draw on the board also breaks eye contact with your audience. *Most instructors discourage or even forbid the use of both for student speakers*, but if you become a teacher, the chalkboard and whiteboard, unlike the dinosaurs, likely will have avoided extinction because they are cheap and easy to use.

Poster Board: Simplicity Itself

A poster board is a very simple medium for visual aids. Available in most college bookstores or stationery outlets, you can draw, stencil, and make graphs or tables using poster board. Making the poster appear professional, however, is a primary challenge. Several guidelines can help. First, all lettering and numbering should be large enough for anyone in the back of the room to see easily. Second, your poster should be neat and symmetrical. Headings, lettering, and numbering should be even, not sloping downward, upward, or any combination that looks like a roller coaster. Use a ruler to keep lines straight. Letters and numbers should be of the same size or font. Third, strive for simplicity. Avoid cluttering the poster with a collage of pictures that meld into a blob of images, unless the assignment requires a collage. Generally, forgo using newspaper clippings whose print is too small and too detailed to read quickly. Resist ornate, flowery borders. Glitter, feathers, and other "accessories" are distracting and rarely beneficial.

Posters are usually attached to an easel for display. Simply standing them on a chalk tray, however, will usually result in the poster curling at the top and flopping onto the ground, unless the poster is made of very stiff, sturdy material. Watching a speaker repeatedly fuss with a poster trying desperately to keep it upright is awkward for everyone. Tape it to a wall if necessary.

Handouts: An Old Standby

Distributing a handout is a popular form of visual aid. Tables, maps, drawings, PowerPoint slides, or even photographs can be copied onto a handout. One significant advantage of a handout is that the listeners can keep it long after the speech has been presented. It can serve as a useful reminder of the information presented. A handout can also include a great quantity of information to be studied carefully as a presentation unfolds (e.g., college budget details).

Handouts have potential disadvantages, however. Passing out a handout in the middle of your speech wastes time and breaks the flow of the speech. If your listeners are busy reading your handout while you are speaking, they will not be attending to your message.

Distribute a handout just prior to your speech if the handout will be an integral part of your presentation. The handout will not distract but will assist audience members to maintain focus and increase understanding of your message. If the audience is large and your speech is short, do not distribute a handout—it is too time-consuming. A handout with names, email addresses, Internet links, and phone numbers of organizations or agencies that can provide additional information on your subject can be made available after your speech.

Video Excerpts: DVDs, YouTube, and Visual Power

An excerpt from a movie, YouTube, or a video segment you shot yourself can be a valuable visual aid. Videos can be dramatic, informative, and moving. They often are great attention grabbers. Videos used during a speech, however, have several limitations. First, the sound on a video will compete with the speaker for attention. Shut off the sound when you are trying to explain a point while the video is playing, unless the video excerpt is very short, such as 30 seconds or less, and sound is essential. Longer video excerpts with sound may be effective in lengthy presentations. Second, a video with its dramatic action can make your speech seem tame, even dull, by comparison. It is tough to compete with a Hollywood production. Third, *a video is not a speech.* There is a real temptation to show a video as a major portion of a speech without any narration or direct reference to it while it is playing.

If you use a video excerpt during your speech, cue it properly so you will not have to interrupt the flow of your presentation by looking for the right place to start the excerpt. Downloading several short excerpts onto a blank DVD is preferable to loading several separate DVDs. Also, downloading any YouTube excerpts onto a blank DVD is less cumbersome and time-consuming to set up and use than accessing the YouTube site or connecting to your thumb drive. YouTube video excerpts should also be embedded into any PowerPoint presentation to avoid interrupting the flow of your presentation by accessing YouTube sites (see *youtube.com* and type "How to embed a YouTube video into PowerPoint 2010" in the search window). Typically, use only a few very short video excerpts (30 seconds) when your speech is short.

Ted Berniers-Lee, credited with inventing the World Wide Web, delivered a TED (Technology, Education, Design) lecture entitled "The Year Open Data Went Worldwide." During his 20-minute lecture, he used slides and brief video excerpts effectively. Since the video excerpts required no sound, he narrated the excerpts, always talking directly to his audience and not at the large video screen behind him. (You can access this lecture at: http://www.ted.com/talks/tim_berniers_lee_the_year_open_data_went_worldwide.html). Harsha Bhogle explained how the rise of cricket paralleled the rise of modern India, effectively using very short video excerpts during a 20-minute TED lecture (see http://www.ted.com/talks/harsha_bhogle_the_rise_of_cricket_the_rise_of_india.html). Since the video excerpts included necessary sound, Bhogle kept the excerpts very short so his presentation did not deteriorate into merely viewing a video without a speech.

Projection Equipment: Blowing It Up

There are several options for projecting images onto a large screen. Slide projectors used to be very common, but they have neared extinction as a visual aid medium, mostly replaced by PowerPoint slide presentations. Kodak stopped manufacturing slide projectors in 2004.

Overhead projectors, despite being an aging technology, continue to be used in some circumstances. Overhead projectors can be used to display enlarged images. They are still around because they are easy to use, mostly problem free, relatively inexpensive, and a flexible piece of equipment. Transparencies are placed on the overhead projector, enlarging a table, map, picture, graph, or drawing. Transparencies are very simple to prepare. Whatever can be photocopied can be made into a transparency. The relative ease with which this equipment can be used tempts speakers to overdo the number of transparencies used during a speech. Be careful not to substitute transparencies for an actual speech.

Document cameras, such as the Elmo series, offer similar advantages of overhead projectors, but they do not require creating transparencies. Almost any image from a magazine, book, pamphlet or a simple object can be projected onto a large screen. They also can magnify very small images a hundredfold, and they allow you to zoom in and out on images. Some versions of this technology have wireless remote control, split-screen, masking, and highlighting capabilities. Becoming familiar with this equipment is essential to using it effectively.

Finally, there are computer projectors. Pictures taken directly from computer software presentations can be shown on a large screen. The time needed to prepare the computer presentation and possible technical breakdowns in the middle of the presentation are potential drawbacks.

Computer-Assisted Presentations: PowerPoint

By now you should be familiar with the many options available for computer-assisted presentations. PowerPoint is probably the most widely available and utilized example of this visual aid medium, although other computer-assisted presentational software options such as Prezi and SlideRocket have emerged more recently. Space does not allow a "how-to" explanation for using PowerPoint. There are several excellent sites on the Internet that provide step-by-step instructions (see www .internet4classrooms.com; or www.microsoft.com/education/ppttutorial.mspx). The biggest drawbacks of PowerPoint presentations are the time it takes to prepare the slides, the potential for glitches to occur during the actual speech, and the tendency to become so enamored with the software capability that it detracts from the actual speech (see Box 13.1).

Consultant Cliff Atkinson (2008), author of *Beyond Bullet Points*, offers several research-based suggestions for improving PowerPoint presentations. Unlike some conventional suggestions, such as the "rule of seven" (no more than seven bulleted lines on a slide or seven words per line), Atkinson translates theory and research on communication into solid advice for improving PowerPoint presentations. First, *do not overwhelm listeners with complicated slides*. Text-heavy slides with numerous bullet points, which Atkinson calls the "grocery list approach," are not visually interesting. Using several different fonts also can be confusing. Second, *do not read the slides to your audience*, and do not wait for your listeners to read lengthy slides. This interrupts the flow of your presentation. Research also shows that reading a list of bulleted points diminishes learning the information (Mayer, 2005; Mitchell, 2009). Attention fades. Third, *narrate your PowerPoint slides*. You tell the story that focuses listeners on your main points as you advance your slides. Fourth, *most slides should have a full-sentence headline at the top with a descriptive graphic (picture) underneath*. Exceptions would be some photographs or cartoons that need no explanation, or slides that convey easy to grasp points. Research shows that full-sentence headlines improve listeners' knowledge and comprehension when compared to sentence fragments or phrase headings (Alley, 2005). A simple but interesting graphic for each slide recognizes that PowerPoint is a *visual* aid, so it should be visually interesting. Seven bulleted points are a snooze. Fifth, *don't get graphic crazy*. Heavy use of animation and clever graphics can make the razzle-dazzle memorable but the main points of your speech opaque and unmemorable. Animation to create humor may be appealing if used infrequently. Finally, *use a remote to advance slides*. Having to press a key on the keyboard chains you to the computer. Either you must stay located at the computer keyboard throughout your presentation, which makes your presentation stilted, or you must keep running back to the keyboard to advance the slides, which can look comical, not professional.

PHOTO 13.2 This is a good slide. It is simple, visually interesting, and relevant. The full-sentence header is not mandatory because the point is very basic, but it is included as a preferred sample. Numbers are used instead of bullet points for clarity. Typically, each "benefit" would be selected separately from this first slide during your explanation, with a new slide and visual image provided for each point.

PHOTO 13.3 Although this slide avoids the bullet point "grocery list" problem, it is a collage not a simple PowerPoint slide. There is no full-sentence header; different font sizes, colors, and typefaces are confusing; there are too many pictures to be useful; far too much text is provided and the extensive text bleeds into images; tight spacing is difficult to read; and italics and underlining are not useful because too much is highlighted. "Breath" also should be "breathe." This slide is a mess.

BOX 13.1 PowerPoint: Lots of Power, Little Point?

The year 2012 marked the twenty-fifth anniversary of PowerPoint, "one of the most elegant, most influential and most groaned-about pieces of software in the history of computers" ("PowerPoint Turns 20," 2007, p. B1). Edward Tufte (2003), Yale political scientist and specialist in graphic display of information, wrote an editorial in *Wired* magazine in 2003 entitled "PowerPoint Is Evil: Power Corrupts, PowerPoint Corrupts Absolutely." Tufte claimed that PowerPoint "elevates format over content, betraying an attitude of commercialism that turns everything into a sales pitch." Tufte even suggested that PowerPoint might have played a role in the Columbia shuttle disaster because vital technical information was swamped in the glitzy PowerPoint slides and endless bullet points. The report by the Columbia Accident

Investigation Board (2003) seemed to agree: "It is easy to understand how a senior manager might read this PowerPoint slide and not realize that it addresses a life-threatening situation." The report then went on to criticize "the endemic use of PowerPoint briefing slides" as a substitute for quality technical analysis. Inventors of the software, Robert Gaskin and Dennis Austin, agree with Tufte's criticisms. "All the things Tufte says are absolutely true. People often make very bad use of PowerPoint" (quoted in "PowerPoint Turns 20," 2007, p. B1).

The heavy reliance on PowerPoint during speeches, what consultant Nancy Stern (2004) calls "slideswiping" and others call "death by PowerPoint," should be discouraged. As Brig. Gen. H. R. McMaster, who banned PowerPoint presentations when he led forces in Iraq, notes, "Some problems in the world are not bullet-izable" (quoted in Bumiller, 2010). Imagine a bullet-point presentation of Martin Luther King's inspiring "I Have a Dream" speech.

"I Have a Dream" (several dreams, actually)—M. L. King
- Dream #1: Nation live true meaning of "all men created equal"
- Dream #2: Sit down at table of brotherhood
- Dream #3: Mississippi: transformed into oasis of freedom/justice
- Dream #4: My 4 children—judged by content of character not color of skin
- Dream #5: Alabama: black and white boys/girls become sisters/brothers

PowerPoint drains the vitality from a powerful, beautifully composed speech (Witt & Fetherling, 2009). No one is likely to feel moved to march for freedom from reading this lifeless laundry list of longed for "dreams."

PowerPoint also can place too much focus on the bells and whistles–the surface "gee whiz" computer capabilities–and too little on the content. As Atkinson (2008) notes, "When you finish the presentation, you want the audience to talk about your special ideas, not your special effects" (p. 323). Consider carefully whether multimedia presentations are appropriate and whether they really enhance the content of your presentation. Too often, speakers obsess about font size and animation instead of concentrating on developing a quality speech.

If you do choose to use PowerPoint, avoid listing every point in your outline. This is tedious and uninteresting. Remember that the power of PowerPoint is in its ability to make presentations far more interesting than your standard chalkboard or whiteboard listing of main points. When PowerPoint becomes little more than a high-tech version of a chalkboard or overhead transparencies, little is gained by using this computer technology. PowerPoint slides should meet the same criteria as visual aids in general (see next section).

There are always exceptions to every rule. A list of bulleted points may be necessary in some circumstances and a single word or phrase header may work well in some situations, but Atkinson's suggestions are excellent guidelines for using PowerPoint effectively. PowerPoint can be a wonderful *visual* aid.

GUIDELINES FOR COMPETENT USE: AIDS NOT DISTRACTIONS

Poorly designed and clumsily presented visual aids will detract, not aid, your speech. Here are some general guidelines for the competent use of visual aids.

Keep Aids Simple

Complex tables, maps, and graphics can work well in print media such as magazines and newspapers. Readers can closely examine a visual aid. Listeners do not have the same option. Complex visual aids do not work well for speeches, especially short ones, where the information needs to be communicated clearly and quickly. Your audience will be intent on figuring out a complex visual aid, not listening to you speak. Keep visual aids simple.

Make Aids Visible

The general rule for visual aids is that people in the back of the room or auditorium should be able to see your visual aid easily. If they cannot, it is not large enough to be effective. Effective font size depends on the size of the screen and the room. A huge screen in a large auditorium requires a larger font size for PowerPoint presentations than for a regular-sized classroom: typically 44 points for headlines, 32 points for main points, and 24 points for subpoints (Earnest, 2007). Font size of 16–20 points usually works well in standard-sized classrooms.

Make Aids Neat, Attractive, and Accurate

Do not embarrass yourself by showing a visual aid of poor quality. Make visual aids neat and attractive. Especially proofread your aids before showing them. Misspelled words or grammatical mistakes on PowerPoint slides, posters, charts, or tables scream "CARELESSNESS!" Tea Party protesters at 2010 rallies carried signs reading: "No Pubic Option," "Politians Are Like Dipers: They Need to be Changed Often," "Get a Brain Morans," and "Crisis of Competnce." Carelessness kills credibility.

PHOTO 13.4 Simple errors on a visual aid can diminish your credibility.

Do Not Block the Audience's View

A very common mistake made even by professional speakers is that they block the audience's view of the visual aid. Standing in front of your poster, graph, drawing, table, or PowerPoint slide while you talk to the visual aid, not to your audience, is awkward and self-defeating. Audience members should not have to stand and move across the room to see a visual aid, crane their necks, or give up in frustration because a speaker's big pumpkin head is blocking their view. Simply stand beside your poster, drawing, graph, or video excerpt while you explain it to the audience. Point the toes of your shoes toward the audience and imagine that your feet are nailed to the ground. If you do not move your feet, you will continue to stand beside, not in front of, your visual aid. *Talk to your audience, not to your visual aid.*

Keep Aids Close to You

Placing a visual aid across the room from where you speak is awkward. This is particularly problematic when using PowerPoint (Atkinson, 2008). You do not

Standing in front of a visual aid and talking to it, not to your audience, are two common mistakes. Speakers need to get their planet-size heads out of the way, stand beside their visual aid, and speak directly to their audience.

want to split the listeners' attention and create the look of a crowd at a tennis match shifting eye contact back and forth from projection screen to you speaking across the room.

Put the Aid Out of Sight When Not in Use

Cover your poster or drawing, graph, or photo when not actually referring to it. Simply leaving it open to view when you no longer make reference to it or showing it before you actually use it distracts an audience. Atkinson (2008) suggests including blank slides between images on PowerPoint slides when you are not referring to them for a while (a minute or more). Shut off the overhead projector, document camera, or video player when you are finished using them.

Practice with Aids

Using visual aids competently requires practice. At first, using a visual aid may seem awkward, even unnatural. Once you have practiced your speech using a visual aid, however, it will seem more natural and less awkward. Practice will also help you work out any problems that might occur before actually giving your speech for real.

Do Not Circulate Your Aids

Do not pass around photos, cartoons, drawings, objects, or anything that can distract your audience from paying attention to you while you are speaking. If audience members want to see your visual aid again, let them approach you after the speech for a second viewing.

Do Not Talk in the Dark

I have had to advise student speakers not to turn off the classroom lights when they are showing video clips during their presentations. When lights are off, the room becomes so dark that they become disembodied voices. The audience cannot see nonverbal elements of their presentation, and it all comes off as just weird. Some professional speakers do the same thing. With a huge screen and PowerPoint slides flashing one after the other, speakers become "little more than well-educated projectionists whose major role is to control the PowerPoint

PHOTO 13.5 You cannot see the speaker's face in the darkness, making his speech little more than a voiceover for PowerPoint slides.

PHOTO 13.6 Do not speak in the dark. Use indirect lighting if room lighting cannot be dimmed.

and video displays projected on the screen" (Nevid, 2011, p. 54). If possible, dim the lights so slides or video excerpts show more effectively without putting everyone in darkness. If there is no dimmer switch to lower the lights, try bringing in a lamp with a low wattage bulb and lighten the room that way with the main lights switched off. If the room is very large and there is no way to dim the lights, try focusing a light on you at a podium so the audience can see you as you speak.

Anticipate Problems

The more complicated your technology, the greater the likelihood that problems will occur before or during your presentation. Projection bulbs burn out unexpectedly, computers crash, programs will not load. Have a backup plan. If the audience is small (30 or fewer), a hard copy of PowerPoint slides, for example, can be prepared just in case your computer fails. Overhead transparencies of slides also can be prepared if the audience is large. Show up early and do a quick test to verify that all systems are GO! If your easel falls over during your presentation, be prepared with a casual remark to lighten the moment ("Just checking to see if everyone is alert; obviously I wasn't"). Think about what might go wrong and anticipate ways to respond.

SUMMARY

Visual aids must be both visually interesting and an actual aid to your speech. Sloppy, poorly prepared, and poorly selected visual aids can bring you ridicule and embarrassment. Always choose and prepare your visual aids carefully. Visual aids can clarify complicated points, gain and maintain audience attention, enhance your credibility, improve your delivery, and make your information memorable. You have many types of visual aids to choose from, but make sure that you do not become enamored with the technologically sophisticated and glitzy aids when you are not well versed in their use and your speech would be diminished by too much flash and not enough substance. Follow the guidelines for using visual aids appropriately and effectively.

14

Informative Speaking

Two theorists speak metaphorically of surfing, swimming, and drowning in information to underline the need to manage it effectively (Crawford & Gorman, 1996). Although discussing information in the context of electronic technology, their metaphors seem applicable to informative speaking. An informative speech with too little information presented is unsatisfying to an audience. This is analogous to surfing, merely skimming the top of a subject without delving deeply. Presenting too much information is analogous to drowning, swamping an audience in a tidal wave of information too voluminous to appreciate or comprehend. An informative speech works best when the speaker swims in the information, finding the right balance between too little and too much information for the audience. In this chapter, the focus is on constructing and presenting a specific type of speech—the informative speech—that must find that right balance between too much and too little information.

Everywhere you look, informative speaking occurs. YouTube and other Internet sites provide access to all manner of informative speeches from education and industry, some great (see especially www.*Ted.com*) and some not so great. Teachers spend the bulk of their time in the classroom speaking informatively. Managers present information at meetings. Religious leaders speak informatively when interpreting religious doctrines, organizing fund drives, charitable activities, and special events. Students give informative presentations in a wide variety of courses and disciplines. Competent informative speaking is a valuable skill.

The principal purpose of this chapter is to explain how you construct and present a competent informative speech. The differences between informative and persuasive speeches, the types of informative speeches, and guidelines and strategies for delivering competent informative speeches are discussed.

DISTINGUISHING INFORMATIVE FROM PERSUASIVE SPEAKING

The overriding difference between an informative and persuasive speech is your general purpose. *The general purpose of an informative speech is to teach your audience something new, interesting, and useful.* You want your listeners to learn. *The general purpose of a persuasive speech is to convince your listeners to change their viewpoint and behavior.* You want your listeners to think and act differently.

Do not think of informative and persuasive speeches as opposites. They differ more by degree than in kind. A teacher, for example, is primarily interested in informing students, but controversial issues arise and advocacy of a particular theory or perspective may occur. So teaching is not purely informative. Persuasive speeches also inform. You often have to teach your audience about the magnitude of a problem that listeners may not have been aware of before advocating solutions. Nevertheless, two specific distinctions between informative and persuasive speeches can help you understand where a speech falls on the informative-persuasive continuum.

Noncontroversial Information: Staying Neutral

Informative speeches do not usually stir disagreement and dissension. It is hard to imagine any audience getting worked into a froth if you offered study tips to improve students' test scores or ways to avoid the common cold, as long as the information is accurate. Some information, however, has the potential to ignite disagreement without prompting. For example, in India, a massive earthquake struck parts of the country on January 26, 2001. The biggest impediment to the distribution of desperately needed aid to the millions afflicted was India's traditional caste system—a social hierarchy, outlawed long ago but still strong in practice, with Brahmans at the top and the "untouchables" at the bottom. As Catholic Relief Services worker Mayuri Mistry explained, "Whatever the distribution of aid, it first goes to the upper caste" (quoted in Coleman, 2001, p. 7A). Simply reporting this to your listeners may outrage many Americans whose cultural values disdain preferential treatment especially in times of crisis, even though it does occur in the United States.

Nevertheless, presenting all relevant sides on an issue in a neutral fashion focuses on teaching something new, interesting, or useful, not on advocating a specific point of view. "I've explained three ways that you can build your finances for the future. Whichever one you choose, know that there is a strong financial future awaiting you" does not advocate; it informs. You are not being told which choice to make. If, however, conclusions are drawn regarding which side is correct after weighing the evidence and a specific choice is advocated, then you are trying to persuade.

Precursor to Persuasion: No Call to Action

An informative speech may arouse your listeners' concern on a subject. This concern may trigger a desire to correct a problem. Your informative speech may act as a precursor, or stepping stone, to a subsequent persuasive speech advocating strong action. If you hear a speech informing you of the pros and cons of hybrid cars, you might be encouraged without any prompting from the speaker to investigate such cars further or even to buy one. If a speaker relates a personal story about the rewards he or she experiences teaching young children, you might begin to consider teaching as a profession, even though the speaker never makes such an appeal.

In some cases, you may be presenting interesting information to your audience without connecting it to any particular issue, but someone in the audience might. For example, do you know who Otis Blackwell was? He died May 6, 2002, at the age of 70. Otis Blackwell was credited with writing more than 1,000 songs that were recorded by such international stars as Elvis Presley, Ray Charles, Billy Joel, The Who, Otis Redding, James Taylor, Peggy Lee, and Jerry Lee Lewis (Edwards, 2002). His songs sold more than 185 million copies. Providing further details about the life of this remarkable African American talent would be an interesting informative speech. Someone listening to such a speech, however, might wonder why mainstream America is mostly oblivious that Blackwell ever lived. A persuasive speech that advocates teaching more African American history to American college students might be triggered by an informative speech on Otis Blackwell.

If you are given an assignment by your teacher to present an informative speech to the class, or are told by your boss to make a report to a committee or group, or are asked to explain a new software package to novice computer users, remember that your focus will be on teaching, not convincing your listeners. The more neutral and even-handed your presentation, the more essentially informative it is. When you take a firm stand, present only one side without critique, or advocate a change in behavior from your listeners, you have moved into persuasive territory.

The competent public speaker recognizes when persuasion is appropriate and when the specific context calls for a presentation more informative in nature. When teachers use the classroom as a platform for personal advocacy, they may step over the not always clear line between informative and persuasive speaking. Advocacy on issues directly relevant to the teaching role, such as advocating the

PHOTO 14.1 Otis Blackwell wrote songs for Elvis and numerous other famous singers but is largely unknown to most Americans.

scientific method as a means of critical thinking, is appropriate. Advocating "correct" political points of view, however, such as who to vote for in an election, can run dangerously close to proselytizing, or converting the "unbelievers," not teaching. Again, *it can be a blurry line that separates informative from persuasive speeches.*

TYPES OF INFORMATIVE SPEECHES

The issue of what constitutes an informative speech becomes clearer by looking at different types. *Informative speeches are about ideas, objects, events, procedures, concepts, and people.* How you approach each of these subjects determines the type of informative speech you present. There is some overlap, but each type has its own unique qualities.

Trying to convince your audience to take a particular action is not an informative speech; it is a persuasive speech.

Reports: Facts in Brief

A **report** is usually a brief, concise, informative presentation that fulfills a class assignment, updates a committee about work performed by a subcommittee, reveals the results of a study, provides recent findings, or identifies the latest developments in a current situation of interest. Students give reports in classes and during meetings of student government. Scientists give reports on research results. Press secretaries give reports, or briefings, to members of the mass media. Military officers give briefings to fellow officers and to the press.

Reports need to be clearly presented. Make sure you have your facts straight and that all information presented is accurate. Complex, detailed information should be summarized succinctly. Present the main points and the most significant specifics. Avoid getting lost in minutia.

Explanations: Deeper Understanding

Unlike a simple report which merely states the facts to an audience that often is already familiar with the topic, such as the press corps at a presidential press conference, speeches that seek to explain are concerned with advancing deep understanding of complex concepts, processes, events, objects, and issues for listeners who are typically unfamiliar with the material presented. For example, Author Elizabeth Gilbert gave a 20-minute TED (Technology, Entertainment, Design) presentation on nurturing creativity and genius (http://www.ted.com/talks/elizabeth_gilbert_on-genius.html). Game designer Jane McGonigal presented a TED lecture on how to make a better world from playing online games such as ones she designed (World without Oil; Superstruct; and Evoke) (http://www.ted.com/talks/jane_mcgonigal_gaming_can_make_a_better_world.html).

The lecture is a common example of informative speeches that explain. Students are most familiar with this type of informative speech, having heard hundreds of lectures from numerous instructors. Unlike reports that typically run about 15 minutes or fewer, lectures often last an hour or more. Also unlike most reports, lectures work best when they are highly entertaining. Attention strategies discussed extensively in Chapter 5 are extremely important to the success of a lecture. Maintaining the attention of listeners for long periods of time is a huge challenge. Teachers, celebrities, famous authors, politicians, consultants, and experts of all types use the lecture platform to share ideas.

Demonstrations: Acting Out

A **demonstration** is an informative speech that shows the audience how to use an object or perform a specific activity. Dance teachers demonstrate dance steps while explaining how best to perform the steps. Cooking and home-improvement television programs are essentially demonstration speeches. Demonstration speeches require the speaker to show the physical object or to display the activity for the audience. A demonstration is not a mere description of objects or activities. If you are going to give a speech on martial arts, do not ask your audience to imagine specific movements and techniques. Show them. A speech on how card tricks and magic are performed must actually demonstrate the trick slowly and clearly so the audience can understand.

Narratives: Storytelling

One morning, a blood vessel burst in neuroanatomist Jill Bolte Taylor's brain. She was 37 years old. As a brain scientist, she realized that she had a rare opportunity to witness her own stroke and understand what was happening while it occurred: movement,

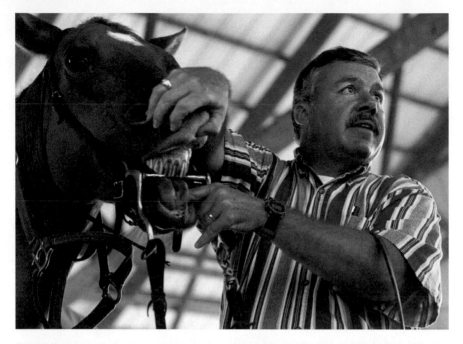

PHOTO 14.2 A live animal may be an effective visual aid for a demonstration speech, but animals can be very difficult to control and are mostly impractical for classroom demonstrations.

speech, memory, self-awareness all became impaired. As she observed, "How many brain scientists have been able to study the brain from the inside out? I've gotten as much out of this experience of losing my left mind as I have in my entire academic career" (quoted in "Jill Bolte Taylor: Neuroanatomist," 2008). She spent 8 years recovering her ability to walk, talk, and think. She tells her amazing story of what it was like experiencing a stroke and what it took to recover from it in a bestselling book entitled: *My Stroke of Insight: A Brain Scientist's Personal Journey.* She also gave an 18-minute narrative presentation at the TED conference in Monterey, California, on February 27, 2008, explaining what her stroke was like and what insights she learned. Her story is intensely moving. By the conclusion, she is in tears, as are many in the audience. It became one of the top ten presentations for the TED organization (see "Jill Bolte Taylor's Stroke of Insight" at *www.TED.com*).

A story well told, such as Dr. Taylor's fascinating journey, can be thoroughly engaging (Hsu, 2008). Taylor's speech is highly engaging. She shows a real human brain with spinal cord attached, a captivating visual aid, and she provides insights about your own brain. Narratives may be about you or about other people. Instructors may give a short presentation at the beginning of a course informing students about number of years spent teaching, where teaching occurred, the joys and

PHOTO 14.3 Neuroanatomist Dr. Jill Bolte Taylor suffered a severe stroke and told her story at a TED lecture entitled "My Stroke of Insight" (also the title of her book).

challenges of teaching, and prospects for teaching in the future. Also relating really dumb things tried in the classroom that went embarrassingly wrong can make a professor seem more human and approachable. Narratives may be historical ("The Struggles of Rosa Parks"), personal ("My Life As a Surgeon"), self-disclosive ("I once lived a life of drug addiction"), or merely amusing ("What It's Like Being a Technophobe"). Narratives are most effective when they entertain an audience.

Speeches that Compare: Balancing the Pros and Cons

Some informative speeches explain serious problems that exist then compare a variety of potential solutions without taking a stand on any of the remedies offered. For example, increasing prices of college textbooks is a recognized national problem. There are several possible solutions: increasing the availability of used books, using open-source public domain materials available for e-readers, establishing textbook rental programs, urging professors to adopt only textbooks that have minimal ancillaries (websites, CDs, etc.), discouraging publishers from producing new editions sooner than every 3–4 years, encouraging customized versions of textbooks, and offering more "stripped down" versions of standard textbooks that can be priced more cheaply than more elaborate versions. Each of these solutions has pros and cons. For instance, expanding the availability of used books means more students can purchase textbooks at three-quarters the cost of a new textbook ($75 used compared to $100 new), but as the availability of used books increases, textbook publishers are pressured to increase the cost of new versions of textbooks to counter losses engendered by used books. Presenting the positives and negatives of various solutions without taking a stand on any of them is structured as an informative speech. You leave it to the audience to make choices based on a balanced presentation of possible remedies for a problem.

These five types of informative speeches can overlap. A report may occasionally veer into a demonstration when listeners appear confused about what is reported. A teacher typically lectures for a majority of a class period, but the teacher may do demonstrations to add variety and make a point more memorable and meaningful. I have used a fairly lengthy demonstration of a polygraph, or lie-detector machine, using student volunteers, to drive home several points related to nonverbal communication and connotative meaning related to words. It never fails to engender interest, even fascination, from the class. Years later, students tell me they still remember that particular demonstration and what it showed.

GUIDELINES FOR COMPETENT INFORMATIVE SPEAKING

In general, informative speeches work best when the information presented is clear, accurate, and interesting instead of opaque, wrong, and boring. Thus, review Chapter 5 on attention, Chapter 7 on outlining and organizing your informative speech, Chapter 10 on reasoning and use of evidence, and Chapter 13 on visual aids. This section provides additional tips for presenting effective informative speeches.

Be Informative: Tell Us What We Do Not Know

Raising the index finger to signify "one" means "two" in Italy–the thumb counts as one. In Japan, however, the upright thumb means "five"; counting begins with the index finger with the thumb as the last digit. Nodding the head up and down means "yes" in the United States, and shaking it side to side means "no." In Bulgaria, Turkey,

Iran, the former Yugoslavia, and Bengal, however, it is the reverse. In Greece, tipping the head back abruptly means "no," but the same gesture in India means "yes" (Axtell, 1998). (Nod your head if you understand all of this.) Did you know these details of cultural differences in nonverbal communication? If not, then you have been informed. If you already knew, then you have not been informed.

Your first guideline for an effective informative speech, and seemingly most obvious, is to provide new information to your listeners. I say seemingly obvious because I have sat through far too many "informative" presentations that never told me a thing I did not know previously, and in some cases the speaker should have known that the points made were trivial and lacked any insight. If your listeners say after your presentation, "I didn't learn a thing," then you have been ineffective. This does not mean that everything you present must be new information, but the emphasis should be on providing information which is not widely known.

Adapt to Your Audience: Topic Choice and Knowledge Base

How do you know whether your informative speech goes beyond what your listeners already know? That requires an analysis of your audience (see Chapter 4).

PHOTO 14.4 To be informative, tell us what we do not know already.

If the topic choice is at your discretion, then choose what will likely interest your listeners and is well suited to their knowledge, concerns, and expectations. If the subject of your speech is too high level, complex, and abstract for the educational level of your audience, then you have chosen poorly. Presenting information on systems theory or thermodynamics will not resonate with very young audiences because the information is well over their heads. Set theory in mathematics will probably baffle a lot of adult audiences. If the choice is not up to you and the topic is very high level, complex, and abstract (a professor teaching quantum physics to students), your challenge is to explain clearly each facet of your subject. Use multiple examples, personal stories, visual aids, metaphors, analogies, and demonstrations to clarify difficult material. Albert Einstein, when faced with explaining his immensely complex theory of relativity to laypeople offered this as a starting point: "When you sit with a nice girl for 2 hours you think it's only a minute. But when you sit on a hot stove for a minute you think it's 2 hours. That's relativity" (quoted in "Famous Quotes and Authors," 2009). Remember that oral style requires simpler language than written style. Strive for language simplicity as discussed in Chapter 12, and avoid highly complex language that may confuse even a well-educated audience.

If your subject is fairly simple and you are addressing an educated audience, be careful not to condescend to your listeners. Acting as though they are third graders is patronizing and will insult them. If your audience is already knowledgeable about your subject, more difficult material can be included earlier and with less need to elaborate extensively.

Avoid Information Overload: Beware the Data Dump

A chief challenge you face constructing an informative speech is not typically too little information available on your subject but too much (Silver, 2012). Separating the useless from the useful information takes effort. The ready availability of huge quantities of information because of computer technologies also can tempt a speaker to provide way too much detail and complexity in a speech. Avoid the tedious "data dump." Know when to quit. Preparation and practice are essential. Prepare a well-organize informative speech, then practice the speech and *time it precisely* while giving it beforehand. Timing your speech will immediately indicate whether you have provided way too much information for the time allotted. Be careful not to offer needless detail. Ask yourself, "Do they really need to know this?"

Tell Your Story Well: Narrative Tips

Stories can be short vignettes or lengthy detailed narratives. Randy Pausch, a 47-year-old Carnegie Mellon University computer science professor who contracted pancreatic cancer in 2007, gave a lecture at his university on September 18, 2007, to a crowd of 500 students, faculty, and friends. In a 75-minute presentation, Pausch told many stories about his life, each relating to his central idea about achieving his childhood dreams. His stories were humorous, poignant, and very entertaining. Although he knew he was dying, he conducted himself as though he were perfectly healthy, at one moment dropping to the floor and doing push-ups both one- and two-handed. When he finished his final lecture, his audience gave him a prolonged, standing ovation. The video of his lecture was seen by millions on YouTube, and it became a book titled *The Last Lecture.*

How do you tell an effective story when giving an informative speech (see Hendricks et al., 1996; Collins & Cooper, 1997)? First, *choose a story that fits your audience.* A story about the challenge and strategies of online poker playing will not likely resonate with an audience that abhors gambling. Second, *make sure that the story fits your purpose and illustrates a key point.* You should not tell sto ries just to entertain if they have no relevance. Third, *keep the stories concise.* Do not get bogged down in details that can become confusing or tedious for your listeners or lose sight of the key theme. If a detail does not advance the story but sidetracks it, cut it. Fourth, *practice telling your story.* Tell it to friends, family

PHOTO 14.5 Randy Pausch delivers his "The Last Lecture" before a packed arena. Knowing he was dying from pancreatic cancer, Pausch nevertheless displayed great storytelling ability and injected humor throughout his presentation. He joked that he had experienced a near-death conversion—he bought an Apple computer.

members, or to anyone who will listen. Fifth, *do not read your story to your listeners.* You want to sound natural not artificial. Sixth, *be animated, even visual when telling a story.* If you are not interested in telling the story, why should your listeners care? Pausch was very engaging because he was unafraid to do push-ups, wear a crazy looking Jabberwocky hat, and walk around with fake arrows in his back while lecturing.

Terry Hersey is a Protestant minister who for almost three decades has presented enormously popular lectures at the annual Religious Education Congress in Anaheim, California. He tells this story often at this conference to make the point that we learn very early in life to fear making mistakes:

> There's a terrific story about a first-grade Sunday school class. The children were restless and fussy. The teacher, in an attempt to get their attention, said, "Okay kids, let's play a game. I'll describe something to you. And you tell me what it is."
>
> The kids quieted down. "Listen. It's a furry little animal with a big bushy tail, that climbs up trees and stores nuts in the winter. Who can tell me what it is? No one said anything. The teacher went on. "You are a good Sunday school class. You know the right answer to this question. It's a furry little animal with a big bushy tail, that climbs up trees and stores nuts in the winter." One little girl raised her hand. "Emily?" Well, teacher," Emily declared, "it sounds like a squirrel to me, but I'll say Jesus". *(see Hersey, 2000, pp. 100–1)*

Unfailingly, when Hersey tells this story, the audience roars with laughter. The story is brief, humorous, fits the audience perfectly because it has religious overtones and a moral to the story, is delivered in an animated style (you had to be there), and is told fluently as though Hersey has told this story many times.

Terry Hersey is a great storyteller because he has clearly practiced the art of telling a narrative. Each of you have stories to tell, whether they be personal experiences, stories told to you by parents, relatives, or friends, or perhaps they are stories you have seen and heard presented on television, on the Internet, or at Sunday sermons. When you are researching your topic, notice clever, amusing, poignant, and powerful stories told by others. You can retell many of these to make a point. "Let me tell you a story" immediately perks up an audience.

For a lengthy example of an informative speech, consult **Appendix A** at the end of this text. The speech is outlined, and then a written text is provided with application of material relevant to making effective informative speeches appearing in the margins.

SUMMARY

A key difference between informative and persuasive speaking is that informative speeches attempt to teach listeners something new, and persuasive speeches, although oftentimes informative, move beyond and attempt to change attitudes and behavior. There are five types of informative speeches that sometimes overlap during the same presentation: those that report, explain, demonstrate, tell a story, or compare pros and cons of a proposal without taking a position. Competent informative speaking is achieved by considering your audience when choosing a topic, organizing carefully, avoiding information overload, keeping your audience interested, using supporting materials competently, and telling stories well.

15

Foundations of Persuasive Speaking

It was the 60th annual convention of the California Federation of Teachers. Keynote speaker Charles Kernaghan, director of the National Labor Committee, was addressing an audience of California teachers. His central idea (theme) was that extreme poverty of much of the world's workforce accrues from economic globalization and the exploitation of workers. His speech was a rousing anti-sweatshop call to arms. Kernaghan held up garments produced overseas, and he told stories of the exploitation of workers who made these garments, most of whom are between the ages of 6 and 16. He argued that young people "have a right to ask, how do the people live who produce the clothes they wear?" ("Anti-sweatshop Activist," 2002, p. 4). Kernaghan discussed the Students Against Sweatshops movement in the United States and its hundreds of chapters on college campuses. The audience cheered when he thundered, "These kids are on fire!" Kernaghan brought his listeners to their feet when he concluded, "There can never be peace without social justice, or in a world with child labor" (p. 4).

Kernaghan's speech was masterful and an enormous success. "Of all the speakers at the 60th annual convention, none stirred delegates as deeply as Charles Kernaghan," reported the article in *California Teacher* ("Anti-sweatshop Activist," 2002, p. 4). His speech was successful for several reasons. First, the CFT convention had social justice as one of its primary themes. As members of a powerful teachers union, listeners were receptive to Kernaghan's message that non-union workers can be and are exploited as "cheap labor." Second, he evidently researched his topic very carefully. He had the facts to support his claims. Third, he used very effective attention strategies. His speech was not a dry recitation of facts and figures; it was a passionate presentation that was at times intense, startling, and vital in its depiction of the plight of garment workers in countries around the world. It aroused anger at injustice. He told stories about young women he interviewed who worked in deplorable sweatshop conditions for $1.38 a day after expenses. Fourth, he ended with a rousing appeal to stamp out exploitation of workers worldwide.

Possessing the persuasive knowledge and skills demonstrated by Kernaghan has practical significance. One study found that when economists totaled the number of people whose jobs depend predominantly on persuading people—lawyers, counselors, managers, administrators, salespersons, and public relations specialists—persuasion accounts for 26% of the gross domestic product of the United States (Bennett, 1995). Individuals often are required to speak persuasively, in courtrooms, classrooms, cultural events, and other venues.

Almost 2,500 years ago, Aristotle systematically discussed persuasion in his influential book *The Rhetoric*. The scientific study of persuasion, however, began less than a century ago in the United States. Much has been learned from this research on persuasion, providing many useful insights for you to learn. Capitalizing on this research and insight, *the primary purpose of this chapter is to explain the foundations of persuasive speaking*. The relationship between attitude change and behavior change, the goals of persuasion, the elaboration likelihood model that explains how persuasion works generally, and the influence of culture on persuasion are discussed. Specific persuasive strategies for public speaking based on an understanding of the foundations of persuasion are discussed in the next chapter.

DEFINING PERSUASION

Persuasion is a communication process of converting, modifying, or maintaining the attitudes and/or behavior of others. In Chapter 4, an **attitude** was defined as "a learned predisposition to respond favorably or unfavorably toward some attitude object" (Gass & Seiter, 2011). "The iPhone is better than the Droid phone" is an attitude and so is "Consistency requires you to be as ignorant today as you were a year ago" (Bernard Berenson). An attitude sets our mind to draw certain judgments.

Although much effort to persuade audiences is aimed at attitude change, behavior of others can change without attitude change. Threats of violence may produce behavioral change without changing attitudes. Forced compliance from threats of physical harm, damage to one's reputation, financial ruin and the like, however, are usually seen as coercion not persuasion.

So what is the difference? *The essential difference between coercion and persuasion is the perception of free choice* (Strong & Cook, 1990; Perloff, 2013). Those who coerce seek to eliminate choice by force, threats of force, or intimidation. Those who seek to persuade do so with logic, evidence, and psychological appeals that leave listeners free to choose whether to change their attitudes and/or their behavior.

ATTITUDE–BEHAVIOR CONSISTENCY

Although attitudes often predict behavior, there is not always a consistent relationship between the two (Perloff, 2013). For example, most Americans think the Ten Commandments should guide our lives and should be posted in public buildings as reminders (Lupu et al., 2007). We embrace them as strong attitudes—killing is wrong, coveting is bad, stealing is immoral, and so forth. Yet everyone violates at least some of the commandments as though they were merely the Ten Suggestions. Thus, our behavior does not always match our attitudes.

Very often, changing attitudes is not sufficient. It is behavior we seek to change. Consider the abstinence-only programs to prevent premarital sex among teenagers. Despite a vigorous campaign to convince teenagers to take a public pledge to

Attitudes and behavior are not always consistent. Thus, changing an attitude will not necessarily change a behavior.

abstain from premarital sex, a careful analysis of data reveals that those who took the "virginity pledge" were just as likely as non-pledgers within a 5-year period to have had premarital sex, but they were less likely to use birth control (Rosenbaum, 2009). If a principal purpose of abstinence-only programs is to prevent teen pregnancy and all the problems associated with it, then this study's results are quite disheartening. The pledge (stated attitude) does not produce the desired behavior. There are other ways to strengthen abstinence-only persuasive efforts (see Jemmott, et al., 2010), but inducing teens to make public pledges of abstinence is, by itself, unlikely to produce actual abstinence.

Why are there inconsistencies in our attitudes and behaviors? Several variables affect how consistent our attitudes and behaviors are likely to be.

Direct Experience: No Second-Hand Attitudes

Attitudes that are formed from direct experience usually conform more closely to actual behavior than those formed more indirectly (Fazio, 1986). When you have encountered a problem in your life, thought about it, felt its implications, and considered appropriate responses, your relevant attitude has been formed through direct experience. Have you ever been unemployed or experienced poverty or had to solicit money from strangers? Have you ever been a small business owner who has worried about high taxes jeopardizing your ability to thrive or even survive? That is direct experience. Your attitudes about food stamps for the poor, unemployment benefits, and business taxation are likely influenced strongly by these directly related experiences. Your behavior toward those similarly disadvantaged is more apt to coincide with these attitudes than if you have only indirect experience of such things (Perloff, 2013).

Even forming relationships with individuals who have experienced problems of discrimination, for example, brings you closer to direct experience of that problem than if you have no such relationships. Several surveys found growing support for same-sex marriage in the United States because of personal relationships respondents have had with gay and lesbian individuals. In a Pew poll, about a third of respondents cited a personal relationship with a gay or lesbian person as the reason they now support same-sex marriage ("Gay Marriage," 2013).

Those attitudes that are shaped more indirectly by media images, what friends and others have told you, or by your participation in discussion on blogging sites tend to be inconsistently related to actual behavior. These "second-hand attitudes" (Gass & Seiter, 2011) derived from indirect experience usually serve as weak predictors of behavior because, when faced with actual situations, the attitudes are more borrowed than personal. For example, it is far easier to ignore panhandlers begging for money when you have never had the desperate, frightening experience of joblessness and homelessness. Directly formed attitudes derived from personal experience are also likely to be more strongly held than second-hand attitudes.

These strong attitudes are more likely to predict behavior than weakly held, borrowed attitudes (Wallace et al., 2005). For instance, you may steadfastly avoid drinking alcohol because you have experienced first-hand what alcoholism can do to a family. Perhaps a parent was alcoholic, became abusive, and provoked constant discord in your family that eventually led to parental divorce. Your attitude about alcohol has been formed directly through personal experience and your attitude about the dangers of alcoholism is strongly held. If your attitude about alcohol is mostly formed indirectly from watching public service announcements on the dangers of alcohol and is only weakly held, however, when prodded to drink by friends and peers, you may cave in to the pressure more easily.

The more directly you can make your audience feel that they are affected by the problem you describe, the greater is the chance that listeners' behavior will move in the direction you advocate in your speech. For example, state budget cuts may seem abstract and even a dull "wonkish" issue, but if you can directly tie such cuts to your student audience's ability to get access to higher education, then you improve your chances of gaining listeners' votes on a state proposition to increase taxes. For example:

> If you don't vote for Proposition X on Tuesday, your annual tuition to attend this college will increase by 25% next year and 35% the following year. Financial aid will not cover such a huge increase. The Legislative Analyst's Office estimated last month on its website that at least 400,000 students in this state will be forced to drop out of college because of these massive tuition hikes. Can you really afford to continue your college education if Proposition X is defeated?

Make your audience "feel the pain."

Social Pressure: Getting Heat from Others

Social pressure has been shown to be a very strong influence on human behavior, and it is a significant reason why your attitudes and behavior may be inconsistent at times (Wallace at al., 2005). You may want to speak up when someone makes a racist or sexist remark, but you may remain quiet if you fear social disapproval from others for being a "troublemaker." You may not particularly enjoy drinking alcohol, but maybe you drink to excess at parties because it is the social expectation of your peer group. A Zogby International survey reported that 56% of the 1,005 college students polled felt group pressure to binge drink ("Poll," 2000; see also "Study Shows," 2012). College students binge drink. They consume 4 to 5 ounces of alcohol in a 2-hour period. They do this primarily to "fit in" with a valued group (Kirn, 1997).

PHOTO 15.1 Binge drinking is heavily influenced by peer pressure. Students may not even like drinking beer (attitude) but will do it to excess (behavior) to "fit in" with a valued group.

Social pressure and fear of disapproval makes standing before an audience and giving a speech that you know will incite a negative reaction very challenging. You want your peers to like and accept you, so you may be tempted to say what you know your audience is comfortable hearing but conflicts with your true attitude. Sometimes, however, you have to take a public stand that will likely invite disapproval. Otherwise, your attitude and behavior are inconsistent.

Effort Required: Degree of Difficulty

Despite the best intentions, attitudes and behavior will often be inconsistent because consistency may require too great an effort to perform the behavior (Wallace et al., 2005). You likely see recycling your cans, bottles, and newspapers as too labor intensive if you have to separate each item into separate bins, load them into the trunks of your cars, then drive to the nearest recycling center to unload the waste. Increasingly, however, communities around the country are recognizing the benefits of curbside recycling. Participation in recycling programs grows explosively when it is no more difficult than hauling a trash bin to the curb in front of your home. The effort required is minimal, so recycling is widespread. According to one survey, 67% of the U.S. population had access to curbside recycling by 2011, and the same percentage of paper is recovered for recycling as a result ("Survey," 2011).

When trying to persuade an audience to act on a problem, find the easiest ways for listeners to express their support. Signing a petition or donating a dollar on the spot after your speech is an easy way to show support. Asking listeners to canvass neighborhoods, call strangers on the phone to solicit support for a cause or a candidate, or raise money for a program are hampered by the effort required to perform the behavior. Far less participation in such activities should be expected as a result.

Consider how student Sean McLaughlin (1996) offers simple, yet effective, solutions for the problem of food poisoning:

> First, wash hands well and wash them often. . . . If you prefer to use sponges and dishcloths, be sure to throw them in the dishwasher two or three times a week. Also, try color coding your sponges—the red one for washing dishes and a blue one for wiping up countertops. . . . Experts also suggest using both sides of a cutting board—one side for meats and the other side for vegetables. And those who wash dishes by hand, be careful. Scrub dishes vigorously with an antibacterial soap and rinse with hot water. Air drying is preferred to drying with a towel. . . . Finally, and perhaps the best advice—don't become lax when it comes to food safety in your home. Don't write your congressperson, write your mom. As we have seen today, re-educating yourself and spreading the word on kitchen safety can significantly reduce chances of food poisoning. (p. 75)

The speaker provides several easy steps that will protect you from food poisoning. One step, air drying dishes, actually reduces labor. Towel drying requires effort; air drying requires merely waiting.

Solutions to serious problems offered in your speech cannot always be simple and easy to implement. Nevertheless, try to suggest ways that even complex solutions can be implemented in relatively simple, straightforward steps.

GOALS OF PERSUASION

Persuasive speaking can have several goals. Choosing the appropriate goal for the situation will largely determine your degree of success or failure.

Conversion: Radical Persuasion

Psychologist Muzafer Sherif and his associates (1965) developed the **social judgment theory** of persuasion to explain attitude change (see also Littlejohn & Foss, 2011). Their theory states that when listeners hear a persuasive message, they compare it with attitudes they already hold. The preexisting attitude on an issue

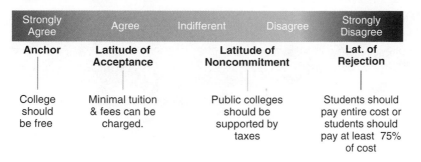

FIGURE 15.1 Social Judgment Theory and Persuasion

serves as an **anchor**, or reference point. Surrounding this anchor is a range of possible attitudes an individual may hold. Positions a person finds tolerable form his or her **latitude of acceptance**. Positions that provoke only a neutral or ambivalent response form the **latitude of noncommitment**. Those positions the person would find objectionable because they are too far from the anchor attitude form the **latitude of rejection**. Figure 15-1 depicts this range of possible opinions on an issue.

Research found that persuasive messages that fall within a person's latitude of rejection almost never produce a change in attitude (Sherif et al., 1965). *The further away a position is from the anchor attitude, the less likely persuasion will be successful* (Sherif et al., 1973; Littlejohn & Foss, 2011). This is especially true when the listener has high ego involvement with the issue. **Ego involvement** refers to the degree to which an issue is relevant or important to a person (Littlejohn & Foss, 2011). Students who work hard for a political candidate, for example, are highly unlikely to vote for the opponent.

Social judgment theory strongly suggests that setting conversion as your goal for persuasion is usually unrealistic. Conversion asks your listeners to move from their anchor position to a completely contradictory position. This is especially unlikely when conversion is sought during a brief persuasive speech. Students often make the attempt to convert the "unbelievers" in speeches on abortion, religion, and other emotionally charged topics. Such efforts are doomed from the start. If your message seeks conversion from your audience, it will likely meet with quick resistance, especially if your listeners have strongly formed attitudes on the subject.

Unless a *significant emotional event* occurs, conversion almost never happens from a single persuasive event. If you have been a strong gun control advocate but experience a home invasion in which your life and those of your loved ones were threatened, you may think seriously about purchasing a hand gun for future protection. Absent such an emotional event, however, conversion from strong gun

Conversion from one strong belief to a contradictory belief is highly unlikely to occur, especially from a single speech. Would appearance pose an identification with the audience issue?

control advocate to a defender of relatively unrestricted gun ownership is unlikely. Hearing a 10-minute persuasive speech, no matter how eloquent, rarely converts anyone holding strong views. Conversion, then, is an unrealistic goal for most persuasive speeches.

Modification: Do Not Ask for the Moon

Research suggests moderate, not extreme, positions relative to a particular audience are most persuasive (Edwards & Smith, 1996). Positions that lie at the outer fringes of a listener's latitude of acceptance may become the new anchor position as a result of a persuasive speech. For example, very restrictive gun control legislation that requires a lengthy waiting period, background checks, and limitations on number of gun purchases annually may be a person's anchor. A strong persuasive speech, however, may realistically modify this person's position to an outright ban on handguns. Once this position is embraced, it may become the new anchor. Subsequent persuasive efforts may move the anchor incrementally until the person eventually accepts a complete ban on ownership of *all guns*. The change in attitude occurs bit by bit. It is rarely a one-time effort. *Modification of attitudes and behavior is an appropriate, realistic goal for a persuasive speech.*

Maintenance: Keep 'Em Coming Back

When most people think of persuasion, changing attitudes and behavior immediately come to mind. Much persuasion, however, does not aim to produce change. Charles Kernaghan's speech to the CFT was mostly "preaching to the choir." Few in that audience of active labor organizers and members would have disagreed with much of what Kernaghan said in his rousing oration. This same speech, however, would likely trigger a much less favorable reaction from an audience composed of Chamber of Commerce members or small business owners who depend on selling inexpensive clothing to stay competitive in a tough business climate.

Most advertising of well-established products, such as Coke or Toyota Camry, aims to maintain buying habits of the public. The goal is to keep consumers purchasing their products over and over and preventing purchases of competing products. In political campaigns, initial persuasion is usually aimed at "securing the base." This means motivating Democrats to keep voting for Democratic candidates and to keep Republicans voting for Republican candidates. The message is "do what you've been doing." Sunday sermons usually change few minds because most people who attend a church service require no such change. They already believe the religious dogmas articulated by the religious leader. "Preaching to the choir," however, can inspire the faithful, energize believers, and reinforce preexisting attitudes.

Part of maintaining current attitudes and behavior of your audience is inducing resistance to **counterpersuasion,** or attacks from an opposing side. Inducing resistance to counterpersuasion helps maintain current attitudes. There are two principal ways you can induce resistance to counterpersuasion. First, *forewarn* your audience members that an attempt to change their attitudes, beliefs, or behavior will occur (Benoit, 1998; Quinn & Wood, 2004). Prosecution and defense attorneys often use forewarning in their opening statements to juries. Here is an example: "The defense will try to appeal to your emotions by presenting her client as a desperate father trying to save his dying child. Don't be fooled. The defendant is a cold, calculating murderer." Forewarning gives your listeners time to generate counter-arguments that thwart attempted persuasion and to rehearse their responses (Gass & Seiter, 2011).

A second way to induce resistance to persuasion is to *inoculate* your audience (McGuire, 1964). When you are inoculated against disease, you are exposed to a weakened version of the virus to trigger an immune response. Likewise, inoculating your audience to counterpersuasion exposes your listeners to a weakened version of counterarguments. Studies aimed at preventing teenagers from starting to smoke cigarettes found that merely mentioning arguments for smoking (e.g., smoking is cool; peers will like you) and then refuting these weakly presented arguments did induce resistance to peer persuasion to start smoking (Pfau & Van Bockern, 1994). There is substantial evidence that inoculation can be an effective way to induce resistance to persuasion (Pfau et al. 2005; Szabo & Pfau, 2002; Wood, 2007).

ELABORATION LIKELIHOOD MODEL

The **elaboration likelihood model** (ELM) of persuasion is an overarching explanation for how listeners cope with the bombardment of persuasive messages by sorting them into those that are important, or central, and those that are less relevant, or peripheral (Petty & Cacioppo, 1986a, 1986b). The *central route* requires mindfulness—the content of the message is scrutinized for careful reasoning and substantial, credible evidence. Counterarguments are considered and weighed. Questions come to mind, and a desire for more information (elaboration) emerges. The *peripheral route* is relatively mindless—little attention is given to processing a persuasive message. The listener looks for mental shortcuts to make quick decisions about seemingly peripheral issues. Credibility, likeability, and attractiveness of a persuader, how other people react to the message, and the consequences that might result from agreeing or disagreeing with the persuader are some of the shortcuts used in the peripheral route (Shadel et al., 2001).

In the aftermath of the 2012 vice-presidential debate between Joe Biden and Paul Ryan, Republican spinmeisters emphasized the frequent "smiles of contempt" exhibited by Biden. These are peripheral cues of influence. Democrats quickly retorted that if you have to focus on smiles and facial expressions, you are tacitly admitting that your candidate lost the debate on substance (central processing). Mainstream and social media are quick to latch on to peripheral cues of persuasion that work for or against an individual or group. The Twitterverse went into hyperdrive during the Biden-Ryan debate, focusing on Biden's flamboyant style of presentation and Ryan's seeming need to drink gallons of water during the debate. A video was released on the Internet afterward showing Ryan drinking substantial quantities of water 22 times during the 90-minute exchange, suggesting that he was extremely nervous. Peripheral cues that an audience views as positive or negative may render carefully prepared arguments relatively inconsequential.

To illustrate the two routes to persuasion working in tandem, consider an example offered by Gass and Seiter (2011). Consider that Michael and Maria are

PHOTO 15.2 Joe Biden's "facial calisthenics" in his 2012 debate against Paul Ryan were peripheral cues that, at times, distracted from his central arguments (Bruni, 2012).

PHOTO 15.3 Senator Marco Rubio delivered the rebuttal to Barack Obama's 2013 State of the Union address. Reaching awkwardly for a drink of bottled water during his speech, however, became a prime peripheral cue that almost entirely obscured the content of his arguments. The blogosphere and Twitterverse concentrated on almost nothing else about his speech.

on a date and about to order dinner at a nice restaurant. The waiter suggests several specials, all of them meat or fish. He even volunteers which one is his favorite. Maria orders first. She is very careful to choose only vegetarian dishes from the menu. She asks the waiter whether an entrée is cooked in animal fat, is there any butter in the pasta, and does the sauce contain any dairy products? Maria turns to Michael and says with an animated delivery that he should eat vegetarian because it is healthier and reduces animal deaths. Michael has no strong opinion on the subject, but he is very attracted to Maria. He tells the waiter, "I'll have what she ordered." Maria used the central route to decide her order. She was very mindful of her decision. She considered her decision very carefully because it was important to her. Michael, on the other hand, used the peripheral route. The decision was relatively unimportant to him so he based his order on a cue unrelated to the menu, the waiter's preference, or the arguments offered by Maria. He ordered vegetarian because he hoped to gain favor with Maria.

Typically, listeners use both central and peripheral routes, called **parallel processing**, when presented with persuasive messages (Petty et al., 1987). The degree to which a receiver emphasizes the central or peripheral route depends primarily on listeners' *motivation* and *ability* to think about and carefully assess the quality of a persuasive message (Petty et al., 2004). Listeners are more motivated to use the central route when the issues affect them personally. They are more likely to use the peripheral route when issues seem tangential to their interests, are largely inconsequential to their lives, and their knowledge of a subject is limited and they are distracted or preoccupied. If you were Michael in the situation above, you are motivated to please your date, not to learn about vegetarianism. Your knowledge of issues related to vegetarianism is superficial at best, and you are distracted by your attraction to your date. It is a wonder you can think at all.

Also, some persuasive messages are too complex and require technical knowledge to evaluate. In such cases, a listener's ability to use central processing is limited. Typically, peripheral cues, such as how other audience members respond to the messages, will be used.

Attitude change produced by the central route tends to be more persistent, resistant to change, and predictive of behavior than attitude change produced by the peripheral route (Petty et al., 2004). If Michael never again went on another outing with Maria, he probably would eat dead cow flesh with relish because his flirtation with vegetarianism was arrived at by peripheral influences.

Clearly, *central processing of persuasive messages should be encouraged* because it is what skeptics do when presented with a persuasive message (see Chapter 9). You can increase central processing when giving speeches by making issues relevant to listeners' lives. Complex, technical issues can be simplified for lay audiences. If listeners understand the basic concepts, they can analyze arguments and evidence presented. Because of time constraints and information overload, however, you sometimes have no choice but to use peripheral processing. Persuasive strategies that typically trigger parallel processing will be discussed in the next chapter.

CULTURE AND PERSUASION

The scientific investigation of persuasive speaking is a peculiarly Western interest. In Asian countries, for instance, spirited debates to influence decision making have been viewed as relatively pointless. Debates create friction and disharmony and usually end inconclusively (Jaffe, 1998). Japan, for example, began implementing a jury-style system in its criminal courts in 2009 (Kawatsu, 2009). This is a momentous change from the long-standing practice of judges making judicial decisions in criminal cases. To acclimate a hesitant populace to the new system, 500 mock trials were held. Nevertheless, 80% of Japanese surveyed about the new jury system expressed dread at the prospect of participating. Japanese reluctance emerges from a deeply rooted cultural revulsion to expressing personal opinions, arguing with others in public, and questioning authority (Onishi, 2007; Tabuchi & McDonald, 2009). Absence of a jury system is not unusual in Asian countries. South Korea, for example, did not institute a jury system until 2008 (Young, 2008).

Persuasive speaking works best when it is adapted to the cultural composition of your audience. Persuasive strategies that may successfully change attitudes and behavior in an individualistic country such as the United States may not be so successful in collectivist countries (Murray-Johnson et al., 2001). **Individualist cultures** emphasize personal autonomy and competitiveness, privacy, individual liberties, and toleration of nonconformity. **Collectivist cultures** emphasize group harmony, intra-group cooperation and conformity, and individual sacrifice for the sake of the group (Hofstede & Hofstede, 2005). One survey showed that 70% of Asian subjects (collectivist) highly valued "an orderly society" but only 11% of Americans (individualist) did, and only 32% of Asians highly valued "individual rights" but 73% of Americans did (cited in Simons & Zielenziger, 1996). Appeals to order should be more persuasive in collectivist cultures and appeals to individual rights should be more persuasive in individualist cultures.

For example, an American ad shows a young man at the wheel of a Cadillac CTS and presents a choice between "The nail that sits up gets hammered down" or "You can be the hammer." The first is an aphorism well known in Japan that expresses a collectivist viewpoint. The second is a clearly individualist viewpoint. Cadillac is obviously appealing to individualist values of American culture to sell cars when the ad implies being the hammer is the preferred position. Such an ad would likely backfire in Japan.

Clearly, your choice of persuasive strategies when giving speeches should be influenced by the diversity of your audience. It is only one element of the complex persuasion equation, but it is an important one.

SUMMARY

When you attempt to persuade an audience you try to convert, modify, or maintain your listeners attitudes and/or behavior. Conversion is the least likely achievable goal when giving a speech. Attitudes do not always predict specific behavior. Reasons for possible inconsistency include whether the attitudes are derived from direct or indirect experience, the degree of effort required to perform the behavior, and the amount of social pressure applied to behave differently from your attitudes. The elaboration likelihood model explains persuasion in general by noting that there are two paths to persuasion. These are the peripheral route that includes likeability, attractiveness, and emotional appeals of the speaker, and the central route that embraces skepticism and its emphasis on reasoning and evidence. Persuasion that works well in American culture may be ineffective in other cultures, especially those that are collectivist.

16

Persuasive Speaking Strategies

Suppose you plan to give a speech convincing your listeners that poor signage is a serious problem warranting a strong solution. You might begin this way:

> "Drop Your Pants Here and You Will Receive Prompt Attention" says the sign outside a laundry. "Kids With Gas Eat Here Free" says another. "Hidden Entrance" reads a third sign. They can be funny, but signs are a critical element of our everyday transit from place to place. Signs such as "Soft Shoulder, Blind Curves, Steep Grade, Big Trucks, Good Luck!" warn us of impending dangers with a touch of humor, but poor signage is no laughing matter. An April 2008 study by psychologists Oliver Clark and Simon Davies from the University of Hull presented at the British Psychological Society conference found that too many signs bunched together can cause accidents. Poor signage shouldn't be life threatening. Therefore, Congress should mandate that all public signs receive advanced governmental approval for clarity, simplicity, and accuracy.

This opening tries to persuade an audience by using humor, appealing to fear, and using evidence. The effectiveness of these or any persuasive strategies are not sure-fire, however, because they must be used under the right conditions.

Consideration of all possible persuasive speaking strategies would require a lengthy book. *The purpose of this chapter is to explore a few of the most prominent and effective persuasive strategies for public speakers.* This chapter discusses how to use these strategies appropriately and effectively.

ENHANCE THE SPEAKER: IDENTIFICATION AND CREDIBILITY

Persuasive speaking begins with enhancing the speaker, or developing **ethos** as Aristotle termed it. Crafty, carefully planned persuasive strategies will not matter if your audience has a problem with you, the speaker. Enhancing your ethos can be accomplished in two primary ways: establishing identification with your audience and bolstering your credibility. Both were discussed extensively in Chapter 4 for a variety of purposes and audiences beyond just the persuasive arena. Both are especially critical when your purpose is to persuade.

Regarding identification, Kenneth Burke (1950) wrote, "You persuade a man [or woman] only insofar as you can talk his language by speech, gesture, tonality, order, image, attitude, idea, identifying your ways with his" (p. 55). Burke considered identification, the affiliation and connection between you and your audience, to be the essence of persuasion (see also Larson, 2012). Enhancing your likeability, developing stylistic similarities, and noting substantive similarities with your audience are ways to create identification, as previously discussed.

You enhance your credibility by appearing competent, trustworthy, and dynamic yet composed. Your credibility has more influence, however, on listeners with weak or nonexistent views on issues than it does on listeners with strong views (Benoit, 1987). Listeners with weak or nonexistent views typically are influenced by peripheral cues such as source credibility. Listeners with strong viewpoints typically require powerful evidence and arguments to influence them via the central route to persuasion.

Humor has been discussed as a superior attention-getting strategy, but it can also enhance identification and credibility. It can influence perceptions of your communication competence (Banas et al., 2012; Wanzer et al., 1996). Humor can also increase your likeability and help establish rapport with your audience (Weinberger & Gulas, 1992). Self-deprecating humor, poking fun at yourself, is especially effective in this regard. At the Al Smith charity dinner just before the 2012 presidential election, Barack Obama made this self-deprecating joke about his lackluster performance in the first presidential debate weeks earlier: "As some of you may have noticed, I had a lot more energy in our second debate. I felt well-rested after the nice long nap I had in the first debate." He added: "I learned that there are worse things that can happen to you on your anniversary than forgetting to buy a gift." Mitt Romney, at the same event also used self-deprecation about his wealth when referring to the black tuxedo and white tie worn during the event: "It's nice to finally relax and wear what Ann and I wear around the house" (quoted in Oppel, 2012). Be cautious, however. Excessive self-deprecation can weaken credibility (see Chapter 5). Inappropriate humor can also do the same (Banas et al., 2012; Derks et al., 1995).

BUILD ARGUMENTS: PERSUASIVE LOGIC AND EVIDENCE

Much has already been said about the structure of arguments and the importance of strong logic and evidence in Chapters 9, 10, and 11. In this section, however, building arguments based on logic and evidence, what Aristotle called **logos**, is addressed with a specific focus on persuasion.

Propositions: Fact, Value, and Policy Claims

The Toulmin structure of an argument, discussed in Chapter 10, begins with a claim. The primary, overriding claim for a persuasive speech is called a **proposition**. A proposition presents a controversial problem, limits issues to what is relevant, and states a desired point of view (Freeley & Steinberg, 2013). The type of proposition depends on your persuasive goal. Do you want to argue factual accuracy, the worth of something, or propose change?

There are three types of propositions relevant to these three goals. There are propositions of fact, value, and policy. A **proposition of fact** alleges a truth, such as "Open carry gun laws would provide significant protection against criminals." Here you would argue factual accuracy. A **proposition of value** calls for a judgment that assesses the worth or merit of an idea, object, or practice, such as "Online classes provide an inferior educational experience for students." Here you want to assign value, or lack thereof. A **proposition of policy** calls for a significant change from how problems are currently handled, such as "Smoking should be banned in all public places." Here your goal is to make important improvements.

An argument, of course, is more than merely asserting a proposition. You must develop and support your grounds or main reasons that justify your proposition. For example, the grounds or main reasons offered to support the proposition that calls for a ban on smoking in public places can include:

1. Second-hand smoke is dangerous to nonsmokers.
2. Second-hand smoke is annoying to nonsmokers.
3. Employees in bars and restaurants cannot escape the smoke.

There is more to persuasion than simply building and presenting just any argument. Arguments and evidence must have a persuasive quality to them.

Persuasive Arguments: Quality and Quantity

The quality and number of arguments advanced for a proposition can be factors in persuasive speaking. One study tested to what degree students could be persuaded that completing comprehensive examinations as a condition for graduating from college is an effective proposal (Petty & Cacioppo, 1984). Students *directly affected* by the proposal were not persuaded by nine weak arguments. In fact, the more weak arguments they heard, the more they disliked the proposal. They were persuaded only when strong arguments were used, especially when many strong arguments were used. For students *unaffected* by the proposal, however, the quality of the arguments was relatively unimportant. They were more persuaded that the proposal was a good idea when nine arguments were presented than when only three were offered, no matter how strong or weak the arguments.

When constructing your persuasive speech, do not be satisfied when you find one or two strong arguments to support your proposition. If several strong arguments emerge when you research your proposition, and time permits, present them all. Several strong arguments can be persuasive to listeners who process your message either peripherally by noting the quantity of supporting arguments or centrally by considering the quality of arguments.

Persuasive Evidence: Statistics versus Narratives

"The use of evidence produces more attitude change than the use of no evidence" (Reynolds & Reynolds, 2002, p. 428). To be persuasive, however, your evidence must be attributed to a highly credible source, be seen by audience members as free of fallacies (see Chapter 10), must gain the attention of your audience and not put your listeners to sleep (see Chapter 11), and should not overwhelm your audience with an excessive abundance (Perloff, 2013).

What about types of evidence? Vivid narratives and examples can be more persuasive than statistics (Glassner, 1999), partly because they typically are more interesting and memorable (Green & Brock, 2000; Kopfman et al., 1998). Finding vivid stories more interesting and memorable, however, does not automatically make them more persuasive than statistics. Research is mixed on which is more persuasive (Allen & Preiss, 1997; Feeley et al., 2006). So what should you conclude? Use both narratives and statistics as your optimum strategy, thereby capitalizing on the strengths of both forms of evidence (Allen et al., 2000).

TRY EMOTIONAL APPEALS: BEYOND LOGIC

Humans are not like Spock or Data on *Star Trek*. Although logic and evidence can be very persuasive, especially for highly involved listeners, emotional appeals—what Aristotle partially meant by **pathos**—are also powerful motivators.

PHOTO 16.1 Using emotional appeals can be a very powerful persuasion strategy.

As social psychologist Drew Westen (2007) observes, "We do not pay attention to arguments unless they engender our interest, enthusiasm, fear, anger, or contempt. . . . 'Reasonable' actions almost always require the integration of thought and emotion . . . " (p. 16). In this section, emotional appeals with special emphasis on fear and anger are discussed.

General Emotional Appeals: Motivating Change

Appeals to sadness, pride, honor, hope, joy, guilt, envy, and shame all have their place as persuasion strategies that ignite emotional reactions and change behavior (Gass & Seiter, 2011). Research, however, on the persuasiveness of these particular emotional appeals is sparse. Nevertheless, there is some evidence that these emotional appeals have persuasive potential (Dillard & Nabi, 2006; Nabi, 2002). Hope, for example, is sometimes a cornerstone of an entire political campaign. Barack Obama's 2008 presidential campaign revolved around a strong appeal to hope, typified in a victory speech the night of the 2008 Iowa caucus:

 We are choosing hope over fear. . . . Hope is what led me here today—with a father from Kenya, a mother from Kansas, and a story that could only happen in the United States of America. Hope is the bedrock of this nation, the belief that our destiny will not be written for us, but by us, by all those men and women who are not content to settle for the world as it is; who have the courage to remake the world as it should be. *("Remarks of Senator Barack Obama," 2008)*

Appeals to hope and other emotions can be persuasive. Unquestionably, however, fear is the number one emotional appeal used to change attitudes and behavior of audiences.

Fear Appeals: Are You Scared Yet?

"Don't put that in your mouth. It's full of germs." "You'll poke your eye out if you run with those scissors." "Never cross the street before looking both ways. You could be killed." From childhood you are undoubtedly familiar with fear appeals. Your parents probably gave you a heavy dose to keep you safe and out of trouble. Fear appeals are used on adults as well. In 2001, Canada began using the most shocking, fear-inducing warnings on cigarette packages ever used anywhere in the world (Bor, 2001). Photos of blackened, bleeding gums, a diseased heart, a lung tumor, or a gangrenous foot appeared on a rotating basis on all cigarette packs along with information on the hazards of smoking.

Do fear appeals work? More research has been conducted on the effectiveness of fear appeals than on all other emotions combined. *In general, the more fear is aroused in listeners, the more vulnerable they feel and the more likely they will be convinced* (Dillard, 1994; Witte & Allen, 1996). This is particularly true when a threat is initially perceived by listeners to be low, so your fear appeal must be strong and the threat must be shown to have a personal impact on your audience to arouse concern.

A study of graphic images of warning on cigarette packages found that they "have the most pronounced short-term impacts on adult smokers, including smokers from groups that have in the past been hard to reach" (Thrasher, et al., 2012). In Montana, a state plagued by methamphetamine use, young people were targeted beginning in 2005 for a barrage of extremely graphic, terrifying video ads of teens hooked on the drug ("Montana Meth Project," 2013). Studies showed that a dramatic shift occurred in attitudes about Meth use among teens as a result. Teens' perceptions of great risk from trying Meth even one time increased substantially to 93% of respondents, and 87% of young adults believed their friends would give them a hard time for using Meth. Behavioral changes also occurred. Teen Meth use declined 63% and Meth-related crime decreased 62% ("Montana Meth Project," 2013). Other states have subsequently followed the Montana Meth persuasive model.

Fear appeals, however, do not always work. Five conditions determine whether high fear appeals used in your speeches will likely produce constructive action (Gass & Seiter, 2007).

First, *your audience must feel vulnerable.* People do not all fear the same things (Witte et al., 2001). Some fear heights while others relish jumping out of planes and sky diving. Teens feel more threatened by social rejection than physical harm caused by drug use (Schoenbachler & Whittler, 1996). Recognizing this, the anti-Meth campaign in Montana tried to create strong social disapproval for Meth use in addition to fear appeals about physical harm ("Montana Meth Project," 2013). There are also cultural differences in what frightens people most. Fear appeals that describe personal harm are persuasive for audiences from individualist cultures. Fear appeals that described harm to the family are persuasive for audiences in collectivist cultures (Witte et al., 2000).

Second, *a clear, specific recommendation for avoiding or lessening the fear is important* (Devos-Comby & Salovey, 2002). A vague recommendation, such as "Get financial aid," is not as effective as a specific recommendation, such as "Fill out this application for a Pell grant," to assuage the fear of having to drop out of school and be left with an uncertain future.

Third, *the recommendation must be perceived as effective* (Cho & Witte, 2004; Keller, 1999). Encouraging your audience to get a flu shot is an effective recommended behavior. Wearing a mask to avoid infection is not nearly as effective and is often impractical. Imagine yourself delivering a speech to a class while everyone wears a mask. When the personal threat is perceived to be high but the solution is viewed as ineffective by listeners, a denial such as "We can't do anything anyway, so why worry?" or a rationalization such as "You've got to die of something" typically neutralizes fear-arousing messages (Goldstein et al., 2008).

Fourth, *listeners must perceive that they can perform the actions recommended.* Again, the effort required to perform the behavior is a key variable. Asking members of your audience to give up sugary sodas entirely for the rest of their lives to avoid dental and health problems may not be possible for most people. The effort is too great. Encouraging your listeners to cut their soda consumption in half, however, may be seen as realistic.

Finally, studies have shown that *fear appeals are more persuasive when combined with high-quality arguments* (Gleicher & Petty, 1992; Rodriguez, 1995). The fear appeal becomes more believable when it is bolstered by credible arguments.

Anger Appeals: Moderately Upset

Arousing anger is often used to persuade listeners. Note how student Hope Stallings (2009) intended to trigger anger: "Now that we understand the catastrophic impact of DPAs [deferred prosecution agreements] on our economy and personal economic well-being, we should be sufficiently angry to do something about it" (p. 15). Attempting to ignite anger in an audience is a common persuasive appeal because anger can provide a strong motivation to act. Double student tuition and watch the student response.

Anger, however, does not always provoke constructive behavior. People sometimes become verbally and/or physically violent when angry. The intensity of the anger is key. Intense anger can short-circuit an individual's ability to think clearly and act responsibly (Fein, 1993). Intensely angry individuals may lash out at any perceived source of their anger, real or imagined (Pfau et al., 2001). Ethically, you would not want to inflame anger in your audience if you suspected a destructive reaction might ensue. As a speaker, you want to keep calm, be unconditionally constructive in your comments even when others are losing their heads, and avoid taunting a heckler in your audience, especially if your audience is predominantly hostile. You could provoke a physical confrontation or even a riot. Arousing anger in your audience can be persuasive but it can also backfire. You want to arouse moderate anger, not rage. Moderate anger can be channeled toward constructive action. Rage can provoke a mob scene.

The **Anger Activism Model** helps explain the relationship between anger and persuasion (Turner et al., 2007; see also Turner, 2006). This model posits that anger provokes desired constructive behavior change when (1) the target audience initially agrees with your persuasion message, (2) the anger produced by your message is fairly strong but not to the point of rage, and (3) your audience members perceive that they can act effectively and constructively to address their anger. Two studies show that if all three of these conditions are met, arousing anger has the potential to motivate appropriate action, even if the action required to quell or satiate the anger is very difficult to perform (Turner et al., 2007).

How can you use moderate anger arousal in a speech? Consider this account:

> Abdullah al-Kidd, a United States citizen and former University of Idaho student and running back for the football team, was detained for more than 2 weeks as a witness in a federal terrorism case in 2003. He was handcuffed, strip-searched, and repeatedly interrogated. There was no evidence of wrongdoing by al-Kidd. He was jailed and then investigated, not the other way around, as required by the U.S. system of justice. A three-judge panel from the 9th Circuit Court ruled in September 2009 that his incarceration was "repugnant to the Constitution and a painful reminder of some of the most ignominious chapters of our national history" (quote in Boone, 2009,

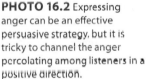

PHOTO 16.2 Expressing anger can be an effective persuasive strategy, but it is tricky to channel the anger percolating among listeners in a positive direction.

p. A5). As a result of the illegal detention, al-Kidd lost a scholarship to graduate school, lost security clearance and subsequently lost a job with a government contractor, lost his passport, and was ordered to live with in-laws in Las Vegas. We should all be angry that our government so blatantly abused one of our citizens.

This story likely arouses appropriate anger on behalf of social justice. That is a first step toward producing constructive change.

Ethics And Emotional Appeals: Is It Wrong To Be Peripheral?

Emotional appeals can be very persuasive, but are they ethical? It depends. Surely, you should be angry about racism, sexism, homophobia, and all manner of injustice, right? Likewise, you should fear terrorism, drunk drivers, food poisoning, and flu pandemics? Emotional appeals are not inherently unethical just because they are not a logical appeal. Emotion in the service of logic and truth can equal constructive action to do good. Emotional appeals motivate action. They also create attention so we might listen more intently to a clearly reasoned and supported argument.

Emotional appeals are ethical as long as they compliment the central route to persuasion (skepticism). Emotional appeals in the service of fabrications, distortions, and rumors are unethical. During the "debate" on health care reform in the summer of 2009, Sarah Palin asserted that a proposal in a congressional bill would require "my parents or my baby with Down Syndrome . . . to stand in front of Obama's death panel so his bureaucrats can decide, based on a subjective judgment of their level of productivity in society, whether they are worthy of health care" (quoted in "Report," 2009). The allegation was explosive but utterly false and was denounced by more than 40 media outlets. *PolitiFact.com*, the nonpartisan fact-checking website of the *St. Petersburg Times* and winner of the 2009 Pulitzer Prize, called it a "pants on fire" lie and voted it "Lie of the Year" (Holan, 2009; "Report," 2009). The nonpartisan Factcheck.org. dubbed it "whopper of 2009" ("Weiner," 2009). A skeptic must ask why any politician would even suggest euthanizing the elderly (e.g., Palin's parents), the most active voting bloc in America? It is completely implausible. The "death panels" allegation, however, scared a lot of older people who showed up at town hall meetings understandably outraged by the misinformation. The "death panels" accusation was a combined fear and anger appeal in the service of dishonesty. That is unethical persuasion.

Similarly, liberal former MSNBC television talk show host Keith Olbermann, on his "Countdown" show, made this wildly unsupported characterization of Scott Brown, a soon to be elected Republican U.S. Senator from Massachusetts: "Scott Brown [is] an irresponsible, homophobic, racist, reactionary, ex-nude model, teabagging supporter of violence against women and against politicians with whom he disagrees" (quoted in Sheppard, 2010). Jon Stewart, on "The Daily Show," ripped Olbermann for wallowing "in the fetid swamp of baseless name-calling." Stewart noted that Olbermann had in past "commentaries" called Chris Wallace "a monkey posing as a newscaster," Rush Limbaugh a "big bag of mashed up jack-ass," and Fox News contributor Michelle Malkin "a mindless, morally bankrupt, knee-jerk, fascistic . . . mashed-up bag of meat with lipstick on it" (quoted in Sheppard, 2010). Olbermann soon after apologized on his show for his "over-the-top" comments.

Name-calling is unethical if there are no solid facts to support the labels. If a person has clearly lied, then you can call them a liar, although this may not be effective persuasion because it can alienate listeners who dislike such abrasive labeling. If a person has not lied, then it is wrong to make the accusation.

Emotional appeals should not be a substitute for logic and evidence. If an emotional appeal contradicts sound logic and solid evidence, then it becomes the tool of the True Believer (see Chapter 9).

FRAME YOUR CASE: SHAPING ATTITUDE AND BEHAVIOR WITH LANGUAGE

Two Catholic priests, Father O'Leary and Father Kelly, strongly disagreed with each other on the question whether smoking and prayer are compatible behaviors. Unable to agree, they each decided to write the Pope, plead their own case, and ask for his wisdom. When they received the Pope's reply, both priests were triumphant. Puzzled that the Pope could agree with both of them when only two contradictory choices seemed available, Father O'Leary asked Father Kelly, "What question did you ask the Pope?" Father Kelly responded, "I asked the Pope if it was permissible to pray while smoking. The Pope said that praying should always be encouraged no matter what you are doing." Father O'Leary chuckled to himself. "Well, I asked the Pope whether it is permissible to smoke while praying, and the Pope said that I should take praying very seriously and not trivialize it by smoking." The way each question was framed by the priests dictated the answer they received from the Pope.

Should you call it *partial-birth abortion* or *late-term abortion*? *Estate tax* or *death tax*? *Undocumented immigrants* or *illegal aliens*? *Income tax fairness* or *class warfare*? Framing matters. **Framing** is the influence wording has on our perception of choices. Much like a photographer frames a picture to communicate a point of view, language frames choices. When a photographer changes the frame from a person as the center of interest to a mere bystander, our thoughts and perception of the picture change. Likewise, changing language that describes or identifies our choices can change how we perceive those choices (Deggans, 2012). As Fairhurst and Sarr (1996) explain, our "frames determine whether people notice problems, how they understand and remember problems, and how they evaluate and act upon them" (p. 4).

Studies abound showing the power of framing (Feinberg & Willer, 2013). When subjects were presented with the option of treating lung cancer with surgery, 84% chose surgery when it was framed in terms of the odds of *living*, but 56% chose surgery when it was framed in terms of the chances of *dying* (McNeil et al., 1982). Most subjects thought condoms were an effective method of preventing AIDS when they were told that condoms have a "95% success rate," but a majority did not view condoms as effective prevention when told that they had a "5% failure rate" (Linville et al., 1992). In these instances the two choices compared have identical outcomes, but they are perceived differently because of how the wording frames them.

Clearly, framing significantly influences our attitudes and behavior. Framing is especially powerful with those who initially view the issue being promoted as one of low importance (Lecheler et al., 2009). Framing alone as a peripheral route to persuasion will likely resonate more with those less informed and less interested initially in an issue. Framing supported by strong evidence and reasoning, however, can crystallize your viewpoint favorably and your opponents viewpoint unfavorably and enhance your persuasive impact enormously.

INDUCE COGNITIVE DISSONANCE: CREATING TENSION

When we want to persuade, one of the most common strategies is to point out inconsistencies between two attitudes or between attitudes and behavior. A student asks her professor for more time on an assignment. The professor says no. The student retorts, "But you gave extra time to Tyrene. Why won't you give me the same extension?" The professor sees herself as a very fair-minded person. Faced with this apparent inconsistency in the treatment of two students, the professor feels tense and uncomfortable. Festinger (1957) called this unpleasant feeling produced by apparent inconsistency **cognitive dissonance**.

Whenever a person holds two inconsistent ideas, beliefs, or opinions at the same time, or when an attitude and a behavior are inconsistent, dissonance likely occurs (McKimmie et al., 2003; Tavris & Aronson, 2007). Parents often confront this persuasive strategy from their children. "Why do I have a curfew? You never gave a curfew to Marianna." We want to be perceived as consistent, not hypocritical or nonsensical, so dissonance emerges when inconsistencies are pointed out to us (McKimmie et al., 2003; Tavris & Aronson, 2007). Cognitive dissonance appears to be common, appearing in a variety of cultures studied (Hoshino-Browne et al., 2005).

"Cognitive dissonance is a motivating state of affairs. Just as hunger impels a person to eat, so does dissonance impel a person to change his [her] opinions or his [her] behavior" (Festinger, 1977, p. 111). *According to this theory, you have to awaken dissonance in listeners for persuasion to occur.* Without dissonance, there is little motivation to change attitudes or behavior. Here is how the strategy works:

> The [persuader] intentionally arouses feelings of dissonance by threatening self-esteem—for example, by making the person feel guilty about something, by arousing feelings of shame or inadequacy, or by making the person look like a hypocrite or someone who does not honor his or her word. Next, the [persuader] offers one solution, one way of reducing this dissonance—by complying with whatever request the [persuader] has in mind. The way to reduce that guilt, eliminate that shame, honor that commitment, and restore

your feelings of adequacy is to give to that charity, buy that car, hate that enemy, or vote for that leader. *(Pratkanis and Aronson, 2001, p. 44)*

Does inducing dissonance change behavior? It is unlikely to be successful with true believers (Walker, 2013), but with others it certainly can be (Aronson et al., 1991; Czopp et al., 2006). Important decisions arouse more dissonance than less important ones (Gass & Seiter, 2011). Pointing out to a teacher that he or she was not consistent when grading a test could elicit varying degrees of dissonance. If the inconsistency involves a single point on a 100-point exam, the teacher can easily downplay the inconsistency as minor and inherent to any subjective grading system. If the inconsistency involves an entire grade difference and seems based on gender bias, however, the dissonance could be quite large.

Notice how Gary Allen (1996), a student at Northeastern State University, uses cognitive dissonance in a speech on drug testing in the military:

> The final problem is caused by a double standard, because a program is only as good as the goal it achieves. While alcohol is universally recognized as the most commonly abused drug, the military does not test for alcohol as regularly as for other drugs . . . Soldiers caught drunk on the job are given 45 days extra duty, that is work that must be performed after the regular duty day, they have a letter put into their permanent file, and they are returned to light duty. Yet the soldier who receives a positive [drug] test result is, currently, kicked out of the military with a dishonorable discharge. Let me say that again. Everyday soldiers are required to undergo a test of their innocence without suspicion of guilt. The soldier who is found guilty is kicked out and marked for life with a dishonorable discharge, while soldiers drunk on the job, endangering everyone's life, are returned to duty with a slap on the hand. (p. 82)

The speaker points out a glaring inconsistency to induce dissonance in the audience. Supporting such a "double standard" is hypocritical and unjust, so the speaker implies. One could argue that there is a big difference between alcohol and other drugs, namely, legality. Nevertheless, concerning possible dangerous effects of use, an inconsistency does seem apparent. Cognitive dissonance can be an effective persuasive strategy (Tavris & Aronson, 2007).

USE THE CONTRAST EFFECT: MINIMIZE THE MAGNITUDE

You are a salesperson and a woman comes into the dress store where you work. Most of your pay is based on commission, so you want to sell as much merchandise as you can at the highest prices possible. Do you show the woman the inexpensive

The contrast effect can make it appear that you are getting a bargain instead of a costly trinket.

dresses first, then gradually show her more expensive dresses, or do you begin with very expensive dresses probably outside of her price range, then show her less expensive dresses? Which will net you the biggest commission? According to research on the contrast effect, you would make a better choice if you began expensive and moved to less expensive (Cialdini, 1993). The **contrast effect** says listeners are more likely to accept a bigger second request or offer when contrasted with a much bigger initial request or offer. If shown a really nice dress that costs $250, most shoppers will balk at purchasing it because it is "so expensive." If shown a $475 dress first, however, then shown the $250 dress, the second dress just seems less expensive by contrast with the first. Once the $250 dress is purchased, "accessorizing" it with $30 worth of jewelry, scarves, or whatever will seem like very little by contrast.

The contrast effect, sometimes referred to as the **door-in-the face strategy**, is used in all types of sales. I once purchased a recliner for $250. It was not "on sale." About 2 months later I was browsing through a furniture store and spotted the identical recliner advertised as part of a "giant blowout sale." The price tag showed $800 marked out, then $600 marked out, then $475 marked out, and finally the "sale price" of $400. A casual customer who had not shopped around might see this recliner as a super bargain. The price had been cut in half. Yet this store was asking $150 more than I paid for the same recliner at the regular price from another store.

Cialdini (1993) provides a stellar, amusing example of the contrast effect in action in parent–child persuasion. Although this example is a letter, you can easily see how this strategy could apply in a persuasive speech.

Dear Mother and Dad:

Since I left for college I have been remiss in writing and I am sorry for my thoughtlessness in not having written before. I will bring you up to date now, but before you read on, please sit down. You are not to read any further unless you are sitting down, okay?

Well, then, I am getting along pretty well now. The skull fracture and the concussion I got when I jumped out the window of my dormitory when it caught on fire shortly after my arrival here is pretty well healed now. I only spent two weeks in the hospital and now I can see almost normally and only get those sick headaches once a day. Fortunately, the fire in the dormitory, and my jump, was witnessed by an attendant at the gas station near the dorm, and he was the one who called the Fire Department and the ambulance. He also visited me in the hospital and since I had nowhere to live because of the burnt-out dormitory, he was kind enough to invite me to share his apartment with him. It's really a basement room, but it's kind of cute. He is a very fine boy, and we have fallen deeply in love and are planning to get married. We haven't set the date yet, but it will be before my pregnancy begins to show.

Yes, Mother and Dad, I am pregnant. I know how much you are looking forward to being grandparents and I know you will welcome the baby and give it the same love and devotion and tender care you gave me when I was a child. The reason for the delay in our marriage is that my boyfriend has a minor infection which prevents us from passing our premarital blood tests and I carelessly caught it from him. I know that you will welcome him into our family with open arms. He is kind and, although not well educated, he is ambitious.

Now that I have brought you up to date, I want to tell you that there was no dormitory fire, I did not have a concussion or skull fracture, I was not in the hospital. I am not pregnant, I am not engaged, I am not infected, and there is no boyfriend. However, I am getting a "D" in American History and an "F" in Chemistry, and I want you to see those marks in their proper perspective.

Your loving daughter,
SHARON

As a strategy to use in a persuasive speech, *the contrast effect works well when presenting your solution to a problem.* For example, say you have argued that taxpayer dollars do not begin to cover the costs of educating college students. You could begin the solution portion of your speech this way:

> Clearly, we cannot expect taxpayers to continue shouldering almost the entire burden of higher education expenses. I think it would be entirely justified if our state legislature immediately doubled tuition for every student in the state. This would provide some tax relief for already over-burdened taxpayers while still covering less than half the cost of educating each student.
>
> Although doubling student tuition is justified, fair, and beneficial, I can see that such a proposal probably isn't entirely practical for a number of reasons, not the least of which is the suddenness of such a large tuition increase. Having weighed the potential merits and demerits of such a proposal, let me propose instead that the state phase in a much smaller tuition increase over the next decade to ease the burden on students and still provide taxpayer relief in the long run.

Peruse the *sample persuasive speech* in **Appendix B** for another example of the contrast effect.

USE A TWO-SIDED ORGANIZATIONAL PATTERN: REFUTATION

Is it better to present arguments in favor of your proposition and ignore opposing arguments (one-sided message), or should you make your case, then refute opposing arguments (two-sided message)? *Two-sided persuasive messages are more effective than one-sided messages in convincing listeners to change attitudes* (Allen, 1991, 1993, 1998). This is true, however, only if you provide effective refutation of opposing arguments. Two-sided but ineffectual refutation actually is less persuasive than one-sided presentations (see also Perloff, 2013).

A two-sided organizational pattern begins with a presentation of main arguments supporting your proposition. After you have laid out your case, you then answer common objections, or opposing arguments, against your case. Answering opposing arguments is called **refutation**. Effective refutation, of course, means that you need to anticipate what an audience might question about your position. Recall that this is an element of the Toulmin structure of an argument discussed in Chapter 10.

There are four steps to refutation. First, *state the opposing argument.* "A common objection to colleges shifting from a semester to a quarter system is that not as much subject matter will be covered each term" is a statement of an opposing argument. Second, *state your reaction to the opposing argument.* "This isn't true. Courses that meet 3 hours per week could meet 5 hours per week under the shorter quarter system" is a statement of response to an opposing argument. Third, *support your response with reasoning and evidence*. Failure to present strong arguments backed by solid evidence may backfire and actually promote more entrenched attitudes instead of changing attitudes (Rucker & Petty, 2004). Weak refutation can be worse than no refutation at all because listeners may deduce that poorly supported counterarguments mean that currently held attitudes are meritorious. Fourth, *indicate what effect, if any, opposing arguments have had on the strength of your case*. If some disadvantage will occur from your proposal, admit it, but weigh the damage against the claimed advantages of your proposal. "No quarter system is perfect. Students will be pressured in some instances to work more intensely in a condensed period of time. Overall, however, the advantages of a quarter system—greater number and variety of courses, more diversity of instructors, better vacation schedules, and greater retention and success rates—far outweigh these minor objections."

There are additional organizational patterns that have persuasive potential. *Monroe's motivated sequence* is one such pattern (see **Appendix B** for a model persuasive speech using this organizational pattern). The problem-solution, problem cause solution, and comparative advantages organization patterns discussed in Chapter 7 also have persuasive potential. All of these, however, are one-sided, not two-sided organizational patterns. You are not answering potential objections to your solutions or claimed advantages. Adding refutation to these patterns (**see Appendix B**) would improve their persuasive potential.

SUMMARY

There are many persuasive strategies a speaker can use. Among these are establishing identification, building credibility, building strong arguments, inducing cognitive dissonance, making emotional appeals, framing, using the contrast effect, and using a two-sided organizational pattern. Competent public speakers will find success if they utilize some or all of these strategies to persuade others. There are conditions that determine the likelihood of success using each strategy, so make sure that you are cognizant of these conditions and that you adapt your persuasive strategy to meet those conditions.

17

Speeches for Special Occasions

Speeches for special occasions should be special. They are different from informative and persuasive speeches. Although a special occasion speech may impart knowledge and information or briefly persuade, that is not its main purpose. Audience expectations are critical to the effectiveness of a special occasion speech. The occasion sets the expectation for the audience, and your primary goal is to meet your audience's expectations. An inspirational occasion requires an inspirational speech. Listeners want to be moved, not merely informed. Listeners at a roast expect to laugh heartily and often. Little effort should be made to offer deep insights or persuade anyone to action.

There are many types of special occasion speeches. *The primary purpose of this chapter is to explore ways to give effective and appropriate special occasion speeches.* A variety of such speeches, including tributes, introductions of featured speakers, award ceremony presentations and acceptance speeches, commencement addresses, and after-dinner speeches are discussed.

TRIBUTE ADDRESSES

Tribute speeches praise or celebrate a person. They honor the person. You hear tribute speeches at retirement parties, birthdays, anniversaries, going-away parties, award ceremonies, and funerals. Principal tribute speeches include toasts, roasts, tributes for colleagues, and eulogies.

Toasts: Raising a Glass in Tribute

A **toast** is a brief tribute to a person or couple. Weddings usually have several toasts offered by the best man and maid of honor, and sometimes by bridesmaids and friends and family members of the bride and groom. Keep them brief. A well-known, oft-quoted Irish toast goes:

> May the road rise to meet you.
> May the wind be always at your back.
> May the sun shine warm upon your face.
> And rains fall soft upon your fields.
> And God hold you in the hollow of His hand.

If so inclined, you could play off this well-known toast and give it your own unique twist, such as:

> May the road rise to meet you, and may you avoid the potholes of life.
> May the wind be always at your back, unless a cool breeze in the face offers refreshment.
> May the sun shine warm on your face, but never burn you.
> And may rain fall softly, washing away any sadness you may feel.

Because a toast is often accompanied by a drink of wine or other alcoholic beverage, be cautious about the effect alcohol can have on your ability to offer a coherent and effective toast. Your toast may follow many others. You do not want to make a fool of yourself and make others uncomfortable. Always be appropriate. Remember, weddings almost always have young children present. Your humor should be playful but G-rated: "To keep your marriage brimming, with love in the wedding cup, whenever you're wrong, admit it; whenever you're right, shut up" (Ogden Nash) or "If I'm the best man, why is she marrying him?" (Jerry Seinfeld) or "Love is an electric blanket with someone else in control of the switch" (Cathy Arlyle). Your toast should also be addressed to the couple. You stand and deliver the toast while everyone else remains seated. At the finish you raise your glass and salute the couple.

Roasts: Poking Fun with Admiration

A **roast** is a purposely humorous tribute to a person. Although the humor can be sarcastic, ribald, even wildly exaggerated, everyone in attendance knows and expects that the entire affair is meant to praise the honoree. You poke fun at the honoree as a way of expressing your admiration and affection for the person. Here are some guidelines:

(1) **Humor is the key ingredient of any roast.** This is not meant to be a serious event. It is supposed to be light-hearted and amusing. Follow the guidelines in Chapter Five on using humor appropriately and effectively.

(2) **Keep the tone positive.** A roast is meant to be a good-natured kidding of the honoree, not an opportunity to embarrass the person in front of friends and relatives.

(3) **Be brief.** This is not your audition for stand-up comedian of the year. Usually, each speaker at a roast addresses the audience for about three to five minutes. Stick to the time limit.

(4) **Finish on a heartfelt, serious note.** Playfully making fun of the honoree should be amusing, but do not forget that a roast is meant to express admiration and affection for the person roasted. "All kidding aside, you know how much I respect and admire my dear friend. He is a beacon of light in a sometimes dark world" is one way to close your roast on a serious note.

Tribute to Colleagues: Honoring the Departing

A tribute to someone leaving due to retirement or simply moving to another place of employment has its own expectations and requirements. The audience may not welcome the departure because a good colleague and friend is leaving, but it should be a cause for a happy send-off. This type of tribute speech, given while the honored person is present, should be light-hearted and should emphasize the contributions and notable qualities that everyone will miss.

Recently, I was asked to give a tribute speech for a friend and long-time colleague. I began this way:

 I'd like to begin this tribute to Jack with a short poem I've written for this occasion. I apologize in advance.

There is a professor named Jack.
Who deserved a most elegant plaque.
With flattering comments and turn of phrase.
Abundant awards and plentiful praise.
But instead he must settle for this sorry rhyme.
Knowing full well that he'll be teaching part-time.
Because try as he might; no matter what he may say
Old teachers never die, they just grade away.

The point of this opening was to create a light-hearted tone, and to be a bit playful. The last line is a glancing reference to the famous line from General Douglas MacArthur in his April 19, 1951 address to the U.S. Congress, "Old soldiers never die, they just fade away." I continued by reflecting on some of my friend's accomplishments during his long career as a teacher and administrator. I finished lightheartedly, as I began, with a "bit of doggerel" or bad poetry:

> The power of one is so often unclear.
> But let voices be raised and perhaps a dark beer.
> To proclaim across campus for all to hear.
> There's one special man whose impact is felt.
> And although his physique is no longer so svelte.
> Our dear friend and colleague will surely be missed.
> But let's all make a vow to steadfastly resist.
> Dwelling long on Jack's parting, no need for redundance.
> And instead wish he and Diane joy in abundance.

No one in the audience expected great poetry from me, and none was evident, but listeners were amused and attentive to hear something a bit different than the previous tribute speeches. Do not be afraid to take a small risk and produce a speech that tries something different. My attempt was greatly appreciated by my friend who recognized immediately that I had put some effort into constructing the tribute. It is the apparent effort that you put into a tribute speech that sends the message, "I care about you and you will be missed."

Eulogies: Praising the Departed

Comedian George Carlin once remarked, "I'm always relieved when someone is delivering a eulogy and I realize I'm listening to it." A **eulogy** is a tribute delivered in praise of a deceased friend or family member. Unlike other tributes where the honored person is present to hear the speech, eulogies pay tribute to someone who has died. Given the sadness that typically surrounds a funeral, your challenge is to show respect for those grieving and provide a sense of closure for those feeling the profound loss of a loved one (Kent, 2007). The word eulogy originates from the Greek word that means "to praise." You want to capture the essence of the person eulogized. For years I required my speech students to deliver their own eulogy, to play the role of someone paying tribute to them after their death. It offered a way of getting in touch with how my students saw themselves, who they wanted to become, and what they would want others to say about them after they died. The assignment was always instructive and often quite moving and insightful.

Eulogies do not have to be somber speeches, or as newscaster Tom Brokaw said at the funeral of his colleague Tim Russert, there would be "some tears, some laughs and the occasional truth" (quoted in Wilson, 2008, p. 2D). Capturing the

PHOTO 17.1 Kate Edwards, daughter of former presidential candidate John Edwards, delivers the eulogy for her mother, Elizabeth. The term "eulogy" is derived from Greek that means "to praise."

essence of the person may mean paying tribute to their infectious sense of humor and their uniqueness as a human being. My father was just such a person, and when he died I delivered his eulogy. I wanted to capture who my father was in life without excessively diminishing his faults or magnifying his admirable qualities. He could be irascible and enormously impatient, yet he could exhibit random acts of stunning kindness. I not only described my father's many acts of kindness, but I also tried to transform his legendary impatience into moments of gentle humor that all could appreciate. Here is an example:

> Dad hated to get behind slow drivers (which was anyone obeying the speed limit). When Dad was in his 70s, he barely slowed down. I remember Mom and Dad picking me up at the airport one time. Dad was driving his Thunderbird. The freeways were jammed, so Dad took a back route home. At one point he was flying down the boulevard. From the back seat I gently inquired: "Dad, when exactly will our flight be leaving the ground?" He reduced his speed only slightly.

Using humor in a eulogy can be tricky. You want to show the utmost respect for the deceased, and you certainly do not want to cause offense for the grieving. Listeners typically welcome gentle humor that humanizes and explores the principal personal characteristics of the deceased.

In constructing an effective and appropriate eulogy, follow these guidelines:

(1) **Your opening should capture attention and set the theme.** A relevant quotation, a short story that reflects the core characteristics of the deceased, or a novel example from the life of the lost loved one are a few possibilities. I began my eulogy at my father's funeral this way: "There's a Jewish saying, 'The only truly dead are those who have been forgotten.' My dad won't be forgotten. One reason is that he was such an unforgettable character."

(2) **Your organizational pattern is typically narrative.** You are briefly telling a story of the person's life, capturing the important plotlines about this character. This is not a mere biography of the person. Do not simply list the person's resume of awards, degrees, professional publications, and the like. Tell a story about what this person was like. Personal attributes are more important and heartfelt than personal accomplishments unless the accomplishments illustrate important and personal laudatory attributes.

(3) **Strive for emotional control.** Your audience already feels grief. A eulogy is a tribute. It should offer uplifting praise. You want the audience to feel a little better not worse after your speech.

(4) **Be balanced and realistic in your praise.** Senator Ted Kennedy, in his eulogy of his brother Robert who was assassinated during his California campaign for president in 1968, chose the perfect line to make this point: "My brother need not be idealized, or enlarged in death beyond what he was in life; to be remembered simply as a good and decent man, who saw wrong and tried to right it, saw suffering and tried to heal it, saw war and tried to stop it" (quoted in "Ted Kennedy's Eulogy," 1968).

(5) **Relate what you will most remember and miss about the person.** Here are a few things I related about my father:

> I will miss his puns—most of them real groaners. I will miss him teaching me golf, or trying to. I will miss Dad and Mom dancing to the big bands on the stereo. I will remember Dad getting up in restaurants, grabbing the coffee pot and serving himself and other customers because the service was too slow. I will remember Dad hip deep in the Oxford Canal, saying "Dammit Dorothy Mae," as if Mom had something to do with his falling into the British muck. Most of all, I will remember Dad's unconditional love, unfailing support, and boundless generosity.

⑥ Finish strong. After telling several stories about my father that illustrated his uniqueness, the final line of my eulogy said this: "Heaven will be a more interesting place now that Dad has entered the Kingdom." This closing statement reflects again on the theme of my father as a unique and unforgettable character and offers mild comfort to those grieving. Ted Kennedy finished his eulogy for his brother Robert this way: "As he [Robert] said many times, in many parts of this nation, to those he touched and who sought to touch him: 'Some men see things as they are and say why. I dream things that never were and say why not'" (quoted in "Ted Kennedy's Eulogy," 1968). When the space shuttle *Challenger* exploded in 1986 with the loss of the entire crew, Ronald Reagan delivered a nationally televised eulogy commemorating our fallen heroes who risked their lives to explore space. Delivering one of the most powerful, touching eulogies ever presented by a president of the United States, a speech ranked eighth on the Top 100 American Speeches of the twentieth century (Lucas & Medhurst, 2008), Reagan captured the essence of the moment with these final few sentences: "The crew of the space shuttle *Challenger* honored us by the manner in which they lived their lives. We will never forget them, nor the last time we saw them, this morning, as they prepared for their journey and waved goodbye and 'slipped the surly bonds of earth' to 'touch the face of God.'" Using the words from a sonnet entitled "High Flight," a poem many pilots know well and some keep on their person, Reagan gave nobility to the deaths of our astronauts in his moving, eloquent finish to his eulogy.

INTRODUCTIONS OF FEATURED SPEAKERS

A **speech of introduction** prepares an audience for a speech to be given by a featured speaker. Sometimes an audience is very familiar with the speaker, requiring a very brief introduction. You want to create enthusiasm for the speaker, but remember that you are not the main focus. Identify who you are if the audience is unfamiliar with you, but place the focus on the speaker being introduced.

If I were introducing American humorist Dave Barry, a well-know personality in many circles, I would keep the introduction very brief because the audience is not excited to hear me speak. They have gathered to hear the featured speaker. I would mostly quote his own self-description taken from his website because it is so amusing, places the focus squarely on him, and sets the mood for his speech. Consider this example:

Thank you for attending this anxiously anticipated event. It is my great honor to introduce to you a man who describes himself in these words: Dave Barry is a humor columnist. He won the Pulitzer Prize for Commentary.

> Many people are still trying to figure out how this happened. Dave has also written a total of 30 books, although virtually none of them contain useful information. In his spare time, Dave is a candidate for president of the United States. If elected, his highest priority will be to seek the death penalty for whoever is responsible for making Americans install low-flow toilets. Anything else I might add about Dave Barry would pale in comparison to his own self-description, so without further ado, please welcome Dave Barry.

Notice that the last statement asks the audience to welcome the speaker. This cues the audience to applaud the speaker as a welcoming gesture.

Less familiar speakers require a bit more information for an audience. You may need to build the speaker's credibility by briefly listing awards, titles, accomplishments, and the like: "Carmen Jimenez has advanced degrees in geotechnical engineering and has investigated some of the worst natural disasters in our recent history, including our own all-too-familiar and tragic collapse of the county's earthen dam. She is a recognized geological expert internationally, and she has won numerous awards for her service to our country." Remember, the audience does not assemble to hear you speak, so keep the credential building short. Also, make sure that you pronounce the speaker's name correctly. If you are unsure, ask the speaker before introducing him or her. Finally, never provide any potentially embarrassing details about the speaker. Making a speaker and the audience uncomfortable at the outset sets an awful tone for the ensuing speech.

As a featured speaker, responding well to an introduction, especially an effusively positive one, can ingratiate you to your audience. Henry Shelton, when General Chairman of the Joint Chiefs of Staff, responded to just such an effusive introduction this way: "Thank you, Mr. Secretary, for that incredible introduction. If I had known you were going to eulogize me, I would have done the only decent thing and died" ("Victory, Honor, Sacrifice," 2001). For more standard introductions, simply offer a gracious thanks, express enthusiasm for appearing before this audience, then begin your speech.

SPEECHES OF PRESENTATION

Awards ceremonies have become commonplace. It is difficult to find a week on television in which there is a total absence of some award program. As journalist and editor Joanne Lipman noted, "Hollywood has its Oscars. Television has its Emmys. Broadway has its Tonys. And advertising has its Clios. And its Andys, Addys, Effies, and Obies. And 117 other assorted awards. And those are just the big ones" (quoted in Foley, 2010). This list does not even include the music entertainment industry, whose awards seem to metastasize uncontrollably.

As a student, you may not have many opportunities to present an award, but you may find occasions on campus and off in which you are responsible for giving a presentation speech. A **speech of presentation** must communicate to the audience assembled the meaning and importance of the award. "The Floyd Younger award for excellence in teaching is offered each year to the one instructor on our campus, chosen by committee from nominations made by his or her colleagues, who has exhibited outstanding effectiveness as a teacher" is an example. Also, a presentation speech should identify why the recipient has earned the award. The following is an example:

> This year's award recipient has taught creative writing on this campus for 15 years. Her students adore her. One student remarked, "I've never had a teacher who was so enthusiastic, so encouraging, so down right fun in class." Another student said this, "She's simply the best instructor in the universe." It is my great pleasure to present the Floyd Younger award for excellence in teaching to Karen Follett.

Present the award to the recipient with your left hand so you are free to shake the recipient's right hand.

SPEECHES OF ACCEPTANCE

How many times have you watched the Academy Awards presentations and heard a winner begin an acceptance speech, "I didn't think I would win, so I didn't prepare a speech"? It is false humility and it is lame. Actors especially should have a prepared script. It is the essence of their business. Some of the worst, most cringe-inducing acceptance speeches have occurred at the Oscars. If you have any inkling that you might win an award, large or small, prepare a brief acceptance speech. Avoid embarrassing yourself.

Your acceptance speech should be appreciative, genuine, and humble. No one wants to hear the winner gloat. "I knew I would win this" or "Boy, I deserve this" does not endear you to the audience. Express your pleasure at receiving the award—"This is such an honor. I am so happy to receive it." Show your appreciation with a simple statement—"Thank you so much for this great honor." Thank the most important people who helped you and those who gave you the award. Thanking your parents for conceiving you is not usually appropriate or effective. Keep the list of those you wish to thank short. Gwyneth Paltrow thanked 23 individuals by name as well as her family, "everybody at Miramax Films," and the "miraculous cast and crew" of "Shakespeare in Love" for her 1998 Oscar ("Gwyneth Paltrow," 1999). Host Billy Crystal, after a series of Oscar winners gave acceptance speeches for *Lord of the Rings*, remarked, "It's now official. There

PHOTO 17.2 Jennifer Lawrence receives the 2013 Critics' Choice Award. Giving an effective acceptance speech can be challenging. You want to express appreciation without being boastful.

is no one left to thank in New Zealand." An audience easily grows restless when a laundry list of people to thank, most of whom may be unknown to audience members, is offered by the award recipient.

COMMENCEMENT ADDRESSES

A **commencement address** is an inspirational speech that occurs at graduation ceremonies. You want to move your listeners to think in news ways, to participate in a cause, or to help your community to solve problems. The primary focus is on engaging your listeners and imparting wisdom. This is no small task. Celebrities, comedians, actors, CEOs of major corporations, politicians, members of the news media, and individuals who have overcome great obstacles in life are invited every year to give commencement addresses at colleges and universities all across the United States. Even presidents of the United States give commencement addresses. As a student, you may be asked to give one type of commencement address, the valedictory speech.

Commencement addresses usually have a serious message to impart to graduates, but the best such addresses blend abundant humor with a serious theme. Barack Obama gave a commencement address at the University of Michigan on May 1, 2010, before 92,000 people. He began: "It is great to be here in the

PHOTO 17.3 Valedictory speeches are examples of commencement addresses delivered by students.

Big House, and may I say 'Go Blue!' I thought I'd go for the cheap applause line to start things off." Obama continued by quoting letters he received from a kindergarten class in Virginia. These youngsters asked him a number of questions, such as "Do you work a lot? "How do you do your job?" and "Do you live next to a volcano?" The last question he read, however, was more serious and became the theme of his address, "Are people being nice?" The rest of his speech developed the theme of the proper role of government in a democracy, and the inability to succeed as a democracy when incivility reigns supreme in our political discourse ("Obama Michigan Graduation Speech," 2010).

Harry Potter author J. K. Rowling, in her 2008 Harvard commencement address, began this way: "The first thing I would like to say is 'thank you.' Not only has Harvard given me an extraordinary honor, but the weeks of fear and nausea I have endured at the thought of giving this commencement address have made me lose weight" ("The Fringe Benefits of Failure," 2008). Her amusing opening tapped beautifully into her theme—fear of failure and the fringe benefits of experiencing failure.

Rock star Bono began his commencement address to graduates at the University of Pennsylvania on May 17, 2004, this way:

> My name is Bono and I am a rock star. Don't get me too excited because I use four letter words when I get excited. I'd just like to say to the parents, your

children are safe, your country is safe . . . Doctor of Laws, wow! I know it's an honor, and it really is an honor, but are you sure? I never went to college, I've slept in some strange places, but the library wasn't one of them. Bono identified the central theme of his speech this way: "So what's the problem that we want to apply all this energy and intellect to? Every era has its defining struggle and the fate of Africa is one of ours. *("Because We Can, We Must," 2004)*

Stephen Colbert delivered a commencement address to graduates at Knox College on June 3, 2006. Not surprisingly, there was abundant humor throughout his presentation. At one point he said, somewhat mocking a cliche heard at so many commencements, "It has been said that children are our future. But does that not also mean that we are their past? You are here to replace us. I don't understand why we're here helping and honoring them. You do not see union workers holding benefits for robots." On a more serious note, Colbert remarked, "Cynicism masquerades as wisdom, but it is the farthest thing from it. Because cynics don't learn anything. Because cynicism is a self-imposed blindness, a rejection of the world because we are afraid it will hurt us or disappoint us. Cynics always say no. But saying 'yes' begins things." He finished on a humorous note, offering advice (sort of) to graduates, that is traditional in commencement addresses: "And lastly, the best career advice I can give you is to get your own TV show. It pays well, the hours are good, and you are famous. And eventually some very nice people will give you a doctorate in fine arts for doing jack squat" ("Stephen Colbert's Address to the Graduates," 2006).

Inspirational commencement addresses should appeal to our better nature. You want to touch deep feelings of your audience, encouraging pure motives and greater effort to achieve a common good. This is a commencement, a new beginning.

AFTER-DINNER SPEECHES

An **after-dinner speech** is a presentation that typically occurs at a formal gathering of some group. After-dinner speeches are not always presented after dinner. Developed in England in the nineteenth century as a formal type of presentation, such speeches were literally delivered right after a dinner, usually to a large gathering for some occasion. More recently, such presentations may occur after a luncheon or even a breakfast gathering of business or civic groups. They probably should be renamed *after-meal speeches* or *post-prandial public speeches* (eh, maybe not), but after-dinner speech remains the common term still used.

An after-dinner speech is meant to entertain. Although your topic can be a serious one, you need to take an amusing approach to it. For example, a speech on vegetarianism could be informative if you describe the pros and cons of eschewing meat, it could be persuasive if you argue forcefully that we should convert to vegetarianism, and it could be an after-dinner speech if you made light of the vegetarian substitutes for meat (e.g., lentil loaf, soy burgers). The tone should be whimsical, not serious. This makes some topics more appropriate than others. AIDS is not a whimsical topic; neither is child abuse, terminal illness, nor torture. "The Most Ridiculous Things People Do With Cell Phones" or "My Top Ten List of Irritating Behaviors in Restaurants" or "The World's Most Pointless Signs" all suggest humorous potential. Again, review the guidelines for using humor effectively and appropriately discussed in Chapter 5.

Despite the whimsical nature of after-dinner speeches, this is not stand-up comedy. Refrain from delivering a series of one-liners unrelated to any theme or thoughtful point. Your after-dinner speech should have a central theme and a serious point relevant to that theme, even though you accomplish this with humor. Often the topic and theme is your choice, or the group that invites you to speak considers you an authority on certain topics and wants you to speak on one of them. The occasion and make-up of your audience may also dictate certain topic choices. If you are speaking before an environmental group, there should be an environmental flavor to your theme (e.g., common mistakes the public makes about the environmental movement in America). Skip the canned jokes. Telling lawyer jokes to a group of attorneys will likely backfire. They probably have heard every lawyer joke ever made. Be original and creative.

SUMMARY

Special occasion speeches are different from informative and persuasive speeches. Each type has its special guidelines for it to be effective and appropriate. In most cases, such speeches work best when they are relatively brief, heartfelt, entertaining, and well suited to audience expectations. Make your special occasion speeches truly special.

A

TEXT OF AN INFORMATIVE SPEECH

(Problem-Cause-Solution Organizational Format)

THE ANNUAL PLAGUE

(Prepared February 2013; about an 8-minute speech)

It killed an estimated 50 million people worldwide and 675,000 Americans, according to the U.S. Department of Health and Human Services website *flu.gov* updated on February 2, 2013 City morgues across the United States became overwhelmed with bodies stacked like cords of wood. Undertakers rapidly ran out of coffins, and graves couldn't be dug fast enough to accommodate the rising death toll, so bodies often lay in homes for days or even weeks. According to Gina Kolata, author of the 1999 book *Flu,* victims of this disease suffered agonizing symptoms that included high fever and violent coughing fits that cracked ribs and spewed blood from victims' mouths. Fluid filled their lungs causing many to drown in their own juices.

What was this terrifying disease? The Black Death of the 14th century revisiting the human species?

Credible source; use of startling statistics gains attention

Credible source; date is fine for historical facts

Vivid description keeps attention; date is fine for historical facts

Transition

Rhetorical questions involve audience, create curiosity

AIDS? Some biological warfare agent? The global killer was the flu! The Spanish flu of 1918–1919 caused a pandemic, or worldwide epidemic.

The previously cited website *flu.gov* notes more recent flu pandemics in its article "Pandemic Flu History." A 1957 "Asian flu" killed almost 70,000 Americans and 2 million worldwide. In 1968, the "Hong Kong flu" killed almost 34,000 Americans. In 2003, the H5N1 avian flu emerged, resulting in the confirmed deaths of 364 people who came in close contact with infected birds. Despite this relatively low human death rate, medical researcher Chris Murray of Harvard University, in a December 20, 2006, issue of *Lancet,* estimates that the H5N1 avian flu could kill as many as 81 million people globally if it were to mutate. No one knows if or when this could happen. Finally, in 2009, the World Health Organization issued a global public health emergency warning of the H1N1 swine flu pandemic. According to a January 25, 2012 CDC article "First Global Estimates of 2009 H1N1 Pandemic Mortality," the H1N1 flu killed as many as 575,000 people worldwide.

Why should we care about flu pandemics of the past? There are two good reasons: (1) a flu pandemic could strike again, and (2) everyone in this room is a potential victim of a deadly flu virus. Consequently, you'll want to listen carefully as I inform you about ways to prevent contracting the flu. My careful and extensive research on this subject leads me to make three main points: First, even seasonal flu viruses are a serious health hazard, second, flu viruses are difficult to combat, and third, there are several ways to prevent the flu.

Let's begin by discussing the serious health hazards produced by a normal flu season. Even ordinary flu viruses that hit the United States every year between the months of October and April are killers. A January 16, 2013, report by the Centers for Disease Control and Prevention, usually referred to simply as the CDC, notes in an article entitled "Flu Vaccinations"

Abbreviated second reference to source

More really startling statistics; stacking statistics for effect

Rhetorical question involves audience, makes transition

Significance of topic to the audience is established

Clear purpose statement

Brief reference to competence

Clear, concise preview of main points; problem-cause-solution organizational pattern used

Transition

Signposting first main point

that flu-associated deaths in the U.S. vary from a low of 3,000 to a high of 49,000 annually.

Most of you won't die from a common flu virus, but you may wish you were dead. Typical flu symptoms include high fever, sore throat, intense muscle aches, congestion, cough, and severe fatigue. My friend Terry once described how he feels when he gets the flu: "It's like being suddenly hit by a speeding car, catapulted into a concrete wall, roasted in an oven, then forced to participate in the Ironman marathon. Death, by comparison, seems pleasant." Symptoms of flu can last from a few days to several weeks. The flu can often lead to severe complications, such as bronchitis and pneumonia, which may require hospitalization.

In addition to the severity of its symptoms, flu is hazardous to humans because it is highly contagious. According to Daniel Haney, science reporter for the Associated Press, in a November 8, 1998, article in the *San Jose Mercury News*, young children are "flu incubators." Haney continues, "In epidemiological terms, children are in the same category as ticks, rats, and mosquitoes: they are vectors of disease." Day care centers and classrooms are flu breeding grounds where sick children spew the virus everywhere by coughing, sneezing, and wiping their runny noses. Children also bring the flu home and infect adult parents, who pass it along to co-workers, and so it spreads throughout the population.

Naturally, we're all interested in why flu is an annual event about as welcome as flies, frogs, and the other plagues God visited upon the ancient Egyptians in the biblical story of the Exodus. This brings me to my second main point, which is that flu viruses are difficult to combat.

Over the centuries, many theories about the causes of the flu emerged. Influenza, flu being the shortened version of this term, reflects the 15th-century astrological belief that the disease was caused by the "influence" of the stars. According to Laurie Garrett,

---

Sidebar annotations:

Startling statistic maintains attention and interest; use of credible source for all statistics

Transition

Vivid use of similes; intensity used to maintain attention

Transition

Credible source; date is fine since phenomenon does not change

Colorful, attention-getting quote

Vivid transition

Signposting main point

Credible source

award-winning author of the 1994 book *The Coming Plague,* prominent American physicians of the time thought the 1918 Spanish flu might have been caused by nakedness, fish contaminated by Germans, dirt, dust, Chinese people, unclean pajamas, open windows, closed windows, old books, or "some cosmic influence."

Historical examples are novel attention getter

Unlike our predecessors and their wrong-headed prejudices and ignorance, we know that a virus causes flu, but a flu virus is difficult to combat. There are many strains, not just a single type. For instance, according to the CDC website *cdc.gov,* there were three strains of flu in 2012–2013: A/California (H1N1), A/Victoria (H3N2), and B/Wisconsin (2010-like-virus). Flu strains are divided into A and B types, with type A usually being more severe, and each is designated by the primary locale where the flu is first reported. There are many strains of flu because flu viruses continually change over time. Thus, your immune system's antibodies produced to fight a previous flu will not combat the disease as well when exposed to a slightly altered virus. Occasionally, a flu strain will mutate, altering the genetic structure of the virus so greatly that human antibodies from previous exposures to flu will be useless. The pandemics of 1918, 1957, 1968, and 2009 were mutated flu strains according to the CDC on its website. The changing structure of flu viruses and their many strains make finding a cure very challenging.

Reference to earlier examples provides continuity to the speech; credible source

Now that you realize how hazardous flu can be and understand that its chief cause is a frequently changing virus, what can be done about the flu? This brings me to my final main point, that there are several ways to prevent catching the flu. First, stay generally healthy. Those in a weakened or vulnerable physical state, such as the very young, the elderly, those with chronic health conditions, and pregnant women, are most likely to catch the flu. All reputable health care professionals encourage a series of preventive steps, including exercise, healthy diet, sufficient rest, frequent hand washing, and avoiding touching your eyes, nose, and mouth. Also, whenever possible avoid large crowds and confined spaces where flu sufferers can

Brief internal summary

Rhetorical question; transition

Signposting main point

Signposting subpoint

spread the disease. Airplanes, classrooms, and offices are flu factories.

Second, a yearly flu shot is an effective preventive. The CDC in an October 13, 2011, article on its website titled "Vaccine Effectiveness" notes that flu shots are 60–90% effective in preventing flu. Younger, healthier individuals typically receive greater protection than older, less healthy individuals. Despite the common belief, a flu shot cannot give you the flu because, as the CDC website explains, flu shots contain no live virus. If you contract the flu soon after receiving the shot, it is because you were exposed to the flu and the vaccine does not provide protection until two weeks after being vaccinated. The most frequent side effect is brief soreness at the site of the shot.

For those who get weak in the knees at the very sight of a syringe, there is FluMist, a vaccine in the form of nasal spray. According to the January 10, 2013, CDC article "CDC Says Take Three Actions," FluMist does contain live virus, so there is a small chance of experiencing flu-like symptoms from the spray. Its side effects are minimal, however, especially when compared to some things people shoot up their noses. Pain phobics take note—it doesn't hurt! Researchers are also working on a pain-free skin patch to inoculate against flu, and a universal flu vaccine that combats all flu types.

None of these options is guaranteed to prevent the flu, so if you do contract this seasonal sickness there are two principal antiviral prescription drugs—Tamiflu and Relenza—that can help you. The same January 10, 2013, CDC article reports that these antiviral drugs are effective in reducing flu symptoms and preventing serious complications if taken soon after the onset of the flu.

In review, I have shown that flu viruses can be hazardous to humans, that combating flu can be difficult because flu viruses can easily change, but that catching the flu can be prevented. I began with a reference

Alliteration for vividness

Signposting subpoint

Credible source; credible statistics

Credible source

Credible source

Alliteration

Abbreviated second citation

Transition to conclusion

Summary of main points

Reference to the spanish flu example in the introduction gives closure to the speech to the 1918 Spanish flu. Author John Barry called the Spanish flu "the deadliest pandemic in history" in his critically acclaimed 2005 book *The Great Influenza*. Nobody knows where the Spanish flu virus went or whether it will surface again. Until we find a lasting cure for the flu, we'll have to be vigilant in our effort to prevent this annual plague.

Quotation as attention-getter

Reference to speech title, "annual plague," makes a memorable finish

B

TEXT OF A PERSUASIVE SPEECH

(Monroe's Motivated Sequence Organization)

This is the text of about a 15-minute persuasive speech. This is a longer speech than most in-class presentations but shorter than many public presentations. This somewhat lengthier speech is presented to provide a more comprehensive illustration of several persuasive strategies.

The speech presented here uses the *Monroe Motivated Sequence* organizational format discussed in Chapter 7. Steps in this sequence are identified in **boldfaced** brackets.

GET BIG MONEY OUT OF COLLEGE SPORTS

(Prepared February 2013)

"We want to put our materials on the bodies of your athletes, and the best way to do that is buy your school. Or buy your coach." So said Sonny Vaccaro in 2001 before shocked members of the Knight Commission on Intercollegiate Athletics. Vaccaro was a slick athletic shoe salesman, sometimes dubbed the "sneaker pimp" by his detractors, who worked for various companies such as Nike, Reebok, and Adidas to establish licensing rights with universities for his products. Asked by Penn State University President Emeritus and Knight Commission member Bryce

Attention step—Monroe's motivated sequence in boldface

Attention step continued

Jordan, "Why should a university be an advertising medium for your industry?" Vaccaro responded, "You sold your souls, and you're going to continue selling them. There's no one of you in this room that's going to turn down any of our money. You're going to take it. I can only offer it." Journalist Taylor Branch in his October 2011 article in *The Atlantic* titled "The Shame of College Sports," remarks, "What Vaccaro said in 2001 was true then, and it's true now: corporations offer money so they can profit from the glory of college athletics, and the universities grab it." He goes on to conclude that "college sports has become very Big Business . . . and corruption is likely to follow."

Intercollegiate athletic programs are being corrupted by massive mountains of money, not only by corporate sponsorships but by the sheer size and cost of athletic programs. The 2011 NCAA report entitled "NCAA Revenues/Expenses" documents that the median athletic budget for the major college athletic programs is almost $47 million annually. That's more than the total operating budget of many small colleges and universities in the United States. The 2010 Knight Commission Report, "Restoring the Balance," projects that by 2020, top intercollegiate athletic program budgets will exceed $250 million annually.

Significance

Is this increasing Big Business model of college sports compatible with the educational mission of institutions of higher learning? Sociology Professor Emeritus Stanley Eitzen, in a December 1, 1997, speech printed in *Vital Speeches,* observed: "Big-time college sport confronts us with a fundamental dilemma. Positively, college football and basketball offer entertainment, spectacle, excitement, festival, and excellence. Negatively, the commercial entertainment function of big-time college sport has severely compromised academia. Educational goals have been superseded by the quest for big money." Professor Eitzen said this more than 15 years ago when the corrupting influence of big money on intercollegiate sports programs was relatively tame by today's standards.

Let's be honest: college athletics, especially Division I-A big-time football and basketball programs, are a commercial entertainment venture far removed from the educational mission of colleges and universities. College sports have become so gigantic that they distort the priorities of colleges and universities and compromise their educational mission. Because this is a serious problem, I will try to convince you that colleges and universities should significantly reduce the scale of their athletic programs.

Proposition of policy

I can guess what some of you are thinking. "He wants to reduce college athletic programs because he's a geek who was always chosen last in the playground draft." Not true! I may not look like an athlete, but I have had a modicum of success playing baseball, earning my share of trophies and accolades. I am also an avid sports fan who roots for the University of Oregon Ducks, San Francisco Forty-Niners, and San Francisco Giants. You may question my choice of teams to support, although I note all three teams' recent success, but I do not propose reducing the scale of college athletics because I hate sports.

Credibility and Identification

I offer several arguments to support my proposal. First, I will show how big-time athletic programs contradict the educational mission of colleges. Second, I will offer a specific plan to rectify this serious problem. Finally, I will respond to primary objections you may have to my proposal.

Preview of main points

Returning to my first argument, that big-time athletic programs contradict the educational mission of colleges, let me begin with what I think we all know is true. The principal mission of a college or university is to provide a quality education for all students. As the 2010 Knight Commission Report on Intercollegiate Athletics notes, "Spending on educational activities should not be compromised to boost sports funding." The NCAA, governing body of collegiate sports programs in the U.S., insists on using the term "student-athlete" in all of its reports and news releases, emphasizing that the priority be given to "student" not "athlete."

Need step

Excessive emphasis on sports programs, however, contradicts the educational mission of colleges in three ways. First, athletic prowess, not academic ability, is often given priority by colleges. According to Donna Desrochers, principal researcher at American Institutes for Research, in her January 2013 report called "Academic Spending Versus Athletic Spending," colleges with big-time athletic programs spend an average of *a million dollars each year* recruiting athletes. They recruit athletes not student scholars. No recruiter cares whether student-athletes have high SAT scores or impressive GPAs as long as they meet the minimum qualifications to play their sport. Gary Gutting notes in his March 15, 2012, *New York Times* article "The Myth of the 'Student-Athlete'" that average SAT scores for college athletes are about 200 points lower than for those of nonathletes. Clearly, athletic prowess, not academic potential, is what counts. Even the student-athletes admit this. A November 2011 NCAA report on goals of student-athletes reported that student-athletes self-identify significantly more with athletics than with academics. In other words, these individuals come to college primarily to play sports.

> Cognitive dissonance

Second, excessive emphasis on athletic programs contradicts the educational mission of colleges because student-athletes and nonathletes alike are harmed by the emphasis placed on athletic ability. So-called student-athletes spend an average of 39–43 hours per week preparing for basketball and football games, significantly more time than they spend on academics, according to the 2011 NCAA report previously cited. Academic success is jeopardized by the excessive time spent on sports. Nonathletes are also adversely affected by the glorification of big-time sports. Admitting less-qualified students because of their athletic abilities prevents other, more academically qualified, students from gaining entrance to some of the best colleges and universities. Some of you may have been denied entrance to the college of your choice and had to settle for a second, third, or even fourth choice because athletes with far weaker academic records were granted preferential admittance. Does this seem fair to you?

> Mild anger appeal

This leads me to my third point, that the primary mission of colleges and universities to educate students is often diminished by athletic department budget deficits. Only 22 NCAA colleges out of 227 Division I schools were self-sustaining, requiring no subsidies from the general budget, based on *USA Today* Sports May 15, 2012, database. The 2010 Knight Commission report concludes: "Reliance on institutional resources to underwrite athletics programs is reaching the point at which some institutions must choose between funding sections of freshman English and funding the football team."

> Continuation of cognitive dissonance

Despite significant deficits, college athletic departments are engaging in out of control spending. Donna Desroachers, previously cited, reports in 2013 that the median expenditure *per athlete* at major colleges is almost $92,000, but median per-student expenditures on academics is less than $14,000. The 2010 Knight Commission report notes that athletic spending since 2005 increased twice as fast as spending on academic programs. Gary Brown, representing the NCAA reported in 2011 that the median deficit of the almost 200 colleges that are not running self-sustaining athletic programs is $7.3 million annually. You've seen your tuition and fees skyrocket recently while sports programs continue to be fat and sassy, experiencing an opulent lifestyle of state-of-the-art facilities and bloated budgets. A May 15, 2012, article in *USA Today* reports that subsidies from student tuition and fees and other sources to cover gigantic athletic budget deficits each year amounted to $2.1 billion in 2011, the latest figures available.

> Use of persuasive evidence; startling and unusual statistics

So what should be done about this problem? Clearly, since football and basketball programs are typically the most costly and the principal source of all these problems, we should eliminate them from all colleges and universities. If we were to eliminate football and basketball, less visible and far less costly sports such as baseball, golf, gymnastics, and field hockey could provide some athletic opportunities for

> Contrast effect

students. Intramural football and basketball programs could be established for those students who prefer such sports, at virtually no cost to the college. Let's face facts—getting the money out of college sports is essential if we are going to solve the problems I've outlined.

Total elimination of football and basketball except for intramural programs solves the problems I've underscored. Perhaps, however, we don't need such a drastic solution. As a sports fan and former athlete, I would be disappointed if colleges dumped their football and basketball programs entirely. I do strongly believe, however, that the big money must be taken out of college sports.

Contrast effect continued

My plan to do this is as follows:

1. There will be no scholarships for students based on athletic ability. Scholarships and grants must be based on academic potential and financial need. This is a strong recommendation of the National Alliance for College Athletic Reform. This is also the current practice of Division III NCAA schools.
2. Student athletes must be admitted according to the same standards as all other students. They must maintain a minimum 2.5 GPA to participate in athletic programs.
3. Team practice sessions and related activities will be limited to no more than 20 hours per week.
4. Absolutely no corporate money goes to athletic programs. No corporate logos or names should appear on any sports facilities, equipment, or apparel of any kind.
5. Football and basketball programs must be self-sustaining.? Ticket sales and sports merchandise will be primary sources of funds. There will be no subsidizing football or basketball programs from a college's general fund. No money from television rights or bowl games will go to college athletic programs. Any revenue earned from television or other media programming must be used for academic programs and for overall athletic programs.

Satisfaction step

6. College coaches must be paid salaries equivalent to any professor. This is the current practice of Ivy League colleges. A 2009 Knight Commission survey of college presidents called escalating salaries of college athletics coaches, especially for football and basketball, "the single largest contributing factor to the unsustainable growth of athletics expenditures." A November 20, 2012, article in *USA Today* reports that major college football coaches' salaries averaged $1.64 million. A December 18, 2012, article in the same source further reports that average pay for football assistant coaches is $201,000. What assistant professor makes anything like that salary at even the most prestigious universities in the U.S.? Full professors, even those with Nobel prizes, typically earn less than assistant football coaches, and this is a travesty that screams "ATHLETICS RULE!" Even coaches for women's basketball, not typically a big revenue producing sport, although lagging far behind the median salaries for men's basketball coaches of $329,300, still is a sizable $171,600, according to an April 2, 2012, *New York Times* article titled "Pay for Women's Basketball Coaches."

7. My plan will be enforced by the NCAA where legally possible, and by all member colleges individually or in concert within each league where anti-trust laws prohibit NCAA action. Enforcement sanctions include probation, suspension, and/or banishment from league play.

Satisfaction step continued

This plan will substantially reduce college athletic programs without eliminating them. I have merely taken the big money out of college sports. Leagues, championships, and bowl games can continue, but without the huge financial incentives to distort the academic mission of colleges. Academic programs will no longer be threatened by huge athletic department debts. Without the big money, colleges can return to their primary mission—to provide a quality education for all students.

In case you're not completely convinced that my plan is a good idea, let me address common objections to my proposal. The first objection might be that disadvantaged student athletes will lose scholarships and be denied a college education. That's true, but the NCAA has cracked down some recently by reducing the number of scholarships a school can offer to athletes if academic performance and graduation rates of athletes sink too low. The NCAA, however, has not gone nearly far enough. Eliminating all athletic scholarships could save money for general scholarships and grants at each college. The net effect on students as a group would be zero. The faces would change, but the same number of students could receive financial help. In addition, if student athletes realize that they cannot play college sports unless they qualify academically, this will provide an incentive for them to take their studies seriously or risk ineligibility.

Two-sided persuasion

A second objection might be that, without scholarships, many academically unprepared student athletes will lose a training ground for a career in professional sports. This may be true, but is it relevant? Should a college be a farm team for professional sports corporations? Why should a college create false hope for athletes, most of whom will never make it into professional sports? Official NCAA statistics reported in a February 10, 2012, *Business Insider* article that the chances of a college student-athlete reaching the pros is less than 2%. It is even less for female athletes, who have fewer professional options. Colleges should not be a party to exploitation of college athletes. Colleges should be working hard to prepare students for important professions because that is their primary mission. They should stop serving as a farm team for professional sports corporations interested only in profit.

Cognitive dissonance

Finally, won't sports fans lose a key source of entertainment if my plan is implemented? This is not true. Notre Dame and USC will still remain archrivals on

Two-sided persuasion

the football field. Bowl games will still exist. Championships will still be contested, simply in scaled-down versions as they once were in the 1950s and 1960s before big money began exerting its corrupting influence. The difference will be that academic programs will not be diminished because of huge deficits from athletic programs, and the academic mission of colleges will not be distorted to pay for a bloated athletic program. The scale of college athletics will be substantially reduced, but the excitement and spectacle can remain.

Imagine what my plan will accomplish. No longer will colleges be tempted or forced to reduce or eliminate an academic program, perhaps a program in your major, to pay for deficits incurred by bloated athletic programs. Millions of dollars in scholarships and grants will be available for academically qualified and needy students. Colleges will no longer serve as mere farm teams for profit-motivated corporations. Colleges will no longer appear hypocritical, espousing an educational mission on one hand while undermining it on the other. Your student fees and tuition will not have to be raised to support a faltering, expensive sports program.

Imagine what will happen if this problem is ignored. Athletic budgets will continue to swell and deficits will rise. Your tuition and fees will increase, academic programs will be cut, and some programs and majors will be eliminated to cover the athletic department deficits. The quality of your education and your opportunities for academic success will be threatened. As the 2001 Knight Foundation Commission report concluded, "If it proves impossible to create a system of intercollegiate athletics that can live honorably within the American college and university, then responsible citizens must join with academic and public leaders to insist that the nation's colleges and universities get out of the business of big-time sports." I submit to you that we have now reached that point.

Two-sided persuasion continued

Visualization step

Mild fear appeal

I began this presentation by quoting Sonny Vaccaro asserting that colleges have sold their souls to corporations for big money. College sports have become too closely connected to corporate interests. Big money has corrupted college athletics and the primary mission of colleges and universities. Colleges need to snatch their souls back from the devil of corporate sponsorships and big money. I have further established that bloated athletic budgets are harmful both to student athletes and nonathletes alike. I have proposed a solution that will work by taking money out of college sports. I have responded to common objections raised against my plan, and these objections have been found meritless. I ask that you support my proposal to significantly reduce college athletic programs. Stop the erosion of academic values and quality. Speak to your Student Senate officers and representatives. Discuss the issues I have raised with the college administration. This college can be a beacon of light signaling the way for other colleges to follow. Change begins with us. Get big money out of college sports!

Action Step

Glossary

Ad hominem fallacy A personal attack on the messenger to avoid the message; a diversionary tactic that is irrelevant to the primary message.

Ad populum fallacy Erroneously basing a claim on popular opinion.

After-dinner speech A humorous presentation that typically occurs at a formal gathering of some group after a meal that is meant to entertain on some topic of interest to an audience.

Alliteration The repetition of the same sound, usually a consonant sound, starting each word in a phrase or sentence.

Ambushing Looking for weaknesses in a speaker's arguments and preparing to pounce on perceived mistakes without listening for understanding of a speaker's message first.

Anchor In social judgment theory, this is the preexisting attitude on an issue that serves as a reference point.

Anecdote A short, entertaining, real-life story used to illustrate a speaker's point.

Anger activism model Explains the relationship between anger and persuasion.

Antithesis A sentence composed of two parts with parallel structure but opposite meanings to create impact.

Appropriateness Behavior that is perceived to be legitimate based on rules that apply to the speaking context.

Argument Implicitly or explicitly presents a claim and provides support for that claim with reasoning and evidence.

Articulation Speaking words clearly and distinctly.

Attention The act of focusing on a specific stimulus to the exclusion of competing stimuli.

Attitude A learned predisposition to respond favorably or unfavorably toward some attitude object.

Belief What a person thinks is true or probable.

Brief example Short instances used to illustrate points in a speech.

Burden of proof The obligation of those making a claim to present compelling evidence and reasoning to support the claim.

Central idea Sometimes referred to as the theme, it identifies the main concept, point, issue, or conclusion that you want the audience to understand, believe, feel, or do.

Cliche A once-vivid expression that has been overused to the point of seeming commonplace.

Cognitive dissonance The unpleasant feeling produced by apparent inconsistency in ideas, beliefs, or opinions; holding two contradictory cognitions simultaneously and feeling uncomfortable when this is pointed out to you.

Coherence Main points of your speech flow directly from the purpose statement and subpoints likewise flow from main points.

Collectivist cultures Cultures that emphasize group harmony, intra-group cooperation and conformity, and individual sacrifice for the sake of the group.

Commencement address An inspirational speech that occurs at graduation ceremonies.

Commitment A passion for excellence; accepting nothing less than the best that you can be and dedicating yourself to achieving that excellence.

Communication A transactional process of sharing meaning with others.

Communication competence Engaging in communication that is perceived to be both effective and appropriate in a given context.

Communication orientation A method of addressing speech anxiety by focusing on making your message clear and interesting to your listeners instead of focusing on being evaluated.

Communication skill The successful performance of a communication behavior and the ability to repeat such a behavior.

Competence An audience's perception of the speaker's knowledge and experience on a topic.

Composure Exhibiting emotional stability, confidence and control while speaking.

Confirmation bias The tendency to seek information that supports one's beliefs and to ignore information that contradicts those beliefs.

Context The environment in which communication occurs; the who, what, where, when, why, and how of communication.

Contrast effect A persuasive strategy that begins with a large request that makes a smaller request seem more acceptable.

Correlation A consistent relationship between two variables.

Counterpersuasion Attacks from an opposing side on an issue of controversy.

Credibility Judgments made by a perceiver concerning the believability of a communicator.

Credibility of evidence Refers to the believability of evidence as determined by consistency and accuracy.

Cynicism Nay-saying, fault-finding, and ridiculing the beliefs of others; often confused with skepticism.

Demographics Characteristics of an audience such as age, gender, culture, ethnicity, and group affiliations.

Demonstration An informative speech that shows an audience how to use an object or perform a specific activity.

Direct question A question asked by a speaker that seeks an overt response from the audience.

Directory An Internet tool where humans edit indexes of Web pages that match, or link with, key words typed in a search window.

Door-in-the-face strategy A persuasive strategy that uses the contrast effect.

Dynamism The enthusiasm, energy, and forcefulness exhibited by a speaker.

Dysfunctional speech anxiety Occurs when the intensity of the fight-or-flight response prevents an individual from giving a speech effectively.

Ego involvement In social judgment theory it refers to the degree to which an issue is relevant or important to a person.

Elaboration likelihood model An overarching perspective on persuasion that explains how listeners cope with the bombardment of persuasive messages by sorting them into those that are important, or central, and those that are less relevant, or peripheral.

Ethics A system for judging the moral correctness of human behavior by weighing that behavior against an agreed upon set of standards of right and wrong.

Ethnocentrism The biased belief that customs, practices, and behaviors of your own culture are superior to any other culture.

Ethos Aristotle's ingredients of speaker credibility consisting of good sense, good moral character, and good will.

Eulogy A tribute delivered in praise of a deceased friend or family member.

Euphemism An indirect or vague word or phrase used to numb us to or conceal unpleasant or offensive realities.

Evidence Statistics, testimony of experts and credible sources, and verifiable facts used to support claims.

Examples Specific instances of a general category of objects, ideas, people, places, actions, experiences, or phenomena.

Extemporaneous speech A speech delivered from a prepared outline or notes.

Extended example A detailed, lengthy example to illustrate a point in a speech.

Fallacy Any error in reasoning and evidence that may deceive your audience.

False analogy A fallacy that occurs when erroneously reasoning from two things with superficial similarities that also have a significant point or points of difference.

Fight-or-flight response The physiological defense-alarm process triggered by stress.

Framing The influence wording has on our perception of choices.

Functional speech anxiety Occurs when the fight-or-flight response is managed and stimulates an optimum presentation.

General purpose Identifies the overall goal of a speech such as to inform, describe, explain, demonstrate, persuade, celebrate, memorialize, entertain, or eulogize.

Graph A visual representation of statistics in an easily understood format.

Hasty generalization A fallacy that occurs when individuals jump to conclusions based on a single example or a handful of examples.

Hypothetical example An example that describes an imaginary situation; one that is created to make a point, illustrate an idea, or identify a general principle.

Identification The affiliation and connection between speaker and audience.

Impromptu speech A speech delivered without preparation, or so it seems.

Individualist cultures Cultures that emphasize personal autonomy and competitiveness, privacy, individual liberties, and toleration of nonconformity.

Inflection Vocal variety used when speaking.

Intensity Concentrated stimuli; an extreme degree of emotion, thought, or activity.

Internal preview Mimics a preview in the Introduction of a speech except it appears in the body of your speech.

Internal summary The reverse of an internal preview; it reminds listeners of points already made in a speech but appears in the body not the conclusion of a speech.

Jargon The specialize language of a profession, trade, or group.

Latitude of acceptance In social judgment theory it is the position a person finds tolerable if not preferable.

Latitude of noncommitment In social judgment theory it is the position that provokes only a neutral or ambivalent response.

Latitude of rejection In social judgment theory it is the position a person finds objectionable because it is too distant from the anchor attitude.

Law of Truly Large Numbers With large enough numbers almost anything is likely to happen to somebody, somewhere, somehow, sometime.

Logos Aristotle's term for building arguments based on logic and evidence to persuade listeners.

Margin of error A measure of the degree of sampling error accounted for by imperfections in sample selection.

Mean The arithmetic average determined by adding the values of all items and dividing the sum by the total number of items.

Measure of central tendency Shows how scores cluster so you can get a sense of what is typically occurring.

Median The middle score in a cluster of numbers.

Metaphor An implied comparison of two seemingly dissimilar things.

Metasearch engine An Internet tool that sends your key word request to several search engines at once.

Mindfulness Occurs when you think about your communication and concentrate on changing what you do to become more effective.

Mindlessness Occurs when you are not cognizant of your communication with others, so no improvement is likely.

Mixed metaphor The use of two or more vastly different metaphors in a single expression.

Mode The most frequent score in the distribution of all scores considered.

Non sequitur Classic type of fallacy in which a conclusion does not follow from its premises.

Parallel processing Using both the central and peripheral routes to persuasion.

Pathos Aristotle's term for emotional appeals to persuade audiences.

Performance An attempt to satisfy an audience of critics whose members are focused on evaluating your presentation.

Persuasion A communication process of converting, modifying, or maintaining the attitudes and/or behavior of others.

Pitch The range of your voice from high to low sounds.

Preview Presents the coming attractions of your speech; identifying the main points of your speech before developing them.

Probability of feared occurrence Likelihood that the feared worst-case scenario while giving a speech would actually happen.

Pronunciation Saying words correctly as indicated in any dictionary based on Standard English rules.

Proposition The primary, overriding claim for a persuasive speech.

Proposition of fact An overriding speech claim that alleges a truth.

Proposition of policy An overriding speech claim that calls for a significant change from how problems are currently handled.

Proposition of value An overriding speech claim that calls for a judgment that assesses the worth or merit of an idea, object, or practice.

Public speaking An act of communication in which a speaker presents a message to an audience on an occasion to achieve a specific purpose.

Random sample A portion of a target population chosen in such a manner that every member of the entire population has an equal chance of being selected.

Rationalization of disconfirmation Inventing superficial, even glib, alternative explanations for contradictory evidence that exposes unwarranted beliefs.

Real example Actual occurrences used in a speech to make a point, illustrate an idea, or identify a general principle.

Reasoning The thought process of drawing conclusions from evidence.

Refutation Answering opposing arguments.

Repetition Stylistic use of language that reiterates the same word, phrase, or sentence, usually with parallel structure.

Report A brief, concise, informative presentation that fulfills a class assignment, updates a committee about work performed by a subcommittee, reveals the results of a study, provides recent findings, or identifies the latest developments in a current situation.

Rhetorical question A question asked by a speaker that the audience answers mentally, but not out loud.

Roast A purposely humorous tribute to a person typically using sarcasm, exaggeration, even ribald humor.

Rule A prescription that indicates what behavior is obligated, preferred, or prohibited in certain contexts.

Search engine An Internet tool that computer generates indexes of Web pages that match, or link with, key words typed in a search window.

Self-deprecation Humor that makes fun of your own failings and limitations.

Self-selected sample Any poll or survey that depends on respondents selecting themselves to participate.

Sensitivity Receptive accuracy whereby one can detect, decode, and comprehend signals in a social environment.

Severity of a feared occurrence Approximated by imagining what would happen if catastrophic failure did occur when giving a speech.

Shared meaning This occurs when both the speaker and receivers have mutual understanding of a message.

Shifting the burden of proof Inappropriately assuming the validity of a claim unless it is proven false by another person who never made the original claim.

Signposts An organizational marker that indicates the structure of a speech and notifies listeners that a particular point is about to be addressed.

Simile An explicit comparison of two seemingly dissimilar things using the words *like* or *as*.

Skepticism A process of inquiry whereby claims are evaluated by engaging in a rigorous examination of evidence and reasoning used to support those claims.

Slang The highly informal speech not in conventional usage.

Social cohesion That which binds us together in mutual liking.

Social judgment theory A theory of persuasion that focuses on how close or distant an audience's position on a controversial issue is from its anchor attitude.

Specific purpose A concise, precise infinitive phrase composed of simple, clear language that encompasses both the general purpose and indicates what the speaker hopes to accomplish with the speech.

Speech anxiety Fear of public speaking and the nervousness that accompanies that fear.

Speech of introduction Prepares an audience for a speech to be given by a featured speaker.

Speech of presentation Communicates to an audience the meaning and importance of an award presented to an individual or group.

Statistics Measures of what is true or factual expressed in numbers.

Stylistic similarity Creating identification with an audience by looking and acting similarly to others.

Substantive similarity Creating identification with an audience by establishing common ground with listeners.

Supporting materials Examples, statistics, and testimony used to bolster a speaker's viewpoint.

Syllogism In formal logic the basic structure of an argument which includes a major premise, minor premise, and conclusion from these two premises.

Systematic desensitization A technique used to control anxiety, even phobias, triggered by a wide variety of stimuli that operates on the principle that relaxation and anxiety are incompatible and do not occur simultaneously.

Table An orderly depiction of statistics, words, or symbols in columns and rows.

Testimony A first-hand account of events or the conclusions offered publicly by experts on a topic.

Toast A brief tribute to a person or couple.

Transactional communication A process in which each person communicating is both a sender and a receiver simultaneously, not merely a sender or a receiver, and all parties influence each other.

Transitions Use of words or phrases to connect what was said with what will be said in a speech.

Tribute speeches Speeches that praise or celebrate a person.

True belief A willingness to accept claims without solid reasoning or valid evidence and to hold these beliefs tenaciously even if a mountain of contradictory evidence proves the belief incorrect.

Trustworthiness Refers to how truthful or honest we perceive a speaker to be.

Uncertainty reduction theory As novelty wears off from experience uncertainty is reduced and anxiety consequently diminishes.

Value The most deeply felt, generally shared view of what is deemed good, right, or worthwhile thinking or behavior.

Variable Anything that can change.

Virtual library A search tool that combines Internet technology and standard library techniques for cataloguing and appraising information.

Visualization Countering negative thoughts of catastrophe when giving a speech with positive images of success.

Vividness effect The outrageous, shocking, controversial, and dramatic events that can distort our perceptions of the facts.

Vocal fillers The insertion of *um, uh, like, you know,* and similar variations that substitute for pauses and often draw attention away from a speaker's message.

Volume The range of your voice from loud to soft.

References

Adler, J. E. (1998, January/February). Open minds and the argument from ignorance. *Skeptical Inquirer*, pp. 41–44.

Adler, R., & Proctor, R. F. (2007). *Looking out, looking in.* Belmont, CA: Thomson-Wadsworth.

Advertising is hazardous to your health. (1986, July). *University of California, Berkeley Wellness Letter*, pp. 1–2.

Airline safety. (2010, March 20). *Funny Humor.* [Online]. Available at: http://www.funnyhumor.com/jokes/586.php

Albers, H. (2012). Pediatric bipolar disorder: A psychological misnomer. In L. G. Schnoor, L. Mayfield, and K. Young (Eds.), *Winning orations.* Mankato, MN: Interstate Oratorical Association.

Aldhous, P. (2012, March 9). Fukushima's fate inspires nuclear safety rethink. *New Scientist.* [Online]. Available at: http://www.newscientist.com/article/dn21556-fukushimas-fate-inspires-nuclear-safety-rethink.html

Allan, K. & Burridge, K. (1991). *Euphemism and dysphemism: Language used as shield and weapon.* New York: Oxford University Press.

Allen, G. (1996). Military drug testing. In L. G. Schnoor & B. Wickelgren (Eds.), *Winning orations,* Mankato, MN: Interstate Oratorical Association..

Allen, M. (1991). Comparing the persuasiveness of one-sided and two-sided messages using meta-analysis. *Western Journal of Speech Communication*, 55, 390–404.

Allen, M. (1993). Determining the persuasiveness of one- and two-sided messages. In M. Allen & R. Preiss (Eds.), *Prospects and precautions in the use of meta-analysis.* Dubuque, IA: Brown & Benchmark.

Allen, M. (1998). Comparing the persuasive effectiveness of one- and two-sided messages. In M. Allen & R. W. Preiss (Eds.), *Persuasion: Advances through meta-analysis.* Creskill, NH: Hampton Press.

Allen, M., & Preiss, R. W. (1997). Comparing the persuasiveness of narrative and statistical evidence using meta-analysis. *Communication Research Reports*, 14, 125–131.

Allen, M., Bruflat, R., Fucilla, R., Kramer, M., McKellips, S., Ryan, D. J., & Spiegelhoff, M. (2000). Testing the persuasiveness of evidence: Combining narrative and statistical forms. *Communication Research Reports*, 17, 331–336.

Alley, M. (2005). *The craft of scientific presentations: Critical steps to succeed and critical errors to avoid.* New York: Springer.

Alter, A. L., Oppenheimer, D. M., Epley, N., & Eyre, R. N. (2007). Overcoming intuition: Metacognitive difficulty activates analytic reasoning. *Journal of Experimental Psychology: General*, 136, 569–576.

American Lung Association (2008, August). Smoking 101 fact sheet. [Online]. Available at: http://www.lungusa.org/site/c.dvLUK900E/b.39853/

Amira, D. (2012, August 14). What the hell did Joe Biden's "Chain" remark mean? *New York Magazine.* [Online]. Available at: http://nymag.com/daily/intel/2012/08/joe-biden-chains-video-black.html

Anderson, G. (2009). Don't reject my homoglobin. In L. G. Schnoor & D. Cronn-Mills (Eds.), *Winning orations.* Mankato, MN: Interstate Oratorical Association.

Anderson, L. V. (2012, July 23). Hot feet: Why don't all firewalkers get burned? *Slate.* [Online]. Available at: http://www.slate.com/articles/health_and_science/explainer/2012/07/tony_robbins_

firewalking_injuries_why_doesn_t_everyone_who_walks_on_hot_coals_get_burned_.html

Anderson, R., & Ross, V. (1994). *Questions of communication: A practical introduction to theory.* New York: St. Martin's Press.

Andeweg, B. A., de Jong, J. C., & Hoeken, H. (1998). May I have your attention? Exordial techniques in informative oral presentations. *Technical Communication Quarterly, 7,* 271–284.

Angier, N. (2002, March 5). One lifetime is not enough for a trip to distant stars. *New York Times.* [Online]. Available at: http://www.nytimes.com/learning/teachers/featured_articles/20020305tuesday.html

Anti-sweatshop activist brings delegates to their feet. (2002, March/April). *California Teacher,* p. 4

Arnold, J. E., Fagnano, M., & Tanenhaus, M. K. (2003). Disfluencies signal thee, um, new information. *Journal of Psycholinguistic Research, 32,* 25–36.

Aronson, E., Fried, C., & Stone, J. (1991). Overcoming denial and increasing the intentions to use condoms through the induction of hypocrisy. *American Journal of Public Health, 81,* 1636–1638.

As "sexiest man alive," you'd think dating would be easier. (2006, December 12). *San Jose Mercury News,* p. 2A.

Assunta, M. & Chapman, S. (2004). Industry sponsored youth smoking prevention programme in Malasia: A case study in duplicity. *Tobacco Control, 13,* 37–42.

Atkinson, C. (2008). *Beyond bullet points: Using Microsoft Office PowerPoint 2007 to create presentations that inform, motivate, and inspire.* Redmond, WA: Microsoft Press.

Axtell, R. (1998). *Gestures: The do's and taboos of body language around the world.* New York: John Wiley.

Axell, R. (2007). *Essential do's and taboos: the complete guide to international business and leisure travel.* New York: Wiley.

Ayres, J. (2005). Performance visualization and behavioral disruption: A clarification. *Communication Reports, 18,* 55–63.

Ayres, J., & Hopf, T. (1995). *Coping with speech anxiety.* Norwood, NJ: Ablex.

Ayres, J., Wongprasert, T. K., Silva, J., Story, T., & Sawant, D. D. (2001). Effects of performance visualization on employment interviews. *Communication Quarterly, 49,* 160–172.

Baesler, E. J., & Burgoon, J. K. (1994). The temporal effects of story and statistical evidence on belief change. *Communication Research, 21,* 582–602.

Bailey, E. (2008, August 7). Celebrities with anxiety: Harrison Ford: Fear of public speaking. *Healthcentral .com.* [Online]. Available at: http://www.healthcentral.com/anxiety/c/22705/36519/celebrities-public

Bailey, J. (2009, June 10). The Palin plagiarism scandal. *Plagiarism Today.* [Online]. Available at: http://www.plagiarismtoday.com/2009/06/10/the-palin-plagiarism-scandal/

Banaji, M. (2011, February). Harnessing the power of *Wikipedia* for scientific psychology: A call to action. *Observor,* pp. 5–6.

Banas, J. A., Dunbar, N., Rodriguez, D., & Liu, S. (2011). A review of humor in education settings: Four decades of research. *Communication Education, 60,* 115–144.

Baram, M. (2009, June 8). Stephen Colbert Iraq show: Gen. Odierno shaves his head. *Huffington Post.* [Online]. Available at: http://www.huffingtonpost.com/2009/06/08/stephen-colbert-iraq-show_n_212388.html

Basic training: Decorum & civility in the House. (2009, September 10). *Committee on Rules-Republican.* [Online]. Available at: http://rules-republicans.house.gov/Educational/Read.aspx?ID=5

Baxter, J. (2012). Women of the corporation: A sociolinguistic perspective of senior women's leadership language in the U.K. *Journal of Sociolinguistics, 16,* 81–107.

Because we can, we must. (2004, May 17). *Almanac Between Issues.* [Online]. Available at: http://www.upenn.edu/almanac/between/2004/commence-b.html

Behnke, R. R., & Sawyer, C. R. (1999a). Milestones of anticipatory public speaking anxiety. *Communication Education*, 48, 1–8.

Behnke, R. R., & Sawyer, C. R. (1999b). Public speaking procrastination as a correlate of public speaking communication apprehension and self-perceived public speaking competence. *Communication Research Reports*, 16, 40–47.

Behnke, R. R., & Sawyer, C. R. (2004). Public speaking anxiety as a function of sensitization and habituation processes. *Communication Education*, 53, 164–173.

Bennett, A. (1995, January 10). Economics meeting: A zillion causes and effects. *Wall Street Journal*, p. B1.

Benoit, W. L. (1987). Argumentation appeals and credibility appeals in persuasion. *Southern Speech Communication Journal*, 52, 181–187.

Benoit, W. L. (1998). Forewarning and persuasion. In M. Allen & R. W. Preiss (Eds.), *Persuasion: Advances through meta-analysis*. Cresskill, NJ: Hampton Press.

Bernieri, F. J. (2001). Toward a taxonomy of interpersonal sensitivity. In J. A. Hall & F. J. Bernieri (Eds.), *Interpersonal sensitivity: Theory and measurement*. Mahwah, NJ: Lawrence Erlbaum Associates.

Best English lesson. (1999, December 26). *Parade*, p. 8,

Beyerstein, B. L. (1998). The sorry state of scientific literacy in the industrialized democracies. *The Learning Quarterly*, 2, 5–11.

Bizony, P. (2009, July 6). It was a fake, right? *Engineering and Technology Magazine*. [Online]. Available at: http://eandt.theiet .org/magazine/2009/12/fake-right.cfm#

Boone, R. (2009, September 5). Court: Ashcroft can be held liable. *San Jose Mercury News*, p. A5.

Bor, J. (2001, January 3). Canadian smokers get stark warning: New labels depict harsh consequences. *San Jose Mercury News*, p. 6A.

Bortfeld, H., Leon, S. D., Bloom, J. E., Schober, M. F., & Brennan, S. E. (2001). Disfluency rates in spontaneous speech:

Effects of age, relationship, topic, role, and gender. *Language and Speech*, 44, 123–147.

Brossart, A. (2009). Don't trust your life to a ratio. In L. G. Schnoor & D. Cronn-Mills (Eds.), *Winning orations*. Mankato, MN: Interstate Oratorical Association.

Bruni, F. (2012, October 11). Big bad Biden. *The New York Times*. [Online]. Available at: http://bruni.blogs.nytimes .com/2012/10/11/big-bad-biden/

Bruskin & Goldring. (1993). America's number 1 fear: Public speaking. In Bruskin & Goldring (Eds.), *Bruskin & Goldring Report*.

Bumiller, E. (2010, April 26). We have met the enemy and he is PowerPoint. *The New York Times*. [Online]. Available at: http:// www.nytimes.com/2010/04/27/world/ 27powerpoint.html?partner=rss&emc=r ss&pagewanted=print

Burke, K. (1950). *A rhetoric of motives*. New York: Prentice-Hall.

Burke, K., & Chapman, B. (2012, December 21). NRA's "ludicrous" proposal to have armed guards at every school would cost $3.3 billion. *New York Daily News*. [Online]. Available at: http://www.nydaily-news.com/new york/nra ludicrous-proposal-cost-3-3b-article-1.1225758

Bush, B. (1990, June 1). Choices and change: Commencement address. *Gifts of Speech*. [Online]. Available at: http://gos.sbc.edu/ b/bush.html

Campbell, S., & Larson, J. (2012). Public speaking anxiety: Comparing face-to-face and web-based speeches. *Journal of Instructional Pedagogies*. [Online]. Available at: http://www.aabi.com/manuscripts/121343 .pdf

Cannon, W. B. (1932). *The wisdom of the body*. New York: Norton.

Carlisle, M. (2011). Bedbugs. In L. G. Schnoor, L. Mayfield, and K. Young (Eds.), *Winning orations*. Mankato, MN: Interstate Oratorical Association.

Carpenter, N. (2004). What you don't know . . . In L. G. Schnoor and B. Wickelgren (Eds.), *Winning orations*. Mankato, MN: Interstate Oratorical Association.

Carroll, R. T. (2010, December 10). Firewalking. *The Skeptic's Dictionary*. [Online]. Available at: http://www.skepdic.com/firewalk.html

Casper, C. (2011). Survivor support. In L. G. Schnoor, L. Mayfield, and K. Young (Eds.), *Winning orations*. Mankato, MN: Interstate Oratorical Association.

Cassata, D. (2012, August 30). Eastwood goes off-script in Romney endorsement. *Associated Press*. [Online]. Available at: http://www.khou.com/news/Eastwood-goes-off-script-in-Romney-endorsement-168096336.html

Castillo, M. (2012, December 21). NRA clear on gun debate stance: Arm schools. *CNN U.S.* [Online]. Available at: http://www.cnn.com/2012/12/21/us/connecticut-school-shooting/index.html

Chabris, C. & Simons, D. (2010). *The invisible gorilla: And other ways our intuitions deceive us*. New York: Crown.

Cheney, G., May, S., & Munshi, D. (2011). *Handbook of communication ethics*. New York: Routledge.

Chesebro, J. L. (2003). Effects of teacher clarity and nonverbal immediacy on student learning, receiver apprehension, and affect. *Communication Education*, 52, 135–147.

Childers, A. (1997). Hormone hell. In L. G. Schnoor & B. Wickelgren (Eds.), *Winning orations*. Northfield, MN: Interstate Oratorical Association.

Childers, T. L., & Houston, M. J. (1984). Conditions for a picture-superiority effect on consumer memory. *Journal of Consumer Research*, 11, 643–654.

Cho, H., & Witte, K. (2004). A review of fear-appeal effects. In J. S. Seiter & R. H. Gass (Eds.), *Perspectives on persuasion, social influence, and compliance gaining*. New York: Pearson.

Cho, Y., Smits, A. J., & Telch, M. (2004). The speech anxiety thoughts inventory: Scale development and preliminary psychometric data. *Behaviour Research and Therapy*, 42, 13–25.

Christenfeld, N. (1995). Does it hurt to say um? *Journal of Nonverbal Behavior*, 19, 171–186.

Christie, S. (2011). Witness harassment: Who watches the watchmen? In L. G. Schnoor, L. Mayfield, and K. Young (Eds.), *Winning orations*. Mankato, MN: Interstate Oratorical Association.

Cialdini, R. (1993). *Influence: Science and practice*. New York: HarperCollins.

Clay, R. A. (2002). Advertising as science. *Monitor on Psychology*, 33, 38–41.

Cliches. (2009, January 28). *Plain English Campaign*. [Online]. Available at: http://www.plainenglish.co.uk/examples/clich.html

Clinton, H. (2011, December 6). Remarks in recognition of International Human Rights Day. *U.S. Department of State*. [Online]. Available at: http://www.state.gov/secretary/rm/2011/12/178368.htm

Coleman, J. (2001, February 8). India's traditional social system is complicating distribution of relief to earthquake survivors. *San Jose Mercury News*, p. 7A.

Collard, M. MacGregor, L. J., & Donaldson, D. I. (2008). Orienting effects of hesitations in speech: Evidence from ERPs. *Journal of Experimental Psychology: Learning, Memory, and Cognition*, 34, 696–702.

Collins, R., & Cooper, P. J. (1997). *The power of story: Teaching through storytelling*. Boston: Allyn & Bacon.

Collins, S. (2013, February 25). Oscar 2013: TV ratings rise with Seth MacFarland as host. *L.A. Times*. [Online]. Available at: http://articles.latimes.com/2013/feb/25/entertainment/la-et-st-oscars-2013-tv-ratings-rise-with-seth-macfarlane-as-host-20130225

Columbia Accident Investigation Board. (2003, August). *Columbia accident investigation report, volume 1*. [Online]. Available: http://www.nasa.gov/columbia/home/CAIB_Vol1.html

Contraception. (2012, September 10). *Centers for Disease Control and Prevention*. [Online]. Available at: http://www.cdc.gov/reproductivehealth/unintended-pregnancy/contraception.htm

Cooper, L. (1960). *The rhetoric of Aristotle: An expanded translation with supplementary examples for students of composition and public speaking.* New York: Appleton Century Crofts.

Corbett, P. B. (2013, January 15). Words we love too much. *The New York Times.* [Online]. Available at: http://afterdeadline .blogs.nytimes.com/2013/01/15/words-we-love-too-much-10/

Crawford, M., & Kaufman, M. R. (2006). Sex differences versus social processes in the construction of gender. In K. Dindia & D. J. Canary (eds.), *Sex differences and similarities in communication.* Mahwah, NJ: Lawrence Erlbaum.

Crawford, W., & Gorman, M. (1996). Coping with electronic information. In J. Dock (Ed.), *The press of ideas: Readings for writers on print culture and the information age.* Boston: St. Martin's Press.

Crescenzo, S. (2005). It's time to admit the hard truth: We're not photographers. *Communication World,* 22, 12–14.

Cronn-Mills, D., & Schnoor, L. C. (2003). Evidence and ethics in individual events: An examination of an AFA-NIET final round. *The National Forensic Journal,* 21, 35–51.

Croucer, S. M. (2004). Like, you know, what I'm saying: A study of discourse marker frequency in extemporaneous and impromptu speaking. *National Forensic Association Journal.* [Online]. Available at: www.nationalforensics.org/journal/vol22no2-3.pdf

Cunningham, V, Lefkoe, M., & Sechrest, L. (2006). Eliminating fears: An intervention that permanently eliminates the fear of public speaking. *Clinical Psychology and Psychotherapy,* 13, 183–193.

Curtis, K. (2002, March 8). Critics nip at attorney's trial tactics. *Santa Cruz Sentinel,* pp. A1, A4.

Cyphert, D. (2009). PowerPoint and the evolution of electronic eloquence: Evidence from the contemporary business presentation. *American Communication Journal.* [Online]. Available at: http://ac-journal .org/journal/2009/Summer/2Power-pointandEvolution.pdf

Czopp, A. M., Monteith, M. J., & Mark, A. Y. (2006). Standing up for change: Reducing bias through interpersonal confrontation. *Journal of Personality and Social Psychology,* 90, 784–803.

Dacey, T. (2008). Water is not free: Think outside the bottle. In L. G. Schnoor & D. Cronin-Mills (Eds.), *Winning orations.* Mankato, MN: Interstate Oratorical Association.

Dahlberg, T. (2010, February 20). Contrive script lacks soul. *Santa Cruz Sentinel,* p. C3).

Danilyuk, A. (2011). Alternatives to imprisonment. In L. G. Schnoor, L. Mayfield, and K. Young (Eds.), *Winning orations.* Mankato, MN: Interstate Oratorical Association.

Davidson, C. (2007, March 19). We can't ignore the influence of digital technologies. *Chronicle of Higher Education,* p. B20.

Davies, J. W. (2011, September 25). Is there any real evidence that people are more afraid of public speaking than dying? *Quora.* [Online]. Available at: http:// www.quora.com/Is-there-any-real-evidence-that-people-are-more-afraid-of-public-speaking-than-dying

Deggans, E. (2012). *Race-baiter: How the media wields dangerous words to divide a nation.* New York: Palgrave Macmillan.

Demasio, N. (2007, January 8). The marvelous and mysterious Marvin Harrison. *Sports Illustrated,* pp. 41–45.

DePino, D. (2012). Lost to silence. In L. G. Schnoor, L. Mayfield, and K. Young (Eds.), *Winning orations.* Mankato, MN: Interstate Oratorical Association.

Derks, P., Kalland, S., & Etgen, M. (1995). The effect of joke type and audience response on the reaction to a joker: Replication and extension. *Humor,* 8, 327–337.

Dershowitz: Knock-knock joke told by Zimmerman's attorney grounds for mistrial. (2013, June 25). *Fox News.* [Online]. Available at: http://www.foxnews .com/us/2013/06/25/dershowitz-knock-knock-joke-told-by-zimmerman-attorney-was-inappropriate/.

Devos-Comby, L., & Salovey, P. (2002). Applying persuasion strategies to alter HIV-relevant thoughts and behavior. *Review of General Psychology*, 6, 287–304.

DiCarlo, M., Johnson, N., & Cochran, P. (2008). Survey and analysis of teacher salary trends 2007. *American Federation of Teachers*. [Online]. Available at: www.aft.org/pdfs/teachers/salarysurvey07.pdf

DiClaudio, D. (2006). *The hypochondriac's pocket guide to horrible diseases you probably already have*. New York: Bloomsbury.

Did HIV-positive mom's beliefs put her children at risk? (2005). *ABC News*. Available at: http://abcnews.go.com/Primetime/print?id=1386737

Dillard, J. P. (1994). Rethinking the study of fear appeals: An emotional perspective. *Communication Theory*, 4, 195–323.

Dillard, J. P., & Nabi, R. L. (2006). The persuasive influence of emotion in cancer prevention and detection messages. *Journal of Communication*, 56, 123–139.

Dindia, K., & Canary (Eds.). (2006). *Sex differences and similarities in communication*. Mahwah, NJ: Lawrence Erlbaum.

Distracted drivers think of themselves as good drivers, research suggests. (2012, May 10). *Science Daily*. [Online]. Available at: http://www.sciencedaily.com/releases/2012/05/120510095812.htm

Dlugan, A. (2008). Speech preparation #7: Choreograph your speech with staging, gestures, and vocal variety. *Six Minutes*. [Online]. Available at: http://sixminutes.dlugan.com/speech-preparation-7-staging-gestures-vocal-variety/

Donald and Rosie (2007, January 8). *Newsweek*, p. 55.

Donald Trump tells FNC: "Rosie O'Donnell's a loser." (2006). *Fox News*. [On-line]. Available at: http://www.foxnews.com/printer_friendly_story/0,3566,237997,00.html

Donovan, K. (2012). Ending the silence. L. G. Schnoor, L. Mayfield, and K. Young (Eds.), *Winning orations*. Mankato, MN: Interstate Oratorical Association.

Dorning, M. (2009, March 7). His words, the president's voice. *Chicago Tribune*. [Online]. Available at: http://www.chicagotribune.com/news/nationworld/chi-favreau-speechwritermar08,0,7344087,print.story

Dowd, M. (2008). *Thank God for evolution: How the marriage of science and religion will transform your life and our world*. New York: Viking.

Driscoll, E. (2011, March 4). Um, like, whatever: College grads lack verbal skills. *Fox Business*. [Online]. Available at: http://www.foxbusiness.com/personal-finance/2011/03/03/um-like-college-grads-lack-verbal-skills/

Driscoll, E. (2013, January 2). The student loan debt crisis: Welcome to the $1 trillion club. *Fox Business*. [Online]. Available at: http://www.foxbusiness.com/personal-finance/2013/01/02/student-loan-debt-crisis-welcome-to-1-trillion-club/

Dunn, G. (2009, June 6). Palin lifts from Gingrich in Anchorage speech. *Huffington Post*. [Online]. Available at: http://www.huffingtonpost.com/geoffrey-dunn/palin-plagiarizes-gingric_b_21228.html

Dux, P. E., Ivanoff, J., Asplund, C. L., Marois, R. (2006). Isolation of a central bottleneck of information processing with time-resolved fMRI. *Neuron*, 52, 1109–1120.

Earnest, W. (2007). *Save our slides: PowerPoint design that works*. Dubuque, IA: Kendall Hunt.

Education: Knowledge and skills for the job of the future. (2013, January 19). *The White House*. [Online]. Available at: http://www.whitehouse.gov/issues/education/higher-education

Edwards, J. (2002, May 8). Songwriter Otis Blackwell, 'Don't Be Cruel' among hits. *Santa Cruz Sentinel*, p. A8.

Edwards, K., & Smith, E. E. (1996). A disconfirmation bias in the evaluation of arguments. *Journal of Personality and Social Psychology*, 71, 5–24.

Eggert, D. (2012, September 7). Jennifer Granholm: "I probably shouldn't have gotten so worked up" in convention speech. *Michigan Live*. [Online]. Available at: http://www

.mlive.com/politics/index.ssf/2012/09/jennifer_granholm_i_probably_s.html

Eiola, A. (2012). Better serving those who served. In L. G. Schnoor, L. Mayfield, and K. Young (Eds.), *Winning orations*. Mankato, MN: Interstate Oratorical Association.

Elder, L. (2000). *The ten things you can't say in America*. New York: St. Martin's Press.

Ellis, A. (1995). Thinking processes involved in irrational beliefs and their disturbed consequences. *Journal of Cognitive Psychotherapy*, 9, 105–116.

Ellis, A. (1996). How I learned to help clients feel better and get better. *Psychotherapy*, 33, 149–151.

Ellis, Y., Daniels, B., & Jauregui, A. (2010). The effect of multitasking on the grade performance of business students. *Research in Higher Education*, 8, 1–10.

End, C. M., Worthman, S., Mathews, M. B., & Wetterau, K. (2010). Costly cell phones: The impact of cell phone rings on academic performance. *Teaching of Psychology*, 37, 55–57.

Engleberg, I. (2002). Presentations in Everyday Life: Linking audience interest and speaker eloquence. *American Communication Journal*. [Online]. Available at: http://ac-journal.org/journal/vol5/iss2/special/engleberg.htm

Erard, M. (2004, January 3). Just like, er, words, not, um, throwaways. *New York Times*. [Online]. Availalbe at: http://www.speech.sri.com/press/nyt-jan03-2004.html

Erard, M. (2008). *Um. . .: Slips, stumbles, and verbal blunders, and what they mean*. New York: Anchor.

Ernst, E. (2012, January/February). Medicines derived from herbs. *Skeptical Inquirer*, pp. 11–13.

Escera, C., Alho, K., Winkler, I., & Naatanen, R. (1998). Neural mechanisms of involuntary attention to acoustic novelty and change. *The Journal of Cognitive Neuroscience*, 10, 590–604.

Evaluating information found on the Internet. (2012, October 15). *John Hopkins University*. [Online]. Available at: http://guides.library.jhu.edu/content.php?pid=198142&sid=1657539

Fact checking the presidential debate in Denver. (2012, October 3). *ABC News*. [Online]. Available at: http://abcnews.go.com/blogs/politics/2012/10/fact-checking-the-presidential-debate-in-denver/

Fairhurst, G. T., & Sarr, R. A. (1996). *The art of framing: Managing the language of leadership*. San Francisco: Jossey-Bass.

Falling cow injures coffee house customer. (2001, July 12). *Santa Cruz Sentinel*, p. A8.

Famous quotes and authors. (2009). [Online]. Available at: http://www.famousquotesandauthors.com/authors/albert_einstein_quotes.html

Faria, M. A. (2002). Guns and violence. *Medical Sentinel*, 7, 112–118.

Fathi, N. (2009, June 23). Woman's death creates symbol of Iran protests. *San Jose Mercury News*, pp. 1A, 6A.

Fazio, R. H. (1986). How do attitudes guide behavior? In R. M. Sorrentino & E. T. Higgins (Eds.), *The handbook of motivation and cognition: Foundations of social behavior*. New York: Guilford Press.

Feeley, T. H., Marshall, H. M., & Reinhart, A. M. (2006). Reactions to narrative and statistical written messages promoting organ donation. *Communication Reports*, 19, 89–100.

Feinberg, M., & Willer, R. (2013). The moral roots of environmental attitudes. *Psychological Science*, 24, 56–62.

Fein, M. L. (1993). *I. A. M. A common sense guide to coping with anger*. Westport, CT: Praeger.

Festinger, L. (1957). *A theory of cognitive dissonance*. Stanford, CA: Stanford University Press.

Festinger, L. (1977). Cognitive dissonance. In E. Aronson (Ed.), *Readings about the social animal*. San Francisco: W. H. Freeman.

Finn, A. N., Sawyer, C. R., & Schrodt, P. (2009). Examining the effect of exposure therapy on public speaking state anxiety. *Communication Education*, 58, 92–109.

Foley, K. (2010, February 5). The award machine. *IN-Business*. [Online]. Available at: http://www.in-business.co.nz/the-award-machine/

Forbes, A. (2012). Prioritize children. In L. G. Schnoor, L. Mayfield, and K. Young (Eds.), *Winning orations*. Mankato, MN: Interstate Oratorical Association.

Ford, P. (2001, September 19). Europe cringes at Bush "crusade" against terrorists. *Christian Science Monitor*. [Online]. Available at: http://www.csmonitor.com/2001/0919/p12s2-woeu.html

Fouhy, B. (2012, January 23). Debates have major impact on GOP presidential race. *Associated Press*. [Online]. Available at: http://cnsnews.com/news/article/debates-have-major-impact-gop-presidential-race

Foulke, E. (2006). Listening comprehension as a function of word rate. *Journal of Communication*, 18, 198–206.

Fox Tree, J. E. (1995). The effects of false starts and repetitions on the processing of subsequent words in spontaneous speech. *Journal of Memory and Language*, 34, 709–738.

France, D. (2000, August 28). The HIV disbeliever. *Newsweek*, pp. 46–48.

Freeley, A. J., & Steinberg, D. L. (2013). *Argumentation and debate: Critical thinking for reasoned decision making*. Belmont, CA: Thomson Wadsworth.

Frobish, T. S. (2000). Jamieson meets Lucas: Eloquence and pedagogical model(s) in *The Art of Public Speaking*. *CommunicationEducation*, 49, 239–252.

Frymier, A. B., Waner, M. B., & Wojtaszczyk, A. M. (2008). Assessing students' perceptions of inappropriate and appropriate teacher humor. *Communication Education*, 57, 266–288.

Full text of remarks from National Rifle Association CEO Wayne LaPierre on gun control debate one week after Newtown school shooting tragedy. (2013, January 6). *Daily News*. [Online]. Available at: http://www.nydailynews.com/news/politics/full-text-nra-remarks-gun-control-debate-newtown-article-1.1225043

Gafni, M. (2013, May 12). Is the end nigh for doomsayer radio network? *San Jose Mercury News*, pp. A1, A19.

Galvan, V. V., Vessal, R. S., & Golley, M. T. (2013). The effects of cell phone conversations on the attention and memory of bystanders. *PLoS ONE*, 8, 1371–1381.

Gantz, J., & Reinsel, D. (2010, May). The digital universe decade—are you ready? *International Data Corporation*.

Gantz, J., & Reinsel, D. (2012, December). The digital universe in 2020: Big data, bigger digital shadows, and biggest growth in the Far East. *International Data Corporation*.

Gardner, L., & Leak, G. (1994). Characteristics and correlates of teacher anxiety among college psychology teachers. *Teaching of Psychology*, 21, 28–32.

Gass, R., & Seiter, J. (2011). *Persuasion, social influence, and compliance gaining*. Boston: Allyn & Bacon.

Gay marriage polls find personal relationships have major impact on support. (2013, March 21). *Huffington Post*. [Online]. Available at: http://www.huffingtonpost.com/2013/03/21/gay-marriage-polls_n_2925240.html?utm_hp_ref=politics

Getter, H., & Nowinski, I. (1981). A free response test of interpersonal effectiveness. *Journal of Personality Assessment*, 45, 301–308.

Glassner, B. (1999). *The culture of fear: Why Americans are afraid of the wrong things*. New York: Basic Books.

Gleicher, F., & Petty, R. (1992). Expectations of reassurance influence the nature of fear-stimulated attitude change. *Journal of Experimental Social Psychology*, 28, 86–100.

Glenn, E. C., Glenn, P. J., & Forman, S. (1998). *Your voice and articulation*. Boston: Allyn & Bacon.

Goldstein, N. J., Martin, S. J., & Cialdini, R. B. (2008). *Yes! 50 scientifically proven ways to be persuasive*. New York: Free Press.

Goldwert, L. (2011, March 17). Americans hoarding potassium iodide pills due to radiation fears; pills protect thyroid, no cure-all. *New York Daily News*. [Online]. Available at: http://www.nydailynews.com/life-style/health/americans-hoarding-potassium-iodide-pills-due-radiation-fears-pills-protect-thyroid-cure-all-article-1.122379

Goodman, E. (2009, July 16). Sotomayor takes one for the supreme team. *San Jose Mercury News*, p. A13.

Goodstein, L. (2008, November 6). Obama made gains among younger evangelical voters, data show. *The New York Times*. [Online]. Available at: www.nytimes.com/2008/11/07/us/politics/07religion.html

Gould, S. J. (1981). *The mismeasure of man.* New York: W. W. Norton.

Govier, T. (2010). *A practical study of argument.* New York: Wadsworth Cengage.

Grace, K. (2000). Unsanitary hotels. In L. G. Schnoor & B. Wickelgren (Eds.), *Winning orations.* Mankato, MN: Interstate Oratorical Association.

Gracely, E. J. (2003, July 24). Why extraordinary claims demand extraordinary proof. *Quackwatch.* [Online]. Available at: http://www.quackwatch.com/01QuackeryRelatedTopics/extraproof.html

Grasgreen, S. (2011 December 6). A heckling occupation. *Inside Higher Ed.* [Online]. Available at: http://www.insidehighered.com/news/2011/12/06/umass-amherst-occupy-protest-resembles-irvine-case

Green, M. C., & Brock, T. C. (2000). The role of transportation in the persuasiveness of public narratives. *Journal of Personality and Social Psychology, 79,* 701–721.

Greengross, G., & Miller, G. F. (2008). Dissing oneself versus dissing rivals: Effects of status, personality, and sex on the short-term and long-term attractiveness of self-deprecating and other-deprecating humor. *Evolutionary Psychology Journal,* 6, 393–408.

Greider, W. (2004, June 28). The Gipper's economy [Ronald Reagan]. *The Nation.* [Online]. Available at: http://www.thirdworldtraveler.com/Ronald_Reagan/Gippers_Economy.html

Griffin, E. (2012). *A first look at communication theory.* New York: McGraw-Hill.

Gruber, J. (2001). Heart disease in women. In L. Schnoor & B. Wickelgren (Eds.), *Winning orations.* Mankato, MN: Interstate Oratorical Association.

Gwyneth Paltrow. (1999, March 21). *The Academy of Motion Picture Arts and Sciences.* [Online]. Available at: http://aaspeechesdb.oscars.org/link/071-3/http://aaspeec

Hahner, J. C., Sokoloff, M. A., & Salesch, S. L. (1997). *Speaking clearly: Improving voice and diction.* New York: McGraw-Hill.

Hall, E. (1981). *Beyond culture.* New York: Doubleday.

Hall, J. A., & Bernieri, F. J. (2001). *Interpersonal sensitivity: Theory and measurement.* Mahwah, NJ: Lawrence Erlbaum Associates.

Hannah, M. (2009, June 26). How will Iranian protests change Twitter? *Mediashift.* [Online]. Available at: http://www.pbs.org/mediashift/2009/06/how-will-Iranian-protests-change-twitter177.html

Hare, W. (2009, March/April). What open-mindedness requires. *Skeptical Inquirer,* pp. 36–39.

Harmon, A. (2001, September 23). The search for intelligent life on the Internet. *The New York Times.* [Online]. Available at: http://www.nytimes.com/2001/09/23/weekinreview/23HARM.html

Harold Camping apologizes for faulty Rapture predictions and retires, report states. (2011, November 1). *Huffington Post.* [Online]. Available at: http://www.huffingtonpost.com/2011/11/01/harold-camping-apologizes-rapture-predictions_n_1069520.html

Harrison, L. E. (2000). Introduction. In L. E. Harrison & S. P. Huntington (Eds.), *Culture matters: How values shape human progress.* New York: Basic Books.

Harry Reid: Mitt Romney "basically paid no taxes" for 12 years. (2012, July 12). *Video Truffle.* [Online]. Available at: http://www.videotruffle.com/2012/07/12/harry-reid-mitt-romney-basically-paid-no-taxes-for-12-years/

Helfand, D. (2001, August 16). "Edspeak" is in a class by itself. *Los Angeles Times.* [Online]. Available at: http://www.scribd.com/doc/91222372/Edspeak-Glossary-of-Education-Terms-Phrases-Buzz-words-And-Jargon-2007

Hendricks, W., Holliday, M., Mobley, R., & Steinbrecher, K. (1996). *Secrets of power presentations*. Franklin Lake, NJ: Career Press.

Hersey, T. (2000). *Soul gardening: Cultivating the good life*. Minneapolis, MN: Augsburg.

Hill, M. (2009, February 4). Ecologists alarmed by rise in bat deaths. *San Jose Mercury News*, p. 8A.

Hinderliter, D. (2012). Collaborative consumption. In L. G. Schnoor, L. Mayfield, and K. Young (Eds.), *Winning orations*. Mankato, MN: Interstate Oratorical Association.

Hofstede, G., & Hofstede, G. J. (2005). *Culture and organizations: Software of the mind*. New York: McGraw-Hill.

Hogan, P. C. (2003). *The mind and its stories: Narrative universals and human emotion*. Cambridge, UK: Cambridge University Press.

Holan, A. D. (2009, December 18). PolitiFact's Lie of the Year: "Death panels." *PolitiFact*. [Online]. Available at: http://www.politifact.com/truth-o-meter/article/2009/dec/18/politifact-lie-year-death-panels/

Holmes, E. A., & Mathews, A. (2005). Mental imagery and emotion: A special relationship? *Emotion*, 5, 489–497.

Holstein, L. (2012). Slavery in the sunshine state. In L. G. Schnoor, L. Mayfield, and K. Young (Eds.), *Winning orations*. Mankato, MN: Interstate Oratorical Association.

Hoppes, S. (2008). Cross at your own risk: America's bridge safety neglect. In L. G. Schnoor & D. Cronin-Mills (Eds.), *Winning orations*. Mankato, MN: Interstate Oratorical Association.

Horowitz, B. (2002). *Communication apprehension: Origins and management*. Albany, NY: Singular.

Hoshino-Browne, E., Zanna, A. S., Spencer, S. J., Zanna, M. P., Kitayama, S., & Lackenbauer, S. (2005). On the cultural guises of cognitive dissonance: The case of Easterners and Westerners. *Journal of Personality and Social Psychology*, 89, 294–310.

Hough, S. (2010). *The Tumultuous Science of Earthquake Prediction*. Princeton, NJ: Princeton University Press.

How we got from 1 to 162 million websites on the internet. (2008, April 4). *Royal Pingdom*. [Online]. Available at: http://royal.pingdom.com/2008/04/04/how-we-got-from-1-to-162-million-websites-on-the-internet

Howard, P. N., Duffy, A., Freelon, D., Hussain, M., Mari, W., & Mazaid, M. (2011). Opening closed regimes: What was the role of social media during the Arab Spring? *Project on Information Technology & Political Islam*.

Hsu, J. (2008, August/September). The secrets of storytelling: Our love for telling tales reveals the workings of the mind. *Scientific American Mind*, pp. 46–51.

Huffington, A. (2011, November 28). Mitt Romney brazenly lies and the media lets him slide. *Huffington Post*. [Online]. Available at: http://www.huffingtonpost.com/ariana-huffington/mitt-romney-ad_b_1117288.html

Hutchinson, S. (2002, March 22). Jury's verdicts reaffirm court of public opinion. *San Jose Mercury News*, p. 9A.

Inman, C. (2010, February 20). Woods' scripted apology perfectly awkward. *San Jose Mercury News*, p. 1D.

Interview: Clifford Nass. (2010, February 2). *Frontline*. [Online]. Available at: http://www.pbs.org/wgbh/pages/frontline/digitalnation/interviews/nass.html

Jaffe, C. (1998). *Public speaking: Concepts and skills for a diverse society*. Belmont, CA: Wadsworth.

Jaksa, J., & Pritchard, M. (1994). *Communication ethics: Methods of analysis*. Belmont, CA: Wadsworth.

Jamieson, K. H. (1988). *Eloquence in an electronic age*. New York: Oxford University Press.

Jamieson, K. H. (1995). *Beyond the double bind: Women and leadership*. Boston: Oxford University Press.

Jemmott, J. B., Jemmott, L. S., & Fong, G. T. (2010). Efficacy of a theory-based abstinence-only intervention over months.

Archives of Pediatrics & Adolescent Medicine, 164, 152–159.

Jensen, J. V. (1997). *Ethical issues in the communication process.* Prospect Heights, IL: Waveland.

Jill Bolte Taylor: Neuroanatomist. (2008, March). *TED.* [Online]. Available at: http://www.ted.com/speakers/jill_bolte_taylor.html

Job outlook 2009—student version. (2009). *National Association of Colleges and Employers.* [Online]. Available at: http://www.jobweb.org/studentarticles.aspx?id=2121

Jodie Foster speech: Retirement speculation at Golden Globes. (2013, January 13). *Huffington Post.* [Online]. Available at: http://www.huffingtonpost.com/2013/01/13/jodie-foster-speech-retirement-_n_2469530.html

Johnson, J. (2012). Water wars: Crisis in the United States. In L. G. Schnoor, L. Mayfield, and K. Young (Eds.), *Winning orations.* Mankato, MN: Interstate Oratorical Association.

Johnson, S. (2008, March 17). Clinton says she's only candidate who can end war. *CNNPolitics.com.* [Online]. Available at: http://www.cnn.com/2008/POLITICS/03/17/clinton.war/

Johnson, S. D., & Miller, A. N. (2002). A cross-cultural study of immediacy, credibility, and learning in the U.S. and Kenya. *Communication Education, 51,* 280–292.

Jones, C. R., Fazio, R. H., & Vasey, M. W. (2012). *Social Psychology & Personality Science, 3,* 556–561.

Jones, J. (2011). The facts about for-profit universities. In L. G. Schnoor, L. Mayfield, and K. Young (Eds.), *Winning orations.* Mankato, MN: Interstate Oratorical Association.

Jorgenson, L. M., & Wahl, K. M. (2000). Psychiatrists as expert witnesses in sexual harassment cases under Daubert and Kumho. *Psychiatric Annals, 30,* 390–396.

Julian Castro's daughter punctuates convention speech with hair toss. (2012, September 6). *The Christian Science Monitor.* [Online]. Available at: http://www.csmonitor.com/The-Culture/Family/2012/0906/Julian-Castro-s-daughter-punctuates-convention-speech-with-hair-toss

Kaleem, J. (2011, March 20). Harold Camping: The man behind "Judgment Day," May 21, 2011. *Huffington Post.* [Online]. Available at: http://www.huffingtonpost.com/2011/05/20/harold-camping-judgment-day-may-21_n_864507.html

Kane, M. J., Brown, L. H., McVay, J. C., Silvia, P. J., Myin-Germeys, I., & Kwapil, T. R. (2007). For whom the mind wanders, and when: An experience-sampling study of working memory and executive control in daily life. *Psychological Science, 18,* 559–656.

Kanye West acts like a jerk at VMAs, Beyonce picks up the pieces. (2009, September 13). *Long Island Press.* [Online]. Available at: http://www.longislandpress.com/2009/09/13/kanye-west-acts-like-a-jerk-at-vmas/

Kates, D. B., Schaffer, H. E., Lattimer, J. K., Murray, G. B., & Cassem, E. H. (1994). Guns and public health: Epidemic of violence or pandemic of propaganda? *Tennessee Law Review, 61,* 513–596.

Kawatsu, H. (2009, May 25). A mixed jury system for Japan. Paper presented at the annual meeting of The Law and Society, Las Vegas, NV. [Online]. Available at: http://www.allacademic.com/meta/p18168_index.html

Kazoleas, D. C. (1993). A comparison of the persuasive effectiveness of qualitative versus quantitative evidence: A test of explanatory hypotheses. *Communication Quarterly, 41,* 40–50.

Keller, P. A. (1999). Converting the unconverted: The effect of inclination and opportunity to discount health-related fear appeals. *Journal of Applied Psychology, 84,* 403–415.

Kelley, M. (2012). The new Catch-22: Unemployment discrimination. In L. G. Schnoor, L. Mayfield, and K. Young (Eds.), *Winning orations.* Mankato, MN: Interstate Oratorical Association.

Kelly, J. R. (2005). The effect of nonverbal behaviors associated with sexual harassment proclivity on women's performance. *Sex Roles: A Journal of Research,* 53, 689–701.

Kelly, L., & Keaten, J. A. (2000). Treating communication anxiety: Implications of the communibiological paradigm. *Communication Education,* 49, 45–57.

Kent, M. L (2007). The rhetoric of funeral oratory and eulogy: Reconciling rheotrics of past and present. Unpublished dissertation. [Online]. Available at: http://faculty-staff.ou.edu/K/Michael.L.Kent-1/PDFs/Funeral_Oratory_And_Eulogy.pdf

Kirka, D. (2009, July 19). Henry Allingham, world's oldest man. *San Jose Mercury News,* p. B8.

Kirkpatrick, P. (2007). Hunting the wild reciter: Elocution and the art of recitation. In J. Damousi & D. Deacon (Eds.), *Talking and listening in the age of modernity: Essays on the history of sound.* Canberra, Australia: ANU E Press.

Kirn, W. (1997, October 3). Drinking to belong. *New York Times,* p. A11.

Kitchen, R. (2007, August 25). Um, like, isn't the Internet wonderful? *San Jose Mercury News,* p. 3A.

Kleck, G. (2005). *Point blank: Guns and violence in America.* Somerset, NJ: Aldine Transaction.

Kolata, G. (1990, February 27). 1-in-a-trillion coincidence, you say? Not really, experts find. *The New York Times,* pp. C1–C2.

Konda, K. J. (2006). The war at home. In L. G. Schnoor & B. Wickelgren (Eds.), *Winning orations.* Mankato, MN: Interstate Oratorical Association.

Kopfman, J. E., Smith, S. W., Ah Yun, J. K., & Hodges, A. (1998). Affective and cognitive reactions to narrative versus statistical evidence organ donation messages. *Journal of Applied Communication Research,* 26, 279–300.

Kraul, C. (2006, December 20). Renowned for longevity, Ecuadoran town changing. *San Jose Mercury News,* p. 16A.

Krieger, L. M. (1999, February 5). Mystery rock injures woman asleep at home. *San Jose Mercury News,* pp. 1B, 4B.

Kurtz, H. (2012, September 4). Michelle Obama's resounding triumph. *The Daily Beast.* [Online]. Available at: http://www.thedailybeast.com/articles/2012/09/04/michelle-obama-s-resounding-triumph.html

Landman, A., Ling, P. M., & Glantz, S. A. (2002). Tobacco industry youth smoking prevention programs: Protecting the industry and hurting tobacco control. *American Journal of Public Health,* 92, 917–930.

Larson, C. U. (2012). *Persuasion: Reception and responsibility.* Belmont, CA: Wadsworth.

Law of truly large numbers. (2012, May 26). *The Skeptic's Dictionary.* [Online]. Available at: http://skepdic.com/lawofnumbers.html

Lecheler, S., de Vreese, C., & Slothuus, R. (2009). Issue importance as a moderator of framing effects. *Communication Research,* 36, 400–425.

Leclaire, J. (2012, March 7). Harold Camping admits Rapture prediction was "sinful statement." *Charisma News.* [Online]. Available at: http://www.charismanews.com/us/32958-harold-camping-admits-rapture-prediction-was-sinful-statement

Lee, Y-T, Jussim, L. J., & McCauley, C. R. (1995). *Stereotype accuracy: Toward appreciating group differences.* American Psychological Association.

Leonhardt, D. (2012, June 22). Old vs. young. *The New York Times.* [Online]. Available at: http://www.nytimes.com/2012/06/24/opinion/sunday/the-generation-gap-is-back.html?pagewanted=all&_r=0

Lese, K. (2012). The kid who cried "Mine": Patent trolls greedy takeover of the technology industry. In L. G. Schnoor, L. Mayfield, and K. Young (Eds.), *Winning orations.* Mankato, MN: Interstate Oratorical Association.

Levander, C. (1998). *Voices of the nation: Women and public speech in nineteenth-century American literature and culture.* Cambridge, UK: Cambridge University Press.

Levine, K. (2001). The dentist's dirty little secret. In L. Schnoor & B. Wickelgren

(Eds.), *Winning orations*, Mankato, MN: Interstate Oratorical Association.

Lewandowsky, S., Ecker, U. K. H., Seifert, C. M., Schwartz, N., & Cook, J. (2012). Misinformation and its correction: Continued influence and successful debiasing. *Psychological Science in the Public Interest*, 13, 106–131.

Lewin, M. R., McNeil, D. W., & Lipson, J. M. (1996). Enduring without avoiding: Pauses and verbal dysfluencies in public speaking fear. *Journal of Psychopathology and Behavioral Assessment*, 18, 387–402.

Lewis, R. D. (1996). *When cultures collide: Managing successfully across cultures.* London: Nicholas Brealey.

Li. C. (1975). *Path analysis: A primer.* Pacific Grove, CA: Boxwood Press.

Lilienfeld, S. O., Ammirati, R., & Landfiled, K. (2009). Giving debiasing away: Can psychological research on correcting cognitive errors promote human welfare? *Perspective on Psychological Science*, 4, 390–398.

Lim, Y. (2012, May 13). Flight attendant adds funny twist to safety demonstration. *The Star Online*. [Online]. Available at: http:thestar.com.my/news/story.asp?file=/2012/5/13/nation/11283698&sec=nation

Lindsey, L. L. M., & Yun, K. A. (2003). Examining the persuasive effect of statistical messages: A test of mediating relationships. *Communication Studies*, 54, 306–322.

Linville, P. W., Fischer, G. W., & Fischoff, B. (1992). Perceived risk and decision-making involving AIDS. In J. B. Pryor & G. D. Reeder (Eds.), *The social psychology of HIV infection.* Hillsdale, NJ: Erlbaum.

Littlejohn, S. W., & Foss, K. A. (2011). *Theories of human communication.* Long Grove, ILL: Waveland Press.

Lucas, S. E., & Medhurst, M. J. (2008). *Words of a century: The top 100 American speeches, 1900–1999.* New York: Oxford University Press.

Lupu, C., Elwood, F., & Davis, E. (2007). Religious displays and the courts. *The Pew Forum on Religion*. [Online]. Available at: http://www.pewforum.org/uploadedfiles/topics/issues/church-state_law/religious-displays.pdf

MacInnis, C. C., MacKinnon, S. P., & MacIntyre, P. D. (2010). The illusion of transparency and normative beliefs about anxiety during public speaking. *Current Research in Social Psychology*. [Online]. Available at: http://www.uiowa.edu/~grpproc/crisp/crisp15_4.pdf

Madison, L., & Boxer, A. B. (2012, January 9). Mitt Romney: "I like being able to fire people" for bad service. *CBS News*. [Online]. Available at: http://www.cbsnews.com/8301-503544_162-57355212-503544/mitt-romney-i-like-being-able-to-fire-people-for-bad-service/

Making ethical decisions: The six pillars of character. (2013). *The Josephson Institute of Ethics*. [Online]. Available at: http://josephsoninstitute.org/MED/MED-2sixpillars.html

Male nurses becoming more commonplace, Census Bureau reorts. (2013, February 25). *U.S. Census Bureau*. [Online]. Available at: http://www.census.gov/newsroom/releases/archives/employment_occupations/cb13-32.html

Mancini, M. (2003). *Selling destinations: Geography for the travel professional.* Clifton Park, NY: Thomson/Selmar Learning.

March 2010 Web server survey. (2010, March). *Netcraft* [Online]. Available at: http://news.netcraft.com/

Martens, T. (2009, September 15). Taylor Swift accepts Kanye West's apology. *Los Angeles Times*. [Online]. Available at: http://latimes.com/music_blog/2009/09/taylor-swift-accepts-kanye-wests-apology.html

Martin, K. A., Moritz, S. E., & Hall, C. R. (1999). Imagery use in sport: A literature review and applied model. *Sport Psychologist*, 13, 245–268.

Martinez, C. (2012). Purchase conflict-free electronics. In L. G. Schnoor, L. Mayfield, and K. Young (Eds.), *Winning orations*. Mankato, MN: Interstate Oratorical Association.

Mattioli, D. (2010, March 23). More men make harassment claims. *The Wall Street Journal*. [Online]. Available at: http://online.wsj.com/article/SB1000142405274870411730457513788143871902 8.html

May, P. (2002, March 22). Jury says it's murder. *San Jose Mercury News*, pp. 1A, 8A.

May, P. (2009, June 22). What's next for Twitter now it's on world stage? *San Jose Mercury News*, p. 6A.

Mayer, L. V. (2003). *Fundamentals of voice and articulation*. New York: McGraw-Hill.

Mayer, R. E. (Ed.). (2005). *The Cambridge handbook of multimedia learning*. Cambridge, MA: Cambridge University Press.

Mayk, V. (2010, November 29). Wilkes University professors examine use of text messaging in the college classroom. *Latest Wilkes News Archives*. [Online]. Available at: http://www.wilkes.edu/pages/194.asp?item=61477

McCoy, S. L., Tun, P. A., Cox, L. C., & Wingfield, A. (2005, July 12). Aging in a fast-paced world: Rapid speech and its effect on understanding. *The ASHA Leader*, pp. 12, 30–31.

McCroskey, J. C., Fayer, J. M., & Richmond, V. P. (1985). Don't speak to me in English: Communication apprehension in Puerto Rico. *Communication Quarterly, 33*, 185–192.

McDonald, J. (1998, January/February). 200% probability and beyond: The compelling nature of extraordinary claims in the absence of alternative explanations. *Skeptical Inquirer, 22*, 45–49.

McGuire, W. (1964). Inducing resistance to persuasion: Some contemporary approaches. In L. Berkowitz (Ed.), *Advances in experimental social psychology*. New York: Academic Press.

McKerrow, R. E., Gronbeck, B. E., Ehninger, D., & Monroe, A. H. (2007). *Principles and types of pubic speaking*. New York: Pearson/Allyn & Bacon.

McKimmie, B. M., Terry, D. J., Hogg, M. A., Manstead, A. S. R., Spears, R., & Doosje, B. (2003). I'm a hypocrite, but so is everyone else: Group support and the reduction of cognitive dissonance. *Group Dynamics: Theory, Research, and Practice, 7*, 214–224.

McLaughlin, S. (1996). The dirty truth about your kitchen: Using common sense to prevent food poisoning. In L. G. Schnoor (Ed.), *Winning Orations*. Northfield, MN: Interstate Oratorical Association.

McNamara, P. (2011, November 2). Wikimedia commissions study to measure accuracy of *Wikipedia*. *Networkworld*. [Online]. Available at: http://www.networkworld.com/community/blog/wikipedia-commissions-study-measure-accuracy-

McNeil, B. J., Pauker, S. G., Sox, H. C., & Tversky, A. (1982). On the elicitation of preferences for alternative therapies. *New England Journal of Medicine, 306*, 1259–1262.

McVay, J. C., & Kane, M. J. (2009). Conducting the train of thought: Working memory capacity, goal neglect, and mind wandering in an executive-control task. *Journal of Experimental Psychology: Learning, Memory, and Cognition, 35*, 196–204.

Meacham, J. (2009, August 14). Hitler and health care don't mix. *Newsweek*, p. 9.

Menzel, K. E., & Carrell, L. J. (1994). The relationship between preparation and performance in public speaking. *Communication Education, 43*, 17–26.

Meyer, D. (2004, July 22). The official start of culture war. *CBS News.com*. Available at: http://www.cbsnews.com/stories/2004/07/21/opinion/meyer/main631126.shtml

Miller, J. (2013, January 14). Ten wildly varying interpretations of Jodie Foster's Golden Globes speech. *Vanity Fair*. [Online]. Available at: http://www.vanityfair.com/online/oscars/2013/01/jodie-foster-golden-globe-speech-coming-out-reviews

Minister accidentally kills self. (1998, October 3). *San Jose Mercury News*, p. A13.

Minchin, J. (2012). Death by doctor: Revealing our hidden health care crisis.

In L. G. Schnoor, L. Mayfield, and K. Young (Eds.), *Winning orations*. Mankato, MN: Interstate Oratorical Association.

Mitchell, O. (2009). New evidence that bullet-points don't work. *Speaking About Presenting*. [Online]. Available at: http://www.speakingaboutpresenting.com/design/new-evidence-bullet-points/

Montana Meth Project (2013). *Meth Project Organization*. [Online]. Available at: http://montana.methproject.org/Results/index.php

Moore, J., & Nattrass (2006, June 4). HIV and AIDS. Available at: http://www.aidstruth.org/

Morello, C., & Mellnik, T. (2012, May 17). Census: Minority babies are now majority in United States. *The Washington Post*. [Online]. Available at: http://articles.washingtonpost.com/2012-05-17/local/35458407 1 minority-babies-census-bureau-demographers-whites

Motley, M. T. (1995). *Overcoming your fear of public speaking: A proven method*. New York: McGraw-Hill.

Motley, M. T. (2011, January 18). Reducing public speaking anxiety: The communication orientation. *YouTube*. [Online]. Available at: http://www.youtube.com/watch?v=GYfHQvi2NAg

Motley, M. T. (1997). COM Therapy. In J. A. Daly, J. C. McCroskey, J. Ayres, T. Hopf, and D. M. Ayres (Eds.), *Avoiding Communication*. Creskill, NJ: Hampton Press.

Murphy, P. (2009, September 14). Two thirds disapprove of Joe Wilson's "You lie!" outburst. *Politics Daily*. [Online]. Available at: http://www.politicsdaily.com/2009/09/14/two-thirds-disapprove-of-joe-wilsons-you-lie-outburst/

Murray, B. (1997, May). How important is teaching style to students? *APA Monitor*, pp. 103.

Murray-Johnson, L., Witte, K., Liu, W., Hubbell, A., Sampson, J., & Morrison, K. (2001). Addressing cultural orientations in fear appeals: Promoting AIDS-protective behaviors among Mexican immigrant and African American adolescents and American and Taiwanese college students. *Journal of Health Communication*, 6, 335–358.

Myers, D. (2004a). *Intuition: Its powers and perils*. Yale University press.

Myers, D. (2004b). *Psychology*. New York: Worth.

Nabi, R. L. (2002). Discrete emotions and persuasion. In J. P. Dillard and M. Pfau (Eds.), *The persuasion handbook: Developments in theory and practice*. Thousand Oaks, CA: Sage.

National Archives and Records Administration. (1987). *Kennedy's inaugural address of 1961*. Washington, D. C.: U.S. Government Printing Office.

National Survey of Student Engagement (2012). *Promoting student learning and institutional improvement: Lessons from NSSE at 13: Annual results 2012*. [Online]. Available at: http://nsse.iub.edu/NSSE_2012_Results/pdf/NSSE_2012_Annual_Results.pdf#page=8

Neal, T. & Brodsky, M. S. (2008). Warmth and competence on the witness stand: Implications for the credibility of male and female expert witnesses. *Journal of the American Academy of Psychiatry and the Law Online*, 40, 488 497.

Nevid, J. S. (2011). Teaching the Millenials. *Observor*. [Online]. Available at: http://www.psychologicalscience.org/index.php/publications/observer/2011/may-june-11/teaching-the-millennials.html

Newport, F. (2012, May 22). Americans, including Catholics, say birth control is morally OK. *Gallup Politics*. [Online]. Available at: http://www.gallup.com/poll/154799/americans-including-catholics-say-birth-control-morally.aspx

Nickerson, R. S. (1998). Confirmation bias: A ubiquitous phenomenon in many guises. *Review of General Psychology*, 2, 175–220.

Noelle, D. (1999, January/February). World's longest firewalk: Physicist leads hot trek for science in Pennsylvania. *Skeptical Inquirer*, 23, 5–6.

Noguchi, S. (2008, June 25). Lifted lines in grads' speeches. *San Jose Mercury News*, pp. 1B; 5B.

Noonan, P. (1998). *Simply speaking: How to communicate your ideas with style, substance, and clarity*. New York: Harper-Collins.

Numbers of Americans killed/wounded, by action. (2011, May 25). *American War Library*. [Online]. Available at: http://www.americanwarlibrary.com/allwars.htm

Obama Michigan graduation speech: Full text. (2010, May 1). *Huffington Post*. [Online]. Available at: http://www.huffingtonpost.com/2010/05/01obama-michigan-graduation_n_559688.html?view=print

O'Brien. (2012, December 21). How much would it cost to put guards with guns in every public school? *The Atlantic*. [Online]. Available at: http://www.theatlantic.com/business/archive/2012/12/how-much-would-it-cost-to-put-guards-every-public-school/266579/

O'Donohue, W. T., & Fisher, J. E. (2008). *Cognitive behavior therapy: Applying empirically supported techniques in your practice*. Hoboken, NJ: John Wiley & Sons.

O'Keefe, D. (1990). *Persuasion: Theory and research*. Newbury Park, CA: Sage.

Onishi, N. (2007, July 16). Japanese wary as they prepare to join juries. *San Jose Mercury News*, p. 8A.

Oppel, R. A. (2012, October 18). Amid brutal campaign, a respite. With Jokes. *New York Times.com* [Online]. Available at: http://www.nytimes.com/2012/10/19/us/politics/obama-romney-roast-each-other-at-al-smith-charity-dinner.html?_r=0

Pashler, H. E. (1998). *The psychology of attention*. Cambridge, MA: MIT Press.

Passer, M.W., & Smith, R. E. (2011). *Psychology: The science of mind and behavior*. New York: McGraw-Hill.

Paulos, J. A. (1994, March). Counting on dyscalculia. *Discourse*, pp. 30–36.

Peoples, S/ (2013, June 2). Gay marriage win a loss for Catholic Church clout. *San Jose Mercury News*, p. A7.

Perloff, R. M. (2013). *The dynamics of persuasion: Communication and attitudes in the 21st century*. New York: Routledge.

Pertaub, D., Slater, M., & Barker, C. (2002). An experiment on public speaking anxiety in response to three different types of virtual audiences. *Presence: Teleoperators and Virtual Environments*, 11, 670–78.

Peterson, C. (2000). The future of optimism. *American Psychologist*, 55, 44–55.

Petrovic, K. (2013, March/April). Closing the book on "open-mindedness." *Skeptical Inquirer*, pp. 53.

Petty, R. E., & Cacioppo, J. (1984). The effects of involvement on responses to argument quantity and quality: Central and peripheral routes to persuasion. *Journal of Personality and Social Psychology*, 46, 69–81.

Petty, R. E., & Cacioppo, J. (1986a). The elaboration likelihood model of persuasion. In L. Berkowitz (Ed.), *Advances in experimental social psychology* (Vol. 19). New York: Academic Press.

Petty, R. E, & Cacioppo, J. (1986b). *Communication and persuasion: Central and peripheral routes to attitude change*. New York: Springer-Verlag.

Petty, R. E., & Wegener, D. T. (1998). Matching versus mismatching attitude functions: Implications for scrutiny of persuasive messages. *Personality and Social Psychology Bulletin*, 24, 227–240.

Petty, R. E., Kasmer, J., Haugtvedt, C., & Cacioppo, J. (1987). Source and message factors in persuasion: A reply to Stiff's critique of the elaboration likelihood model. *Communication Monographs*, 54, 233–249.

Petty R. E., Rucker, D. D., Bizer, G. Y., Cacioppo, J. T. (2004). The Elaboration Likelihood Model in persuasion. In J. S. Seiter & R. H. Gass (Eds.), *Perspectives on persuasion, social influence, and compliance*. New York: Pearson.

Pew Research Center. (2004, February 24). A global generation gap. [Online]. Available at: http://people-press.org/commentary/?analysisid=86

Pew Research Center. (2009, June 29). Growing old in America: Expectations vs. reality. [Online]. Available at: http://pewresearch.org/pubs/1296/aging-survey-expectations-versus-reality

Peyser, M. (2006, February 13). The truthiness teller. *Newsweek*. [Online]. Available at: http://www.democraticunderground.com/discuss/duboard.php?az=view_all&address=364x334537

Pfau, M., & Van Bockern, S. (1994). The persistence of inoculation in conferring resistance to smoking initiation among adolescents: The second year. *Human Communication Research*, 20, 413–430.

Pfau, M., Ivanov, B., Houston, B., Haigh, M., Sims, J., Gilchrist, E., Russell, J., Wigley, S., Eckstein, J., & Richert, N. (2005). Inoculation and mental processing: The instrumental role of associative networks in the process of resistance to counterattitudinal influence. *Communication Monographs*, 72, 414–441.

Pfau, M., Szabo, E. A., Anderson, J., Morrill, J., Zubric, J., & Wan, H. (2001). The role and impact of affect in the process of resistance to persuasion, *Human Communication Research*, 27, 216–252.

Phefan, N. (2011). A disease we can cure. In L. G. Schnoor, L. Mayfield, and K. Young (Eds.), *Winning orations*. Mankao, MN: Interstate Oratorical Association.

Pitts, L. (2011, March 6). Prominent blogger dismisses accuracy as "no big deal." *San Jose Mercury News*, p. A13.

Poldrack, R. (2010, Summer). Novelty and testing: When the brain learns and why it forgets. *Nieman Reports*. [Online]. Available at: http://www.nieman.harvard.edu/reports/article/102397/Novelty-and-Testing-When-the-Brain-Learns-and-Why-It-Forgets.aspx

Polisetti, S. (2012). The loss of Native American culture. In L. G. Schnoor, L. Mayfield, and K. Young (Eds.), *Winning orations*. Mankato, MN: Interstate Oratorical Association.

Politics. (2007). *MSNBC*. [Online]. Available at: www.msnbc.msn.com/id/11009379/

Poll. (2012, April 9). *Daily Kos*. [Online]. Available at: http://www.dailykos.com/

Poll: College students feel pressure to drink. (2000, June 20). *San Jose Mercury News*, p. 9A.

Poole, M. (2009, July 27). A's great Henderson cool at Cooperstown. *San Jose Mercury News*, pp. 1A; 6A.

Pornpitakpan, C. (2004). The persuasiveness of source credibility: A critical review of five decades' evidence. *Journal of Applied Social Psychology*, 34, 243–281.

Post-ABC poll: Broad support for gun restrictions, armed guards in schools-January 10–13. (2013, January 16). *The Washington Post*. [Online]. Available at: http://www.washingtonpost.com/politics/polling/postabc-poll-broad-support-gun-restrictions/2013/04/12/c8f74d38-5e95-11e2-8acb-ab5cb77e95c8 page.html

Powell, T. (2012). It's not the addict, it's the drug: Redefining America's War on Drugs. In L. G. Schnoor, L. Mayfield, and K. Young (Eds.), *Winning orations*. Mankato, MN: Interstate Oratorical Association.

PowerPoint turns 20, as its creators ponder a dark side to success. (2007, June 20). *Wall Street Journal*, p. B1.

Pratkanis, A., & Aronson, E. (2001). *The age of propaganda: The everyday use and abuse of persuasion*. New York: W. H. Freeman.

President George W. Bush to the 300th graduating class of Yale University. (2001, May 22). *Everything2*. [Onine]. Available at: http://www.everything2.com/index.pl?node_id=1056073

Prochow, H. V. (1944). *Great stories from great lives*. New York: Harper & Brothers.

Pryor, J. H., Eagan, K., L., Blake, L. P., Hurtado, S., Berdan, J., & Case, M. H. (2012). *The American freshman: National norms fall 2012*. [Online]. Available at: http://heri.ucla.edu/monographs/TheAmericanFreshman2012.pdf

Quick Facts. (2012, December 10). *United States Census Bureau*. [Online]. Available at: http://quickfacts.census.gov/qfd/states/00000.html

Quinn, J. M., & Wood, W. (2004). Fore-warnings of influence appeals: Inducing resistance and acceptance. In E. S. Knowles & J. A. Linn (Eds.), *Resistance and persuasion*. Mahwah, NJ: Lawrence Erlbaum Associates.

Quinones, E. (1999, August 1). Companies learn the value of storytelling. *New York Times*, p. 4.

Radford, B. (2013, July/August). Is there a 100C grain of truth to homeopathy? *Skeptical Inquirer*, pp 33–34.

Radosh, D. (2005, February 28). The pictures: One billion. *New Yorker*, p. 32.

Rand, H. (1998, February 15). Science, non-science and nonsense. *Vital Speeches of the Day*, pp. 282–284.

Reguillo, R. (2013, January 8). Human mic: Technologies for democracy. *North American Congress on Latin America*. [Online]. Available at: http://nacla.org/news/2013/1/8/human-mic-technologies-democracy

Remarks of Senator Barack Obama. (2008, January 3). *Obama News & Speeches*. [Online]. Available at: http://www.barackobama.com/2008/01/03/remarks_of_senator_barack_obam_39.php

Report: The media have debunked the death panels more than 40 times. (2009, August 15) *MediaMatters for America*. [Online]. Available at: http://mediamatters.org/research/200908150001

Rey, P. J. (2012, January 3). Why we disrupt. *Inside Higher Ed*. [Online]. Available at: http://www.insidehighered.com/views/2012/01/03/essay-why-occupy-movement-disrupts-speakers-campus

Reynolds, R. A., & Reynolds, J. L. (2002). Evidence. In J. E. Dillard & M. Pfau (Eds.), *The persuasion handbook: Developments in theory and practice*. Thousand Oaks, CA: Sage.

Richmond, V. P., & McCroskey, J. C. (1995). *Communication: Apprehension, avoidance, and effectiveness*. Boston: Allyn & Bacon.

Roach, J. (2013). 8.7 ideas in earthquake prediction. *NBC News*. [Online]. Available at: http://www.nbcnews.com/id/30075875/ns/technology_and_science/t/ideas-earthquake-prediction/

Robinson, E. (2009, September 15). Joe Wilson's transgression, Tea Party protesters and the Wall Street casino. *The Washington Post*. [Online}. Available at: http://www.washingtonpost.com/wp-dyn/content/discussion/2009/09/09/DI2009090901377.html

Roby, D. E. (2009, Summer). Teacher leadership skills: An analysis of communication apprehension. *FindArticles*. [Online]. Available at: http://www.questia.com/library/1G1-201209726/teacher-leadership-skills-an-analysis-of-communication

Rodriguez, J. (1995). Confounds in fear arousing persuasive messages: Do the paths less traveled make all the difference? Unpublished doctoral dissertation, Michigan State University, East Lansing, MI.

Romney says he paid at least 13% taxes for last 10 years. (2012). *CNBC*. [Online]. Available at: http://politicalticker.blogs.cnn.com/2012/08/16/romney-says-he-paid-at-least-13-in-taxes-for-last-ten-years/

Ropeik, D. (2008, April 13). How risky is flying? *NOVA*. [Online]. Available at: http://www.pbs.org/wgbh/nova/planecrash/risky.html

Rosenbaum, J. E. (2009). Patient teenagers? A comparison of the sexual behavior of virginity pledgers and matched non-pledgers. *Pediatrics*, 123, 110–120.

Rucker, D. D., & Petty, R. E. (2004). When resistance is futile: Consequences of failed counterarguing for attitude certainty. *Journal of Personality and Social Psychology*, 86, 219–235.

Ruet, B. (2006). Sudan's forgotten war. In L. Schnoor & B. Wickelgren (Eds.), *Winning orations*. Mankato, MN: Interstate oratorical Association.

Ruggeiro, V. (1988). *Teaching thinking across the curriculum*. New York: Harper & Row.

Ruiter, R. A. C., Kessels, L. T. E., Jansma, B. M., & Brug, J. (2006). Increased attention for computer-tailored health communications: An event-related potential study. *Health Psychology*, 25, 300–306.

Ryland, K. (2012). Needed: Vaccines against exemptions. In L. G. Schnoor, L. Mayfield, and K. Young (Eds.), *Winning orations*. Mankato, MN: Interstate Oratorical Association.

Rymer, R. (1993). *Genie: An abused child's flight from silence*. New York: Harper-Collins.

Sagan, C. (1996). *The demon-haunted world: Science as a candle in the dark*. New York: Random House.

Same-sex mariage detailed tables. (2013, March). *Pew Research Center for the People and the Press*. [Online]. Available at: www.people-press.org/. . .detailed_tables/Gay%20marriage%20detailed%20tables.pdf

Sandburg, C. (1944). *Abraham Lincoln: the prairie years and the war years*. New York: Houghton Mifflin Harcourt.

Sanders, A. F. (1983). Toward a model of stress and human performance. *Acta Psychologica*, 53, 61–97.

Savitsky, K. & Gilovich, T. (2003). The illusion of transparency and the alleviation of speech anxiety. *Journal of Experimental Social Psychology*, 39, 618–625.

Schacter, S., Christenfeld, N., Ravina, B., & Bilbous, F. (1991). Speech disfluency and the structure of knowledge. *Journal of Personality and Social Psychology*, 60, 362–367.

Schittekatte, M. & Van Hiel, A. (1996). Effects of partially shared information and awareness of unshared information on information sampling. *Small Group Research*, 27, 431–449.

Schoenbachler, D. D., & Whittler, T. E. (1996). Adolescent processing of social and physical threat communications. *Journal of Advertising*, 25, 37–54.

Seligman, M. (1991). *Learned optimism*. New York: Knopf.

Shadel, W. G., Niaura, R., & Abrams, D. B. (2001). How do adolescents process smoking and antismoking advertisements? A social cognitive analysis with implications for understanding smoking initiation.

Review of General Psychology, 5, 429–444.

Sheppard, N. (2010, January 22). Stewart blasts Olbermann for Brown Rants, Defends Michelle Malkin. *NewsBusters*. [Online]. Available at: http://newsbusters.org/blogs/noel-sheppard/2010/01/22/stewart-blasts-olbermann-brown-rants-defends-michelle-malkin

Sherif, C. W., Kelly, M., Rodgers, H. L., Sarup, G., & Tittler, B. I. (1973). Personal involvement, social judgment and action. *Journal of Personality and Social Psychology*, 27, 311–328.

Sherif, M., Sherif, C., & Nebergall, R. (1965). *Attitude and attitude change: The social judgment-involvement approach*. Philadelphia: Saunders.

Sherman, E. (2009), March/April). Science and antiscience in America: Why it matters. *Skeptical Inquirer*, pp. 32–35.

Shermer, M. (2002). *Why people believe weird things: Pseudoscience, superstition, and other confusions of our time*. New York: Owl Books.

Shermer, M. (2013, February 1). What is skepticism, anyway? *Huffington post*. [Online]. Available at: http://www.huffingtonpost.com/michael-shermer/what-is-skepticism-anyway_b_2581917.html

Shimanoff, S. B. (1980). *Communication rule: Theory and research*. Beverly Hills, CA: Sage.

Silver, N. (2012). *The signal and the noise: Why so many predictions fail—but some don't*. New York: The Penguin Press.

Simons, G. G., & Zielenziger, M. (1996, March 3). Culture clash dims U.S. future in Asia. *San Jose Mercury News*, p. 1A.

Simpson, P. A., & Stroh, L. K. (2004). Gender differences: Emotional expression and feelings of personal inauthenticity. *Journal of Applied Psychology*, 89, 715–721.

Smith, S. M., & Shaffer, D. R. (1995). Speed of speech and persuasion: Evidence for multiple effects. *Personality and Social Psychology Bulletin*, 21, 1051–1060.

Solomon, D. (2005, September 25). Funny about the news. *The New York Times*.

[Online]. Available at: http://www.nytimes.com/2005/09/25/magazine/25questions.html?_r=1

Soraghan, M. (2009, September 11). Speaker Pelosi agrees to plan to scold Rep. Wilson for "You lie" outburst. *The Hill*. [Online]. Available at: http://thehill.com/home-news/house/58331-dems-lay-plans-to-scold-wilson

Spiegler, M. D., & Guevremont, D. C. (1998). *Contemporary behavior therapy*. Pacific Grove, CA: Brooks/Cole.

Spitzberg, B. H. (2000). A model of intercultural communication competence. In L. A. Samovar & R. E. Porter (Eds.), *Intercultural communication: A reader*.

Spitzberg, B., & Hecht, M. (1984). A component model of relational competence. *Human Communication Research, 10*, 575–599.

Stallings, H. (2009). Prosecution deferred is justice denied. In L. G. Schnoor & D. Cronn-Mills (Eds.), *Winning orations*. Northfield, MN: Interstate Oratorical Association.

Stephen Colbert's address to the graduates. (2006, June 5). *AlterNet*. [Online]. Available at: http://www.alternet.org/story/37144/stephen_colbert%27s_address_to_the_graduates

Stern, N. (2004). Just say no to PowerPoint: Enough is enough. [Online]. Available at: http://www.eitforum.com/696.php

Sternberg, S. (2007, November 29). Unnecessary CT scans exposing patients to excessive radiation. *USA Today*, p. 1A.

Steward, C. (2009a, July 24). Rickey takes his speech to school. *San Jose Mercury News*, pp. C1, C5.

Stovall, S. (2012). Juvenile crime from deleterious environmental conditions. In L. G. Schnoor, L. Mayfield, and K. Young (Eds.), *Winning orations*. Mankat, MN: Interstate Oratorical Association.

Streich, L. (2012). 4-H Four-Gotten. In L. G. Schnoor, L. Mayfield, and K. Young (Eds.). *Winning orations*. Mankato, MN: Interstate Oratorical Association.

Strong, W., & Cook, J. (1990). *Persuasion: Strategies for speakers*. Dubuque, IA: Kendall/Hunt.

Study shows your teen's binge drinking could be caused by peer pressure. (2012, January 2). *Female Network*. [Online]. Available at: http://www.femalenetwork.com/family-parenting/study-shows-your-teens-binge-drinking-could-be-caused-by-peer-pressure/

Sunstein, C., & Zeckhauser, R. (2009). Overreaction to fearsome risks. In E. Michel-Kerjan and P. Slovic (Eds.), *The irrational economist: Future directions in behavioral economics and risk management*, Washington, DC: Public Affairs Press.

Surprenant, J. (2012). ALEC: Stopping the puppet master. In L. G. Schnoor, L. Mayfield, and K. Young (Eds.), *Winning orations*. Mankato, MN: Interstate Oratorical Association.

Survey: Eighty-seven percent of U.S. population can recycle paper. (2011, January 27). Resource Recycling. [Online]. Available at: http://resource-recycling.com/node/890

Suter, E. A. (1994). Guns in the medical literature—a failure of peer review. *Journal of the Medical Association of Georgia, 83*, 133–159.

Svoboda, E. (2009, February/March). Avoiding the big choke. *Scientific American Mind*, pp. 36–41.

Szabo, E. A., & Pfau, M. (2002). Nuances in inoculation: Theory and applications. In J. P. Dillard & M. Pfau (Eds.), *The persuasion handbook: Developments in theory and practice*. Thousand Oaks, CA: Sage.

Taber, C. S., & Lodge, M. (2006). Motivated skepticism in the evaluation of political beliefs. *American Journal of Political Science, 50*, 755–769.

Tabuchi, H., & McDonald, M. (2009, August 7). In first return to Japan court, jurors convict and sentence. *The New York Times*. [Online]. Available at: http://www.nytimes.com/2009/08/07/world/asia/07japan.html?_r=1&pagewanted=print

Tan Chin Keok, R. (2010). Public speaking: A case study of speech anxiety in L1 and L2. *Seminar Penyelidikan Pendidikan Pasca Ijazah*, 25–27.

Tannen, D. (2003, January 5). Hey, did you catch that? Why they're talking as fast as they can. *Washington Post*, pp. B1, B4.

Taraborelli, D. (2012, July, 2012). Seven years after Nature, pilot study compares *Wikipedia* favorably to other encyclopedias in three languages. *Wikimedia*. [Online]. Available at: http://blog.wikimedia.org/2012/08/02/seven-years-after-nature-pilot-study-compares-wikipedia-favorably-to-other-encyclopedias-in-three-languages/

Tavris, C., & Aronson, E. (2007). *Mistakes were made (but not by me)*. New York: Harcourt.

Ted Kennedy's eulogy of brother Robert, St. Patrick's Cathedral, New York City, June 8, 1968. (2009, August 26). *New York Daily News*. [Online]. Available at: http://nydailynews.com/news/politics/2009/08/26/2009-08-26_ted_kennedys_eulogy_of_brother_robert_1968.html

Tennant, V. (2012, April 23). Cell phone usage numbers, trends & stats. *Vitalyvt.com*. [Online]. Available at: http://vitalyvt.com/cell-phone-usage-numbers-trends-stats/

The evidence that HIV causes AIDS (2010, January 14). Available at: http://www.niaid.nih.gov/topics/hivaids/understanding/howhivcausesaids/pages/hivcausesaids.aspx

The fringe benefits of failure, and the importance of imagination. (2008, June 5). *Harvard Magazine*. [Online]. Available at: http://harvardmagazine.com/commencement/the-fringe-benefits-failure-the-importance-imagination

This year's freshmen at 4-year colleges: Highlights of a survey. (2010, January 21). *The Chronicle of Higher Education*. [Online]. Available at: http://chronicle.com/article/This-Years-Freshmen-at-4-Year/63672/

Thomma, S. (2009, August 30). Paranoid political rumors flourish. *San Jose Mercury News*, p. A9.

Thompson, E. (1960). An experimental investigation of the relative effectiveness of organization structure in oral communication. *Southern Speech Journal*, 26, 59–69.

Thomson, J. (2008, October 24). A quarter of people fear public speaking more than dying—here's how to beat your fear. *Smartcompany*. [Online]. Available at: http://www.smartcompany.com.au/Free-Articles/The-Briefing/20081024

Thrasher, J. F., Carpenter, M. J., Andrews, J. O. et al. (2012). Cigarette warning label policy alternatives and smoking-related health disparities. *American Journal of Preventive Medicine*, 43, 590–600.

Tincher, J. (2007, February 27). About our live votes and surveys. *NBCNews.com*. [Online]. Available at: http://www.nbcnews.com/id/3704453/#.UQhfaRwQ3Is

Titsworth, B.S. (2004). Students' notetaking: The effects of teacher immediacy and clarity. *Communication Education*, 53, 305–320.

Tolchin, M., & Tolchin, S. (1973). *Clout: Woman power and politics*. New York: Coward, McCann & Georghepon.

Top ten skills for job candidates. (2013, April 3). *National Association of Colleges and Employers*. [Online]. Available at: http://www.naceweb.org/s04032013/top-10-job-skills.aspx

Touching base with clichés, 24/7. (2004, March 24). *CNN International .Com*. [Online]. Available at: http://edition.cnn.com/2004/WORLD/europe/03/24/plain.english/

Toulmin, S. E. (1958). *The uses of argument*. Cambridge: Cambridge University press

Transcript: Hillary Clinton's prime-time speech. (2009, July 24). *NPR*. [Online]. Available at: http://www.npr.org/templates/story/story.php?storyId=94003143

Trump versus Rosie: The war continues (2006, December 21). *The Showbuzz* [Online]. Available at: http://www.cbsnews.com/2100-207_162-2287402.html

Tufte, E. (2003, September). PowerPoint is evil: Power corrupts, PowerPoint corrupts Absolutely. *Wired*. [Online]. Available at: http://www.wired.com/wired/archive/11.09/ppt2_pr.html

Turner, M. (2006). Using emotion in risk communication: The Anger Activism

Model. *Public Relations Review*, 33, 114–119.

Turner, M., Bessarabova, E., Sipek, S., & Hambleton, K. (2007, May 23). *Does message-induced anger facilitate or debilitate persuasion? Two tests of the Anger Activism Model.* Paper presented at the annual meeting of the International Communication Association, San Francisco, CA.

Turner, S. A., & Silvia, P. J. (2006). Must interesting things be pleasant? A test of competing appraisal structures. *Emotion*, 6, 670–674.

TV or not TV. (1993, April 19). *San Jose Mercury News*, p. 5E.

Twenty eight distracting mannerisms that must be avoided. (2011, March 29). *Basic Public Speaking*. [Online]. Available at: http://basicpublicspeaking.blogspot.com/2011/03/28-distracting-mannerisms-that-must-be.html

United Kingdom: Gun facts, figures and the law. (2013). *GunPolicy.org*. [Online]. Available at: http://www.gunpolicy.org/firearms/region/united-kingdom

U.S. Geological Survey. (2013). Earthquakes with 1,000 or more deaths since 1900. [Online]. Available at: http://earthquake.usgs.gov/earthquakes/world/world_deaths.php

Vaccine effectiveness: Do vaccines work? (2010). *National Network for Immunization Information*. [Online]. Available at: http://www.immunizationinfo.org/parents/why-immunize

Vaccine effectiveness: How well does the flu vaccine work? (2013, January 6). *Centers for Disease Control and Prevention*. [Online]. Available at: http://www.cdc.gov/flu/about/qa/vaccineeffect.htm

Verlinden, J. (2005). *Critical thinking and everyday argument.* Belmont, CA: Wadsworth/Thomson.

Victory, honor, sacrifice. (Henry H. Shelton address) (transcript) (2001, August 1). *Vital Speeches of the Day.* [Online]. Available at: http://www.accessmylibrary.com/coms2/summary_0286_28267884_ITM

Von Muhlenen, A., Rempel, M. I., Enns, J. T. (2005). Unique temporal change is the key to attentional capture. *Psychological Science*, 16, 979–986.

Wakefield, M., Terry-McElrath, Y., Emery, S., et al. (2006). Effect of televised, tobacco company—funded smoking prevention advertising on youth smoking-related beliefs, intentions, and behavior. *American Journal of Public Health*, 96, 1–7.

Waldman, M., & Stephanopoulos, G. (2003). *My fellow Americans: The most important speeches of America's presidents, from George Washington to George W. Bush.* New York: Sourcebooks Media Fusion.

Walker, J. (2013, March/April). Understanding believers' cognitive dissonance. *Skeptical Inquirer*, pp. 50–52.

Wallace, D. S., Paulson, R. M., Lord, C. G., Bond, C. F. (2005). Which behaviors do attitudes predict? Meta-analyzing the effects of social pressure and perceived difficulty. *Review of General Psychology*, 9, 214–227.

Wanzer, M. B., Booth-Butterfield, M., & Booth-Butterfield, S. (1996). Humor and social attraction: Are funny people more popular? An examination of humor orientation, loneliness, and social attraction. *Communication Quarterly*, 44, 42–52.

Wasserman, D. (2013). 2012 national popular vote tracker. [Online]. Available at: https://docs.google.com/spreadsheet/lv?key=0AjYj9mXElO_QdHpla0loWE1jOFZRbnhJZkZpVFNKeVE&toomany=true#gid=19

Weinberger, M. G., & Gulas, C. S. (1992). The impact of humor in advertising: A review. *Journal of Advertising*, 21, 35–59.

Weiner, R. (2009, December 27). Death panels lie on Factcheck.org's "Whoppers of 2009." *The Huffington Post*. [Online]. Available at: http://www.huffingtonpost.com/2009/12/27/death-panels-lie-on-factc_n_404284.html

Weingarten, G. (1994, September 27). I'm absolutely sure: You need a marshmallow enema. *San Jose Mercury News*, p. B7.

Weir, B. (2012, July 12). Gun deaths: A familiar American experience. *ABCNews*.

[Online]. Available at: http://abcnews.go.com/blogs/headlines/2012/07/gun-deaths-a-familiar-american-experience/

Weisberg, J., & Ivins, M. (2004). *The deluxe election edition Bushisms: The first term, in his own words.* New York: Fireside Books.

Wells, G. L., Wright, E. F., & Bradfield, A. L. (1999). Witnesses to crime: Social and cognitive factors governing the validity of people's reports. In R. Roesch, S. D. Hart, & J.R.P. Ogloff (Eds.), *Psychology and law: The state of the discipline.* New York: Kluwer.

Werner, S. (2005). Mandatory minimum sentencing. In L. G. Schnoor & B. Wickelgren (Eds.), *Winning orations.* Mankato, MN: Interstate Oratorical Association.

Westen, D. (2007). *The political brain: The role of emotion in deciding the fate of the nation.* New York: Public Affairs.

Westen, D., Blagov, P., Harenski, K., Kilts, C., & Hamann, S. (2006). The neural basis of motivated reasoning: An fMRI study of emotional constraints on political judgment during the U.S. presidential election of 2004. *Journal of Cognitive Neuroscience,* 18, 1947–1958.

White, D. (1998, December 30). Stupid things really said by famous people. *San Jose Mercury News,* p. E5.

Who was Neda? Slain woman an unlikely martyr. (2009, June 24). *CNN.com/world.* [Online]. Available at: http://www.cnn.com/2009/WORLD/meast/06/23/iran.neda.profile/

Wikipedia statistics. (2013, June). [Online]. Available at: http://stats.wikimedia.org/EN/TablesArticlesTotal.htm.

Wilgoren, J. (2002, October 31). Memorial for Wellstone assumes spirit of rally. *New York Times.* [Online]. Available at: http://www.nytimes.com/2002/10/30/us/2002-campaign-mourning-minnesota-memorial-for-wellstone-assumes-spirit-rally.html?n=Top%2fReference%2fTimes%20Topics%2fPeople%2fW%2fWellstone%2c%20Paul

Wilms, T. (2012, September 18). It is time for a "parental control, no texting while driving" phone. Forbes.

Wilson, C. (2008, June 19). Russert gets a final toast from Washington. *USA Today,* p. 2D.

Wilson, J. F. (2003). *Biological foundations of human behavior.* Belmont, CA: Wadsworth.

Wilson, T. D. (2002). *Strangers to ourselves: Discovering the adaptive unconscious.* Cambridge: Harvard University press.

Wiseman, R. (2007). *LaughLab.* [Online]. Available: www.laughlab.co.uk/home.html.

Witt, C., & Fetherling, D. (2009). *Real leaders don't do PowerPoint: How to sell yourself and your ideas.* New York: Crown Forum.

Witt, P. L., & Behnke, R. R. (2006). Anticipatory speech anxiety as a function of public speaking assignment type. *Communication Education,* 55, 167–177.

Witt, P. L., Brown, K. C., Roberts, J. B., Weisel, J., Sawyer, C. R., & Behnke, R. R. (2006). Somatic anxiety patterns before, during, and after giving a public speech. *Southern Communication Journal,* 71, 87–100.

Witte, K., & Allen, M. (1996, November). When do scare tactics work? A meta-analysis of fear appeals. Paper presented at the annual meeting of the Speech Communication Association, San Diego, CA.

Witte, K., Meyer, G., & Martell, D. (2001). *Effective health risk messages: A step-by-step guide.* Thousand Oaks, CA: Sage.

Witte, K., Murray-Johnson, L., Hubbell, A. P., Liu, W. Y., Sampson, J., & Morrison, K. (2000). Addressing cultural orientations in fear appeals: Promoting AIDS-protective behaviors among Hispanic immigrant and African-American adolescents, and American and Taiwanese college students. *Journal of Health Communication,* 6, 1023.

Wnek, A. (2012). Untitled. In L. G. Schnoor, L. Mayfield, and K. Young (Eds.), *Winning orations.* Mankato, MN: Interstate Oratorical Association.

Wolpe, J. (1990). *The practice of behavior therapy.* Tarrytown, NY: Pergamon Press.

Wong, Y. J., Pituch, K. A., & Rochlen, A. B. (2006). Men's restrictive emotionality:

An investigation of associations with other emotion-related constructs, anxiety, and underlying dimensions. *Psychology of Men & Masculinity*, 7, 113–126.

Wood, M. L. M. (2007). Rethinking the inoculation analogy: Effects on subjects with differing preexisting attitudes. *Human Communication Research*, 33, 357–378.

Wray, R. (2010, May 3). Goodbye petabytes, hello zettabytes. *Guardian*. [Online]. Available at: http://www.guardian.co.uk/technology/2010/may/03/humanity-digital-output-zettabyte/print

Wright, D. B., Memon, A., Skagerberg, E. M., & Gabbert, F. (2009). When eyewitnesses talk. *Current Directions in Psychological Science*, 18, 174–178.

Young, L. J. (2008, April 9). South Korea adopts jury system. *UPI Asia Online*. [Online]. Available: http://www.upiasia.com/Society_Culture/2008/04/09/south_korea_adopts_jury_system/1409/?view=print

Young, M. J., Behnke, R. R., & Mann, Y. M. (2004). Anxiety patterns in employment interviews. *Communication Reports*, 17, 49–57.

Zhang, Q. (2005). Immediacy, humor, power distance, and classroom communication apprehension in Chinese college classrooms. *Communication Quarterly*, 53, 109–124.

Zinsser, W. (1985). *On writing well*. New York: Harper & Row.

Credits

Chapter 15
p. 232: © Marcy Wieland; p. 235: © The Washington Post/Getty Images; p. 238: © Marcy Wieland; p. 241 (top): © AP Photo/Charlie Neibergall; p. 241 (bottom): © AP Photo

Chapter 16
p. 249: © Peter Turnley/CORBIS; p. 253: © Boston Globe/Getty Images; p. 258 © Marcy Wieland

Chapter 17
p. 266: © Raleigh News & Observer/Getty Images; p. 271: Photo by Matt Sayles/Invision/AP Photo; p. 272: © AP Photo

Index